P9-DTV-392

A Marvelous Work and a Wonder

A Marvelous Work and a Wonder

LeGrand Richards
of the Council of the Twelve
The Church of Jesus Christ of Latter-day Saints

Wherefore the Lord said, Forasmuch as this people draw near me with their mouth, and with their lips do honour me, but have removed their heart far from me, and their fear toward me is taught by the precept of men:

Therefore, behold, I will proceed to do a marvellous work among this people, even a marvellous work and a wonder: for the wisdom of their wise men shall perish, and the understanding of their prudent men shall be hid.

—Isaiah 29:13-14.

Published by Deseret Book Company, Salt Lake City, Utah, 1973

Lithographed by

DESERET PRESS

in the United States of America

PREFACE

At the conclusion of Elder LeGrand Richards' presidency of the Southern States Mission of The Church of Jesus Christ of Latter-day Saints in 1937, he left with the missionaries an outline entitled, "The Message of Mormonism." This outline was prepared to assist the missionaries in their study and presentation of the gospel in a systematic and logical manner. It has since been used in a number of missions and by stake missionaries. Repeated requests and suggestions that it be printed have influenced the decision to enlarge upon the original outline and have it published in book form. It is here presented under the title "A Marvelous Work and A Wonder."

Recently a letter was received from the president of a mission requesting permission to use this outline. The letter is quoted in part:

> For some time I have been dreaming over a program of subjects for the missionaries to use in their contacts and follow-ups with investigators, subjects with a natural sequence that will make their message more effective and intelligible.

> This morning I was cleaning out a drawer and ran across the answer to my dreams—dust covered and neglected. It was a mimeographed booklet entitled, "The Message of Mormonism," by LeGrand Richards. I have read it through, and it embodies just the thing I would like to place in the hands of each missionary.

> Would it be agreeable to you if I make copies of it for this purpose? It is excellent and would be effective in stimulating systematic study and regulated presentations.

An added encouragement to publish this outline came through a request from a teacher at Brigham Young University for permission to mimeograph and use it in his work at that institution. He had been using the outline for the past eight years as a missionary, as a seminary teacher, and at Brigham Young University where he was doing graduate work in religion, teaching three two-hour classes. An excerpt from his letter follows:

In all my Church work I have found this the most helpful of introductions to the restored gospel. I have often thought that this outline, by all means, ought to be circulated in all the missions of the Church in order that all missionaries might profit by its use, because it presents such a clear and comprehensive picture of the message we have for the world, and also it presents it in such a logical order . . . I consider it excellent. In fact, the best I have seen, and I am writing this with the hope that it will get more, yes, much more publicity and circulation. I have tested it now for eight years in active Church work and found it not wanting.

When this outline was first given to the missionaries of the Southern States Mission, a letter accompanied it with added suggestions for the presentation of the gospel message, which included the following:

By us the gospel is to be preached in all the world *as a witness* to all nations. (See Matt. 24:14; Rev. 14:6-7.)

We are the fishers and hunters the Lord promised to send forth in the last days to fish and hunt Israel "from every mountain, and from every hill, and out of the holes of the rocks." (See Jer. 16:16.)

We are sent out two and two as the seventy of old (See Luke 10:1) with this instruction from the Master:

And into whatsoever house ye enter, first say, Peace be to this house.

And if the son of peace be there, your peace shall rest upon it: if not, it shall turn to you again.

And in the same house remain, eating and drinking such things as they give: for the labourer is worthy of his hire. *Go not from house to house.* (Luke 10:5-7.)

In these words and those which follow in this chapter the Master indicated that those who receive his servants receive him. He seems to want to impress the seventy that when their peace rests upon a house the Lord has done his part of the work, and he then leaves the responsibility to his servants to remain there and deliver the whole message so it can stand as a witness for or against them; and hence the instruction: *"Go not from house to house."* Too often, because of lack of experience and preparation, our missionaries run away from their work instead of running to it. Ask yourself this question: "In how many homes have I explained our message in detail and completeness so it could stand as a witness against those who heard it?"

If we tell our story we have a right to be heard, regardless of the hundreds of Christian denominations already existent in the land.

If we properly tell our story, there is no need for argument, which should remove the fear from the heart of the missionary. Missionaries have usually felt that they were going forth to argue or debate and should be prepared; but if they are prepared to tell our story intelligently and enthusiastically, their hearers will become listeners and questioners.

By explaining a few principles of the gospel we have not delivered our message as a witness against the people, any more than a man has built a house by laying the foundation. How can a person judge as to the beauty of the house when the foundation only is laid, or even when part of the sidewalls are built? The same rule applies in the presentation of the gospel—how can a man judge as to its truth before he has heard it?

When we find a home where "the son of peace be there," we should have a definite aim to visit that home once a week for at least six months. If we will do this and present our message in a systematic and orderly manner, the people will either join the Church or admit that the message is true, but their social and family standing will not permit their accepting it, if they have followed with interest your presentation, realizing, of course, that the spirit of the Lord must accompany your efforts since "the letter killeth, but the spirit giveth life." (See II Cor. 3:6.)

In submitting this outline it is realized there are many things worthy of discussion which have not been mentioned. Some subjects may take more than one visit to present properly. However, these suggestions should be helpful in presenting the message in a systematic and impressive manner.

It is the writer's experience that where reference is made to the Bible, it is wise to invite the investigator to turn to the passage in his own Bible and read with you. It is much more impressive than where the missionary quotes or reads from his own Bible only.

This book has been prepared and published without any monetary remuneration to the author: It is dedicated to the great missionary work of The Church of Jesus Christ of Latter-day Saints which is so dear to the author's heart.

REFERENCES AND ABBREVIATIONS

Books within the Authorized (King James) Version of the Holy Bible are designated by name or by their accepted abbreviations.

I Nephi; II Nephi; III Nephi; Moroni; Mormon; Ether; and *Alma* are books within The Book of Mormon.

P. of G. P., Moses, (Abraham—Joseph Smith), refers to The Book of Moses, or to The Book of Abraham, or to the Writings of Joseph Smith within the Pearl of Great Price.

D. & C. 3:9-11 refers to the book, Doctrine and Covenants, Section 3, verses 9-11.

D.H.C. 2, pp. 40-48 refers to the Documentary History of the Church, Volume two, pages forty to forty-eight.

All other references are given in full within the text and are self-explanatory.

USE OF ITALICS

All italics used throughout the text are the author's and indicate his selection of titles, words, and phrases needing emphasis to assist the reader in his study of truth as presented herein.

ACKNOWLEDGMENTS

The following acknowledgments are not intended to imply, directly or indirectly, any endorsement of this work, or to relieve the author of his full responsibility therefor.

The invaluable assistance rendered by my dear friend and associate, Lee A. Palmer, in editing the manuscript, and in following through with the details of publication, is acknowledged with the deepest feeling of gratitude.

Valuable suggestions and comments from members of the Publication Committee of the Church are gratefully acknowledged.

For the generous and competent assistance of Doyle L. Green, Marba C. Josephson, and Elizabeth J. Moffitt, Managing Editor, Associate Managing Editor, and Manuscript Editor, respectively, of *The Improvement Era,* the writer will ever be most grateful.

Appreciation is also expressed to my secretary, Mable S. Chapman, for copying and recopying the manuscript preparatory to the publication of this work.

LEGRAND RICHARDS

Salt Lake City, Utah
December 1, 1950

CONTENTS

CHAPTER 16

The Prophecies of Jeremiah Concerning the Gathering of Israel—Israel to be Gathered in Small Numbers—Judah to be Gathered to Jerusalem—Ephraim to be Gathered to the Land of America—Latter-day Saints Fulfil Jeremiah's Prophecy—The Prophecies of Isaiah Concerning Latter-day Israel—The Lord's House Established in the Top of the Mountains—Coming of the Railroad and Airplane Speeds the Gathering of Israel—Does Introduction of Irrigation Fulfil Prophecy? The Desert Made to Blossom as the Rose

CHAPTER 17

Elias and the Spirit of Elias—Elijah, Elias, and John, Three Persons

CHAPTER 18

The Voice of Warning Unto All People—Preaching the Kingdom of God—Every Nation to Hear the Word of the Lord

CHAPTER 19

One Heaven and One Hell—Many Mansions, or Degrees, in Heaven—Celestial Glory—Terrestrial Glory—Telestial Glory—Variation in the Degrees of Glory—With Definitions —Sons of Perdition—All Are Heirs of Salvation—Saved by Grace—Exaltation Dependent upon Good Works—Salvation Defined

CHAPTER 20

Man in the Spirit World—The Council in Heaven—Satan and His Angels—The Sons of God Shouted for Joy—Prophets Chosen Before Birth—The Antemortal Calling

A MARVELOUS WORK AND A WONDER

CHAPTER 1

THE POSITION OF THE CHURCH OF JESUS CHRIST OF LATTER-DAY SAINTS

The position of The Church of Jesus Christ of Latter-day Saints will be discussed from the point of view that it is the only Christian church that does not depend entirely upon the Bible for its teachings. Had all the Bibles in the world been destroyed, the doctrines and teachings of the Church would have been found to conform to Bible teachings, since they were received by direct revelation from God. We appeal to the Bible to prove that the truths received through the restoration of the gospel are in accord with its teachings.

Statement of Nationally Prominent Commentator

It has been said that one of our nationally prominent commentators once made the statement over the radio that he had been asked what message could be broadcast to the world that would be considered more important than any other. After giving the matter much thought and consideration he came to the conclusion that to be able to announce that a man who had lived upon the earth, had died, and had returned again with a message from God would be the most important message that could be broadcast to the world. This being true the Latter-day Saints have the most important message for the world today. In the western part of the state of New York in 1936 they erected a monument upon the Hill Cumorah to such a person, Moroni, a prophet of God, who lived upon the American continent four hundred years after Christ. This is the only such monument in the world today.

A Missionary Church

This explains why The Church of Jesus Christ of Latter-day Saints must, of necessity, be a missionary church, and why our missionaries take their message to other Christians, even though they are often criticized for so doing with the query, "Why do you not go to the heathens? We already have Christianity." The answer must obviously be: "Because we believe in a restored, revealed religion and Church."

Classification of Christian Churches

The Christian churches of today may be generally classified as follows:

1. The Catholic Church, contending that the Church has had an uninterrupted existence upon the earth since originally founded by Jesus Christ.

2. Protestant churches founded by the reformers who contend that the original Church fell into apostasy, and therefore, through a study of the Bible, have attempted to return to the original teachings and practices of the Church. The number of these churches is an evidence of how impossible it is to agree upon the teachings of the Bible when left to the wisdom of man to interpret and understand them. Because of this lack of unity, churches have continued to multiply in a further effort to return to what they consider the original teachings of the Christ.

3. Those who believe that the Church established by

Jesus Christ while upon the earth, fell into an apostate condition as predicted by the Apostles, and that the Church could not be reestablished upon the earth merely through a reformation but only through a restoration.

The Church of Jesus Christ of Latter-day Saints stands alone in this latter classification, except for only small apostate groups that have broken away from this Church.

In considering these claims it is obvious that if the first be true, there is no excuse for the existence of any other Christian church. If the original Church had gone astray, could a reformation restore its power? Can a living branch be taken from a dead tree? Or, must there be a new planting, a restoration?

A Catholic Utterance

In a pamphlet, entitled *The Strength of the Mormon Position*, the late Elder Orson F. Whitney, of the Council of the Twelve Apostles, related the following incident under the heading, "A Catholic Utterance":

> Many years ago a learned man, a member of the Roman Catholic Church, came to Utah and spoke from the stand of the Salt Lake Tabernacle. I became well-acquainted with him, and we conversed freely and frankly. A great scholar, with perhaps a dozen languages at his tongue's end, he seemed to know all about theology, law, literature, science and philosophy. One day he said to me: "You Mormons are all ignoramuses. You don't even know the strength of your own position. It is so strong that there is only one other tenable in the whole Christian world, and that is the position of the Catholic Church. The issue is between Catholicism and Mormonism. If we are right, you are wrong; if you are right, we are wrong; and that's all there is to it. The Protestants haven't a leg to stand on. For, if we are wrong, they are wrong with us, since they were a part of us and went out from us; while if we are right, they are apostates whom we cut off long ago. If we have the apostolic succession from St. Peter, as we claim, there is no need of Joseph Smith and Mormonism; but if we have not that succession, then such a man

as Joseph Smith was necessary, and Mormonism's attitude is the only consistent one. It is either the perpetuation of the gospel from ancient times, or the restoration of the gospel in latter days."

Elder James E. Talmage and the Congress of Religious Philosophies

In an address in the Salt Lake Tabernacle, Sunday, October 10, 1915, the late Elder James E. Talmage, of the Council of the Twelve Apostles, told of a notable religious gathering held in San Francisco in July, 1915. It was held in connection with the Panama-Pacific International Exposition known as the Congress of Religious Philosophies. Three days were devoted to this congress with three meetings each day. The days were designated respectively, "Christian Day, Hindu Day, and Oriental Day." It was the plan of the organizers to invite to the platform representatives of any and all religious organizations claiming a distinctive status, or professing a philosophical basis for their belief, such as would give them a distinct identity.

Representatives of the Roman Catholic and Greek Catholic churches were invited to participate, a representative of Protestantism, and a representative of The Church of Jesus Christ of Latter-day Saints.

The representative of the Roman Catholic Church failed to appear. The representative of the Greek Catholic Church pleaded for a union with the Roman Catholic Church and suggested that the schism of the past be forgotten, that the chasm be bridged, and that the Greek Catholics come back into the fold and acknowledge the Pope as their common shepherd.

The address of the representative of Protestantism was a plea for church unity. He argued in favor of demolishing the barriers or erasing the lines of demarcation by which the many Protestant organizations of the day are now divided.

Elder James E. Talmage added: "I speak advisedly and after mature consideration when I say that the Mormon Church [The Church of Jesus Christ of Latter-day Saints] was the only Christian organization there present that had a definite, distinct, and unqualified philosophical basis to proclaim." He had questioned the organizing officials of the congress, first as to their reasons for extending to the Church in Salt Lake City so cordial an invitation to be represented, and second, as to why Christian sects generally were not given a place upon the program. The answer was to the effect (1) that a program providing for the presentation of the philosophies of Christian organizations would be incomplete were The Church of Jesus Christ of Latter-day Saints left out, (2) that they regarded the various so-called Christian churches as sectarian divisions, not characterized by any distinctive philosophical claims, and that if all that they asserted be admitted as true, their claims would not entitle them to recognition in such a gathering. (For full report of Elder Talmage's presentation, see the pamphlet, *The Philosophical Basis of Mormonism*.)

The Most Important Message to the World

If heavenly messengers (prophets who have lived upon this earth) have visited this earth in this dispensation, bringing messages from God, as claimed by the Prophet Joseph Smith, then we have the most important message that can go out to the world today, which invites investigation. If such messengers really came, they must have contributed that which is worthy a divine messenger and which was not already in possession of mortal man.

With this thought in mind, we shall proceed to analyze the contribution of these heavenly messengers. We suggest the reader assume the position of judge and jury, withholding his verdict until the evidence herein presented has been fully considered.

CHAPTER 2

THE VISIT OF THE FATHER AND THE SON

On the morning of a beautiful spring day in 1820 there occurred one of the most important and momentous events in this world's history. God, the Eternal Father and His Son, Jesus Christ, appeared to Joseph Smith and gave instructions concerning the establishment of the kingdom of God upon the earth in these latter days. Joseph Smith has left us a detailed account of this glorious experience:

Joseph Smith's Own Story

Owing to the many reports which have been put in circulation by evil-disposed and designing persons, in relation to the rise and progress of the Church of Jesus Christ of Latter-day Saints, all of which have been designed by the authors thereof to militate against its character as a Church and its progress in the world—I have been induced to write this history, to disabuse the public mind, and put all inquirers after truth in possession of the facts, as they have transpired, in relation both to myself and the Church, so far as I have such facts in my possession.

In this history I shall present the various events in relation to this Church, in truth and righteousness, as they have transpired, or as they at present exist, being now the eighth year since the organization of the said Church.

I was born in the year of our Lord one thousand eight hundred and five, on the twenty-third day of December, in the town of Sharon, Windsor county, State of Vermont. . . . My father, Joseph Smith, Sen., left the State of Vermont, and moved to Palmyra, Ontario (now Wayne) county, in the State of New York, when I was in my tenth year, or thereabouts. In about four years after my father's arrival in Palmyra, he moved with his family into Manchester, in the same county of Ontario—

His family consisting of eleven souls, namely, my father, Joseph Smith; my mother, Lucy Smith (whose name, previous to her marriage, was Mack, daughter of Solomon Mack); my brothers, Alvin (who died November 19th, 1824, in the 27th year of his age), Hyrum, myself, Samuel Harrison, William, Don Carlos; and my sisters, Sophronia, Catherine, and Lucy.

Some time in the second year after our removal to Manchester, there was in the place where we lived an unusual excitement on the subject of religion. It commenced with the Methodists, but soon became general among all the sects in that region of country. Indeed, the whole district of country seemed affected by it, and great multitudes united themselves to the different religious parties, which created no small stir and division amongst the people, some crying, "Lo, here!" and others, "Lo, there!" Some were contending for the Methodist faith, some for the Presbyterian, and some for the Baptist.

For, notwithstanding the great love which the converts to these different faiths expressed at the time of their conversion, and the great zeal manifested by the respective clergy, who were active in getting up and promoting this extraordinary scene of religious feeling, in order to have everybody converted, as they were pleased to call it, let them join what sect they pleased; yet when the converts began to file off, some to one party and some to another, it was seen that the seemingly good feelings of both the priests and the converts were more pretended than real; for a scene of great confusion and bad feeling ensued—priest contending against priest, and convert against convert; so that all their good feelings one for another, if they ever had any, were entirely lost in a strife of words and a contest about opinions.

I was at this time in my fifteenth year. My father's family was proselyted to the Presbyterian faith, and four of them joined that church, namely, my mother, Lucy; my brothers Hyrum and Samuel Harrison; and my sister Sophronia.

During this time of great excitement my mind was called up to serious reflections and great uneasiness; but though my feelings were deep and often poignant, still I kept myself aloof from all these parties, though I attended their several meetings as often as occasion would permit. In process of time my mind became somewhat partial to the Methodist sect, and I felt some desire to be united with them; but so great were the confusion and strife among the different denominations, that it was impossible for a person young as I was, and so unacquainted with men and things, to come to any certain conclusion who was right and who was wrong.

My mind at times was greatly excited, the cry and tumult were so great and incessant. The Presbyterians were most decided against the Baptists and Methodists, and used all the powers of both reason and sophistry to prove their errors, or, at least, to make the people think they were in error. On the other hand, the Baptists and Methodists in their turn were equally zealous in endeavoring to establish their own tenets and disprove all others.

In the midst of this war of words and tumult of opinions, I often said to myself: What is to be done? Who of all these parties are right; or, are they all wrong together? If any one of them be right, which is it, and how shall I know it?

While I was laboring under the extreme difficulties caused by the contests of these parties of religionists, I was one day reading the Epistle of James, first chapter and fifth verse, which reads: *If any of you lack wisdom, let him ask of God, that giveth to all men liberally, and upbraideth not; and it shall be given him.*

Never did any passage of scripture come with more power to the heart of man than this did at this time to mine. It seemed to enter with great force into every feeling of my heart. I reflected on it again and again, knowing that if any person needed wisdom from God, I did; for how to act I did not know, and unless I could get more wisdom than I then had, I would never know; for the teachers of religion of the different sects understood the same passages of scripture so differently as to destroy all confidence in settling the question by an appeal to the Bible.

At length I came to the conclusion that I must either remain in darkness and confusion, or else I must do as James directs, that is, ask of God. I at length came to the determination to "ask of God," concluding that if he gave wisdom to them that lacked wisdom, and would give liberally, and not upbraid, I might venture.

So, in accordance with this, my determination to ask of God, I retired to the woods to make the attempt. It was on the morning of a beautiful, clear day, early in the spring of eighteen hundred and twenty. It was the first time in my life that I had made such an attempt, for amidst all my anxieties I had never as yet made the attempt to pray vocally.

After I had retired to the place where I had previously designed to go, having looked around me, and finding myself alone, I kneeled down and began to offer up the desires of my heart to God. I had scarcely done so, when immediately I was seized upon by some power which entirely overcame me, and had such an astonishing influence over me as to bind my tongue so that I could not speak. Thick darkness gathered around me, and it seemed to me for a time as if I were doomed to sudden destruction.

But, exerting all my powers to call upon God to deliver me out of the power of this enemy which had seized upon me, and at the very moment when I was ready to sink into despair and abandon myself to destruction—not to an imaginary ruin, but to the power of some actual being from the unseen world, who had such marvelous power as I had never before felt in any being— just at this moment of great alarm, I saw a pillar of light exactly over my head, above the brightness of the sun, which descended gradually until it fell upon me.

It no sooner appeared than I found myself delivered from the enemy which held me bound. When the light rested upon me I saw two Personages, whose brightness and glory defy all description, standing above me in the air. One of them spake unto me, calling me by name, and said, pointing to the other— *This is My Beloved Son. Hear Him!*

My object in going to inquire of the Lord was to know which of all the sects was right, that I might know which to join. No sooner, therefore, did I get possession of myself, so as to be able to speak, than I asked the Personages who stood above me in the light, which of all the sects was right—and which I should join.

I was answered that I must join none of them, for they were all wrong; and the Personage who addressed me said . . . "they draw near to me with their lips, but their hearts are far from me; they teach for doctrines the commandments of men, having a form of godliness, but they deny the power thereof."

He again forbade me to join with any of them; and many other things did he say unto me, which I cannot write at this time. When I came to myself again I found myself lying on my back, looking up into heaven. When the light had departed, I had no strength; but soon recovering in some degree, I went home. And as I leaned up to the fireplace, mother inquired what the matter was. I replied, "Never mind, all is well—I am well enough off." I then said to my mother, "I have learned for myself that Presbyterianism is not true." It seems as though the adversary was aware, at a very early period of my life, that I was destined to prove a disturber and an annoyer of his kingdom: else why should the powers of darkness combine against me? Why the opposition and persecution that arose against me, almost in my infancy?

Some few days after I had this vision, I happened to be in company with one of the Methodist preachers, who was very active in the before mentioned religious excitement; and, conversing with him on the subject of religion, I took occasion to give him an account of the vision which I had had. I was greatly surprised at his behavior; he treated my communication not only lightly, but with great contempt, saying it was all of the devil, that there were no such things as visions or revelations in these days; that all such things had ceased with the apostles, and that there would never be any more of them.

I soon found, however, that my telling the story had excited a great deal of prejudice against me among professors of religion, and was the cause of great persecution, which continued to increase; and though I was an obscure boy, only between fourteen and fifteen years of age, and my circumstances in life such as to make a boy of no consequence in the world, yet men of high standing would take notice sufficient to excite the public mind against me, and create a bitter persecution; and this was common among all the sects—all united to persecute me.

It caused me serious reflection then, and often has since, how very strange it was that an obscure boy, of a little over fourteen years of age, and one, too, who was doomed to the necessity of obtaining a scanty maintenance by his daily labor, should be thought a character of sufficient importance to attract the attention of the great ones of the most popular sects of the day, and in a manner to create in them a spirit of the most bitter persecution and reviling. But strange or not, so it was, and it was often the cause of great sorrow to myself.

However, it was nevertheless a fact that I had beheld a vision. I have thought since, that I felt much like Paul, when he made his defense before King Agrippa, and related the account of the vision he had when he saw a light, and heard a voice; but still there were but few who believed him; some said he was dishonest, others said he was mad; and he was ridiculed and reviled. But all this did not destroy the reality of his vision. He had seen a vision, he knew he had, and all the persecution under heaven could not make it otherwise; and though they should persecute him unto death, yet he knew, and would know to his latest breath, that he had both seen a light and heard a voice speaking unto him, and all the world could not make him think or believe otherwise.

So it was with me. I had actually seen a light, and in the midst of that light I saw two Personages, and they did in reality speak to me; and though I was hated and persecuted for saying that I had seen a vision, yet it was true; and while they were persecuting me, reviling me, and speaking all manner of evil against me falsely for so saying, I was led to say in my heart: Why persecute me for telling the truth? I have actually seen a vision; and who am I that I can withstand God, or why does the world think to make me deny what I have actually seen? For I had seen a vision; I knew it, and I knew that God knew it, and I could not deny it, neither dared I do it; at least I knew that by so doing I would offend God, and come under condemnation. (P. of G. P. Joseph Smith 2:1-25.)

This was the prophet's first vision. From this we learn among other truths, that God the Father and his Son, Jesus Christ, are two separate and distinct personages, and that man is literally created in the image of God.

The Worship of False Gods

The great sin of the ages has been the worship of false gods, hence the first of the ten commandments written by God, himself, upon the tablets of stone amid the thunder and lightning of Sinai: "Thou shalt have no other Gods before me." (Exod. 20:3.)

When Moses led the children of Israel to the promised land, he told them that they should be, in coming generations, scattered among the heathen nations: "And there ye shall serve gods, the work of men's hands, wood and stone, which *neither see, nor hear, nor eat, nor smell.*" (Deut. 4:28) Then Moses promised them that "in the latter days" when they were in tribulation, if they would seek after the Lord their God they should find him, if they would seek him with all their hearts and with all their souls. (See Deut. 4:29-30.)

Could the Gods made by the hands of man, taught and worshiped by the Christian churches of the world at the time Joseph Smith received his glorious vision, *see* or *hear* or *eat* or *smell?*

The Strange Gods of Christendom

A few quotations will indicate the general beliefs in Christendom during the early history of The Church of Jesus Christ of Latter-day Saints:

The God of the Catholic Church was described as follows:

Q. What is God?

A. God is a Spirit, eternal, independent, infinite and immutable, who is present everywhere, who seeth all things and governs the universe.

Q. Why do you say that he is a Spirit?

A. Because he is a supreme intelligence, *who has neither body, nor figure, nor color, and who cannot fall under the senses.* (Rev. P. Collot, *Doctrine and Scriptural Catechism of the Catholic Church,* Published in Montreal, quoted from *Liahona,* Vol. 23, No. 14, p. 268.)

The Methodist Church worships this kind of God:

There is but one living and true God, everlasting, *without body or parts,* of infinite power, wisdom and goodness, the maker and preserver of all things, visible and invisible; and in unity of this Godhead there are three persons, of one substance, power and eternity, the Father, the Son and the Holy Ghost. (*Methodist Discipline,* published in Toronto, 1886, quoted from *Liahona,* Vol. 23, No. 14, P. 269.)

Let us examine the description of the God of the Presbyterian Church:

> There is but one living and true God, who is infinite in being and perfection, a most pure *spirit, invisible, without body, parts or passions,* immutable, immense, eternal, *incomprehensible,* almighty, most wise, most holy, most free, most absolute, working all things according to the counsel of his immutable and righteous will, for his own glory; most loving, gracious, merciful, long-suffering, abundant in goodness and truth, forgiving iniquity, transgression and sin; the rewarder of them that diligently seek him; and with all most just and terrible in his judgments; hating all sin, and who will by no means clear the guilty. (*Presbyterian Church Confession of Faith,* Chap. 2, Art. 1, quoted from *Liahona,* Vol. 23, No. 14, p. 269.)

These are but typical examples of the Gods worshiped by Christian churches during the nineteenth century. Here are the Gods which Moses told Israel they would encounter as they were scattered among the nations—Gods "which neither *see,* nor *hear,* nor *eat,* nor *smell.*" How could a God without body, parts, or passions, be expected either to see, hear, eat or smell? How could any child of God be expected to understand, much less to love and be loved by, such an "incomprehensible" God as the above tenets would lead him to worship?

Compare the certain knowledge and information Joseph Smith obtained regarding the personality of God and his Son, Jesus Christ, during the few moments he talked with them face to face, with the Council of Nicaea which was convened by Emperor Constantine in the year 325 A.D. when 318 bishops spent four weeks in debate on the true divinity and personality of the Son of God, and the equality of Christ with God, before they could become sufficiently united to make a public declaration on the matter.

Could You Gaze into Heaven Five Minutes?

Consider carefully the words of the Prophet Joseph Smith:

> Could you gaze into heaven five minutes, you would know

more than you would by reading all that ever was written on the subject. (D. H. C. Vol. 6, p. 50.)

The appearance of the Father and the Son to Joseph Smith is vividly portrayed in the words of the song, "Joseph Smith's First Prayer":

O how lovely was the morning!
Radiant beamed the sun above
Bees were humming, sweet birds singing,
Music ringing thro' the grove,
When within the shady woodland,
Joseph sought the God of love.

Humbly kneeling, sweet appealing—
'Twas the boy's first uttered prayer—
When the pow'rs of sin assailing
Filled his soul with deep despair,
But undaunted still, he trusted
In his heav'nly Father's care.

Suddenly a light descended,
Brighter far than noon-day sun,
And a shining, glorious pillar
O'er him fell, around him shone,
While appeared two heav'nly beings,
God the Father and the Son.

"Joseph, this is my Beloved,
Hear Him." oh, how sweet the word!
Joseph's humble prayer was answered,
And he listened to the Lord;
Oh, what rapture filled his bosom,
For he saw the living God.

—George Manwaring

The visit of the Father and the Son to Joseph Smith opened the door to the establishment of the kingdom of God upon the earth in this dispensation which was the greatest event of the nineteenth century.

CHAPTER 3

PERSONALITY OF THE FATHER AND THE SON

Man Created in the Image and Likeness of God

The simple story told by the Prophet Joseph Smith of his interview with the Father and the Son makes it easy to understand the teachings of the Bible relating to this important matter. It must be remembered, however, that this knowledge was not obtained by the prophet through a study of the Bible. We take the Bible merely to prove that his story harmonizes fully with the teachings thereof, some of which we shall now consider:

> And God said, Let us make man in our own image, after our likeness: and let them have dominion over the fish of the sea, and over the fowl of the air, and over the cattle, and over all the earth, and over every creeping thing that creepeth upon the earth.

> So *God created man in his own image,* in the image of God created he him; male and female created he them. (Gen. 1:26-27.)

Attempts have been made to explain that this creation was only in the spiritual image and likeness of God, but after reading Joseph Smith's simple story, one wonders how a historian could have made a more clearcut, understandable statement of what actually happened in the creation of man, especially when one reads:

> And Adam lived an hundred and thirty years, and begat a son *in his own likeness,* after his image; and called his name Seth. (Gen. 5:3.)

Joseph Smith found that he was as literally in the image and likeness of God and Jesus Christ, as Seth was in the likeness and image of his father Adam.

Moses' Testimony of the Personality of God

This also makes the experience of Moses and his associates and seventy of the elders of Israel seem so reasonable and easy to understand:

> Then went up Moses, and Aaron, Nadab, and Abihu, and seventy of the elders of Israel.
>
> And they saw the God of Israel: and there was under his feet as it were a paved work of sapphire stone, and as it were the body of heaven in his clearness. (Exod. 24:9-10.)
>
> And it came to pass, as Moses entered into the tabernacle, the cloudy pillar descended, and stood at the door of the tabernacle, and the Lord talked with Moses.
>
> And all the people saw the cloudy pillar stand at the tabernacle door: and all the people rose up and worshipped, every man in his tent door.
>
> And *the Lord spake unto Moses face to face*, as a man speaketh unto his friend . . . (Exod. 33:9-11.)

Could any historian be expected to describe this event any more clearly than to say that the Lord and Moses talked with each other *"face to face*, as a man speaketh unto his friend"? Does anyone need to be told how a man speaks to his friend? The Father and the Son spoke with Joseph Smith "face to face, as a man speaketh unto his friend." There is only one thing that made this possible and that is the fact that God did create man in his own image and likeness. Could any other image or likeness have been half so wonderful?

Paul's Testimony of the Personality of God

Paul, the Apostle, tried to make clear what kind of personage God was by telling us that his Son, Jesus Christ, was "the brightness of his glory, and the express image of his person," and that he "sat down on the right hand of the Majesty on high." (See Heb. 1:3.) This of course, could only have been possible when his Father did have a form on whose right hand he could sit.

Stephen's Testimony of the Personality of God

Paul's description of God gives real meaning to the words of Stephen, when he was being stoned to death by his enemies:

> But he, being full of the Holy Ghost, looked up stedfastly into heaven, and saw the glory of God, and Jesus standing on the right hand of God,
>
> And said, Behold, I see the heavens opened, and the Son of man standing on the right hand of God. (Acts 7:55-56.)

Thus he saw two separate and distinct personages, the one, the Son, standing on the right hand of the other, the Father.

John's Testimony of the Personality of God

This accords also with the report of John's baptism of Jesus:

> And Jesus, when he was baptized, went up straightway out of the water: and, lo, the heavens were opened unto him, and he saw the Spirit of God descending like a dove, and lighting upon him:
>
> And lo a voice from heaven, saying, This is my beloved Son, in whom I am well pleased. (Matt. 3:16-17.)

Here each of the three members of the Godhead are distinctly and separately mentioned: (1) Jesus coming up out of the water; (2) the Holy Ghost descending like a dove; (3) the voice of the Father from heaven expressing his love and approval of his Beloved Son. How could one possibly believe these three to be one person without body or form?

The Resurrected Lord

Consideration should now be given to the resurrected Lord. Unless he now has his body of flesh and bone that was laid away in the tomb, he must have died a second time, for when Mary Magdalene and the other Mary came to the sepulchre to see the body of Jesus, they found that an angel of the Lord had descended from heaven and was sitting on the stone which he had rolled back from the door:

> His countenance was like lightning, and his raiment white as snow: . . .

> And the angel answered and said unto the women, Fear not ye: for I know that ye seek Jesus, which was crucified.

> He is not here: for he is risen, as he said. Come, see the place where the Lord lay. (Matt. 28:3, 5-6.)

Following his resurrection Jesus appeared to many. While the eleven Apostles were gathered together at Jerusalem discussing what had happened:

> . . . Jesus himself stood in the midst of them, and saith unto them, Peace be unto you.

> But they were terrified and affrighted, and supposed that they had seen a spirit.

> And he said unto them, Why are ye troubled? and why do thoughts arise in your hearts?

> Behold my hands and my feet, that it is I myself: handle me, and see; for a spirit hath not flesh and bones, as ye see me have. (Luke 24:36-39.)

To further prove that he had his body, he took a piece of broiled fish and of honeycomb and did eat before them.

With his resurrected body he ascended to heaven in the presence of five hundred of the brethren:

> . . . he was seen of above five hundred brethren at once . . . (I Cor. 15:6.)

His Apostles saw Him ascend into heaven and the "two men (who) stood by them in white apparel" affirmed the fact:

> And while they looked stedfastly toward heaven as he went up, behold, two men, stood by them in white apparel;

Which also said, Ye men of Galilee, why stand ye gazing up into heaven? this same Jesus, which is taken up from you into heaven, shall so come in like manner as ye have seen him go into heaven. (Acts 1:10-11.)

If Jesus and his Father are one in spirit without body or form, so large that he fills the universe and so small that he dwells in each heart, as so many believe and as the churches teach, then what meaning has the resurrection which is commemorated each Easter in the Christian churches, and what did he do with his body after he showed it to his Apostles and others?

Joseph Smith's Testimony of the Personality of Jesus

Joseph Smith did again behold the same Jesus as was seen ascending into heaven after his resurrection. This is the testimony given of him by Joseph Smith and Sidney Rigdon, following a vision they received at Hiram, Ohio, February 16, 1832:

And while we meditated upon these things, the Lord touched the eyes of our understandings and they were opened, and the glory of the Lord shone round about.

And we beheld the glory of the Son, on the right hand of the Father, and received of his fulness:

And saw the holy angels, and them who are sanctified before his throne, worshiping God, and the Lamb, who worshiped him forever and ever.

And now, after the many testimonies which have been given of him, this is the testimony, last of all, which we give of him: That he lives!

For we saw him, even on the right hand of God; and we heard the voice bearing record that he is the Only Begotten of the Father—

That by him, and through him, and of him, the worlds are and were created, and the inhabitants thereof are begotten sons and daughters unto God. (D. & C. 76:19-24.)

Note how this parallels Joseph Smith's first vision and the testimony of the Father at Jesus' baptism. The Father spoke of his Son—two separate and distinct persons. The Father must have had a voice or he could not have spoken.

This testimony shall now stand as a witness unto all to whom it shall come, until he shall again return to reign as "Lord of lords and King of kings." (See Rev. 17:14.)

An understanding of the reality of his existence and personality gives real meaning to his promise found in Christ's Sermon on the Mount: "Blessed are the pure in heart: for they shall *see* God." (Matt. 5:8.)

Scriptures Often Misunderstood Concerning the Personality of God

There are a few statements in the Bible which have been misunderstood and have led to a misconception of the personality and form of God and of his Son, Jesus Christ. Brief consideration might be given to some of them:

> No man hath seen God at any time; the only begotten Son, which is in the bosom of the Father, he hath declared him. (John 1:18.)

> No man hath seen God at any time. If we love one another, God dwelleth in us, and his love is perfected in us. (I John 4:12.)

In the Inspired Version of the Bible, as rendered by the Prophet Joseph Smith, he gives us the following:

> And no man hath seen God at any time, *except he hath borne record of the Son;* for except it is through him no man can be saved. (John 1:19.)

He also gives us the rendition of I John 4:12 as follows:

> No man hath seen God at any time, *except them who believe.* If we love one another, God dwelleth in us, and his love is perfected in us.

The Prophet Joseph Smith's understanding of the true meaning of these scriptures was made plain in a revelation received by him from the Lord at Hiram, Ohio, November, 1831:

> For no man has seen God at any time in the flesh, except quickened by the Spirit of God. (D. & C. 67:11.)

This doctrine was further clarified in the Visions of Moses as revealed to the Prophet Joseph Smith:

> But now mine own eyes have beheld God; but not my natural, but my spiritual eyes, for my natural eyes could not have beheld, for I should have withered and died in his presence; *but his glory was upon me; and I beheld his face,* for I was transfigured before him. (P. of G. P. Moses 1:11.)

It is thus plain that man can only see God when *"quickened by the Spirit of God."* This is apparently what John had in mind in the following statement:

> It is written in the prophets, And they shall be all taught of God. Every man therefore that hath heard, and hath learned of the Father, cometh unto me.
>
> Not that any man hath seen the Father, *save he which is of God, he hath seen the Father.* (John 6:45-46.)

Paul spoke of God as an "invisible God":

> In whom we have redemption through his blood, even the forgiveness of sins:
>
> Who is the image of the *invisible God,* the firstborn of every creature. (Col. 1:14-15.)

Further study of Paul's teachings indicates that he had the same understanding as John; that while God is *invisible* to men generally, he is not invisible to the prophets, for he indicated that Moses saw the *invisible God:*

> By faith he forsook Egypt, not fearing the wrath of the king: for he endured, as seeing him who is invisible. (Heb. 11:27.)

John also referred to God as a spirit, which is confusing to some:

> God is a Spirit: and they that worship him must worship him in spirit and in truth. (John 4:24.)

This should not be confusing since we are all spirits, clothed with bodies of flesh and bones. John says we are to "worship him in spirit and in truth." He would not, however, imply that our spirits should leave our bodies so that we can worship him "in spirit."

Paul declared: "But he that is joined unto the Lord is one spirit." (I Cor. 6:17.) We are spirits in the same sense that John had in mind when he said, "God is a Spirit."

The Oneness of the Father and the Son

There has been much misunderstanding regarding the oft repeated statement that Jesus and his Father are one. A careful reading of the seventeenth chapter of John should clarify this matter fully. As Jesus was about to be offered up, he prayed unto his Father and thanked him for his Apostles, and prayed, "that they may be one, as we are." (See John 17:11.) Then he added:

> Neither pray I for these alone, but for them also which shall believe on me through their word;
>
> That they all may be one; as thou, Father, art in me, and I in thee, that they also *may be one in us;* that the world may believe that thou hast sent me. (John 17:20-21.)

Now it is very apparent that Jesus was not speaking of oneness of personage but oneness of purpose, for he further prayed that they might be with him, which would be unnecessary if the oneness referred to was of personage instead of purpose:

> Father, I will that they also, whom thou hast given me, be with me where I am; that they may behold my glory, which thou

hast given me: for thou lovedst me before the foundation of the world. (John 17:24.)

Again it is evident that the *oneness* referred to has no reference to oneness of personage, for if Jesus and his Father were one in person, how absurd to think that Jesus would pray unto himself, or that he would love himself before the foundation of the world.

And this is life eternal, that they might know thee the only true God, and Jesus Christ, whom thou hast sent. (John 17:3.)

This true knowledge of God, and his Son, Jesus Christ, has come again to the world in this dispensation, not through a study of the Bible, but through the actual appearance of these heavenly personages to the boy, Joseph Smith, as he has so eloquently testified.

CHAPTER 4

FALSE DOCTRINES AND UNIVERSAL APOSTASY

Apostasy from the Truth

A second great truth was revealed in the visitation of the Father and the Son to the Prophet Joseph Smith through the announcement made by the Savior of the world in answer to Joseph Smith's question as to which of the churches he should join. He was told he should join none of them, for they were all wrong. The Personage who addressed him said:

> . . . "they draw near to me with their lips, but their hearts are far from me; they teach for doctrines the commandments of men, having a form of godliness, but they deny the power thereof." (P. of G. P. Joseph Smith 2:19.)

This pronouncement brought to the boy Joseph Smith the information he so much desired, for, more than anything else, he wanted to know which of all the churches he should join, and it was to obtain this information that he went to the Lord in prayer.

Erroneous Teachings of the Christian Churches

One erroneous teaching of many Christian churches is: *By faith alone we are saved.* This false doctrine would relieve man from the responsibility of his acts other than to confess a belief in God, and would teach man that no matter how great the sin, a confession would bring him complete forgiveness and salvation. What the world needs is more preaching of the necessity of abstaining from sin and living useful and righteous lives and less preaching of forgiveness of sin. This would then be a different world. The truth is that men must repent of their sins and forsake them before they can expect forgiveness. Even when our sins are forgiven, God cannot reward us for the good we have not done.

The Prophet Mormon, who lived upon the American continent about 400 A.D., foretold the coming of the plates from which the Book of Mormon should be translated and described the condition of the churches which should then be found among the people:

> Yea, it shall come in a day when the power of God shall be denied, and churches become defiled and be lifted up in the pride of their hearts; yea, even in a day when leaders of churches and teachers shall rise in the pride of their hearts, even to the envying of them who belong to their churches . . .
>
> Yea, it shall come in a day when there shall be churches built up that shall say: Come unto me, and for your money you shall be forgiven of your sins. (Mormon 8:28, 32.)

Doctrine of Predestination

Again, there is the erroneous doctrine of predestination, that without any act on our part some are predestined to eternal life and some to eternal damnation, and that no matter in which class we find ourselves, there is nothing we can do about it. A complete analysis of this doctrine forces one to the conclusion that, if true, God would be responsible for all the sin and iniquity in the world since the belief is that all our acts were pre-determined before we were born, whether they be good or evil.

In his effort to destroy truth, Satan could hardly have hoped to deceive men more effectively and completely than to take from them a consciousness of their responsibilities through the teaching of such doctrines.

One Heaven and One Hell

Then again, there is the false teaching of one heaven and one hell, with the thought that all who reach heaven will share alike, and the same with those who are assigned to hell.

The truth, as restored through the Prophet Joseph Smith, emphasizes the fact that every man will receive according to his works; that there is a glory like the sun, another like the moon, and still another like the stars, and that the glory to which he shall be assigned will be determined by the things he does and the life he lives.

God Cannot Be a God of Confusion

Sane thinking leads one to the conclusion that God cannot be the author of confusion; that two contradictory organizations could not originate with him, for God cannot be divided against himself. According to Paul:

> And he gave some, apostles; and some, prophets; and some, evangelists; and some, pastors and teachers;
>
> For the perfecting of the saints, for the work of the ministry, for the edifying of the body of Christ:
>
> Till we all *come in the unity of the faith,* and of the knowledge of the Son of God, unto a perfect man, unto the measure of the stature of the fulness of Christ:
>
> That we henceforth be no more children, tossed to and fro, and carried about with every wind of doctrine, by the *sleight of men,* and cunning craftiness, whereby they lie in wait to deceive. (Eph. 4:11-14.)

When Joseph Smith commenced his search for truth, it soon became apparent that the Christian churches had not "come in the unity of the faith." Paul indicated they were "carried about with every wind of doctrine, by the sleight of men." Hence the statement of the Savior to Joseph Smith, that all their creeds were wrong.

In the reading of the scriptures men would discover truths that were not to be found in the existing churches. They would gather a group together and then organize a church without any direct call or ordination from God. Hence the Christian sects multiplied until they numbered hundreds. Such leaders would emphasize one certain principle, and then organize a church around that one thought: for instance, spiritual gifts, apostles, worship on the seventh day, etc.

Mission of the True Church

The mission of the true Church, under divine inspiration and leadership, should bring together into one Church all the truths that are to be found in all other Christian churches, as well as those which have been overlooked, or ignored, and eliminate all error and man-made doctrines. This is what the Lord did in restoring his Church to the earth through the instrumentality of the Prophet Joseph Smith.

Contemporary Opinions Affirming the Great Apostasy

The idea that the churches had gone astray and lost their vitality and authority accords with the judgment of some of our greatest thinkers, and with prophecies of the Holy Scriptures, as the following references will indicate:

In a work prepared by seventy-three noted divines and Bible students, we read:

> We must not expect to see the church of Holy Scripture actually existing in its perfection on the earth. It is not to be found thus perfect either in the collected fragments of Christendom, or still less in any one of those fragments. (Dr. William Smith, *Smith's Dictionary of the Bible*, Houghton Mifflin Company, Boston, Mass.)

Thus these seventy-three learned men, in effect, confirm the statement of Jesus to Joseph Smith—that all their creeds were wrong.

Roger Williams, pastor of the oldest Baptist Church in America at Providence, Rhode Island, refused to continue as pastor on the grounds that there was—

> . . . no regularly constituted church of Christ, on earth, nor any person authorized to administer any church ordinance, nor can there be until new apostles are sent by the great head of the Church, for whose coming, I am seeking. (*Picturesque America,* p. 503.)

Had Roger Williams been privileged to live to know the Prophet Joseph Smith and hear his message, he would have found that which he was seeking.

Dr. Harry Emerson Fosdick described the decadent condition of the Christian church in these words:

> A religious reformation is afoot, and at heart it is the endeavor to recover for our modern life the religion of Jesus as against the vast, intricate, largely inadequate and often positively false religion about Jesus. Christianity today has largely left the religion which he preached, taught and lived, and has substituted another kind of religion altogether.
>
> If Jesus should come back to earth now, hear the mythologies built up around him, see the creedalism, denominationalism, sacramentalism, carried on in his name, he would certainly say, "If this is Christianity, I am not a Christian." (*Liahona,* Vol. 23, No. 22, p. 424.)

These and similar statements of ministers from various nations would certainly seem to corroborate the statement of the Savior to Joseph Smith, and should motivate thinking seekers after truth to want to hear the remainder of the Prophet's story.

Bible Predictions Foretelling the Great Apostasy

Now, let us consider the scriptural predictions that the time and conditions we have considered would come:

This know also, that *in the last days* perilous times shall come.

For men shall be lovers of their own selves, covetous, boasters, proud, blasphemers, disobedient to parents, unthankful, unholy,

Without natural affection, trucebreakers, false accusers, incontinent, fierce, despisers of those that are good,

Traitors, heady, highminded, lovers of pleasures more than lovers of God;

Having a form of Godliness, but denying the power thereof: from such turn away. (II Tim. 3:1-5.)

Now we beseech you, brethren, by the coming of our Lord Jesus Christ, and by our gathering together unto him.

That ye be not soon shaken in mind, or be troubled, neither by spirit, nor by word, nor by letter as from us, as that the day of Christ is at hand.

Let no man deceive you by any means: for that day shall not come, except there come a falling away first, and that man of sin be revealed, the son of perdition;

Who opposeth and exalteth himself above all that is called God, or that is worshipped; so that he as God sitteth in the temple of God, shewing himself that he is God. (II Thess. 2:1-4.)

For the time will come when they will not endure sound doctrine; but after their own lusts shall they heap to themselves teachers, having itching ears;

And they shall turn away their ears from the truth, and shall be turned unto fables. (II Tim. 4:3-4.)

From the above it is very evident that the Apostle Paul was privileged to see our time and describe in advance the very conditions the Savior referred to in his denunciation of the churches to Joseph Smith, and as admitted by prominent ministers of the day. He indicated that these conditions were to exist in *"the last days,"* that men would have *"itching ears,"* and thus gather to themselves teachers after their own hearts and thus "turn away their ears from the truth." He states further that men cannot look for the second promised advent of the Christ except there be a "falling away first," so that all we have said is but an announcement that the events predicted have come to pass.

When the Apostle John was banished upon the Isle of Patmos, he saw the power that would be given to Satan:

> And it was given unto him to make war with the saints, and to overcome them: and power was given him over all kindreds, and tongues, and nations. (Rev. 13:7.)

From this, it is evident that all kindreds, and tongues, and nations should succumb to this evil power, which we will further understand more fully when we find that John saw the bringing back of the gospel to the earth to be preached to every nation, kindred, tongue and people. (See Rev. 14:6-7.)

To understand this scripture properly, it should be remembered that the followers of Christ were called *saints*. (See Eph. 2:19; II Cor. 8:4; I Cor. 14:33.)

Knowing how universal this departure from the truth should be, enables one to understand some of the prophecies of the ancient prophets as recorded in the Old Testament:

> Behold, the days come, saith the Lord God, that I will send a famine in the land, not a famine of bread, nor a thirst for water, but of hearing the words of the Lord:
>
> And they shall wander from sea to sea, and from the north even to the east, they shall run to and fro to seek the word of the Lord, and shall not find it. (Amos 8:11-12.)

In light of the words of Jesus: "Seek and ye shall find," there can be but one explanation why they would not be able to find the word of the Lord, even though they would seek "from sea to sea, and from the north even to the east." The answer is, as Amos indicated, that the Lord would send a "famine in the land," a famine for hearing the word of the Lord.

The Prophet Micah saw the day when there would be "no answer of God." He described the apostate condition of Israel as follows:

> Thus saith the Lord concerning the prophets that make my people err, that bite with their teeth, and cry, Peace; and he that putteth not into their mouths, they even prepare war against him.
>
> Therefore night shall be unto you, that ye shall not have a vision; and it shall be dark unto you, that ye shall not divine; and the sun shall go down over the prophets, and the day shall be dark over them.
>
> Then shall the seers be ashamed, and the diviners confounded: yea, they shall all cover their lips; for there is no answer of God . . .
>
> The heads thereof judge for reward, and the priests thereof teach for hire, and the prophets thereof divine for money: yet will they lean upon the Lord, and say, Is not the Lord among us? none evil can come upon us. (Micah 3:5-7,11.)

Isaiah had a similar vision of what was to happen to Israel:

> Behold, the Lord maketh the earth empty, and maketh it waste, and turneth it upside down, and scattereth abroad the inhabitants thereof.
>
> And it shall be, as with the people, so with the priest; as with the servant, so with his master; as with the maid, so with her mistress; as with the buyer, so with the seller; as with the lender, so with the borrower; as with the taker of usury, so with the giver of usury to him.
>
> The land shall be utterly emptied, and utterly spoiled: for the Lord hath spoken this word.
>
> The earth mourneth and fadeth away, the world languisheth and fadeth away, the haughty people of the earth do languish.
>
> The earth also is defiled under the inhabitants thereof; *because they have transgressed the laws, changed the ordinances, broken the everlasting covenant.*
>
> Therefore hath the curse devoured the earth, and they that dwell therein are desolate: therefore the inhabitants of the earth are burned, and few men left. (Isa. 24:1-6.)

Isaiah understood the displeasure of the Lord that would rest upon the inhabitants of the earth for having "transgressed the laws, changed the ordinance, broken the everlasting covenant," and in light of the destructive powers of the recently discovered atom bomb and other scientific developments along this line, it is not difficult to understand that the predicted destruction could result in there being "few men left" upon the earth.

Paul also shared with the prophets a full understanding of the Lord's displeasure with those who should assume to change the truths of his gospel:

> But though we, or an angel from heaven, preach any other gospel unto you than that which we have preached unto you, let him be accursed. (Gal. 1:8.)

In explaining the condition of the Christian world as the Savior replied to Joseph Smith's query as to which church he should join, he repeated the statement revealed to Isaiah, (See Isa. 29:13-14.) This condition was to be followed by the Lord proceeding to do a marvelous work and a wonder among the children of men.

> Wherefore the Lord said, Forasmuch as this people draw near me with their mouth, and with their lips do honour me, but have removed their heart far from me, and their fear toward me is taught by the precept of men:
>
> Therefore, behold, I will proceed to do a marvellous work among this people, even a marvellous work and a wonder; for the wisdom of their wise men shall perish, and the understanding of their prudent men shall be hid. (Isa. 29:13-14.)

Since the departure from the true gospel of Christ was to be universal, as the prophets foretold, and since such universal apostasy was confirmed in the statement of Jesus made to Joseph Smith, it would follow that a restoration would be necessary. Such a restoration is the message of The Church of Jesus Christ of Latter-day Saints.

CHAPTER 5

A MARVELOUS WORK AND A WONDER TO COME FORTH

Necessity for a Restoration

We have already pointed out that the prophets foresaw a universal departure from the truth, and that such a condition obtained in the world at the time Joseph Smith went into the woods to pray. This being true, a restoration of the gospel must necessarily follow if the world were not to be left in spiritual darkness. Peter declared:

> We have also a more sure word of prophecy; whereunto ye do well that ye take heed, as unto a light that shineth in a dark place, until the day dawn, and the day star arise in your hearts: (II Peter 1:19.)

It now seems proper that we should consider the words of the prophets. We refer first to the words of Isaiah already quoted in the last chapter, since the visit of the Father and the Son to Joseph Smith marked the first step in the *marvelous work and a wonder* the Lord promised to bring forth:

> Wherefore the Lord said, Forasmuch as this people draw near me with their mouth, and with their lips do honour me, but have removed their heart far from me, and their fear toward me is taught by the precept of men:
>
> Therefore, behold, I will proceed to do a marvellous work among this people, even a marvellous work and a wonder: for the wisdom of their wise men shall perish, and the understanding of their prudent men shall be hid. (Isa. 29:13-14.)

What would really constitute a marvelous work and a wonder? Why should not honest lovers of truth welcome the pronouncement of such a work? Should any generation reject revealed truth when sent from heaven, even as they rejected the Christ when he came among men? Why does it seem so much easier to accept and believe in the dead prophets than in living prophets?

The Restitution of All Things

In the accomplishment of this promised marvelous work and a wonder, the Lord had in mind a "restitution of all things" and moved upon Peter to so prophesy to those who had crucified his Lord:

> Repent ye therefore, and be converted, that your sins may be blotted out, when the times of refreshing shall come from the presence of the Lord;
>
> And he shall send Jesus Christ, which before was preached unto you:
>
> Whom the heaven must receive until the times of restitution of all things, which God hath spoken by the mouth of all his holy prophets since the world began. (Acts 3:19-21.)

Let us analyze this promise: (1) that their great sin might be forgiven; (2) that the Lord would send to them again that same Jesus which had been before preached unto them; (3) that there would be a "restitution of all things, which God hath spoken by the mouth of all his holy prophets since the world began."

When looking for the second coming of the Christ as herein promised, we must realize that he will not come before there is a "restitution of all things." It is obvious that there cannot be a restitution of that which has not been taken away. Therefore, this scripture is another very plain prediction of apostasy—the taking of the gospel from the earth—with a promise of a complete restoration of all things spoken by all the holy prophets since the world began.

It was the time of such a complete restitution that Paul must have had in mind when he wrote to the Ephesians:

> Having made known unto us the mystery of his will, according to his good pleasure which he hath purposed in himself:
>
> That in the dispensation of the fullness of times he might gather together in one all things in Christ, both which are in heaven, and which are on earth; even in him. (Eph. 1:9-10.)

It is the pronouncement of The Church of Jesus Christ of Latter-day Saints that this is the Dispensation of the Fulness of Times, and that through the "restitution of all things" the Lord has made provision to "gather together in one all things in Christ, both which are in heaven, and which are on earth." This "restitution of all things" will, however, not be complete until the end of the thousand years of the personal reign of Christ upon the earth when death will be destroyed. (See I Cor. 15:-24-26.) There is no other such plan in the world today.

God's Kingdom in the Latter-Days

When the Lord gave the Prophet Daniel the interpretation of King Nebuchadnezzar's dream, he saw the rise and fall of the kingdoms of the world which makes an interesting study for its accuracy. The important thing, however, was his observation that in the "latter days" the God of heaven would set up a kingdom that ultimately would subdue all other kingdoms and would become as a great mountain and fill the whole earth:

> Daniel answered in the presence of the king, and said, The secret which the king hath demanded cannot the wise men, the astrologers, the magicians, the soothsayers, shew unto the king;
>
> But there is a God in heaven that revealeth secrets, and maketh known to the king Nebuchadnezzar what shall be in the *latter days.* Thy dream, and the visions of thy head upon thy bed are these. . . .
>
> Thou sawest till that a stone was cut out without hands, which smote the image upon his feet that were of iron and clay, and brake them to pieces.

. . . and the stone that smote the image became a great mountain, and filled the whole earth. . . .

And in the days of these kings *shall the God of heaven set up a kingdom, which shall never be destroyed:* and the kingdom shall not be left to other people, but it shall break in pieces and consume all these kingdoms, and it shall stand for ever. (Dan. 2:27-28, 34-35, 44.)

The establishment of his kingdom by "the God of heaven" was to be the greatest event "in the latter days." Though small and insignificant as its beginning would be, its ultimate destiny is to fill the whole earth, with Christ our Lord at its head. The kingdom was to be given to the saints of the Most High that they might possess it forever.

With all our present day (latter-day) development and progress, scientific and otherwise, why should we not be concerned with the promised spiritual development? Daniel gave us the sure word of prophecy:

I saw in the night visions, and, behold, one like the Son of man came with the clouds of heaven, and came to the Ancient of days, and they brought him near before him.

And there was given him dominion, and glory, and a kingdom, that all people, nations, and languages, should serve him: his dominion is an everlasting dominion, which shall not pass away, and his kingdom that which shall not be destroyed. . . .

But the saints of the most High shall take the kingdom, and possess the kingdom for ever, even for ever and ever. (Dan. 7:13-14, 18.)

In a revelation to the Prophet Joseph Smith February 24, 1834, the Lord said:

But verily I say unto you, that I have decreed a decree which my people shall realize, inasmuch as they hearken from this very hour unto the counsel which I, the Lord their God, shall give unto them.

Behold they shall, for I have decreed it, begin to prevail against mine enemies from this very hour.

> And by hearkening to observe all the words which I, the Lord their God, shall speak unto them, they shall never cease to prevail until the kingdoms of the world are subdued under my feet, and the earth is given unto the saints, to possess it forever and ever. (D. & C. 103:5-7.)

In our consideration of the apostasy, we referred to what the Lord showed to John while he was on the Isle of Patmos. He saw that power would be given to Satan "to make war with the saints, and to overcome them: and power was given him over all kindreds, and tongues, and nations." (See Rev. 13:7.)

John experienced these further prophetic visions:

> After this I looked, and, behold, a door was opened in heaven: and the first voice which I heard was as it were of a trumpet talking with me; which said, Come up hither, and I will shew thee things which must be *hereafter.* (Rev. 4:1.)

Restoration of the Gospel Foretold

John not only saw that Satan's power would be universal for a season, but he saw a recommitment to the earth of the "everlasting gospel" which was to be preached to all people:

> And I saw another angel fly in the midst of heaven, having the *everlasting gospel* to preach unto them that dwell on the earth, and to every nation, and kindred, and tongue, and people,
>
> Saying with a loud voice, Fear God, and give glory to him; for the hour of his judgment is come: and worship him that made heaven, and earth, and the sea, and the fountains of waters. (Rev. 14:6-7.)

If there had been any nation, kindred, tongue, or people upon the earth still in possession of "the everlasting gospel," it would not have been necessary that an angel bring it back to the earth. This angel was also to call the inhabitants of the earth back to a worship of the God that "made heaven, and earth, and the sea, and the fountains of waters." We have already pointed out that the everlasting gospel was to be taken from the earth, and it is now our witness that it has been returned to the earth by the angel, through the Prophet Joseph Smith, from the God of heaven.

The Prophet Malachi also saw this promised day of restoration through messengers sent from God, which he described in these words:

> Behold, I will send my messenger and he shall prepare the way before me: and the Lord, whom ye seek, shall suddenly come to his temple, even the messenger of the covenant, whom ye delight in: behold, he shall come, saith the Lord of hosts. (Mal. 3:1.)

A full consideration of this verse and those following indicates that this promise had reference to the second coming of Jesus Christ and not to his first coming, since he is to come suddenly to his temple, which he did not do at his first coming.

The Calling of Joseph Smith

The promises herein referred to concerning the establishment of a "latter day" kingdom through the sending of heavenly messengers, and the restoration of the "everlasting gospel" to be preached in all the world, could not be fulfilled without someone upon the earth to whom such restoration and commitments could be made.

This brings us to another great truth we learn from the visit of the Father and the Son to the boy Joseph Smith, i.e., that prophets are never self-sent—they must be called and sent of God:

> Surely the Lord God will do nothing, but he revealeth his secret unto his servants the prophets. (Amos 3:7.)

Thus with Joseph Smith selected by the Lord, we are now prepared to consider what he revealed to his chosen prophet.

Criticism has been expressed because the boy, Joseph Smith, was only in his fifteenth year when the Father and the Son appeared unto him. Let us consider the words of Jesus:

> No man also seweth a piece of new cloth on an old garment: else the new piece that filled it up taketh away from the old, and the rent is made worse.
>
> And no man putteth new wine into old bottles: else the new wine doth burst the bottles, and the wine is spilled, and the bottles will be marred: but new wine must be put into new bottles. (Mark 2:21-22.)

We would not expect the Lord to select a man who had been steeped in the traditions and doctrines of men for such individual would be too difficult to teach. As Jesus said, the new wine would burst the bottles, and the wine be spilled. However, by selecting the lad, Joseph Smith, the Lord could teach him as he would, and it would truly be new wine in a new bottle without conflict with the old. Thus we see that the Lord has his own way of doing things. Surely this is his divine right and his privilege:

> For my thoughts are not your thoughts, neither are your ways my ways, saith the Lord.
>
> For as the heavens are higher than the earth, so are my ways higher than your ways, and my thoughts than your thoughts. (Isa. 55:8-9.)

There is another reason why it does not seem inconsistent that the Lord selected a mere boy, for we all lived in the spirit before we were born in the flesh. The Lord knew us and knew the nature of our spirits and the measure of our integrity. That is why he selected Jesus Christ "before the world was" to be the Redeemer of the world:

> And now, O Father, glorify thou me with thine own self with the glory which I had with thee before the world was. (John 17:5.)

This is the reason why Jeremiah was called to be a prophet unto the nations:

> Before I formed thee in the belly I knew thee; and before thou camest forth out of the womb I sanctified thee, and I ordained thee a prophet unto the nations. (Jer. 1:5.)

Now, of course, Jeremiah could not have been so called and ordained before he was born if he did not exist. We will speak more of this subject later; and we will learn that Joseph Smith was also selected before he was born, as was Jeremiah.

This makes it easy to understand why the "everlasting gospel" could not be discovered through reading the Bible alone—the old bottles full of old wine could not contain the new wine. So glorious was to be the day when the Lord would "proceed to do a marvellous work among this people, even a marvellous work and a wonder," that he had to select one free from all exposure to the unsound philosophies of men. That is why our original statement is consistent:

That this is the only Christian church in the world that did not have to rely upon the Bible for its organization and government; that had all the Bibles in the world been destroyed we would still be teaching the same principles and administering the same ordinances as introduced and taught by Jesus and the prophets. True, we take the Bible to prove that these principles and ordinances accord with divine truths of all ages, but if we had no Bible we would still have all the needed direction and information through the revelations of the Lord "to his servants the prophets" in these latter-days.

CHAPTER 6

THE COMING FORTH OF THE BOOK OF MORMON

Visit of Angel Moroni to Joseph Smith

At this point it seems proper that we should let Joseph Smith tell his own story of what happened from the time the Father and his Son, Jesus Christ, appeared to him in the spring of 1820 until the first messenger was sent from heaven to further instruct him:

> I had now got my mind satisfied so far as the sectarian world was concerned—that it was not my duty to join with any of them, but to continue as I was until further directed. I had found the testimony of James to be true—that a man who lacked wisdom might ask of God, and obtain, and not be upbraided.
>
> I continued to pursue my common vocations in life until the twenty-first of September, one thousand eight hundred and twenty-three, all the time suffering severe persecution at the hands of all classes of men, both religious and irreligious, because I continued to affirm that I had seen a vision.
>
> During the space of time which intervened between the time I had the vision and the year eighteen hundred and twenty-three—having been forbidden to join any of the religious sects of the day, and being of very tender years, and persecuted by those who ought to have been my friends and to have treated me kindly, and if they supposed me to be deluded to have endeavored in a proper and affectionate manner to have reclaimed me—I was left to all kinds of temptation; and, mingling with all kinds of society, I frequently fell into many foolish errors, and displayed the weakness of youth, and the foibles of human nature; which, I am sorry to say, led me into divers temptations, offensive in the sight of God. In making this confession, no one need suppose me guilty of any great or malignant sins. A disposition to commit such was never in my nature. But I was guilty of levity, and sometimes associated with jovial company, etc., not

consistent with that character which ought to be maintained by one who was called of God as I had been. But this will not seem very strange to anyone who recollects my youth, and is acquainted with my native cheery temperament.

In consequence of these things, I often felt condemned for my weakness and imperfections; when, on the evening of the above-mentioned twenty-first day of September, after I had retired to my bed for the night, I betook myself to prayer and supplication to Almighty God for forgiveness of all my sins and follies, and also for a manifestation to me, that I might know of my state and standing before him; for I had full confidence in obtaining a divine manifestation, as I previously had one.

While I was thus in the act of calling upon God, I discovered a light appearing in my room, which continued to increase until the room was lighter than at noonday, when immediately a personage appeared at my bedside, standing in the air, for his feet did not touch the floor.

He had on a loose robe of most exquisite whiteness. It was a whiteness beyond anything earthly I had ever seen; nor do I believe that any earthly thing could be made to appear so exceedingly white and brilliant. His hands were naked, and his arms also, a little above the wrist; so, also, were his feet naked, as were his legs, a little above the ankles. His head and neck were also bare. I could discover that he had no other clothing on but this robe, as it was open, so that I could see into his bosom.

Not only was his robe exceedingly white, but his whole person was glorious beyond description, and his countenance truly like lightning. The room was exceedingly light, but not so very bright as immediately around his person. When I first looked upon him, I was afraid; but the fear soon left me.

He called me by name, and said unto me that he was a messenger sent from the presence of God to me, and that his name was Moroni; that God had a work for me to do; and that my name should be had for good and evil among nations, kindreds, and tongues, or that it should be both good and evil spoken of among all people.

He said there was a book deposited, written upon gold plates, giving an account of the former inhabitants of this continent, and the source from whence they sprang. He also said that the fulness of the everlasting Gospel was contained in it, as delivered by the Savior to the ancient inhabitants;

Also, that there were two stones in silver bows—and these stones, fastened to a breastplate, constituted what is called the Urim and Thummim—deposited with the plates; and the possession and use of these stones were what constituted "seers" in ancient or former times; and that God had prepared them for the purpose of translating the book.

After telling me these things, he commenced quoting the prophecies of the Old Testament. He first quoted part of the third chapter of Malachi; and he quoted also the fourth or last chapter of the same prophecy, though with a little variation from the way it reads in our Bibles. Instead of quoting the first verse as it reads in our books, he quoted it thus:

For behold, the day cometh that shall burn as an oven, and all the proud, yea, and all that do wickedly shall burn as stubble; for they that come shall burn them, saith the Lord of Hosts, that it shall leave them neither root nor branch.

And again, he quoted the fifth verse thus: *Behold, I will reveal unto you the Priesthood, by the hand of Elijah the prophet, before the coming of the great and dreadful day of the Lord.*

He also quoted the next verse differently: *And he shall plant in the hearts of the children the promises made to the fathers, and the hearts of the children shall turn to their fathers. If it were not so, the whole earth would be utterly wasted at his coming.*

In addition to these, he quoted the eleventh chapter of Isaiah, saying that it was about to be fulfilled. He quoted also the third chapter of Acts, twenty-second and twenty-third verses, precisely as they stand in our New Testament. He said that that prophet was Christ; but the day had not yet come when "they who would not hear his voice should be cut off from among the people," but soon would come.

He also quoted the second chapter of Joel, from the twenty-eighth verse to the last. He also said that this was not yet fulfilled, but was soon to be. And he further stated that the fulness of the Gentiles was soon to come in. He quoted many other passages of scripture, and offered many explanations which cannot be mentioned here.

Again, he told me, that when I got those plates of which he had spoken—for the time that they should be obtained was not yet fulfilled—I should not show them to any person; neither the breastplate with the Urim and Thummim; only to those to whom I should be commanded to show them; if I did I should be destroyed. While he was conversing with me about the plates, the vision was opened to my mind that I could see the place where the plates were deposited, and that so clearly and distinctly that I knew the place again when I visited it.

After this communication, I saw the light in the room begin to gather immediately around the person of him who had been speaking to me, and it continued to do so until the room was again left dark, except just around him; when, instantly I saw, as it were, a conduit open right up into heaven, and he ascended till he entirely disappeared, and the room was left as it had been before this heavenly light had made its appearance.

I lay musing on the singularity of the scene, and marveling greatly at what had been told to me by this extraordinary messenger; when, in the midst of my meditation, I suddenly discovered that my room was again beginning to get lighted, and in an instant, as it were, the same heavenly messenger was again by my bedside.

He commenced, and again related the very same things which he had done at his first visit, without the least variation; which having done, he informed me of great judgments which were coming upon the earth, with great desolations by famine, sword, and pestilence; and that these grievous judgments would come on the earth in this generation. Having related these things, he again ascended as he had done before.

By this time, so deep were the impressions made on my mind, that sleep had fled from my eyes, and I lay overwhelmed in astonishment at what I had both seen and heard. But what was my surprise when again I beheld the same messenger at my bedside, and heard him rehearse or repeat over again to me the same things as before; and added a caution to me, telling me that Satan would try to tempt me (in consequence of the indigent circumstances of my father's family), to get the plates for the purpose of getting rich. This he forbade me, saying that I must have no other object in view in getting the plates but to glorify God, and must not be influenced by any other motive than that of building his kingdom; otherwise I could not get them.

After this third visit, he again ascended into heaven as

before, and I was again left to ponder on the strangeness of what I had just experienced; when almost immediately after the heavenly messenger had ascended from me for the third time, the cock crowed, and I found that day was approaching, so that our interviews must have occupied the whole of that night.

I shortly after arose from my bed, and, as usual, went to the necessary labors of the day; but, in attempting to work as at other times, I found my strength so exhausted as to render me entirely unable. My father, who was laboring along with me, discovered something to be wrong with me, and told me to go home. I started with the intention of going to the house; but, in attempting to cross the fence out of the field where we were, my strength entirely failed me and I fell helpless on the ground, and for a time was quite unconscious of anything.

The first thing that I can recollect was a voice speaking unto me, calling me by name. I looked up, and beheld the same messenger standing over my head, surrounded by light as before. He then again related unto me all that he had related to me the previous night, and commanded me to go to my father and tell him of the vision and commandments which I had received.

I obeyed; I returned to my father in the field, and rehearsed the whole matter to him. He replied to me that it was of God, and told me to go and do as commanded by the messenger. I left the field, and went to the place where the messenger had told me the plates were deposited; and owing to the distinctness of the vision which I had concerning it, I knew the place the instant that I arrived there.

Convenient to the village of Manchester, Ontario county, New York, stands a hill of considerable size, and the most elevated of any in the neighborhood. On the west side of this hill, not far from the top, under a stone of considerable size, lay the plates, deposited in a stone box. This stone was thick and rounding in the middle on the upper side, and thinner towards the edges, so that the middle part of it was visible above the ground, but the edge all around was covered with earth.

Having removed the earth, I obtained a lever, which I got fixed under the edge of the stone, and with a little exertion raised it up. I looked in, and there indeed did I behold the plates, the Urim and Thummim, and the breastplate, as stated by the messenger. The box in which they lay was formed by laying stones together in some kind of cement. In the bottom of the box were laid two stones crossways of the box, and on these stones lay the plates and the other things with them.

I made an attempt to take them out, but was forbidden by the messenger, and was again informed that the time for bringing them forth had not yet arrived, neither would it, until four years from that time; but he told me that I should come to that place precisely in one year from that time, and that he would there meet with me, and that I should continue to do so until the time should come for obtaining the plates.

Accordingly, as I had been commanded, I went at the end of each year, and at each time I found the same messenger there, and received instruction and intelligence from him at each of our interviews, respecting what the Lord was going to do, and how and in what manner his kingdom was to be conducted in the last days. . . .

At length the time arrived for obtaining the plates, the Urim and Thummim, and the breastplate. On the twenty-second day of September, one thousand eight hundred and twenty-seven, having gone as usual at the end of another year to the place where they were deposited, the same heavenly messenger delivered them up to me with this charge: that I should be responsible for them; that if I should let them go carelessly, or through any neglect of mine, I should be cut off; but that if I would use all my endeavors to preserve them, until he, the messenger, should call for them, they should be protected.

I soon found out the reason why I had received such strict charges to keep them safe, and why it was that the messenger had said that when I had done what was required at my hand, he would call for them. For no sooner was it known that I had them, than the most strenuous exertions were used to get them from me. Every stratagem that could be invented was resorted to for that purpose. The persecution became more bitter and severe than before, and multitudes were on the alert continually to get them from me if possible. But by the wisdom of God, they remained safe in my hands, until I had accomplished by them what was required at my hand. When, according to arrangements, the messenger called for them, I delivered them up to him; and he has them in his charge until this day, being the second day of May, one thousand eight hundred and thirty-eight.

The excitement, however, still continued, and rumor with her thousand tongues was all the time employed in circulating falsehoods about my father's family, and about myself. If I were to relate a thousandth part of them, it would fill up volumes. The persecution, however, became so intolerable that I was under the necessity of leaving Manchester, and going with my wife to Susquehanna County, in the State of Pennsylvania. While preparing to start—being very poor, and the persecution so heavy upon us that there was no probability that we would ever be otherwise—in the midst of our afflictions we found a friend in a gentleman by the name of Martin Harris, who came to us and gave me fifty dollars to assist us on our journey. Mr. Harris was a resident of Palmyra township, Wayne County, in the State of New York, and a farmer of respectability.

By this timely aid was I enabled to reach the place of my destination in Pennsylvania; and immediately after my arrival there I commenced copying the characters off the plates. I copied a considerable number of them, and by means of the Urim and Thummim I translated some of them, which I did between the time I arrived at the house of my wife's father, in the month of December, and the February following.

Sometime in this month of February, the aforementioned Mr. Martin Harris came to our place, got the characters which I had drawn off the plates, and started with them to the city of New York. For what took place relative to him and the characters, I refer to his own account of the circumstances, as he related them to me after his return, which was as follows:

"I went to the city of New York, and presented the characters which had been translated, with the translation thereof, to Professor Charles Anthon, a gentleman celebrated for his literary attainments. Professor Anthon stated that the translation was correct, more so than any he had before seen translated from the Egyptian. I then showed him those which were not yet translated, and he said they were Egyptian, Chaldaic, Assyriac, and Arabic; and he said they were true characters. He gave me a certificate, certifying to the people of Palmyra that they were true characters, and that the translation of such of them as had been translated were also correct. I took the certificate and put into my pocket, and was just leaving the house, when Mr. Anthon called me back, and asked me how the young man found out that there were gold plates in the place where he found them. I answered that an angel of God had revealed it unto him."

"He then said to me, 'Let me see that certificate.' I accordingly took it out of my pocket and gave it to him, when he took it and tore it to pieces, saying that there was no such thing now as ministering of angels, and that if I would bring the plates to him he would translate them. I informed him that part of the plates were sealed, and that I was forbidden to bring them. He replied, 'I cannot read a sealed book.' I left him and went to Dr. Mitchell, who sanctioned what Professor Anthon had said respecting both the characters and the translation."

On the 5th day of April, 1829, Oliver Cowdery came to my house, until which time I had never seen him. He stated to me that having been teaching school in the neighborhood where my father resided, and my father being one of those who sent to the school, he went to board for a season at his house, and while there the family related to him the circumstances of my having received the plates, and accordingly he had come to make inquiries of me.

Two days after the arrival of Mr. Cowdery (being the 7th of April) I commenced to translate the Book of Mormon, and he began to write for me. (P. of G. P. Joseph Smith 2:26-54, 59-67.)

Professor Charles Anthon Fulfils Isaiah's Prophecy

From the words of the radio commentator, to which we referred, such a story from Moroni, a prophet of God who lived upon the earth about 400 A.D., and who returned to the earth with a message from God, should constitute the greatest message that could possibly be broadcast to the world.

It has been said that if the plates from which the Book of Mormon was translated had been found by one plowing in his field and had been given to some college to be translated, that it would have been considered the greatest event of the nineteenth century. But, true to form, men are loath to accept anything that bears relationship to the miraculous or is reported to have come from a divine source.

This was evidenced in the experience related above by the Prophet Joseph Smith of the visit of Martin Harris to Professor Charles Anthon of New York, when Martin Harris presented to him some copy of the characters which appeared upon the gold plates.

When Professor Anthon said, as recounted above, "I cannot read a sealed book," he did not realize that he was literally fulfilling the prophecy of Isaiah:

> And the vision of all is become unto you as the words of a book that is sealed, which men deliver to one that is learned, saying, Read this, I pray thee: and he saith, I cannot; for it is sealed. (Isa. 29:11.)

Moroni's Prediction Concerning Joseph Smith

One of the important statements of the Angel Moroni to Joseph Smith was—

> He called me by name, and said unto me that he was a messenger sent from the presence of God to me, and that his name was Moroni; that God had a work for me to do; and that my name should be had for good and evil among all nations, kindreds, and tongues, or that it should be both good and evil spoken of among all people. (P. of G. P. Joseph Smith 2:33.)

This remarkable statement was made by the Angel Moroni, September 21, 1823, when Joseph Smith was not yet eighteen years of age, and six and one-half years before the Church was organized. Who, except a messenger from the presence of the Lord, would dare make such a statement today of any young man eighteen years of age? To be able to make a statement that a young man who had achieved great success in his schoolwork was destined to become prominent among his fellows, might be done with reasonable accuracy, but to be able to say of this young man who had scarcely seen the inside of a schoolroom, that his "name should be had for good and evil among all nations, kindreds and tongues, and that it should be both good and evil spoken of among all people," could only be done by one who understood the purposes of the Almighty as they were related to the divine mission of Joseph Smith.

The missionaries of the Church realize how completely the prediction of Moroni has been fulfilled. They have gone to all nations carrying the restored gospel message, and like the Prophet Joseph Smith, they have been persecuted, evil spoken of, imprisoned, and some have been put to death because they have borne witness that Joseph Smith was a prophet sent of God. While multitudes have reviled the prophet and called him an impostor and false prophet, the humble and meek of the earth who have heard and accepted the call of the missionaries, have gathered together and worshiped the Lord as he has revealed to the Prophet Joseph Smith. With joy and thanksgiving they have sung the song:

> Praise to the man who communed with Jehovah!
> Jesus anointed "that Prophet and Seer"—
> Blessed to open the last dispensation;
> Kings shall extol him, and nations revere.

> —W. W. Phelps

History has recorded a complete fulfilment of this prediction of Moroni concerning the life of Joseph Smith, for he, himself, was imprisoned and caused to stand trial many times on concocted charges which had been brought against him, mostly instigated by ministers of religion. In no case, however, was he found guilty of the charges preferred until his enemies are reported to have said: "If the law will not reach them, powder and ball can." (D.H.C. Vol. 6, p. 594.) Accordingly, Joseph Smith, and his brother Hyrum, were shot to death by a wicked mob at Carthage Jail, Illinois, June 27, 1844.

Some thought this would end the work of the Prophet Joseph Smith, established under divine revelation from heaven, but the works of a prophet are not so easily terminated:

> All the Prophets who have ever spoken upon the earth were insulted by men, and men will insult those who are to come. We can recognize Prophets by this, that smeared with mud and covered with shame, they pass among men, bright-faced, speaking out what is in their hearts. No mud can close the lips of those who must speak. Even if the obstinate prophet is killed, they cannot silence him. His voice multiplied by the echoes of his death will be heard in all languages and through all the centuries. (Giovanni Papini, *Life of Christ,* p. 93, Harcourt, Brace and Company, Inc. New York.)

The voice of the Prophet Joseph Smith has continued to be heard until his living followers today number more than one million souls, not counting those who have passed away, nor those who believed his message but have not had the courage to accept it because of the unfavorable attitude of relatives and friends, and the public generally, toward the Church which he established under the revelations of the Lord.

The Book of Mormon Prophets Commanded to Keep Records

The most important phases of Moroni's visit and message to Joseph Smith were: (1) to acquaint him with the existence of the gold plates containing the history of the early inhabitants of the Americas; (2) to reveal the words and teachings of the prophets who lived among them; (3) to proclaim the future destiny of the remnants of that people (the American Indians or Lamanites); (4) to declare that this land of America is "a land which is choice above all other lands" (See I Nephi 2:20.) and that upon it shall be established the New Jerusalem, according to the promise of the prophets.

We learn that the prophets who lived among the people upon this land of America were instructed by the Lord to keep records, that the Prophet Mormon, the father of Moroni, made an abridgment of all these records, from which the Book of Mormon was translated. The book bears the name of the great prophet, Mormon.

Moroni's introduction to his abridgment, taken from the introductory page of the Book of Mormon, is as follows:

> Wherefore, it is an abridgment of the record of the people of Nephi, and also of the Lamanites—Written to the Lamanites, who are a remnant of the house of Israel; and also to Jew and Gentile—Written by way of commandment, and also by the spirit of prophecy and of revelation—Written and sealed up, and hid up unto the Lord, that they might not be destroyed—To come forth by the gift and power of God unto the interpretation thereof—Sealed by the hand of Moroni, and hid up unto the Lord, to come forth in due time by way of the Gentile—The interpretation thereof by the gift of God.
>
> An abridgment taken from the Book of Ether also, which is a record of the people of Jared, who were scattered at the time the Lord confounded the language of the people, when they were building a tower to get to heaven—Which is to show unto the remnant of the House of Israel what great things the Lord hath done for their fathers; and that they may know the covenants of the Lord, that they are not cast off forever—And also to the convincing of the Jew and Gentile that *Jesus* is the *Christ, the Eternal God*, manifesting himself unto all nations—And now, if there are faults they are the mistakes of men; wherefore, condemn not the things of God, that ye may be found spotless at the judgment-seat of Christ.

From this it will be noted that one of the chief purposes for which this record has been preserved is for "the convincing of the Jew and Gentile that Jesus is the Christ, the Eternal God, manifesting himself unto all nations."

The Book of Mormon, A New Witness for Christ

It is general knowledge that faith in Jesus Christ as the Son of God, the Redeemer of the world, is waning, both among clergy and laity. In February, 1934, the Northwestern University, School of Education, Chicago, Illinois, sent a questionnaire to five hundred Protestant ministers, which revealed many modifications in religious beliefs. Of this number twenty-six percent or 130 of the five hundred ministers were opposed to the Deity of Jesus. (*The Deseret News,* Feb. 8, 1934.) *If* such be the result with the ministers, what can be expected from the laity? Such a condition would seem to indicate the great wisdom of God in providing a new witness of the divine mission of his Son, that he was in very deed "the Christ, the Eternal God, manifesting himself unto all nations."

Such is the testimony of the Book of Mormon. The Lord did not leave Joseph Smith's testimony regarding the plates from which this book was translated, and the inspired translation thereof, to stand alone, for as the Apostle Paul stated:

> ... In the mouth of two or three witnesses shall every word be established. (II Cor. 13:1.)

Testimony of the Three Witnesses to The Book of Mormon

Read the inspired testimony of the three witnesses to The Book of Mormon:

> Be It Known unto all nations, kindreds, tongues, and people, unto whom this work shall come: That we, through the grace of God the Father, and our Lord Jesus Christ, have seen the plates which contain this record, which is a record of the people of Nephi, and also of the Lamanites, their brethren, and also of the people of Jared, who came from the tower of which hath been spoken. And we also know that they have been translated by the gift and power of God, for his voice hath declared it unto us; wherefore we know of a surety that the work is true. And we also

testify that we have seen the engravings which are upon the plates; and they have been shown unto us by the power of God, and not of man. And we declare with words of soberness, that an angel of God came down from heaven, and he brought and laid before our eyes, that we beheld and saw the plates, and the engravings thereon; and we know that it is by the grace of God the Father, and our Lord Jesus Christ, that we beheld and bear record that these things are true. And it is marvelous in our eyes. Nevertheless, the voice of the Lord commanded us that we should bear record of it; wherefore, to be obedient unto the commandments of God, we bear testimony of these things. And we know that if we are faithful in Christ, we shall rid our garments of the blood of all men, and be found spotless before the judgment-seat of Christ, and shall dwell with him eternally in the heavens. And the honor be to the Father, and to the Son, and to the Holy Ghost, which is one God. Amen.

Oliver Cowdery
David Whitmer
Martin Harris

Each of these three witnesses passed from this life to meet his reward with a confirmation of the truth of his testimony upon his lips. Why should the world doubt? The testimony of three such men would convict any man in the courts of our land, and the testimony of these witnesses will stand against those who have heard it and who have refused to accept the truth.

The Lord's Promise Concerning The Book of Mormon

We should not overlook the promise contained in the last chapter of The Book of Mormon:

> And when ye shall receive these things, I would exhort you that ye would ask God, the eternal Father, in the name of Christ, if these things are not true; and if ye shall ask with a sincere heart, with real intent, having faith in Christ, he will manifest the truth of it unto you, by the power of the Holy Ghost. (Moroni 10:4.)

Thousands and tens of thousands have put this promise to the test and have witnessed its veritable fulfilment. Only God could make and fulfil such a promise.

CHAPTER 7

THE BOOK OF MORMON FULFILS BIBLE PROPHECIES

Possible Reasons for Erroneous Assumption that No Other Scriptures Are to Come Forth

When the plates which had been delivered to Joseph Smith by the Angel Moroni had been translated and published as the Book of Mormon, its distribution was met by much opposition, particularly by the ministers of the day who warned their followers against reading it. This, of itself, seems rather absurd, for if it were the work of man, as they claimed, their followers might have been counseled to read it and learn for themselves of its falsity. They were told the canon of scripture was complete; that we would never have more than that contained in the Holy Bible. They often quoted:

> For I testify unto every man that heareth the words of the prophecy of this book, If any man shall add unto these things, God shall add unto him the plagues that are written in this book:

> And if any man shall take away from the words of the book of this prophecy, God shall take away his part out of the book of life, and out of the holy city, and from the things which are written in this book. (Rev. 22:18-19.)

At first reading, one might be justified in assuming that the Apostle John meant that no other scripture would be added to the Bible, and this particularly in view of the fact that it is contained in the last chapter of the Bible as we now have it. It is easy to understand, however, that this interpretation is erroneous when one realizes, according to Bible scholars, (1) that this revelation was written sometime between 64 and 96 A.D.; (2) that John, himself, wrote his gospel (The Gospel According to St. John) at a much later date at Ephesus; (3) that at that time the books of the Bible were not compiled as we now have them. (See *Bible Helps,* S. Bagster & Sons, Lt'd., London, pp. 86 and 110.) It must, therefore, be understood that John was warning against adding to or taking from the revelations he had received and written while banished upon the Isle of Patmos. This does not, however, prevent the Lord from adding to what he had revealed.

By referring to the words of Moses we find evidence that no other conclusion is tenable, else we would be compelled to reject all the books of the Bible from Deuteronomy on:

> Ye shall not add unto the word which I command you, neither shall ye diminish ought from it, that ye may keep the commandments of the Lord your God which I command you. (Deut. 4:2.)

> What things soever I command you, observe to do it: thou shalt not add thereto, nor diminish from it. (Deut. 12:32.)

The Lord's Prophecy Concerning Other Scriptures

The Lord understood that Satan would put it into the hearts of the children of men to refuse to accept this new volume of scripture, the Book of Mormon, and so declared himself through the American Prophet, Nephi:

> But behold, there shall be many—at that day when I shall proceed to do a marvelous work among them, that I may remember my covenants which I have made unto the children of men, that I may set my hand again the second time to recover my people, which are of the house of Israel;

> And also, that I may remember the promises which I have made unto thee, Nephi, and also unto thy father, that I would remember your seed; and that the words of your seed should

proceed forth out of my mouth unto your seed; and my words shall hiss forth unto the ends of the earth, for a standard unto my people, which are of the house of Israel;

And because my words shall hiss forth—many of the Gentiles shall say: A Bible! A Bible! We have got a Bible, and there cannot be any more Bible.

But thus saith the Lord God: O fools, they shall have a Bible; and it shall proceed forth from the Jews, mine ancient covenant people. And what thank they the Jews for the Bible which they receive from them? Yea, what do the Gentiles mean? Do they remember the travels, and the labors, and the pains of the Jews, and their diligence unto me, in bringing forth salvation unto the Gentiles?

O ye Gentiles, have ye remembered the Jews, mine ancient covenant people? Nay; but ye have cursed them, and have hated them, and have not sought to recover them. But behold, I will return all these things upon your own heads; for I the Lord have not forgotten my people.

Thou fool, that shall say: A Bible, we have got a Bible, and we need no more Bible. Have ye obtained a Bible save it were by the Jews?

Know ye not that there are more nations than one? Know ye not that I, the Lord your God, have created all men, and that I remember those who are upon the isles of the sea; and that I rule in the heavens above and in the earth beneath; and I bring forth my word unto the children of men, yea, even upon all the nations of the earth?

Wherefore murmur ye, because that ye shall receive more of my word? Know ye not that the testimony of two nations is a witness unto you that I am God, that I remember one nation like unto another? Wherefore, I speak the same words unto one nation like unto another. And when the two nations shall run together the testimony of the two nations shall run together also.

And I do this that I may prove unto many that I am the same yesterday, today, and forever; and that I speak forth my words according to mine own pleasure. And because that I have spoken one word ye need not suppose that I cannot speak another; for my work is not yet finished; neither shall it be until the end of man, neither from that time henceforth and forever.

Wherefore, because that ye have a Bible ye need not suppose that it contains all my words; neither need ye suppose that I have not caused more to be written.

For I command all men, both in the east and in the west, and in the north, and in the south, and in the islands of the sea, that they shall write the words which I speak unto them; for out of the books which shall be written I will judge the world, every man according to their works, according to that which is written.

For behold, I shall speak unto the Jews and they shall write it; and I shall also speak unto the Nephites and they shall write it; and I shall also speak unto the other tribes of the house of Israel, which I have led away, and they shall write it; and I shall also speak unto all nations of the earth and they shall write it.

And it shall come to pass that the Jews shall have the words of the Nephites, and the Nephites shall have the words of the Jews; and the Nephites and Jews shall have the words of the lost tribes of Israel; and the lost tribes of Israel shall have the words of the Nephites and the Jews.

And it shall come to pass that my people, which are of the house of Israel, shall be gathered home unto the lands of their possessions; and my word also shall be gathered in one. And I will show unto them that fight against my word and against my people, who are of the house of Israel, that I am God, and that I covenanted with Abraham that I would remember his seed forever. (II Nephi, Chapter 29.)

From this revelation we are justified in assuming that there are other scriptures besides those contained in the Bible and in the Book of Mormon. Jesus enlightens us further on this subject:

And other sheep I have, which are not of this fold: them also I must bring, and they shall hear my voice; and there shall be one fold, and one shepherd. (John 10:16.)

A writer on the life of Christ has indicated that he could find no excuse for this passage of scripture, since he knew of no other sheep except those to whom Jesus ministered. Some have explained that it must have been the Gentiles, but Jesus indicated: " . . . I am not sent but unto the lost sheep of the house of Israel." (Matt. 15:24.)

Jesus Visited His Other Sheep

It should be noted that Jesus did not minister unto the Gentiles although he did send his Apostles unto them after his crucifixion. This leaves us with the question unanswered, so far as the Bible is concerned: Who were the other sheep he promised to visit? For this information we must look to the restoration of the gospel and the coming forth of the Book of Mormon.

After Jesus had been crucified and had ascended unto his Father, he visited his "other sheep" in America, known as the Nephites, and there chose twelve disciples and organized his Church, as he had done among the Jews, an account of which is given in some detail in Third Nephi of the Book of Mormon, often referred to as the Fifth Gospel, from which we quote:

> And now it came to pass that when Jesus had spoken these words, he said unto those twelve whom he had chosen:
>
> Ye are my disciples; and ye are a light unto this people, who are a remnant of the *house of Joseph*.
>
> And behold, this is the land of your inheritance; and the Father hath given it unto you.
>
> And not at any time hath the Father given me commandment that I should tell it unto your brethren at Jerusalem.
>
> Neither at any time hath the Father given me commandment that I should tell unto them concerning the other tribes of the house of Israel, whom the Father hath led away out of the land.
>
> This much did the Father command me, that I should tell unto them:
>
> That other sheep I have which are not of this fold; them also I must bring, and they shall hear my voice; and there shall be one fold, and one shepherd.
>
> And now, because of stiffneckedness and unbelief they understood not my word; therefore I was commanded to say no more of the Father concerning this thing unto them.
>
> But, verily, I say unto you that the Father hath commanded me, and I tell it unto you, that ye were separated from among

them because of their iniquity; therefore it is because of their iniquity that they know not of you.

And verily, I say unto you again that the other tribes hath the Father separated from them; and it is because of their iniquity that they know not of them.

And verily I say unto you, that ye are they of whom I said: Other sheep I have which are not of this fold; them also I must bring, and they shall hear my voice; and there shall be one fold, and one shepherd.

And they understood me not, for they supposed it had been the Gentiles; for they understood not that the Gentiles should be converted through their preaching.

And they understood me not that I said they shall hear my voice; and they understood me not that the Gentiles should not at any time hear my voice—that I should not manifest myself unto them save it were by the Holy Ghost.

But behold, ye have both heard my voice, and seen me; and ye are my sheep, and ye are numbered among those whom the Father hath given me. (III Nephi 15:11-24.)

From this we learn who the other sheep were whom Jesus told his disciples at Jerusalem he would visit, and that they were a remnant of the house of Joseph. Jesus further explains that he has still other sheep "which are not of this land, neither of the land of Jerusalem" (See III Nephi 16:1) whom he must visit. Since we do not yet know who or where they are, we will now concern ourselves with the remnant of the house of Joseph, and we will see what the Bible has to say about this branch of the house of Israel.

The House of Judah and the House of Joseph

A study of the promises of the Lord to Abraham, Isaac, and Jacob (Israel), and to his twelve sons, whom we understand to be the heads of the twelve tribes of the house of Israel, indicates clearly that the outstanding promises were given unto Judah and Joseph. Much confusion and misapplication exists in the minds of many with respect to the use of the name *Israel.* Many think of it, even today, as referring to the Jews or to the house of Judah, forgetting that Judah was only one of the twelve sons of Israel. Reuben was the eldest son, but because of his transgression the birthright was taken from him and given to the sons of Joseph:

> Now the sons of Reuben the firstborn of Israel, (for he was the firstborn; but forasmuch as he defiled his father's bed, his birthright was given unto the sons of Joseph the son of Israel: and the genealogy is not to be reckoned after the birthright.
>
> For Judah prevailed above his brethren, and of him came the chief ruler; but the birthright was Joseph's.) (I Chron. 5: 1-2.)

Speaking of the relative importance and position of Judah and Joseph, Paul said:

> For it is evident that our Lord sprang out of Juda; of which tribe Moses spake nothing concerning priesthood. (Heb. 7:14.)

When these promises and blessings are understood, it is clear that the blessings of Joseph, who received the birthright, gave him preference over all the sons of Israel including Judah. It is probably due to the fact that Judah and his descendants (the Jews) have held together that they have come to be regarded as the only Israelites. In earlier days, Israel was divided, Judah comprising the smaller group, the larger group being called "Israel";

> And Joab gave up the sum of the number of the people unto the king: and there were in Israel eight hundred thousand valiant men that drew the sword; and the men of Judah were five hundred thousand men. (II Sam. 24:9.)
>
> And the Lord said, I will remove Judah also out of my sight, as I have removed Israel, and will cast off this city Jerusalem which I have chosen, and the house of which I said, My name shall be there. (II Kings 23:27.)

Under Ephraim, Israel was led into the north at the time the Kingdom of Israel was overthrown by the Assyrians about 721 B.C., and never returned. They were sifted among the nations:

> ... I will not utterly destroy the house of Jacob, saith the Lord.
>
> For, lo, I will command, and I will sift the house of Israel among all nations, like as corn is sifted in a sieve, yet shall not the least grain fall upon the earth. (Amos 9:8-9.)

Then Amos promised that after this sifting they shall be gathered again. (See Amos 9:14-15.) In a later discussion we will consider the gathering of Israel in the latter-days as promised by the prophets.

Moses Blessed Joseph

Let us now consider more in detail the promises made to Joseph and his seed. We will find that not only were their promises greater than those made to Judah, but also that Joseph and Judah were to be separated into two great divisions as we have already pointed out. Joseph, after the sifting of Israel, was to be given a new land separate and apart from the promised land occupied principally by Judah.

Moses "blessed the children of Israel before his death." (See Deut. Chapter 33.) The reader is referred to the account of the blessings with the suggestion they be read carefully noting particularly the import and significance of Joseph's blessing as compared with the blessings of his brothers. Let us give specific consideration to Joseph's blessing:

> And of Joseph he said, *Blessed of the Lord be his land,* for the precious things of heaven, for the dew, and for the deep that coucheth beneath,
>
> And for the precious fruits brought forth by the sun, and for the precious things put forth by the moon,
>
> And for the chief things of the ancient mountains, and for the precious things of the lasting hills,
>
> And for the precious things of the earth and fulness thereof,

and for the good will of him that dwelt in the bush: let the blessing come upon the head of Joseph, and upon the top of the head of him that was separated from his brethren.

His glory is like the firstling of his bullock, and his horns are like the horns of unicorns: with them he shall push the people together to the ends of the earth: *and they are the ten thousands of Ephraim, and they are the thousands of Manasseh.* (Deut. 33:13-17.)

When this blessing was given by Moses, the patriarch, it is clear that he first had in mind the new land that would be given to Joseph which would be abundantly blessed of the Lord to produce precious fruits of the land and the precious things of the lasting hills and of the ancient mountains.

When the descendants of Joseph were led to this land of America about 600 B.C., they were told that it would be a land choice above all other lands. The reading of Moses' blessing to Joseph indicates that Moses was impressed with this fact and attempted to so describe it. He further indicated that it would be in the "ancient mountains" and "lasting hills." The land to which they were led was in the western part of South, Central, and North America, in the Rocky Mountains, which accurately answers Moses' description.

Then Moses further indicated that the good will of him who dwelt in the bush (referring to the God of Israel who dwelt in the burning bush—see Exodus 3:2) would be upon Joseph who was separated from his brethren. Then he refers to his glory as like "the firstling of his bullock," or the firstborn or heir of his father, and we have already pointed out how Joseph became heir to the birthright. Moses looked beyond to the power and authority that should be given to Joseph's seed and added: "he shall push the people together to the ends of the earth: and they are the ten thousands of Ephraim, and they are the thousands of Manasseh." (See Deut. 33:17.) This seems to look forward to the establishment of the kingdom of God in the earth in the latter-days, which we have previously outlined, and the gathering of Israel which we will later discuss.

Jacob (Israel) Blessed Joseph

The great patriarch Jacob called his children to him and blessed them just prior to his death:

And Jacob called unto his sons, and said, Gather yourselves together, that I may tell you that which shall befall you *in the last days.*

Gather yourselves together, and hear, ye sons of Jacob: and hearken unto Israel your father. (Gen. 49:1-2.)

It is suggested the reader study the entire chapter noting the great difference in the respective blessings.

Now let us give careful consideration to the special blessing Joseph received from his father:

Joseph is a fruitful bough, even a fruitful bough by a well; whose branches run over the wall:

The archers have sorely grieved him, and shot at him, and hated him:

But his bow abode in strength, and the arms of his hands were made strong by the hands of the mighty God of Jacob; (from thence is the shepherd, the stone of Israel:)

Even by the God of thy father, who shall help thee; and by the Almighty, who shall bless thee with blessings of heaven above, blessings of the deep that lieth under, blessings of the breasts, and of the womb;

The blessings of thy father have prevailed above the blessings of my progenitors unto the utmost bound of the everlasting hills: they shall be on the head of Joseph, and on the crown of the head of him that was separate from his brethren. (Gen. 49:22-26.)

This blessing is very similar to that given by Moses, and begins with reference to the land to which Joseph's seed would go: "A fruitful bough by a well; whose branches run over the wall." It seems consistent to assume that the ocean was regarded as the wall over which Joseph's branches were to run "unto the utmost bound of the everlasting hills." Then Jacob indicated that Joseph would be blessed "with the blessings of heaven above . . . blessings of the breasts, and of the womb," indicating that his posterity would be great, and that his blessings would prevail above the blessings of his progenitors.

Significance of Joseph's Dream

Add Joseph's dream to these two blessings, when he saw his brothers' sheaves do obeisance to his sheaf. Then he dreamed that the sun and the moon and the eleven stars made obeisance to him. (See Gen. 37:5-10; 44:14.) Now ask yourself these questions:

1. Does the Bible record promises to any other man equal to these promises, except the promise that through the loins of Judah the Christ would come into the world?

2. Does the Bible record the fulfilment of these promises? If so, where?

3. It is generally conceded that the Bible is a record of the Jews, but where is the record of Joseph and his seed?

4. Is it consistent to assume that God would make greater promises to Joseph and his seed than to any other group of the eleven sons of Jacob (Israel) and his seed, and then make no provision that a record should be kept of the fulfilment of those promises?

The Stick of Joseph (The Book of Mormon)

The Lord did not overlook this very important matter but made adequate provision that a record should be kept of his hand-dealings with Joseph and his seed beginning with his two sons, Ephraim and Manasseh:

> The word of the Lord came again unto me, saying,
>
> Moreover, thou son of man, take thee one stick, and write upon it, For Judah, and for the children of Israel his companions: then take another stick, and write upon it, For Joseph, the stick of Ephraim, and for all of the house of Israel his companions:
>
> And join them one to another into one stick; and they shall become one in thine hand.
>
> And when the children of thy people shall speak unto thee, saying, Wilt thou not shew us what thou meanest by these?
>
> Say unto them, Thus saith the Lord God; Behold, I will take the stick of Joseph, which is in the hand of Ephraim, and the tribes of Israel his fellows, and will put them with him, even with the stick of Judah, and make them one stick, and they shall be one in mine hand,
>
> And the sticks whereon thou writest shall be in thine hand before their eyes. (Ezek. 37:15-20.)

In ancient times it was the custom to write on parchment and roll it on a stick. Therefore, when this command was given, it was the equivalent of directing that two books or records should be kept. A careful reading will indicate that it would be in coming generations (verse 18) when their children would ask the meaning of this commandment, when the Lord would "take the stick of Joseph, which is in the hand of Ephraim, and the tribes of Israel his fellows, and will put them with him, even with the stick of Judah, and make them one stick, and they shall be one in mine hand."

Note that the Lord said he would do this and would make them *one* in his hand. Now, granting that the Bible is the stick of Judah, where is the stick of Joseph? Can anyone answer? God commanded that it should be kept and that it should be kept to record the fulfilment of his greater promises to Joseph. It would naturally be a record kept in another land, since Joseph was to be "separate from his brethren." It is plain from the reading of this scripture that the record of Judah, or the Holy Bible would remain with the people, and that the record of Joseph would be joined unto it, and that the two would become one.

Should anyone object to God doing the very thing he promised Ezekiel he would do? Could this promise be fulfilled in a more simple and perfect manner than it was through the coming forth of the Book of Mormon? God led a branch of the house of Joseph to America and commanded them to keep records of all their doings. He then commanded his prophet, Moroni, to hide this sacred record in the Hill Cumorah in the western part of the state of New York, U. S. A. Centuries later he sent Moroni back to deliver the record to Joseph Smith and gave him power to translate it with the assistance of the Urim and Thummim. Now, the two records have been joined together, constituting a complete fulfilment of another great prophecy. Again, who should object to God doing the thing he promised to do? Until someone can explain where the record of Joseph is, the Book of Mormon stands unrefuted in its claim to be "the stick of Joseph."

A Voice from the Dust

Isaiah saw the coming forth of this record as the voice of one that has a familiar spirit whispering out of the dust:

> Woe to Ariel, to Ariel, the city where David dwelt! add ye year to year; let them kill sacrifices.
>
> Yet I will distress Ariel, and there shall be heaviness and sorrow: and it shall be unto me as Ariel.
>
> And I will camp against thee round about, and will lay siege against thee with a mount, and I will raise forts against thee.
>
> And thou shalt be brought down, and shalt speak out of the

ground, and thy speech shall be low out of the dust, and thy voice shall be, as of one that hath a familiar spirit, out of the ground, and thy speech shall whisper out of the dust. (Isa. 29: 1-4.)

Isaiah saw the downfall of Ariel, or Jerusalem, at a time far in the future, "add ye year to year." Then he seems to have been carried away in vision to witness a similar destruction of the cities of Joseph, "and it shall be unto me as Ariel." Then he describes how they would be besieged and forts would be raised against them; they would be brought down and would speak out of the ground. Their speech would be low out of the dust; their voice would be as one that hath a familiar spirit, out of the ground; their speech would whisper out of the dust. Now, obviously, the only way a dead people could speak "out of the ground" or "low out of the dust" would be by the written word, and this the people did through the Book of Mormon. Truly it has a familiar spirit, for it contains the words of the prophets of the God of Israel.

The Prophet Nephi describes this event in these words:

> After my seed and the seed of my brethren shall have dwindled in unbelief, and shall have been smitten by the Gentiles; yea, after the Lord God shall have camped against them around about, and shall have laid siege against them with a mount, and raised forts against them; and after they shall have been brought down low in the dust, *even that they are not,* yet the words of the righteous shall be written, and the prayers of the faithful shall be heard, and all those who have dwindled in unbelief shall not be forgotten.

> For those who shall be destroyed shall speak unto them out of the ground, and their speech shall be low out of the dust, and their voice shall be as one that hath a familiar spirit; for the Lord God will give unto him power, that he may whisper concerning them, even as it were out of the ground; and their speech shall whisper out of the dust.

> For thus saith the Lord God: They shall write the things

which shall be done among them, and they shall be written and sealed up in a book, and those who have dwindled in unbelief shall not have them, for they seek to destroy the things of God. (II Nephi 26:15-17. Compare with Isa. 29:1-4.)

Isaiah did not only see the destruction of this people; that they would be brought down; that they would speak out of the ground; that their speech would be as one that hath a familiar spirit, whispering out of the dust; but he saw also that this whole vision was represented by a sealed book:

And the vision of all is become unto you as the words of a book that is sealed, which men deliver to one that is learned, saying, Read this, I pray thee: and he saith, I cannot; for it is sealed. (Isa. 29:11.)

After this vision closed, the word of the Lord came again unto Isaiah informing him of the marvelous work and a wonder he would bring forth:

Wherefore the Lord said, Forasmuch as this people draw near me with their mouth, and with their lips do honour me, but have removed their heart far from me, and their fear toward me is taught by the precept of men:

Therefore, behold, I will proceed to do a marvellous work among this people, even a marvellous work and a wonder: for the wisdom of their wise men shall perish, and the understanding of their prudent men shall be hid. (Isa. 29:13-14.)

The bringing forth of the Book of Mormon is a "marvellous work and a wonder," and the wise men and prudent men of the world cannot account for it in any other way than the story told by Joseph Smith, and he did not get it, neither could he have gotten it, by reading the Bible only. He received it by revelation from the Lord through the Angel Moroni.

CHAPTER 8

EVIDENCES OF THE DIVINITY OF THE BOOK OF MORMON

Testimony of Witnesses

We have considered the Book of Mormon as a companion volume of scripture (the stick of Joseph, a record of the "other sheep" Jesus promised to visit) which the Lord promised he would join unto the Bible (the stick of Judah) and make them one in his hand. Now it seems proper that we should mention briefly a few of the evidences of the divinity of the Book of Mormon.

One of the greatest evidences is the testimony of the three witnesses to whom the Angel Moroni showed the plates and bore witness that they were translated by the gift and power of God. This testimony we have already quoted in its entirety; it appears in the front of each copy of the Book of Mormon, together with the testimony of the eight witnesses, to whom Joseph Smith was permitted to show the plates. Not one of these witnesses ever denied his testimony, even though each was subjected to much persecution and ridicule.

"Translated by the Gift and Power of God"

Let us give consideration to the statement of the Lord to the witnesses that the plates were "translated by the gift and power of God." When Moroni told Joseph Smith of the record deposited in the Hill Cumorah, he said:

Also, that there were two stones in silver bows—and these stones, fastened to a breastplate, constituted what is called the Urim and Thummim—deposited with the plates; and the possession and use of these stones were what constituted "seers" in ancient or former times; and that God had prepared them for the purpose of translating the book. (P. of G. P. Joseph Smith 2:35.)

It was through the use of the Urim and Thummim that Joseph Smith was able to translate, into English, from the gold plates, the Book of Mormon, consisting of over five hundred printed pages, in about sixty days time, from April 7, 1829 to the first week in June, 1829. We doubt if any other writer has ever written even a book of fiction of such magnitude in anything like such a short period of time.

The Urim and Thummim

Would it be unfair to ask what the spiritual leaders of Joseph Smith's day knew about the Urim and Thummim? Would Joseph Smith, of himself, have thought of claiming that he translated the Book of Mormon with the assistance of the Urim and Thummim? Yet, the use of the Urim and Thummim was known to the prophets of old:

Urim and Thummim, (i.e., 'Light and Perfection') mentioned as the means by which the High Priest inquired of the Lord, Ex. 28:30; Lev. 8:8; Nu. 27:21; Deut. 33:8; I Sam. 28:6. The Urim and Thummim were clearly material objects of some kind; it has been suggested that they were (I) stones in the High Priest's breastplate, (II) sacred dice, (III) little images of "truth" and "justice" such as are found hung around the neck of an Egyptian priest's mummy. The Urim and Thummim did not exist after the Captivity—Ezra 2:63. (*A Concise Biblical Encyclopedia*, p. 154.)

Since the Urim and Thummim was used by the ancient prophets as a means by which they inquired of the Lord; and since it was preserved by the hand of the Lord and delivered to Joseph Smith along with the gold plates, it would demonstrate the wisdom of God in preserving it for this sacred purpose. These facts account for the statement of the scribes for the Prophet Joseph Smith, that they wrote as he dictated, and that he made no corrections. Follow the testimony of Oliver Cowdery, the chief scribe:

> I wrote, with my own pen, the entire Book of Mormon (save a few pages) as it fell from the lips of the Prophet Joseph, as he translated it by the gift and power of God, by the means of the Urim and Thummim. . . . I beheld with my eyes, and handled with my hands, the gold plates from which it was transcribed. . . . That book is true. (Roberts, *Comprehensive History of the Church*, Vol. 1, p. 139.)

Origin of the American Indians

The Book of Mormon gives a very definite account of who the American Indians are and how they came to the western hemisphere. The first people accounted for, who occupied this land of America, were the Jaredites who left the Tower of Babel at the time of the confounding of their language and the scattering of the people. They were led to America by the Lord:

> And the Lord said, Behold, the people is one, and they have all one language; and this they begin to do: and now nothing will be restrained from them, which they have imagined to do.
>
> Go to, let us go down, and there confound their language, that they may not understand one another's speech.
>
> So the Lord scattered them abroad from thence upon the face of all the earth: and they left off to build the city. (Gen. 11:6-8.)

In view of the statement "the Lord scattered them abroad from thence upon the face of all the earth," it is not unreasonable to assume that some of the people were scattered to the land of America, for certainly it is a part of "all the earth."

The Jaredites became extinct through their failure to

keep the commandments of the Lord. For an account of this people, see the Book of Ether in the Book of Mormon.

Lehi and his family were led from Jerusalem 600 B.C. by the hand of God to the land of America and have since continued to occupy the land. However, shortly after their arrival here, because of the wickedness of the followers of two of the sons of Lehi—Laman and Lemuel—the Lord placed the curse of a dark skin upon them:

> And he had caused the cursing to come upon them, yea, even a sore cursing, because of their iniquity. For behold, they had hardened their hearts against him, that they had become like unto a flint; wherefore, as they were white, and exceeding fair and delightsome, that they might not be enticing unto my people the Lord God did cause a skin of blackness to come upon them.

> And thus saith the Lord God: I will cause that they shall be loathsome unto thy people, save they shall repent of their iniquities.

> And cursed shall be the seed of him that mixeth with their seed; for they shall be cursed even with the same cursing. And the Lord spake it, and it was done. (II Nephi 5:21-23.)

Those who were thus cursed succeeded in destroying all the white people, save 24 souls, about 384 A.D. It was at this time that Mormon deposited in the Hill Cumorah all the records which had been entrusted to him except a few plates which he gave to his son Moroni. (See Mormon, Chapter 6).

About 420 A.D., Moroni placed these plates with those his father Mormon had already deposited in the hill. (See Moroni 10:1-2). It was from these latter plates that the Book of Mormon was translated by Joseph Smith.

The dark-skinned people who occupied this land of America from that time on were called, in the Book of

Mormon, "Lamanites," which are the people known generally as the American Indians, all of whom are of the house of Israel, as we have already indicated.

It is, therefore, to be assumed that since the Book of Mormon is a record or history of this ancient American people, that quite a complete account may be expected of their origin and travels, their wars and contentions, the lives and teachings of their prophets, and prophecies as to the future destiny of this land of America.

One of the most interesting features of the entire book is an account of Jesus' visit to the inhabitants of the land of America following his crucifixion and ascension, including an account of the destructions that took place at the time of his crucifixion which literally changed the face of the entire land: Mountains were thrown up; tempests and whirlwinds raged; cities were sunk; buildings were leveled by violent earthquakes, "the face of the whole earth became deformed." (See III Nephi, Chap. 8.)

Modern archeological research has accounted for many of these buried cities; uncovered cement highways mentioned in the Book of Mormon; located temples and other magnificent buildings erected by those people who reached a high stage of civilization and culture in the land of America. The traditions of the Indians confirm these facts.

Washoe Indian Legend

Typical of these traditions is the following Washoe Indian Legend which seems to have preserved the story of the disappearance of the great intermountain lake. This immense "sheet" of water was called Lahonitan. Its existence in the past is attested by the fossilized remains of animals that have been found in various parts of the basin, as well as by other unmistakable evidences. The Indian legend is related as follows:

Long time, heap long time. Maybe one hundred years, injun no sabe, white man sabe. My grandfather's father, he heap old man. Maybe two, three hundred years, me dunno, Carson Valley, Waso Valley, Truskee Valley, Long Valley, Pilamid Lake, Lublock, eblywhere all water, plenty pish, plenty duck. Big pish too, now no see him no more, all go away, no come back.

Wasu Injun, he lib big mountains (pointing to the Comstock and Pyramid range.) Sometime Wasu Indian take em boat go see Piutee, maybe Piutee he take em boat go see Wasu Indian, Yash he good friend, all time.

Pointing to the Sierra to the west of Washoe Valley, the old Indian continued:

Big mountain all time pire, plenty 'boom, 'boom, heap smoke, injun heap flaid! Byme bye, one day, mountain heap smoke, heap noise, glound too much shake, Injun heap flaid, pall down, plenty cly. He sun ebly day come up (pointing to the northeast) he go down, (pointing to the southwest.) One day no come up, Injun no sabe, mountain heap smoke, glound plenty shake, wind blow, water heap mad. *Maybe two, tlee day sun he no come,* injun no eat, no sleep, all time, cly, cly. Yash, heap flaid. Byme bye water make plenty noise, go plenty fast like Tlukee Liver; water go down, down, mountain come up, come up, plenty mud, plenty pish die, byme bye sun come back over this mountain (pointing to the southeast) he go down ober there (pointing to the northwest.) Yash, white man sabe, injun no sabe,

Maybe two, tlee week, mud he dly up, Piutee. Wasu Injun walk, no more boat. All water he go; maybe little water Pilamid Lake, Honey Lake, Wasu Lake, too much mountain, he come purty quick. Yash, injun no sabe, water, big pish no come back. No see him no more. (Mrs. M. M. Garwood, *Progressive West Magazine,* reprinted in *Deseret Semi-Weekly News,* February 5, 1906.)

The narrative is lacking in detail, but it is sufficiently clear to indicate that the aborigines of this country have preserved, in legendary form, some account of the terrible cataclysms that have convulsed the American continents.

Nephi's Testimony

Now read an account of this same incident as related in Third Nephi of the Book of Mormon and you will note that the two accounts agree on practically every detail, even to the length of time in which the sun failed to come up. This is the account given by Nephi of the happenings upon the American continent at the time the Savior was crucified:

> But behold, there was a more great and terrible destruction in the land northward; for behold, the whole face of the land was changed, because of the tempest and the whirlwinds, and the thunderings and the lightnings, and the exceeding great quaking of the whole earth;
>
> And the highways were broken up, and the level roads were spoiled, and many smooth places became rough.
>
> And many great and notable cities were sunk, and many were burned, and many were shaken till the buildings thereof had fallen to the earth, and the inhabitants thereof were slain, and the places were left desolate. . . .
>
> And thus the face of the whole earth became deformed, because of the tempests, and the thunderings, and the lightnings, and the quaking of the earth. . . .
>
> And it came to pass that there was thick darkness upon all the face of the land, insomuch that the inhabitants thereof who had not fallen could feel the vapor of darkness;
>
> And there could be no light, because of the darkness, neither candles, neither torches; neither could there be fire kindled with their fine and exceedingly dry wood, so that there could not be any light at all;
>
> And there was not any light seen, neither fire, nor glimmer, neither the sun, nor the moon, nor the stars, for so great were the mists of darkness which were upon the face of the land.
>
> And it came to pass that it did last for the space of three days that there was no light seen; and there was great mourning and howling and weeping among all the people continually; yea, great were the groanings of the people, because of the darkness and the great destruction which had come upon them. (III Nephi 8:12-14, 17, 20-23.)

In considering the marked similarity in these two accounts, it should be remembered that the Book of Mormon was published in 1829, and this Indian Legend in 1906. What is the explanation if neither of them be true?

Supplementary Reading

It is not the writer's purpose to attempt to consider in detail the archeology and ethnology of the Americas which contribute so much corroborative evidence in support of the Book of Mormon. For a study of such evidences as (1) that this land has been occupied by different peoples at widely separated periods; (2) that the traditions found among the native races of America, seeming to come from common stock, are closely allied to, if not identical with, the Israelites; (3) that the ancient inhabitants of the American continents had a knowledge of such major Biblical events as the creation, the building of the Tower of Babel, the flood, the life and crucifixion of the Savior, the second coming of the Redeemer, the administration of the sacrament, etc., the reader is referred to *Seven Claims of the Book of Mormon,* by John A. Widtsoe and Franklin S. Harris, Jr., *Articles of Faith,* by James E. Talmage, *Ancient America and the Book of Mormon,* by Hunter and Ferguson.

Contemporary Effort to Establish the Origin of the American Indian

The following article of interest was released from Los Angeles by the Associated Press, October 22, 1936, and appeared in *The Deseret News,* Salt Lake City, Utah, on that date under the caption: "Former President Hoover Will Aid Pan-American School Project."

A vision of creating a new world center of culture for North and South America is nearing fruition, it was revealed here by Dr. William A. Kennedy of Lima, Peru.

He announced that Herbert Hoover has agreed to serve on a board comprised of representatives from the twenty-one republics of the Americas and the Dominion of Canada, and that the goal of $30,000,000 in initial endowments is near.

A charter for this Pan-American University will be granted within a few months by the government of Peru and sent to the other republics for endowment, he said.

One of the interesting branches of the American internation institution will be research into the archaeology of the Americas, particularly the Inca civilization and the extension of the Mayan civilization, about which new material is constantly being brought to light.

"I expect to leave on my return to Lima within two or three weeks with pledges for $1,500,000 in endowments from the people in the United States," Dr. Kennedy said. "I came to Southern California with $1,250,000 subscribed in the east and middle west and have met with a most enthusiastic response here.

"Other nations of the Americas have agreed to match the contribution from this country, and we have $30,000,000 in unconditional endowments. Within ten years we expect to have $60,000,000 to $70,000,000 endowments!"

From this it is evident that the expenditure of sixty to seventy million dollars is not regarded as too great a price to pay for added information regarding the early inhabitants of the Americas. It can hardly be expected that even the expenditure of this amount of money will furnish the historical information and data now contained in the Book of Mormon. In addition, the Book of Mormon contains a record of the teachings of inspired prophets who ministered among the people, and prophetic predictions as to the future destiny of this land.

A Choice Land

Behold, this is a choice land, and whatsoever nation shall possess it shall be free from bondage, and from captivity, and from all other nations under heaven, if they will but serve the God of the land, who is Jesus Christ, who hath been manifested by the things which we have written. (Ether 2:12.)

But behold, this land, said God, shall be a land of thine inheritance, and the Gentiles shall be blessed upon the land.

And this land shall be a land of liberty unto the Gentiles, and there shall be no kings upon the land, who shall raise up unto the Gentiles.

And I will fortify this land against all other nations.

And he that fighteth against Zion shall perish, saith God.

For he that raiseth up a king against me shall perish, for I, the Lord, the king of heaven, will be their king, and I will be a light unto them forever, that hear my words. (II Nephi 10: 10-14.)

And now I, Moroni, proceed to finish my record concerning the destruction of the people of whom I have been writing.

For behold, they rejected all the words of Ether; for he truly told them of all things, from the beginning of man; and that after the waters had receded from off the face of this land it became a choice land above all other lands, a chosen land of the Lord; wherefore the Lord would have that all men should serve him who dwell upon the face thereof;

And that it was the place of the New Jerusalem, which should come down out of heaven, and the holy sanctuary of the Lord.

Behold, Ether saw the days of Christ, and he spake concerning a New Jerusalem upon this land.

And he spake also concerning the house of Israel, and the Jerusalem from whence Lehi should come—after it should be destroyed it should be built up again, a holy city unto the Lord; wherefore, it could not be a new Jerusalem for it had been in a time of old; but it should be built up again, and become a holy city of the Lord; and it should be built unto the house of Israel.

And that a New Jerusalem should be built up upon this land, unto the remnant of the seed of Joseph, for which things there has been a type.

For as Joseph brought his father down into the land of Egypt, even so he died there; wherefore, the Lord brought a remnant of the seed of Joseph out of the land of Jerusalem, that he might be merciful unto the seed of Joseph that they should perish not, even as he was merciful unto the father of Joseph that he should perish not.

Wherefore, the remnant of the house of Joseph shall be built upon this land; and it shall be a land for their inheritance; and they shall build up a holy city unto the Lord, like unto the Jerusalem of old; and they shall no more be confounded, until the end come when the earth shall pass away. (Ether 13:1-8.)

A high government official, after reading the Book of Mormon, made the following statement:

Of all the American religious books of the Nineteenth Century, it seems probable that the Book of Mormon was the most powerful. It reached perhaps only one per cent of the people of the United States but it affected this one per cent so powerfully and lastingly that all the people of the United States have been affected especially by its contribution to opening up one of our greatest frontiers.

A Tourist's Testimony

In July 1934, after visiting on Temple Square in Salt Lake City, where he obtained a copy of the Book of Mormon, a tourist wrote the following letter:

I have been a minister of the Methodist Church in . . . for 37 years. I have built up a library of the greatest books in the world, costing me more than $12,000. But I have found here in the Book of Mormon a library more valuable than all the collections of books in the world because it is the word of God.

Dr. Willard Richards' Testimony

It was reported that when Dr. Willard Richards, who was in jail with the Prophet Joseph Smith when he and his brother were martyred, and who later became a counselor to Brigham Young in the First Presidency of the Church, first saw a copy of the Book of Mormon, he opened it in the center and read a few pages. He closed the book with this statement: "That book was either written by God or the devil, and I am going to find out who wrote it." Accordingly, he read the book through twice in the next ten days, whereupon, he replied: "The devil could not have written it—it must be from God."

The Promised Witness to the Truth of The Book of Mormon

It is a regrettable thing that the world moves so slowly in the acceptance of truth. With such a marvelous book in our midst, the companion volume of scripture the Lord commanded Ezekiel to write, (the stick of Joseph) which he declared he would join to the stick of Judah, (our present Bible) why is the world so unwilling to accept it?

In this brief presentation of the message of the Angel Moroni to the Prophet Joseph Smith, we have not attempted to present the teachings of the Book of Mormon, or the history contained therein. We have contented ourselves with an effort to show that it has a place, yes, an important place, in the religious literature of the world; that God himself commanded the record should be kept; that it should be preserved; and that it should be brought forth in due season. The sending of Moroni to deliver the gold plates to Joseph Smith with the Urim and Thummim for their translation constitutes one of the most important messages that could possibly be broadcast to the world. It is hoped that this presentation will encourage many with a desire to read the Book of Mormon and put to the test the Lord's promise contained therein:

And when ye shall receive these things, I would exhort you that ye would ask God, the Eternal Father, in the name of Christ, if these things are not true; and if ye shall ask with a sincere heart, with real intent, having faith in Christ, he will manifest the truth of it unto you, by the power of the Holy Ghost. (Moroni 10:4.)

CHAPTER 9

RESTORATION OF PRIESTHOOD AUTHORITY

Visit of John the Baptist

Next, in chronological order, came the visit of the heavenly messenger, John the Baptist, who, under the direction of Peter, James, and John appeared to Joseph Smith and Oliver Cowdery and ordained them to the Aaronic Priesthood. Following is Joseph Smith's own account of this heavenly visitation and ordination:

Two days after the arrival of Mr. Cowdery (being the 7th of April) I commenced to translate the Book of Mormon, and he began to write for me.

We still continued the work of translation, when, in the ensuing month (May, 1829), we on a certain day went into the woods to pray and inquire of the Lord respecting baptism for the remission of sins, that we found mentioned in the translation of the plates. While we were thus employed, praying and calling upon the Lord, a messenger from heaven descended in a cloud of light, and having laid his hands upon us, he ordained us, saying:

Upon you my fellow servants, in the name of Messiah, I confer the Priesthood of Aaron, which holds the keys of the ministering of angels, and of the gospel of repentance, and of baptism by immersion for the remission of sins; and this shall never be taken again from the earth until the sons of Levi do offer again an offering unto the Lord in righteousness.

He said this Aaronic Priesthood had not the power of laying on hands for the gift of the Holy Ghost, but that this should be conferred on us hereafter; and he commanded us to go and be baptized, and gave us directions that I should baptize Oliver Cowdery, and that afterwards he should baptize me.

Accordingly we went and were baptized. I baptized him first, and afterwards he baptized me—after which I laid my hands upon his head and ordained him to the Aaronic Priesthood, and afterwards he laid his hands on me and ordained me to the same Priesthood—for so we were commanded.

The messenger who visited us on this occasion and conferred this Priesthood upon us, said that his name was John, the same that is called John the Baptist in the New Testament, and that he acted under the direction of Peter, James, and John, who held the keys of the Priesthood of Melchizedek, which Priesthood, he said, would in due time be conferred on us, and that I should be called the first Elder of the Church, and he (Oliver Cowdery) the second. It was on the fifteenth day of May, 1829, that we were ordained under the hand of this messenger, and baptized. (P. of G. P. Joseph Smith 2:67-72.)

From this visit of John the Baptist, we learn these great truths:

1. That one must be ordained to the necessary priesthood by one having authority before he can administer the ordinances of the gospel.

2. That the Aaronic Priesthood holds the keys of:
   a. The ministering of angels;
   b. The gospel of repentance;
   c. Baptism by immersion for the remission of sins.

3. That this priesthood "shall never be taken again from the earth until the sons of Levi do offer again an offering unto the Lord in righteousness."

4. That while the Aaronic Priesthood is divine authority from God, its administration is limited; it "had not the power of laying on hands for the gift of the Holy Ghost"; that in conferring this priesthood upon Joseph Smith and Oliver Cowdery, John the Baptist acted under the direction of Peter, James, and John, who held the keys of the priesthood of Melchizedek which should thereafter be conferred upon them.

Restoration of the Melchizedek Priesthood

Therefore, in order that there might be a "restitution of all things, which God hath spoken by the mouth of all his holy prophets since the world began," (See Acts 3:21) it was necessary that these two priesthoods be restored again to men upon this earth.

Not long after this glorious event transpired, Peter, James, and John, Apostles of the Lord Jesus Christ, conferred upon Joseph Smith and Oliver Cowdery the Melchizedek Priesthood, including the Holy Apostleship as promised by John, the Baptist, which gave them the necessary authority to organize the Church and kingdom of God upon the earth in this dispensation. Accordingly, The Church of Jesus Christ of Latter-day Saints was organized with six members at Fayette, Seneca County, New York, on the sixth day of April, 1830.

Aaronic and Melchizedek Priesthoods

An understanding of the Aaronic or Levitical Priesthood, sometimes called the Lesser Priesthood, and the Melchizedek Priesthood, and the functions and administrations of each, is very necessary to a proper understanding of the gospel of Jesus Christ and the Church he established upon the earth.

The question might be asked: "Under which order of priesthood do the present Christian churches claim to operate—the Aaronic or Melchizedek?" A satisfactory answer to this question could not be expected from any of them. The only reason we are in a position to make proper explanation is that John the Baptist brought back to this earth the Aaronic or Levitical Priesthood and conferred it upon the heads of Joseph Smith and Oliver Cowdery. The Apostles, Peter, James, and John, brought the Melchizedek Priesthood in like manner. All doubt and misunderstanding has thus been removed, and we are therefore able to understand the scriptures dealing with this important subject. Could there be any subject more important than to understand the meaning and purpose of the priesthood of God and how it is obtained, since it holds the keys and rights to officiate in his name and administer unto his children the saving ordinances of the gospel of Jesus Christ? How could anyone suppose that without this priesthood authority there could be any authorized Church of Jesus Christ upon the earth?

> If therefore perfection were by the Levitical priesthood, (for under it the people received the law,) what further need was there that another priest should rise after the order of Melchizedec, and not be called after the order of Aaron?
>
> For the priesthood being changed, there is made of necessity a change also of the law. . . .
>
> For it is evident that our Lord sprang out of Judah; of which tribe Moses spake nothing concerning priesthood. . . .
>
> For he testifieth, Thou art a priest for ever after the order of Melchizedec. . . .
>
> But this man, because he continueth ever, hath an unchangeable priesthood. (Heb. 7:11-12, 14, 17, 24.)

This explanation should make it plain that the law or schoolmaster to lead the people unto Christ was administered by the Levitical or Aaronic Priesthood. However, perfection cannot be obtained through this priesthood alone, as Paul explained. Therefore, it was necessary for the Lord to send another priest after the order of Melchizedek. The priesthood thus being changed, there was "of necessity a change also of the law." The fulness of the gospel of Jesus Christ, therefore, was introduced by him to take the place of the law of Moses.

Limitations of the Aaronic Priesthood

John the Baptist understood this fully, for his ministry was under the authority of the Aaronic Priesthood which held the keys of administering the ordinance of baptism by immersion for the remission of sins. When he was sent to prepare "the way of the Lord," he did not attempt to confer the Holy Ghost by the laying on of hands. He taught that one mightier than he would come, and "he shall baptize you with the Holy Ghost, and with fire." (See Matt. 3:11.)

This is the explanation he gave to Joseph Smith and Oliver Cowdery when he conferred the Aaronic Priesthood upon them and commissioned them to baptize each other by immersion for remission of their sins. He told them that this priesthood "had not the power of laying on hands for the gift of the Holy Ghost," but that this would be conferred on them later.

Nature of the Melchizedek Priesthood

In a revelation on priesthood given through the Prophet Joseph Smith on March 28, 1835, the Lord stated:

> There are, in the church, two priesthoods, namely, the Melchizedek and Aaronic, including the Levitical Priesthood.
>
> Why the first is called the Melchizedek Priesthood is because Melchizedek was such a great high priest.
>
> Before his day it was called the Holy Priesthood, after the order of the Son of God.
>
> But out of respect or reverence to the name of the Supreme Being, to avoid the too frequent repetition of his name, they, the church, in ancient days, called that priesthood after Melchizedek, or the Melchizedek Priesthood.
>
> All other authorities or offices in the church are appendages to this priesthood.
>
> But there are two divisions or grand heads—one is the Mel-

chizedek Priesthood, and the other is the Aaronic or Levitical Priesthood. (D. & C. 107:1-6.)

The Apostle Paul also understood what a great high priest Melchizedek was, and made this explanation:

> For this Melchizedec, king of Salem, priest of the most high God, who met Abraham returning from the slaughter of the kings, and blessed him;
>
> To whom also Abraham gave a tenth part of all; first being by interpretation King of righteousness, and after that also King of Salem, which is, King of peace;
>
> Without father, without mother, without descent, having neither beginning of days, nor end of life; but made like unto the Son of God; abideth a priest continually. (Heb. 7:1-3.)

This last verse has been much misunderstood, some assuming that Paul meant Melchizedek was without father or mother, or descent, having neither beginning of days, nor end of life. However, in a revelation on the subject of priesthood given through the Prophet Joseph Smith, September 22, 1832, the Lord made it plain that it is the priesthood and not Melchizedek that is without beginning of days or end of years:

> Which priesthood continueth in the church of God in all generations, and is without beginning of days or end of years. (D. & C. 84:17.)

Calling and Ordination Necessary to Authority

Now that we have established the necessity for priesthood authority, we will consider the scriptural evidences that men must be ordained to the priesthood to minister in the things of God—they cannot assume this authority or receive it from one who does not possess it. This is why it was necessary for John the Baptist to bring back the Aaronic or Levitical Priesthood, and for Peter, James, and John to bring again the Melchizedek Priesthood, both of which were conferred upon Joseph Smith and Oliver Cowdery:

> For every high priest taken from among men is ordained for men in things pertaining to God, that he may offer both gifts and sacrifices for sins: . . .
>
> And no man taketh this honour unto himself, but he that is called of God, as was Aaron.
>
> So also Christ glorified not himself to be made an high priest; but he that said unto him, Thou art my Son, to day have I begotten thee.
>
> As he saith also in another place, Thou art a priest for ever after the order of Melchizedec. (Heb. 5:1, 4-6.)

Could anything be said with greater plainness: "For every high priest taken from among men is ordained for men in things pertaining to God." Then how can a man be a high priest if he is not so ordained?

"And no man taketh this honour unto himself but he that is called of God as was Aaron." (Heb. 5:4.) How was Aaron called? The Lord spoke unto Moses saying:

> And take thou unto thee Aaron thy brother, and his sons with him, from among the children of Israel, that he may minister unto me in the priest's office. . . .
>
> And thou shalt put them upon Aaron thy brother, and his sons with them; and shalt anoint them, and consecrate them, and sanctify them, that they may minister unto me in the priest's office. (Exod. 28:1, 41.)

Therefore, Aaron did not call or ordain himself.

"So also Christ glorified not himself to be made an high priest;" (see Heb. 5:5) but was chosen and appointed by his Father an high priest forever, and after being so called and appointed, he proceeded to call others:

> Then Jesus said unto them [the twelve] again, Peace be unto you: as my Father hath sent me, even so send I you. . . .
>
> Whose soever sins ye remit, they are remitted unto them; and whose soever sins ye retain, they are retained. (John 20:21,23.)

And he *ordained* twelve, that they should be with him, and that he might send them forth to preach,

And to have power to heal sicknesses, and to cast out devils. (Mark 3:14-15.)

The Apostles of Jesus did not call or ordain themselves—Jesus called them, and ordained them, and sent them forth to minister as his Father had sent him.

The Calling and Ordination of Paul

The calling of Saul (afterwards called Paul, Acts 13:9) to the ministry, including his subsequent ordination, presents a vivid example of the order of heaven in such matters since the pattern was given by the voice of Jesus:

And as he [Saul] journeyed, he came near Damascus: and suddenly there shined round about him a light from heaven:

And he fell to the earth, and heard a voice saying unto him, Saul, Saul, why persecutest thou me?

And he said, Who art thou, Lord? And the Lord said, I am Jesus whom thou persecutest: it is hard for thee to kick against the pricks.

And he trembling and astonished said, Lord, what wilt thou have me to do? And the Lord said unto him, Arise, and go into the city, and it shall be told thee what thou must do. (Acts 9:3-6.)

Notwithstanding the fact that Jesus spoke to Saul personally, that did not qualify him to engage in the ministry and administer the ordinances of the gospel. It was necessary for him to regain his sight by the laying on of Ananias' hands and to be baptized by him. Even though the Lord had indicated to Ananias that Saul was a chosen vessel unto him to bear his name before the gentiles, kings, and the children of Israel, it was nevertheless necessary that he should be ordained to this ministry sometime later, after he had declared before the disciples and others what he had seen and heard.

Now there were in the church that was at Antioch certain prophets and teachers; as Barnabas, and Simeon . . . and Saul.

As they ministered to the Lord, and fasted, the Holy Ghost said, Separate me Barnabas and Saul for the work whereunto I have called them.

And when they had fasted and prayed, *and laid their hands on them*, they sent them away. (Acts 13:1-3)

We assume that there are many in the world today who would consider themselves fully called and ordained had they seen and heard what Paul saw and heard on the way to Damascus. But not so with Paul, neither with Joseph Smith! They had to be ordained by one having authority. And so must all men who would authoritatively engage in the ministry. Joseph Smith learned this great truth, not by reading the Bible, but through the visitations of John the Baptist, and of Peter, James and John. Hence the fifth Article of Faith of The Church of Jesus Christ of Latter-day Saints, as penned by the Prophet Joseph Smith:

We believe that a man must be called of God, by prophecy and by the laying on of hands, by those who are in authority to preach the Gospel and administer in the ordinances thereof.

The Church of Jesus Christ "A Royal Priesthood"

Peter, in speaking of the Church in his day, said:

But ye are a chosen generation, a *royal priesthood*, an holy nation, a peculiar people; and ye should shew forth the praises of him who hath called you out of darkness into his marvellous light. (I Peter 2:9.)

From this and the revelations of the Lord to the Prophet Joseph Smith, in restoring the priesthood to the earth again in this dispensation, the Lord has made it plain that all male members of the Church, who live worthily, may receive the priesthood and thus become an active force in establishing the Church and kingdom of God in the earth, a part of that "royal priesthood" to which Peter referred; that they may all be united in showing forth "the praises of him who hath called you out of darkness into his marvellous light." These men are not trained specially for the ministry, any more than were the Apostles of old. But they develop the gifts and talents with which God has endowed them through the service they render and the gift of the Holy Ghost.

Paul understood this also when he said:

> For ye see your calling, brethren, how that not many wise men after the flesh, not many mighty, not many noble, are called:
>
> But God hath chosen the foolish things of the world to confound the wise; and God hath chosen the weak things of the world to confound the things which are mighty;
>
> And base things of the world, and things which are despised, hath God chosen, yea, and things which are not, to bring to naught things that are:
>
> That no flesh should glory in his presence. (I Cor. 1:26-29.)

In addition to all of its local officers, the Church of this dispensation, since its organization, has sent into the mission field in the neighborhood of seventy thousand missionaries, all of the type to which Paul referred. This great host of missionaries represents an unpaid ministry as was the priesthood in the days of Christ and his Apostles.

As of December 1, 1972, out of a Church population of 3,227,790 men, women, and children, there were 401,229 male members holding the Aaronic Priesthood, and 382,037 male members holding the Melchizedek Priesthood in the stakes of the Church. Where else in all the world is there such a "royal priesthood" as Peter called the Church of his day?

It was this practice to ordain to the priesthood, and

call into service all who were worthy and willing to serve, that led Jesus to say, when he sent the seventy, two and two before his face into every city and place, whither he himself would come:

> ... The harvest truly is great, but the labourers are few: pray ye therefore the Lord of the harvest, that he would send forth labourers into his harvest. (Luke 10:2.)

Offices in the Priesthood

There is so much to be done that the Lord placed many officers in his Church, and divided the Aaronic and Melchizedek Priesthoods into many divisions, that there may be a place suited to each man's capacity.

In the Aaronic Priesthood there are the following divisions: deacons, teachers, and priests. There are bishops when they are direct descendants of Aaron, otherwise they are chosen from among the high priests of the Melchizedek Priesthood.

In the Melchizedek Priesthood there are the following divisions and offices: elders, seventies, high priests, evangelists or patriarchs, apostles, and prophets.

All of the above-named officers are mentioned in the New Testament in connection with the primitive Church of Christ. However, only a few of them are now to be found in the existing branches of modern Christianity. It is our impression that were this complete organization offered to the churches of today, they would not know what to do with them all. They would not know the difference in the calling of an elder, high priest, deacon, teacher, or priest, nor the difference in their respective ministrations. Neither would they know how many of each are required to make a quorum or how a quorum should be organized and governed. Neither would we know this were we dependent upon the Bible only for this information. But we are not so dependent, for all this we have received through the revelations of the Lord in connection with the restoration of the priesthood in this dispensation through the Prophet Joseph Smith. (See D. & C. Sections 13, 20, 84, 107, 121.)

The Church Should Be Fully Organized

Paul fully understood the importance of a complete organization when he said:

> And he gave some, apostles; and some, prophets; and some, evangelists; and some, pastors and teachers;
>
> For the perfecting of the saints, for the work of the ministry, for the edifying of the body of Christ:
>
> Till we all come in the unity of the faith, and of the knowledge of the Son of God, unto a perfect man, unto the measure of the stature of the fulness of Christ:
>
> That we henceforth be no more children, tossed to and fro, and carried about with every wind of doctrine, by the sleight of men, and cunning craftiness, whereby they lie in wait to deceive. (Eph. 4:11-14.)

It surely appears as if the Christian world has been "tossed to and fro, and carried about with every wind of doctrine, by the sleight of men, and the cunning craftiness, whereby they lie in wait to deceive." Who would say that it is not because they have done away with the officers whom God placed in the Church to bring them to a unity of the faith? What more could be expected?

The Future of The Church of Jesus Christ

With its limited Church membership, already The Church of Jesus Christ of Latter-day Saints, with most of its male membership over the age of twelve years holding some office in the priesthood, is attracting great attention. When the general conferences of the Church are held in Salt Lake City, the great Tabernacle and Assembly Hall on Temple Square are filled beyond capacity with members of the priesthood alone at the general priesthood meeting. These men serve the Church without compensation, except a very few who give their entire time to the service of the Church, who receive only a living allowance. From the most highly trained educators, the most efficient and successful businessmen, the most qualified and experienced scientists, agriculturists, contractors, and mechanics, to the laboring man himself —each is at the call of his Church, and his services and training may be called for in the service of the Church and of his fellow men, and, in most cases, without even the thought that he should be compensated. It is considered an honor to be able to serve the interests of the Church. Highly successful businessmen, professional men, and farmers, leave their businesses, their professional work, their farms, and their families and at their own expense travel to the far countries of the world to labor for a few years in the great missionary cause of the Church. There is nothing like it in this world today. They must be like the saints of Peter's time which led him, when calling them "a royal priesthood," to add "a peculiar people," for in this respect also we are a very "peculiar people."

If you were to travel up and down through Latter-day Saint communities and were to stop and visit with a farmer working in his field, you would probably find that he is the bishop of his ward or the president of his stake, or an elder, seventy, or high priest. This would likely be as true were you to stop and visit with the banker, postmaster, owner or clerks in the stores, workers in the shops and factories, or the barber who may serve you at his chair.

Labor disturbances, therefore, do not find so fruitful a field among us, for how can our men meet weekly in their priesthood meetings where every man is a brother, and at the same time participate in labor disturbances when his brother's interests are at stake? Some industries recognizing this fact are seeking to establish themselves in our midst to avoid labor disturbances. To a true Latter-day Saint the priesthood of God is the greatest union in the world. Can you visualize a day when this kingdom of God shall spread throughout the world as Daniel declared (See Daniel 2:44), and all men everywhere, united in the bonds of the holy priesthood will devote their strength and talents to the welfare of their fellow men and the establishment of the kingdom of God in the earth?

These great truths we would not have understood had it not been for the restoration of the Aaronic Priesthood by John the Baptist and the Melchizedek Priesthood by Peter, James, and John. We use the Bible to show that the things revealed are in accord therewith and make it possible for us to understand them.

Further information concerning the responsibilities and activities of the priesthood will be given in succeeding chapters.

CHAPTER 10

THE ORDINANCE OF BAPTISM

We have established the need for the Aaronic Priesthood to preach the gospel of repentance and administer to the repentant one the ordinance of baptism by immersion for the remission of sins. Now let us consider the experience Joseph Smith related when he and Oliver Cowdery baptized each other under the direction of John the Baptist, and compare this with the teachings of that day and with the Holy Scriptures.

The Baptism of Joseph Smith and Oliver Cowdery

Let us refer again to Joseph Smith's own story in which he informs us that while he and Oliver Cowdery were engaged in translating the Book of Mormon they went into the woods to inquire of the Lord respecting baptism for the remission of sins which they found mentioned in the translation of the plates. It was in answer to their prayers that a messenger from heaven descended in a cloud of light and laid his hands upon their heads and conferred upon them the priesthood of Aaron and commanded them to go and be baptized. He gave directions that Joseph should baptize Oliver and that afterwards Oliver should baptize Joseph. This messenger said his name was John, the same that is called John the Baptist in the New Testament, and that he acted under the direction of Peter, James, and John.

Hundreds of books have been written on the subject of baptism. Who should be baptized, adults or children? What is the purpose of baptism? What is the correct mode of baptism— by immersion, sprinkling, or pouring?

But in this one grand and glorious experience Joseph Smith and Oliver Cowdery learned more about these matters from John the Baptist, who was sent to prepare the way of the Lord, and who was privileged to baptize the Son of God, than they could have learned had they read all the books that have ever been written on the subject of baptism.

In keeping with the commandment of John the Baptist, and under his direction, these two young men baptized each other by immersion, for the remission of their sins, May 15, 1829, presumably in the Susquehanna River in the western part of the state of New York. This should put an end to all controversy on this subject as to how baptism should be performed and the divine purpose thereof.

In April 1830, the month the Church was organized, Joseph Smith received a revelation on Church organization and Church government:

> No one can be received into the church of Christ unless he has arrived unto the years of accountability before God, and is capable of repentance.
>
> Baptism is to be administered in the following manner unto all those who repent—
>
> The person who is called of God and has authority from Jesus Christ to baptize, shall go down into the water with the person who has presented himself or herself for baptism, and shall say, calling him or her by name: Having been commissioned of Jesus Christ, I baptize you in the name of the Father, and of the Son, and of the Holy Ghost. Amen.
>
> Then shall he immerse him or her in the water, and come forth again out of the water. (D. & C. 20:71-74.)

Little Children Not to be Baptized

From this revelation we first learn that no man can be received into the Church of Jesus Christ unless he has arrived unto the years of accountability before God and is capable of repentance. This, obviously, eliminates infants and little children, for they have not arrived at the age of accountability before God; neither are they capable of repentance.

In a revelation given through Joseph Smith in November 1831, the Lord gave further light and instruction in this matter:

> And again, inasmuch as parents have children in Zion, or in any of her stakes which are organized, that teach them not to understand the doctrine of repentance, faith in Christ the Son of the living God, and of baptism and the gift of the Holy Ghost by the laying on of the hands, when eight years old, the sin be upon the heads of the parents.
>
> For this shall be a law unto the inhabitants of Zion, or in any of her stakes which are organized.
>
> And their children shall be baptized for the remission of their sins *when eight years old,* and receive the laying on of hands. (D. & C. 68:25-27.)

Thus the Lord himself fixed the age of accountability at eight years, at which age children who have been taught by their parents as commanded are to be baptized.

The Prophet Mormon wrote to his son, Moroni, on this subject as follows:

> And now, my son, I speak unto you concerning that which grieveth me exceedingly; for it grieveth me that there should disputations rise among you.
>
> For, if I have learned the truth, there have been disputations among you concerning the baptism of your little children.
>
> And now, my son, I desire that ye should labor diligently, that this gross error should be removed from among you; for, for this intent I have written this epistle.
>
> For immediately after I had learned these things of you I inquired of the Lord concerning the matter. And the word of the Lord came to me by the power of the Holy Ghost, saying:
>
> Listen to the words of Christ, your Redeemer, your Lord and your God. Behold, I came into the world not to call the righteous

but sinners to repentance; the whole need no physician, but they that are sick; wherefore, little children are whole, for they are not capable of committing sin; *wherefore the curse of Adam is taken from them in me,* that it hath no power over them; and the law of circumcision is done away in me.

And after this manner did the Holy Ghost manifest the word of God unto me; *wherefore, my beloved son, I know that it is solemn mockery before God, that ye should baptize little children.*

Behold I say unto you that this thing shall ye teach—repentance and baptism unto those who are accountable and capable of committing sin; yea, teach parents that they must repent and be baptized, and humble themselves as their little children, and they shall all be saved with their little children.

And their little children need no repentance, neither baptism. Behold, baptism is unto repentance to the fulfilling the commandments unto the remission of sins.

But little children are alive in Christ, even from the foundation of the world; if not so, God is a partial God, and also a changeable God, and a respecter to persons; for how many little children have died without baptism!

Wherefore, if little children could not be saved without baptism, these must have gone to an endless hell.

Behold I say unto you, that he that supposeth that little children need baptism is in the gall of bitterness and in the bonds of iniquity; for he hath neither faith, hope, nor charity; wherefore, should he be cut off while in the thought, he must go down to hell.

For awful is the wickedness to suppose that God saveth one child because of baptism, and the other must perish because he hath no baptism.

Wo be unto them that shall pervert the ways of the Lord after this manner, for they shall perish except they repent. Behold, I speak with boldness, having authority from God; and I fear not what man can do; for perfect love casteth out all fear.

And I am filled with charity, which is everlasting love; wherefore, all children are alike unto me; wherefore, I love little children with a perfect love; and they are all alike and partakers of salvation.

For I know that God is not a partial God, neither a changeable being; but he is unchangeable from all eternity to all eternity.

Little children cannot repent; wherefore, it is awful wickedness to deny the pure mercies of God unto them, for they are all alive in him because of his mercy.

And he that saith that little children need baptism denieth the mercies of Christ, and setteth at naught the atonement of him and the power of redemption. (Moroni 8:4-20.)

It is strange, indeed, that so many churches should have practiced the principle of infant baptism when there is no account of any such baptisms having been performed in the Church of Jesus Christ in primitive days, nor any instructions given that it should be done. Obviously, any such instructions would have to be given to the parents for the children, since infants cannot act for themselves.

In a revelation given through the Prophet Joseph Smith in September 1830, the Lord, in speaking on this subject said:

But, behold, I say unto you, that little children are redeemed from the foundation of the world through mine Only Begotten;

Wherefore, they cannot sin, for power is not given unto Satan to tempt little children, until they begin to become accountable before me. (D. & C. 29:46-47.)

The Fallacy of Infant Baptism

The erroneous conception of the need of baptizing infants is, no doubt, due to the teachings of the churches of the day that little children are answerable for the original sin of Adam and Eve or the sins of their parents. This concept cannot be true as we have already pointed out from the revelations of the Lord through the Prophet Joseph Smith, for Jesus died to atone for the sins over which we have no control:

For as in Adam all die, even so in Christ shall all be made alive. (I Cor. 15:22.)

Jesus Christ redeemed all from the fall; he paid the price; he offered himself as a ransom; he atoned for Adam's sin, leaving us responsible only for our own sins. One of our Articles of Faith states:

> We believe that men will be punished for their own sins, and not for Adam's transgression.

The Apostle John understood this doctrine:

> I write unto you, little children, because your sins are forgiven you for his name's sake. (I John 2:12.)

Children to be Blessed

The question may then be asked: If children are not to be baptized until they reach the age of accountability (eight years) what, if anything, should be done for them? The Lord answered this question in a revelation through Joseph Smith, the Prophet, in April, 1830:

> Every member of the church of Christ having children is to bring them unto the elders before the church, who are to lay their hands upon them in the name of Jesus Christ, and bless them in his name. (D. & C. 20:70.)

How perfectly this all accords with the teachings and practice of Jesus when he ministered among men:

> And they brought young children to him, that he should touch them; and his disciples rebuked those that brought them.
>
> But when Jesus saw it, he was much displeased, and said unto them, Suffer the little children to come unto me, and forbid them not: for of such is the kingdom of God.
>
> Verily I say unto you, Whosoever shall not receive the kingdom of God as a little child, he shall not enter therein.
>
> And he took them up in his arms, put his hands upon them, and blessed them. (Mark 10:13-16.)

It is quite apparent that the disciples of Jesus must have felt the unworthiness of little children to command the personal attention of their Master, even as present-day ministers of religion must feel in requiring that they be baptized. In this, Jesus was "much displeased." He is

equally displeased with the so-called infant baptisms being performed today. He set the example by suffering the
little children to be brought unto him. He took them up
in his arms, put his hands upon them, and blessed them.
This is his pattern and commandment to his Church of
this dispensation. As we have already pointed out, Joseph
Smith did not get this information from reading the Bible
or any other book written on this subject, but by the
revelations of the Lord to him.

Baptism by Immersion for Remission of Sins

We have shown that Joseph Smith and Oliver
Cowdery were baptized by immersion for remission of
their sins, as directed by John the Baptist, and that in a
revelation to Joseph Smith the Lord indicated how baptism should be performed, giving even the words to be
used by the one officiating in performing the ordinance.
(See D. & C. 20:72-74.)

We will now consider the pattern given and the purpose of baptism as introduced by John the Baptist in this
dispensation, the same as was taught and practiced in the
primitive Church. Jesus himself set the example "to fulfil
all righteousness":

> Then cometh Jesus from Galilee to Jordan unto John, to be
> baptized of him.
>
> But John forbad him, saying, I have need to be baptized of
> thee, and comest thou to me?
>
> And Jesus answering said unto him, Suffer it to be so now:
> for thus it becometh us to fulfil all righteousness. Then he suf-
> fered him.
>
> And Jesus, when he was baptized, went up straightway out
> of the water: and, lo, the heavens were opened unto him, and he
> saw the Spirit of God descending like a dove, and lighting upon
> him:
>
> - -And lo a voice from heaven, saying, This is my beloved Son,
> in whom I am well pleased. (Matt. 3:13-17.)

It requires a considerable stretch of the imagination to think Jesus would go to John at the River Jordan and then go down into the river, only to have a little water sprinkled or poured upon his head. "When he was baptized, he went up straightway out of the water." He could not come up out of the water unless he had been in the water, and he would not have gone into the water to be sprinkled or poured. He had to go into the water to be immersed or baptized. What does the word *baptize* mean anyway? It is taken from the Greek *bapto* or *baptizo* and means to dip or to immerse. In discussing the principle of baptism, Jesus and his Apostles could just as easily have referred to sprinkling or pouring if that had been satisfactory, but they did not. Not a little water, but "much water" was needed for the ordinance of baptism:

> And John also was baptizing in Aenon near to Salim, because there was much water there: and they came, and were baptized. (John 3:23.)

John could have found sufficient water for sprinkling or pouring, almost anywhere. He could have gone to those desiring baptism, but they came to locations he selected "because there was much water there" where he could really baptize or immerse them.

Paul indicated that there is "One Lord, one faith, one baptism." (Eph. 4:5.)

If there is but one baptism, then answer the question Jesus put to the high priests:

> The baptism of John, whence was it? from heaven, or of men? And they reasoned with themselves, saying, If we shall say, From heaven; he will say unto us, Why did ye not then believe him?
>
> But if we shall say, Of men; we fear the people; for all hold John as a prophet. (Matt. 21:25-26.)

Since the baptism of John was from heaven, all men

should be willing to accept it. John's baptism was by immersion for the remission of sins:

> John did baptize in the wilderness, and preach the baptism of repentance for the remission of sins.
>
> And there went out unto him all the land of Judaea, and they of Jerusalem, and were all baptized of him in the river of Jordan, confessing their sins. (Mark 1:4-5.)

Could this account be written more plainly?—they "were all baptized of him *in the river of Jordan.*" There is only one baptism, and that is John's baptism, and it was performed *in the river,* not *by the* river.

Repentance to Precede Baptism

> And he [John] came into all the country about Jordan, preaching the baptism of repentance for the remission of sins. (Luke 3:3.)
>
> Then said he to the multitude that came forth to be baptized of him, O generation of vipers, who hath warned you to flee from the wrath to come?
>
> Bring forth therefore fruits worthy of repentance, and begin not to say within yourselves, We have Abraham to our father: for I say unto you, That God is able of these stones to raise up children unto Abraham. (Luke 3:7-8.)

It is, therefore, clear that remission of sins comes only through baptism when one has truly repented of his sins; that baptism, without repentance, is not a means by which one can "flee from the wrath to come."

Peter held out this same promise of forgiveness of sins through repentance and baptism to those to whom he preached on the day of Pentecost:

> Now when they heard this, they were pricked in their heart, and said unto Peter and to the rest of the apostles, Men and brethren, what shall we do?
>
> Then Peter said unto them, Repent, and be baptized every one of you in the name of Jesus Christ for the remission of sins, and ye shall receive the gift of the Holy Ghost.
>
> For the promise is unto you, and to your children, and to all

that are afar off, even as many as the Lord our God shall call. (Acts 2:37-39.)

What a glorious promise! Is there any honest seeker after truth who would not want to reach out his soul and accept of such an invitation for himself and his loved ones as here extended by Peter? In addition to knowing what we should do when seeking after the blessings and gifts of God, we should know where to find those who hold his Holy Priesthood and are thus authorized, through proper ordination, to officiate in his name. The reason we are not confused in these matters is that they were revealed to Joseph Smith through the restoration of the gospel. We use the Bible to show that these revealed truths are in harmony with its teachings.

Baptism, a Requisite to Salvation

After Jesus' resurrection he spoke to his eleven Apostles:

And he said unto them, Go ye into all the world, and preach the gospel to every creature.

He that believeth and is baptized shall be saved; but he that believeth not shall be damned. (Mark 16:15-16.)

This is but a confirmation of what the Savior said to Nicodemus before the crucifixion. Therefore, when he declared, while hanging on the cross, "It is finished," (John 19:30) he did not mean that his gospel should not continue to be preached by those he sent to minister for the salvation of his children, as some maintain:

There was a man of the Pharisees, named Nicodemus, a ruler of the Jews:

The same came to Jesus by night, and said unto him, Rabbi, we know that thou art a teacher come from God: for no man can do these miracles that thou doest, except God be with him.

Jesus answered and said unto him, Verily, verily, I say unto thee, Except a man be born again, he cannot see the kingdom of God.

Nicodemus saith unto him, How can a man be born when he is old? can he enter the second time into his mother's womb, and be born?

Jesus answered, Verily, verily, I say unto thee, Except a man be born of water and of the Spirit, he cannot enter into the kingdom of God. . . .

Nicodemus answered and said unto him, How can these things be?

Jesus answered and said unto him, Art thou a master of Israel, and knowest not these things? (John 3:1-5, 9-10.)

Baptism, a Second Birth

If one cannot *see* or *enter* into the kingdom of God without being born again, it is very important that we should fully understand what the Savior had in mind. Since he indicated that this second birth should be "of water and of the spirit," it is obvious that He had in mind the matter of being baptized in water and receiving the Holy Ghost following baptism, for how similar to our first birth this second birth really is. When one is first born into this life, his body comes forth out of water; the spirit takes possession thereof; and he is literally born of water and of spirit. Were this not so, how could he be born again of water and of the spirit?

Paul discussed this rebirth in this manner:

Know ye not, that so many of us as were baptized into Jesus Christ were baptized into his death?

Therefore we are buried with him by baptism into death: that like as Christ was raised up from the dead by the glory of the Father, even *so we also should walk in newness of life.*

For if we have been planted together in the likeness of his death we shall be also in the likeness of his resurrection:

Knowing this, that our old man is crucified with him, that the body of sin might be destroyed, that henceforth we should not serve sin. (Rom. 6:3-6.)

This seems very plain. When "we are *buried* with him by baptism into death," (which of course could not be true were we sprinkled or had water poured on us) we are born again of water when we come forth from this watery grave, and our sins having been remitted, we "should walk in a newness of life." We can only walk in newness of life when we are born again. Our "old man" of sin is therefore crucified with him, and we are born again, in similitude of his resurrection.

Baptism of Cornelius

The experience of Cornelius of Caesarea, a devout man who feared God, and prayed to him always, (See Acts 10:1-4) teaches quite a lesson.

Should an angel of God appear to one in our day with such a message, most religious teachers would not worry about his need of baptism. But not so with the Lord who sent the angel to tell Cornelius to send men to Simon Peter and "he shall tell thee what thou oughtest to do." (See Acts 10:5-6.)

The Lord then gave Peter a vision of a vessel or sheet let down from heaven, containing all manner of wild beasts and fowls and creeping things. Peter was hungry and a voice came unto him saying:

> . . . Rise, Peter; kill, and eat.
>
> But Peter said, Not so, Lord; for I have never eaten any thing that is common or unclean.
>
> And the voice spake unto him again the second time, What God hath cleansed, that call not thou common. (Acts 10:13-15.)

This was because Cornelius was the first of the Gentiles to accept the word of God. After they had related to each other their experiences which had brought them together, Peter preached Christ and the baptism of John to him and his company. They accepted his message; the

Holy Ghost rested upon them; they spoke with tongues and magnified God. Then answered Peter:

> Can any man forbid water, that these should not be baptized, which have received the Holy Ghost as well as we?
>
> And he commanded them to be baptized in the name of the Lord. . . . (Act 10:47-48.)

From this we learn that no matter how righteous one may be who seeks after truth, the Lord directs him to one of his servants who has been ordained to the priesthood, so that he can be baptized at his hands and be instructed.

This was also true with respect to Saul (Paul), to which we have already referred. Even though the Savior spoke to him on the road to Damascus, the Lord directed him to go into the city of Damascus, where the Lord instructed one of his servants, Ananias, what to do. Ananias first restored Paul's sight by the laying on of hands, and then baptized him. Paul was later ordained to the ministry. (See Acts 9; 13:1-3.)

John's Baptism Confirmed in These Latter Days

Now these are exactly the same steps taken by the Lord with respect to Joseph Smith and Oliver Cowdery when they went into the woods to inquire about baptism by immersion for the remission of sins. The only difference being that there was no one upon the earth holding the priesthood of God with authority to administer the ordinance of baptism unto them. Therefore, the Lord sent the resurrected John the Baptist, who conferred the priesthood of Aaron upon them, which priesthood held the keys of baptism by immersion for the remission of sins. John then commanded them to baptize each other.

Again, Joseph Smith and Oliver Cowdery did not obtain this information from reading the Bible but from the revelations of the Lord to them and by their own experiences through obedience to divine instruction.

We have now given consideration to the principal points of interest covered by the visit of John the Baptist to Joseph Smith and Oliver Cowdery on May 15, 1829. John did inform them that the Aaronic Priesthood held the keys of "the ministering of angels," the truth of which will be fully evidenced in consideration of the further visits of heavenly messengers in connection with the recommitment to this earth of the necessary keys and authority for a complete "restitution of all things which God hath spoken by the mouth of all his holy prophets since the world began." (See Acts 3:21.)

CHAPTER 11

THE MISSION OF THE HOLY GHOST

When John the Baptist conferred the Aaronic Priesthood on Joseph Smith and Oliver Cowdery May 15, 1829, he told them that the Aaronic Priesthood had not the power of laying on hands for the gift of the Holy Ghost, but that this power would thereafter be conferred upon them. He further stated that he acted under the direction of Peter, James, and John, who held the keys of the Priesthood of Melchizedek, which priesthood, he said, would, in due time, be conferred on them. (See P. of G. P. Joseph Smith 2:70-72.)

In fulfilment of John's promise, and soon after the first ordination, Peter, James, and John, ancient apostles of the Lord Jesus Christ, conferred upon Joseph Smith and Oliver Cowdery the priesthood of Melchizedek in the wilderness of Fayette, Seneca County, New York. Among other things, this higher priesthood gave them the promised power of "laying on hands for the gift of the Holy Ghost," which we will now discuss.

Laying on of Hands for the Gift of the Holy Ghost

So far as we know, there was no church upon the earth that taught and practiced the principle of "laying on hands for the gift of the Holy Ghost," at the time John the Baptist informed Joseph Smith and Oliver Cowdery that the Aaronic Priesthood had not this power. Not only did John the Baptist make it plain that this was a principle of the gospel, but in further revelations to the Prophet Joseph Smith, the Lord also confirmed the truth of this statement.

In December 1830, the Lord spoke to the Prophet Joseph Smith:

> But now I give unto thee a commandment, that thou shalt baptize by water, and they shall receive the Holy Ghost by the laying on of the hands, even as the apostles of old. (D. & C. 35:6.)

A similar commission was given by the Lord through Joseph Smith, the prophet in March 1831, to a number of the elders of the Church:

> Wherefore, I give unto you a commandment that ye go among this people, and say unto them, like unto mine apostle of old, whose name was Peter:
>
> Believe on the name of the Lord Jesus, who was on the earth, and is to come, the beginning and the end;
>
> Repent and be baptized in the name of Jesus Christ, according to the holy commandment, for the remission of sins;
>
> And whoso doeth this shall receive the gift of the Holy Ghost, by the laying on of the hands of the elders of the Church. (D. & C. 49:11-14.)

From the date of the organization of The Church of Jesus Christ of Latter-day Saints, admission to membership has been through baptism by immersion for the remission of sins, and the laying on of hands for the gift of the Holy Ghost. In the revelation last referred to, the Lord, through the Prophet Joseph Smith, instructed the elders of the Church to go among the people and instruct them as did Peter of old. Let us examine the holy scriptures to ascertain what Peter did instruct the people to do.

On the day of Pentecost when there was an outpouring of the spirit of the Lord, those who heard the preaching of Peter—

> . . . were pricked in their heart, and said unto Peter and to the rest of the apostles, Men and brethren, what shall we do?

Then Peter said unto them, Repent, and be baptized every one of you in the name of Jesus Christ for the remission of sins, and ye shall receive the gift of the Holy Ghost.

For the promise is unto you, and to your children, and to all that are afar off, even as many as the Lord our God shall call. (Acts 2:37-39.)

Wherein does this instruction from Peter differ from that given to Joseph Smith and Oliver Cowdery by John the Baptist; and subsequently, by Peter, James, and John; and in the revelation of the Lord to the elders of the Church through the Prophet Joseph Smith?

In this Biblical account of Peter's sermon, the only thing lacking is the statement wherein he promises them that they shall receive the gift of the Holy Ghost, that they shall receive it by the laying on of hands. This omission was undoubtedly an inadvertence or brevity in reporting this event, for the scriptures are definite enough in the statement that Peter understood the Holy Ghost was bestowed by the laying on of hands. This is evident in Peter's participation in the ordinance of "laying on of hands" for the bestowal of the Holy Ghost in the case of those baptized by Philip at Samaria:

Then Philip went down to the city of Samaria, and preached Christ unto them.

And the people with one accord gave heed unto those things which Philip spake, hearing and seeing the miracles which he did.

For unclean spirits, crying with loud voice, came out of many that were possessed with them: and many taken with palsies, and that were lame, were healed.

And there was great joy in that city.

But there was a certain man, called Simon, which beforetime in the same city used sorcery, and bewitched the people of Samaria, giving out that himself was some great one:

To whom they all gave heed, from the least to the greatest, saying, This man is the great power of God.

And to him they had regard because that of long time he had bewitched them with sorceries.

But when they believed Philip preaching the things concerning the kingdom of God, and the name of Jesus Christ, they were baptized, both men and women.

Then Simon himself believed also: and when he was baptized, he continued with Philip, and wondered, beholding the miracles and signs which were done.

Now when the apostles which were at Jerusalem heard that Samaria had received the word of God, they sent unto them Peter and John:

Who, when they were come down, prayed for them, that they might receive the Holy Ghost:

(For as yet he was fallen upon none of them: only they were baptized in the name of the Lord Jesus.)

Then laid they their hands on them, and they received the Holy Ghost.

And when Simon saw that through laying on of the apostles' hands the Holy Ghost was given, he offered them money,

Saying, Give me also this power, that on whomsoever I lay hands, he may receive the Holy Ghost.

But Peter said unto him, Thy money perish with thee, because thou hast thought that the gift of God may be purchased with money. (Acts 8:5-20.)

How could this truth be stated with greater plainness? How did the people of Samaria receive the word of God? By being baptized! Why were Peter and John sent unto them? Because the people had not yet received the Holy Ghost—they had been baptized only in the name of the Lord Jesus! Why did Philip not bestow the Holy Ghost upon them? Because, presumably, he was authorized to exercise only the functions of the Aaronic Priesthood, as was John the Baptist, who explained to Joseph Smith and Oliver Cowdery that the Aaronic Priesthood "had not the power of laying on hands for the gift of the Holy Ghost!"

If men could take this honor unto themselves, Simon would not have offered them money to purchase this power when he saw that the Holy Ghost was given by laying on of the Apostles' hands. Why have the Christian churches of today forsaken this glorious principle? Because they have not understood the scriptures, and being without revelation and the priesthood of God, they have had to depend upon their own interpretation of the scriptures for their guidance.

A Scripture Misunderstood

The scripture that has probably been most confusing in this matter was the statement of Jesus to Nicodemus:

> Marvel not that I said unto thee, Ye must be born again.
>
> The wind bloweth where it listeth, and thou hearest the sound thereof, but canst not tell whence it cometh, and whither it goeth: so is every one that is born of the Spirit. (John 3:7-8.)

This has been interpreted to mean that the spirit of the Holy Ghost comes and goes at will without any doing of ours, or the performance of any ceremony, such as the laying on of hands. There is no justification for such interpretation in the light of many scriptural passages to the contrary already referred to. True it is that we cannot see the spirit come or go any more than we can see the wind, even though we can hear its sound and feel its movement. But when the Holy Ghost is conferred upon us by the laying on of hands by one having authority, even though he cannot be seen by the mortal eye, his workings are discernible in the life and conduct of the worthy recipient.

John the Baptist understood that the gift of the Holy Ghost could only be received through the instrumentality of one commissioned to convey it:

> . . . There cometh one mightier than I after me, the latchet of whose shoes I am not worthy to stoop down and unloose.
>
> I indeed have baptized you with water: but he shall baptize you with the Holy Ghost. (Mark 1:7-8.)

If the Holy Ghost were to fall upon men at will, what need was there for Jesus to follow John, baptizing with the Holy Ghost?

The People of Ephesus Receive the Holy Ghost by the Laying on of Hands

Paul understood that the Holy Ghost was conferred by the laying on of hands:

> And it came to pass, that, while Apollos was at Corinth, Paul having passed through the upper coasts came to Ephesus: and finding certain disciples,
>
> He said unto them, Have ye received the Holy Ghost since ye believed? And they said unto him, We have not so much as heard whether there be any Holy Ghost.
>
> And he said unto them, Unto what then were ye baptized? And they said, Unto John's baptism.
>
> Then said Paul, John verily baptized with the baptism of repentance, saying unto the people, that they should believe on him which should come after him, that is, on Christ Jesus.
>
> When they heard this, they were baptized in the name of the Lord Jesus.
>
> And when Paul had laid his hands upon them, the Holy Ghost came on them; and they spake with tongues, and prophesied. (Acts 19:1-6.)

This shows that Peter and John at Samaria and Paul at Ephesus were in perfect accord in understanding that the Holy Ghost should be conveyed by the laying on of hands. Paul gave further emphasis to this ordinance:

> Therefore leaving the principles of the doctrine of Christ, let us go on unto perfection; not laying again the foundation of repentance from dead works, and of faith toward God,

Of the doctrine of baptisms, *and of laying on of hands,* and of resurrection of the dead, and of eternal judgment. (Heb. 6:1-2.)

It will be seen that this foundation is in full accord with the gospel as restored in these latter days and as taught by the Apostles of old. How then can there be any question? The Apostles were taught by the Savior himself, and there could be no misunderstanding. Certain of them were sent back to the earth in this dispensation by the Lord to re-establish the same principles, the same foundation, and the same gospel of Jesus Christ in these latter-days, through the instrumentality of the Prophet Joseph Smith. How then is it possible to omit such an important part of the foundation of the gospel of Christ and yet be justified in claiming to have his gospel? What would happen to a building were one side of the foundation omitted? The Apostles understood fully that there would be those who would come among the people teaching their own ideas and changing the doctrines they had taught. The people were warned against such false teachers:

Whosoever transgresseth, and abideth not in the doctrine of Christ, hath not God. He that abideth in the doctrine of Christ, he hath both the Father and the Son.

If there come any unto you, and bring not this doctrine, receive him not into your house, meither bid him God speed. (II John 9-10.)

Personality and Mission of the Holy Ghost

Having considered the principle of laying on of hands for the gift of the Holy Ghost, it now seems proper that we should consider the gifts and functions of the Holy Ghost:

If ye love me, keep my commandments.

And I will pray the Father, and he shall give you another Comforter, that he may abide with you for ever;

Even the Spirit of truth; whom the world cannot receive, because it seeth him not, neither knoweth him; but ye know him; for he dwelleth with you, and shall be in you. . . .

But the Comforter, which is the Holy Ghost, whom the Father will send in my name, he shall teach you all things, and bring all things to your remembrance, whatsoever I have said unto you. (John 14:15-17, 26.)

Nevertheless I tell you the truth; It is expedient for you that I go away: for if I go not away, the Comforter will not come unto you; but if I depart, I will send him unto you. . . .

I have yet many things to say unto you, but ye cannot bear them now.

Howbeit when he, the Spirit of truth, is come, he will guide you into all truth: for he shall not speak of himself; but whatsoever he shall hear, that shall he speak: and he will shew you things to come.

He shall glorify me: for he shall receive of mine, and shall shew it unto you. (John 16:7,12-14.)

There are a few fundamental truths we learn from these statements by the Savior:

1. That he, his Father, and the Holy Ghost are three distinct personages, and that their oneness referred to in the scriptures is only oneness of purpose and desire, else why should Jesus pray unto his Father and promise that the Father would send another comforter. There cannot be another unless there is already one. Jesus is the one comforter, and surely he would not pray unto himself, asking that he (himself) send himself as "another comforter."

2. That the Holy Ghost is a male personage. Note how often Jesus refers to the Holy Ghost as "he" and "him," in the above quotations. He is a male personage of spirit as was Jesus before he was born of the Virgin Mary. Note Jesus' own statement:

I have glorified thee on the earth: I have finished the work which thou gavest me to do.

And now, O Father, glorify thou me with thine own self with the glory which I had with thee before the world was. (John 17:4-5.)

"Before the world was," Jesus was with the Father and shared his glory. But he was a personage of spirit until he was born into the world. It was while Jesus had his spirit body that he created this earth under the direction of his Father. (See John 1:1-14.) Likewise, the Holy Ghost in his spirit body has his assignment of responsibility as the third member of the Godhead, which assignment is that of a comforter. While Jesus does not explain why he and the Holy Ghost cannot remain on the earth and serve together, nevertheless he does make this fact clear:

. . . It is expedient for you that I go away: for if I go not away, the Comforter will not come unto you. . . . (John 16:7.)

When Nephi was shown, by the spirit of the Lord, the dream his father had seen, Nephi asked him the interpretation thereof:

And it came to pass after I had seen the tree, I said unto the spirit: I behold thou hast shown unto me the tree which is precious above all.

And he said unto me: What desirest thou?

And I said unto him: To know the interpretation thereof— for I spake unto him as a man speaketh; for I beheld that he was in the form of a man; yet nevertheless, I knew that it was the Spirit of the Lord; and he spake unto me as a man speaketh with another. (I Nephi 11:9-11.)

3. The third important truth we learn is: That the *gift* of the Holy Ghost comes not to the world, but only to those upon whom this gift has been conferred by the laying on of hands by those ordained to this authority: (See "Limited Ministrations of the Holy Ghost Without Laying on of Hands," in this chapter.)

And I will pray the Father, and he shall give you another Comforter, that he may abide with you for ever;

Even the Spirit of truth; whom the world cannot receive, because it seeth him not, neither knoweth him: but ye know him; for he dwelleth with you, and shall be in you. (John 14:16-17.)

4. Still another great truth we learn is that the reception of the Holy Ghost enables one to understand the truths of the spirit:

I have yet many things to say unto you, but ye cannot bear them now.

Howbeit when he, the Spirit of truth, is come, he will guide you into all truth: for he shall not speak of himself; but whatsoever he shall hear, that shall he speak: and he will shew you things to come.

He shall glorify me: for he shall receive of mine, and shall shew it unto you. (John 16:12-14.)

How the Holy Ghost Ministers

Since the Holy Ghost is a personage of spirit in the form of man (See I Nephi 11:11) and hence confined in his personage to a limited space, the question is often asked: How can he be a comforter to all who have received the laying on of hands for the gift of the Holy Ghost, scattered as they may be, among all nations of men?

The following illustration may help to explain how this may be possible: The sun is millions of miles away from the earth; it is a body of specific dimensions; yet, when its morning rays stream through our windows, we remark, The sun is in our room. A similar statement might also be made by a person thousands of miles away. Yet it is obvious that neither is correct, for the sun remains millions of miles away. Only the influence which the sun radiates is in our room.

It does not seem consistent to assume that anything which God has created, no matter how wonderful, can equal in power or influence the Creator himself. Why, then, is there anything unreasonable or difficult to understand in assuming that spiritual power and influence, and even information, such as Jesus promised that the Holy Ghost, or Comforter, would convey, can emanate from him and be received by us, even though he, in person, be far removed from us?

The radio of our modern age should help us to understand this phenomenon. A person's voice traveling through the air can encircle the globe in the flash of a second through the power which God has created.

What then can be the possibilities of the operation or ministry of the Holy Ghost, God's agency for communicating unto those who are "not of the world," but unto whom the promise of the Holy Ghost is given by one having the authority of God?

Mission of the Holy Ghost

. . . he shall teach you all things and bring all things to your remembrance, whatsoever I have said unto you. (John 14:26.)

. . . he shall testify of me. (John 15:26.)

. . . he will guide you into all truth . . . and he will shew you things to come.

. . . he shall receive of mine, and shall shew it unto you. (John 16:13-14.)

. . . he will reprove the world of sin, and of righteousness, and of judgment. (John 16:8.)

For the Holy Ghost shall teach you in the same hour what ye ought to say. (Luke 12:12.)

But ye shall receive power, after that the Holy Ghost is come upon you. . . . (Acts 1:8.)

. . . the Spirit searcheth all things, yea, the deep things of God. (I Cor. 2:10.)

. . . even so the things of God knoweth no man, but the Spirit of God. (I Cor. 2:11.)

The Spirit itself beareth witness with our spirit, that we are the children of God: (Rom. 8:16.)

But the fruit of the Spirit is love, joy, peace, longsuffering, gentleness, goodness, faith,

Meekness, temperance: . . . (Gal. 5:22-23.)

And these signs shall follow them that believe; In my name shall they cast out devils; they shall speak with new tongues;

They shall take up serpents; and if they drink any deadly thing, it shall not hurt them; they shall lay hands on the sick, and they shall recover. (Mark 16:17-18.)

Now there are diversities of gifts, but the same Spirit. . . .

But the manifestation of the Spirit is given to every man to profit withal.

For to one is given by the Spirit the word of wisdom; to another the word of knowledge by the same Spirit;

To another faith by the same Spirit; to another the gifts of healing by the same Spirit;

To another the working of miracles; to another prophecy; to another discerning of spirits; to another divers kinds of tongues; to another the interpretation of tongues:

But all these worketh that one and the selfsame Spirit, dividing to every man severally as he will. (I Cor. 12:4, 7-11.)

All these gifts and ministrations of the spirit belong in the true Church, and they have been enjoyed in rich measure by the faithful members of The Church of Jesus Christ of Latter-day Saints since its organization April 6, 1830.

Limited Ministrations of the Holy Ghost Without Laying on of Hands

From the revelations given of the Lord to Joseph Smith and Oliver Cowdery in this dispensation, and from accounts given in the scriptures, it is very evident that the gift of the Holy Ghost is conferred only by the laying on of hands by those having divine authority from God. It must, nevertheless, be understood that the Holy Ghost is the medium through whom God and his Son, Jesus Christ, communicate with men upon the earth, unless the message is of sufficient importance to justify the sending of heavenly messengers or by personal visitation, as was the case in certain of the experiences of Joseph Smith. Hence the promise of Moroni first referred to, that all men to whom the Book of Mormon should come, who would ask God, the Eternal Father, in the name of Christ, asking with a sincere heart, having faith in Christ, that he would manifest the truth of it unto them by the power of the Holy Ghost. Thus the Holy Ghost enlightens their minds and gives them to know the truth when they have faith in Christ and seek sincerely in order that they may accept and obey the truth. However, there is no promise that the Holy Ghost will remain as a comforter and companion with even such as they, except upon their acceptance of the truth and their obedience to its requirements.

In his Sermon on the Mount, Jesus said:

And blessed are they which do hunger and thirst after righteousness: for they shall be filled. (Matt. 5:6.)

Jesus made this even more plain when he visited the Nephites on the American continent:

Blessed are all they who do hunger and thirst after righteousness, for they shall be filled with the Holy Ghost. (III Nephi 12:6.)

In fulfilment of these promises, when his servants are sent to teach the truth, the Holy Ghost gives men and women to know the truth of such teachings and to lead them to the acceptance thereof when in their hearts they earnestly seek after righteousness. Hence, upon the day of Pentecost, when the multitude heard Peter preaching Christ and him crucified, it was the Holy Ghost who caused them to be "pricked in their heart," and to say to Peter and the rest of the Apostles, "Men and brethren, what shall we do?" (Acts 2:37.)

> Then Peter said unto them, Repent, and be baptized every one of you in the name of Jesus Christ for the remission of sins, and ye shall receive the *gift* of the Holy Ghost. (Acts 2:38.)

Therefore, while they had received the Holy Ghost to convince them of the truth as preached by Peter, nevertheless, they had not received the Holy Ghost as a *gift*. Peter offered the Holy Ghost to them that believed, and "there were added unto them about three thousand souls" who were baptized that day. (See Acts 2:41.)

The Apostle Paul said:

> How then shall they call on him in whom they have not believed? and how shall they believe in him of whom they have not heard? and how shall they hear without a preacher?
>
> And how shall they preach except they be sent? . . .
>
> So then faith cometh by hearing, and hearing by the word of God. (Rom. 10:14-15, 17.)

What is it that causes men to have faith when they are seeking after righteousness and when they hear the word of God from those who are sent unto them? It is the impressions of the Holy Ghost. Every elder in the Church knows how he prays for the Holy Ghost to rest upon those to whom he preaches the word of God in his missionary labors; that they might have faith to believe and repent of their sins; that they might be baptized for the remission of their sins and receive the gift of the Holy Ghost.

In studying the subject of baptism we considered the case of Cornelius, the first of the gentiles to be admitted to the fold of Christ through baptism. He was a righteous man who "gave much alms to the poor, and prayed to God always," so that an angel of God came to him and directed him to Peter, a servant of God, who would tell him what he should do. Then the Lord had to prepare Peter to administer the ordinances of the gospel to him by showing him a vision of all manner of four-footed and wild beasts, and creeping things and fowls of the air let down from heaven in a vessel. Then Peter was commanded to kill and eat, to which he replied: "Not so, Lord, for I have never eaten anything that is common or unclean." And the voice said: "What God hath cleansed, that call not thou common." (See Acts 10:14-15.) This vision was shown to Peter three times. When Peter met Cornelius and they had exchanged accounts of their experiences:

> Then Peter opened his mouth, and said, Of a truth I perceive that God is no respecter of persons:
>
> But in every nation he that feareth him, and worketh righteousness, is accepted with him. . . .
>
> While Peter yet spake these words, the *Holy Ghost* fell on all them which heard the word.
>
> And they of the circumcision which believed were astonished, as many as came with Peter, because that on the Gentiles also was poured out the gift of the Holy Ghost.
>
> For they heard them speak with tongues, and magnify God. Then answered Peter,
>
> Can any man forbid water, that these should not be baptized, which have received the Holy Ghost as well as we?
>
> And he commanded them to be baptized in the name of the Lord. . . . (Acts 10:34-35, 44-48.)

It is evident from the reading of this chapter that Peter was not so much impressed by the fact that Cornelius had seen an angel of God, of his worthiness for baptism, as he was when the Lord permitted the Holy

Ghost to rest upon him. This fully convinced Peter that he should call nothing unclean or common which God had cleansed. For such an important mission as this, there seems ample justification that the Lord should send the Holy Ghost as his messenger to convince Peter of the worthiness of this man and his associates to be baptized.

The Spirit of God or the Spirit of Christ

We have considered the mission and operations of the Holy Ghost as the third personage of the Godhead. We have indicated that men can receive the gift of the Holy Ghost only through obedience to the command-ments of the Lord, and by the laying on of hands by those who are in authority to administer in the ordinances of the gospel. Jesus made it plain that the world cannot re-ceive the Holy Ghost whom he describes as "the Spirit of truth":

And I will pray the Father, and he shall give you another Comforter, that he may abide with you for ever;

Even the Spirit of truth; *whom the world cannot receive,* because it seeth him not, neither knoweth him: but ye know him; for he dwelleth with you, and shall be in you. (John 14:16-17.)

We have also considered limited operations of the Holy Ghost, which seem to be confined to those who seek after righteousness, and where the Lord has some special message to convey. In such cases, however, the Holy Ghost does not come as a gift to remain with the in-dividual, as is the case where one receives the gift of the Holy Ghost by the laying on of hands.

The question may then be asked: Has the Lord made no provision for inspiring and directing those who are not entitled to receive the gift of the Holy Ghost? We answer, Yes, the Lord has made such provision. In the words of the Apostle John:

> In the beginning was the Word, and the Word was with God, and the Word was God.
>
> The same was in the beginning with God.
>
> All things were made by him; and without him was not any thing made that was made.
>
> In him was life; *and the life was the light of men.*
>
> And the light shineth in darkness; and the darkness comprehended it not.
>
> There was a man sent from God, whose name was John.
>
> The same came for a witness, to bear witness of the Light, that all men through him might believe.
>
> He was not that Light, but was sent to bear witness of that Light.
>
> *That was the true Light, which lighteth every man that cometh into the world. . . .*
>
> And the Word was made flesh, and dwelt among us, (and we beheld his glory, the glory as of the only begotten of the Father,) full of grace and truth. (John 1:1-9,14.)

It is thus evident that Jesus Christ created all things, and that he "was the true Light, which *lighteth every man* that cometh into the world." Thus not one of our Father's children is born in spiritual darkness. This must have been what the Apostle Paul had in mind:

> (For not the hearers of the law are just before God, but the doers of the law shall be justified.
>
> For when the Gentiles, which have not the law, do by nature the things contained in the law, these, having not the law, are a law unto themselves:
>
> Which shew the work of the law written in their hearts, their conscience also bearing witness, and their thoughts the mean while accusing or else excusing one another.) (Rom. 2:13-15.)

It will thus be seen that even where the law is not given and understood, that through this light "which lighteth every man that cometh into the world," that all men have "the law written in their hearts," and that their consciences bear witness of right and wrong.

It must have been this spirit the Prophet Joel spoke of when he said:

> And it shall come to pass afterward, that I will pour out my spirit upon all flesh; and your sons and your daughters shall prophesy, your old men shall dream dreams, your young men shall see visions:
>
> And also upon the servants and upon the handmaidens in those days will I pour out my spirit.
>
> And I will shew wonders in the heavens and in the earth, blood, and fire, and pillars of smoke.
>
> The sun shall be turned into darkness, and the moon into blood, before the great and the terrible day of the Lord come. (Joel 2:28-31.)

In a revelation to the Prophet Joseph Smith at Kirtland, Ohio, September 22, 1832, the Lord spoke of this spirit in these words:

> For you shall live by every word that proceedeth forth from the mouth of God.
>
> For the word of the Lord is truth, and whatsoever is truth is light, and whatsoever is light is Spirit, even the Spirit of Jesus Christ.
>
> *And the Spirit giveth light to every man that cometh into the world; and the Spirit enlighteneth every man through the world, that hearkeneth to the voice of the Spirit.* (D. & C. 84:44-46.)

Three months after the above revelation was given, the Lord gave further light on this same question in a revelation to Joseph Smith:

> He that ascended up on high, as also he descended below all things, in that he comprehended all things, that he might be in all and through all things, the light of truth;
>
> Which truth shineth. This is the light of Christ. As also he is in the sun, and the light of the sun, and the power thereof by which it was made.
>
> As also he is in the moon, and is the light of the moon, and the power thereof by which it was made;

As also the light of the stars, and the power thereof by which they were made;

And the earth also, and the power thereof, even the earth upon which you stand.

And the light which shineth, which giveth you light, is through him who enlighteneth your eyes, which is the same light that quickeneth your understandings;

Which light proceedeth forth from the presence of God to fill the immensity of space—

The light which is in all things, which giveth life to all things, which is the law by which all things are governed, even the power of God who sitteth upon his throne, who is in the bosom of eternity, who is in the midst of all things. (D. & C. 88:6-13.)

In presenting the teachings of his father Mormon, the Prophet Moroni said:

For behold, the Spirit of Christ is given to every man, that he may know good from evil; wherefore, I show unto you the way to judge; for every thing which inviteth to do good, and to persuade to believe in Christ, is sent forth by the power and gift of Christ; wherefore ye may know with a perfect knowledge it is of God. (Moroni 7:16.)

In a sermon in the Salt Lake Tabernacle, March 16, 1902, President Joseph F. Smith spoke of the operations of the Spirit of God or the Spirit of Christ, and the difference between them and the operation or mission of the Holy Ghost as follows:

It is by the power of God that all things are made that have been made. It is by the power of Christ that all things are governed and kept in place that are governed and kept in place in the universe. It is the power which proceeds from the presence of the Son of God throughout all the works of his hands, that giveth light, energy, understanding, knowledge, and a degree of intelligence to all the children of men, strictly in accordance with the words in the Book of Job: "There is a spirit in man; and the inspiration of the Almighty giveth them understanding." It is this inspiration from God, proceeding throughout all his creations, that enlighteneth the children of men; and it is nothing more nor less than the spirit of Christ, that enlighteneth the mind, that quickeneth the understanding, and that prompteth the children of men to do that which is good and to eschew that which is evil; which quickens the conscience of man and gives him intelligence to judge between good and evil, light and darkness, right and wrong.

But the Holy Ghost, who bears record of the Father and the Son, who takes of the things of the Father and shows them unto men, who testifies of Jesus Christ, and of the everlasting God, the Father of Jesus Christ, and who bears witness of the truth—this Spirit, this Intelligence, is not given unto all men until they repent of their sins and come into a state of worthiness before the Lord. Then they receive the gift of the Holy Ghost by the laying on of the hands of those who are authorized of God to bestow his blessings upon the heads of the children of men. The Spirit spoken of in that which I have read is that Spirit which will not cease to strive with the children of men until they are brought to the possession of the greater light and intelligence. Though a man may commit all manner of sin and blasphemy, if he has not received the testimony of the Holy Ghost, he may be forgiven by repenting of his sins, humbling himself before the Lord, and obeying in sincerity the commandments of God. As it is stated, "Every soul who forsaketh his sins and cometh unto me, and calleth on my name, and obeyeth my voice, and keepeth my commandments shall see my face and know that I am." He shall be forgiven, and receive of the greater light; he will enter into a solemn covenant with God, into a compact with the Almighty, through the Only Begotten Son, whereby he becomes a son of God, an heir of God, and a joint heir with Jesus Christ. Then, if he shall sin against the light and knowledge he has received, the light that was within him shall become darkness, and oh, how great will be that darkness! Then, and not till then, will this Spirit of Christ that lighteth every man that cometh into the world cease to strive with him, and he shall be left to his own destruction.

The question is often asked, Is there any difference between the Spirit of the Lord and the Holy Ghost? The terms are frequently used synonymously. We often say the Spirit of God when we mean the Holy Ghost; we likewise say the Holy Ghost when we mean the Spirit of God. The Holy Ghost is a personage in the Godhead, and is not that which lighteth every man that cometh into the world. It is the Spirit of God which proceeds through Christ to the world, that enlightens every man that comes into the world, and that strives with the children of men, and will continue to strive with them, until it brings them to a knowledge of the truth and the possession of the greater light and testimony of the Holy Ghost. If, however, he receive that greater light, and then sin against it, the Spirit of God will cease to strive with him, and the Holy Ghost will wholly depart from him. Then will he persecute the truth; then will he seek the blood of the innocent; then will he not scruple at the commission of any crime, except so far as he may fear the penalties of the law, in consequence of the crime upon himself. (Joseph F. Smith, *Gospel Doctrine*, Fifth edition, pp. 66-68.)

Nephi saw the spirit of God rest upon a man whom we understand to be Columbus and lead him to this land:

And I looked and beheld a man among the Gentiles, who was separated from the seed of my brethren by the many waters; *and I beheld the Spirit of God, that it came down and wrought upon the man;* and he went forth upon the many waters, even unto the seed of my brethren, who were in the promised land. (I Nephi 13:12.)

Columbus had not received the laying on of hands for the gift of the Holy Ghost, but the time had come, as seen by Nephi over two thousand years before, when this land, which God had hidden from the eyes of other nations, (See II Nephi 1:8) should be prepared to receive the restoration of the gospel of Jesus Christ.

Such an important mission would seem to call for special inspiration from the Lord, as Nephi states when he "beheld the Spirit of God, that it came down and wrought upon the man." President Joseph F. Smith, as we have herein indicated, states that the terms: "Spirit of God and the Holy Ghost are frequently used synonymously." Therefore, it could have been the Spirit of God or the Holy Ghost that "wrought upon the man."

Nephi also saw the spirit of God move upon others in like manner:

And it came to pass that I beheld the Spirit of God, that it wrought upon other Gentiles; and they went forth out of captivity, upon the many waters. (I Nephi 13:13.)

This, no doubt, included the Pilgrim Fathers and others who first settled this land. These were great events in the unfolding of God's plans with respect to the Dispensation of the Fulness of Times or the latter-day gospel dispensation, which fully justified the sending of the spirit of God to move upon the minds and hearts of men to bring about the purposes of the Almighty. Such things have transpired through the ages to assist in achieving his purposes.

No doubt the reformers and those who gave us the Holy Bible, were also inspired in preparation for the restoration of the gospel.

The knowledge of all these things, as the reader will note, comes not to us primarily through reading the Bible, but through the revelations of the Lord in these latter-days. We use the Bible to show that these teachings are completely in accord therewith.

CHAPTER 12

SETTING UP THE KINGDOM OF GOD UPON THE EARTH

A Recommitment of the Keys of the Kingdom

In a revelation to Joseph Smith in September 1830 the Lord referred to the ordination of Joseph Smith and Oliver Cowdery to the Melchizedek Priesthood by Peter, James, and John, and then referred to the *keys* that had been restored to Joseph Smith by the various prophets of former days:

And also with Peter, and James, and John, whom I have sent unto you, by whom I have ordained you and confirmed you to be apostles, and especial witnesses of my name, and bear the keys of your ministry and of the same things which I revealed unto them;

Unto whom I have committed the keys of my kingdom, and a dispensation of the gospel for the last times; and for the fulness of times, in which I will gather together in one all things, both which are in heaven, and which are on earth;

And also with all those whom my Father hath given me out of the world. (D. & C. 27:12-14.)

A careful consideration of this revelation indicates a very complete and comprehensive commitment to Joseph Smith and Oliver Cowdery of the keys of the kingdom held by Peter, James, and John when Jesus left the kingdom in their hands following his resurrection, after he had ministered among them.

They were, therefore, ordained Apostles of the Lord Jesus Christ; they became special witnesses of his name; they received the keys of the kingdom and a dispensation of the gospel for the last time, and for the fulness of times, in which the Lord promised to gather together in one all things, both which are in heaven and which are on earth. The Lord indicated that there is also a work to be done with those whom the Father had given him "out of the world."

This all embraces great and important responsibilities and activities in connection with the new gospel dispensation. It seems proper that we should first consider the organization of the Church of Jesus Christ. All of the details in connection with the organization of the Church were not given by Peter, James, and John, but they did restore the keys and the authority of the priesthood so essential to the establishment of the kingdom. The organization was perfected through revelation to the Prophet Joseph Smith as the membership of the Church increased, making such organization possible and necessary.

Organization and Name of the Church in These Latter Days

In keeping with a revelation from the Lord to the Prophet Joseph Smith, The Church of Jesus Christ of Latter-day Saints was organized April 6, 1830, at the home of Peter Whitmer, Sr., in Fayette, Seneca County, New York. Six members made up the original membership of the Church—Joseph Smith, Oliver Cowdery, Hyrum Smith, Peter Whitmer, Jr., David Whitmer, and Samuel H. Smith. At this time Joseph Smith was sustained as the first elder of the Church and Oliver Cowdery as the second elder, as John the Baptist had indicated they should be at the time he conferred the Aaronic Priesthood upon them May 15, 1829. (See D. & C. 20:1-4.)

In a revelation to Joseph Smith April 26, 1838, after

the Lord addressed himself to the Presidency of the Church and others he added:

> And also unto my faithful servants who are of the *high council of my church in Zion,* for thus it shall be called and unto all the elders and people of my *Church of Jesus Christ of Latter-day Saints, scattered abroad in all the world;*
>
> For thus shall my church be called in the last days, even *The Church of Jesus Christ of Latter-day Saints.* (D. & C. 115:3-4.)

The designation "Latter-day Saints" is to differentiate between the members of The Church of Jesus Christ of this dispensation and those of the Church established by Jesus in the Meridian of Time.

The matter of the name his Church should bear was of great importance to the Savior. Not only was this name revealed to Joseph Smith as indicated above, but also in reporting the visit of Jesus to the Nephites in America, following his ascension, when he had organized his Church among them, the Book of Mormon records their inquiry and the Lord's reply as to what the name of his Church should be:

> And Jesus again showed himself unto them, for they were praying unto the Father in his name; and Jesus came and stood in the midst of them, and said unto them: What will ye that I shall give unto you?
>
> And they said unto him: Lord, we will that thou wouldst tell us the name whereby we shall call this church; for there are disputations among the people concerning this matter.
>
> And the Lord said unto them: Verily, verily, I say unto you, why is it that the people should murmur and dispute because of this thing?
>
> Have they not read the scriptures, which say ye must take upon you the name of Christ, which is my name? For by this name shall ye be called at the last day;
>
> And whoso taketh upon him my name, and endureth to the end, the same shall be saved at the last day.
>
> Therefore, whatsoever ye shall do, ye shall do it in my name; therefore ye shall call the church in my name; and ye shall call

upon the Father in my name that he will bless the church for my sake.

And how be it my church save it be called in my name? For if a church be called in Moses' name then it be Moses' church; or if it be called in the name of a man then it be the church of a man; but if it be called in my name then it is my church, if it so be that they are built upon my gospel. (III Nephi 27:2-8.)

Thus the name of the Church was not obtained through study or research, but by revelation direct from the Lord. Does it not seem incredible that of all the churches in the world, there was not one that bore his name when the Lord restored his Church in this dispensation?

Members of the Primitive Church Called Saints

There seems to be a common misunderstanding today that the designation "saints" should be applied only to those members or officers in Christian churches who have distinguished themselves in such a manner that their names should be canonized. This, however, is an obvious error, since all the followers of Christ in former days were called "saints," as a careful study of the following scriptures indicate:

Paul, called to be an apostle of Jesus Christ through the will of God, and Sosthenes our brother,

Unto the church of God which is at Corinth, to them that are sanctified in Christ Jesus, called to be *saints*, with all that in every place call upon the name of Jesus Christ our Lord. . . . (I Cor. 1:1-2.)

For God is not the author of confusion, but of peace, as in all churches of the *saints*. (I Cor. 14:33.)

Praying us with much intreaty that we would receive the gift, and take upon us the fellowship of the ministering to the *saints*. (II Cor. 8:4.)

To all that be in Rome, beloved of God, called to be *saints*: Grace to you and peace from God our Father, and the Lord Jesus Christ. (Rom. 1:7.)

Now therefore ye are no more strangers and foreigners, but fellowcitizens with the *saints,* and of the household of God. (Eph. 2:19.)

But fornication, and all uncleanness, or covetousness, let it not be once named among you, as becometh *saints.* (Eph. 5:3.)

Salute every *saint* in Christ Jesus. The brethren which are with me greet you.

All the *saints* salute you, chiefly they that are of Caesar's household. (Phil. 4:21-22.)

Dare any of you, having a matter against another, go to law before the unjust, and not before the *saints?*

Do ye not know that the *saints* shall judge the world? and if the world shall be judged by you, are ye unworthy to judge the smallest matters? (I Cor. 6:1-2.)

And the graves were opened; and many bodies of the *saints* which slept arose. (Matt. 27:52.)

Beloved, when I gave all diligence to write unto you of the common salvation, it was needful for me to write unto you, and exhort you that ye should earnestly contend for the faith which was once delivered unto the *saints.* (Jude 1:3.)

From the above it is very apparent that the followers of Jesus were called saints; that they were so addressed by the Apostles notwithstanding their weaknesses; and that the Lord placed officers in his Church "for the perfecting of the *Saints.* " (See Eph. 4:12.)

The Psalmist was privileged to see our day when the Lord would come to judge his people; when he would send forth his truth to the inhabitants of the earth; when he would gather his *saints* together unto Zion. (See Ps. 50:1-5.)

In Daniel's interpretation of Nebuchadnezzar's dream, he explains that in the latter-days when the kingdoms of this world would begin to crumble, the God of heaven would set up a kingdom that would never be destroyed but would stand forever (See Dan. 2:28-45); he describes the coming of the Son of man unto whom this kingdom would be delivered; he states that all nations would serve and obey the God of heaven (See Dan. 7:13-14). Speaking further of this latter-day kingdom: "But the *saints* of the most High shall take the kingdom, and possess the kingdom for ever, even for ever and ever." (See Dan. 7:18.)

Now, it is obvious that a kingdom cannot be delivered unto the Son of Man when he comes to take his rightful place to rule over all nations, unless a kingdom is prepared for him. The kingdom, according to Daniel, is to be given to "the *saints* of the most High" that they might "possess the kingdom for ever, even for ever and ever."

Thus, it will be observed, that as the name of the Church is given of God, so also is the designation "saints," given to the members of his Church.

Priesthood Authority in Church Government

In the revelations of the Lord to the Prophet Joseph Smith, he makes known the fact that the Melchizedek Priesthood "has power and authority over all the offices in the church in all ages of the world." Therefore, when Joseph Smith and Oliver Cowdery received this priesthood under the hands of Peter, James, and John, they received the keys and authority necessary to organize completely The Church of Jesus Christ, and the quorums of the priesthood:

> And this greater priesthood administereth the gospel and holdeth the key of the mysteries of the kingdom, even the key of the knowledge of God.
>
> Therefore, in the ordinances thereof, the power of godliness is manifest.
>
> And without the ordinances thereof, and the authority of the priesthood, the power of godliness is not manifest unto men in the flesh. (D. & C. 84:19-21.)

The power and authority of the higher, or Melchizedek

Priesthood, is to hold the keys of all the spiritual blessings of the church—

To have the privilege of receiving the mysteries of the kingdom of heaven, to have the heavens opened unto them, to commune with the general assembly and church of the Firstborn, and to enjoy the communion and presence of God the Father, and Jesus the mediator of the new covenant. (D. & C. 107:18-19.)

The Melchizedek Priesthood holds the right of presidency, and has power and authority over all the offices in the church in all ages of the world to administer in spiritual things. (See D. & C. 107:8.)

The Quorum of the First Presidency

If the Church is to function in perfect form, as the human body, as the Apostle Paul has indicated (See I Cor. 12:12-31), who is to stand at the head of the Church upon the earth until it is delivered unto the Son of Man at his coming? It seems proper that a president (prophet), or presidency (prophets), should be appointed by him to direct all the activities of the Church and of the priesthood, through whom he can speak and reveal his mind and will to the entire Church, without having to do this to individual units that might be established throughout the world. The Lord has done this very thing in providing that three high priests be appointed and ordained to form a quorum of the presidency of The Church of Jesus Christ of Latter-day Saints. On this subject the Lord has thus spoken:

Of the Melchizedek Priesthood, three Presiding High Priests, chosen by the body, appointed and ordained to that office, and upheld by the confidence, faith, and prayer of the church, form a quorum of the Presidency of the Church. (D. & C. 107:22.)

And again, the duty of the President of the office of the High Priesthood is to preside over the whole church, and to be like unto Moses—

Behold, here is wisdom; yea, to be a seer, a revelator, a

translator, and a prophet, having all the gifts of God which he
bestows upon the head of the church. (D. & C. 107:91-92.)

This presidency, with additional counselors as appointed by the President for specific needs, presides over
the High Priesthood, and directs all the affairs of the
Church, being also the court of final appeal in the
Church. They are prophets, seers, and revelators.

We find no direct statement in the Bible to the effect
that a presidency of the Church was appointed by the
Savior to stand at the head of the Church after his departure. However, the fact that he sent Peter, James, and
John back to the earth in this dispensation to restore the
Melchizedek Priesthood, and the keys thereof, including
the holy apostleship, would indicate that they held a position of preference over the other Apostles, which, by virtue of their administration in this dispensation, would
indicate that they were the presidency of the Melchizedek Priesthood and of the Church in the meridian of
time, following the ascension of Jesus.

If this assumption is correct, it will also explain why
Jesus took these three Apostles, Peter, James, and John
up into an high mountain apart—

> And was transfigured before them: and his face did shine as
> the sun, and his raiment was white as the light.
>
> And, behold, there appeared unto them Moses and Elias
> talking with him. . . .
>
> . . . and behold a voice out of the cloud, which said, This is
> my beloved Son, in whom I am well pleased; hear ye him. (Matt.
> 17:2-3, 5.)

Certainly one cannot read this account without feeling that these three Apostles had a sanctification and
preparation for their ministry such as the other Apostles
did not have. What other consistent explanation can be
given for the preference shown Peter, James, and John
over their brethren of the Apostles? Of this glorious
event, the Prophet Joseph Smith stated:

The Priesthood is everlasting. The Savior, Moses, and Elias, gave the keys to Peter, James, and John, on the mount, when they were transfigured before him. (D.H.C. Vol. 3, p. 387.)

The Quorum of the Twelve Apostles

The Lord made plain the duties and responsibilities of the Quorum of the Twelve Apostles in his Church in these latter-days. He indicated that they officiate under the direction of the First Presidency of the Church and that they form a quorum "equal in authority and power" to the presidency. The wisdom of the Lord in this matter is evident, for when the quorum of the Presidency is disorganized by the death of the president, the Quorum of the Twelve Apostles holds all the keys and authority necessary to reorganize the presidency:

The twelve traveling councilors are called to be the Twelve Apostles, or special witnesses of the name of Christ in all the world—thus differing from other officers in the church in the duties of their calling.

And they form a quorum, equal in authority and power to the three presidents previously mentioned. (D. & C. 107:23-24.)

The twelve are a Traveling Presiding High Council, to officiate in the name of the Lord, under the direction of the Presidency of the Church, agreeable to the institution of heaven; to build up the church, and regulate all the affairs of the same in all nations, first unto the Gentiles and secondly unto the Jews. (D. & C. 107:33.)

The duty and calling of the twelve Apostles are, therefore, "to build up the Church and regulate all the affairs of the same, in all nations" under the direction of the First Presidency of the Church. The twelve Apostles are also prophets, seers, and revelators.

The calling and appointment of the Quorum of the Twelve Apostles in his Church is in complete accord with the responsibilities bestowed upon the original twelve who ministered under the direction of the Savior when he was upon the earth, and following his crucifixion, as the following quotations indicate:

And when it was day, he called unto him his disciples and of them he chose twelve, whom also he named apostles. (Luke 6:13.)

Then the eleven disciples went away into Galilee, into a mountain where Jesus had appointed them.

And when they saw him, they worshipped him: but some doubted.

And Jesus came and spake unto them, saying, All power is given unto me in heaven and in earth.

Go ye therefore, and teach all nations, baptizing them in the name of the Father, and of the Son, and of the Holy Ghost:

Teaching them to observe all things whatsoever I have commanded you: and lo, I am with you alway, even unto the end of the world. (Matt. 28:16-20.)

Then the same day at evening, being the first day of the week, when the doors were shut where the disciples were assembled for fear of the Jews, came Jesus and stood in the midst, and saith unto them, Peace be unto you.

And when he had so said, he shewed unto them his hands and his side. Then were the disciples glad, when they saw the Lord.

Then said Jesus to them again, Peace be unto you: *as my Father hath sent me, even so send I you. . . .*

Whose soever sins ye remit, they are remitted unto them; and whose soever sins ye retain, they are retained. (John 20:19-21, 23.)

Ye have not chosen me, but I have chosen you, and ordained you, that ye should go and bring forth fruit, and that your fruit should remain: that whatsoever ye shall ask of the Father in my name, he may give it you. (John 15:16.)

And I will give unto thee the keys of the kingdom of heaven: and whatsoever thou shalt bind on earth shall be bound in heaven: and whatsoever thou shalt loose on earth shall be loosed in heaven. (Matt. 16:19.)

From these quotations it is clear that all power was given Jesus in heaven and upon earth, and that he chose twelve Apostles and ordained them and sent them forth in the ministry with the same power and authority which he himself had received from his Father, even the keys of the kingdom of heaven.

How different is the ministry of the churches of to-day. Men do not wait to be chosen and ordained and sent forth to minister, but they, themselves, do the choosing, and their preparation for the ministry comes not by virtue of their ordination by one having authority from God, but by their graduation from seminaries of learning established by men for such purposes. How things have changed! Who is responsible for the changes—God or man?

There are those who think that the Lord only intended to have the original twelve Apostles, but this position is not tenable, for if Apostles were ever necessary in the Church, they would continue to be necessary until the work assigned them is completed. Paul informs us what this assignment is and its objective:

And he gave some, apostles; and some, prophets; and some evangelists; and some, pastors and teachers;

For the perfecting of the saints, for the work of the ministry, for the edifying of the body of Christ:

Till we all come in the unity of the faith, and of the knowledge of the Son of God, unto a perfect man, unto the measure of the stature of the fulness of Christ:

That we henceforth be no more children, tossed to and fro, and carried about with every wind of doctrine, by the sleight of men, and cunning craftiness, whereby they lie in wait to deceive. (Eph. 4:11-14.)

Are the saints perfected? Is the work of the ministry completed? Has the body of Christ, his Church, been fully edified? Have we all come in the unity of the faith? In light of the many Christian creeds, can we claim that the people of the world have ceased to be "tossed to and fro, and carried about with every wind of doctrine, by the sleight of men, and cunning craftiness, whereby they lie in wait to deceive?" Who can say that the reason these objectives have not been achieved is not due to the fact that the officers the Lord placed in his Church to bring about this accomplishment were done away with by men?

The Apostle Paul indicated that the Church was built upon the foundation of Apostles and prophets:

> Now therefore ye are no more strangers and foreigners, but fellowcitizens with the saints, and of the household of God;
>
> And are built upon the foundation of the *apostles* and *prophets,* Jesus Christ himself being the chief corner stone. (Eph. 2:19-20.)

It is plain, therefore, that it was the Lord's intention to keep the Quorum of the Twelve Apostles complete, for after Judas Iscariot betrayed the Lord, Matthias was called to take his place:

> And they prayed, and said, Thou, Lord, which knowest the hearts of all men, shew whether of these two thou hast chosen,
>
> That he may take part of this ministry and *apostleship,* from which Judas by transgression fell, that he might go to his own place.
>
> And they gave forth their lots; and the lot fell upon Matthias; and he was numbered with the *eleven apostles.* (Acts 1:24-26.)

The Apostles understood that the quorum was to be kept complete. Paul and Barnabas were called to be Apostles after the calling of the original twelve:

> Which when the apostles, Barnabas and Paul, heard of, they rent their clothes, and ran in among the people. . . . (Acts 14:14; see also Acts 13:1-4.)

James, the Lord's brother, was also called to the apostleship after the first twelve were appointed:

> But other of the apostles saw I none, save James the Lord's brother. (Gal. 1:19; see also Mark 6:3.)

Since Apostles were essential in the Church which Jesus Christ established in the meridian of time, why should they not continue to be necessary wherever his recognized Church is upon the earth? To a thinking person it should be obvious that as the Church grows, the need for Apostles to direct the work would be even more essential.

Even with the limited information the Bible gives on this subject, it is very apparent that had the Church which Jesus organized in person, continued among men, the Quorum of the Twelve Apostles would have been kept complete to direct it.

The High Priest

Following the restoration of keys and powers of the Melchizedek Priesthood to Joseph Smith and Oliver Cowdery, as the Church increased in numbers, the Lord revealed to the Prophet Joseph Smith the proper organization of the priesthood into divisions and quorums. Of the calling of a *high priest* he said:

High priests after the order of the Melchizedek Priesthood have a right to officiate in their own standing, under the direction of the presidency, in administering spiritual things, and also in the office of an elder, priest (of the Levitical order), teacher, deacon, and member. . . .

The *high priest* and elder are to administer in spiritual things, agreeable to the covenants and commandments of the church; and they have a right to officiate in all these offices of the Church when there are no higher authorities present. (D. & C. 107:10, 12.)

Every president of the high priesthood (or presiding elder), bishop, high councilor, and *high priest*, is to be ordained by the direction of a high council or general conference. (D. & C. 20:67.)

But, as a *high priest* of the Melchizedek Priesthood has authority to officiate in all the lesser offices he may officiate in the office of bishop when no literal descendant of Aaron can be found, provided he is called and set apart and ordained unto this power, under the hands of the First President of the Melchizedek Priesthood. (D. & C. 68:19.)

There are many other revelations and references pertaining to the calling of a high priest, but since the purpose of this discussion is to show that the same organization of the priesthood has been re-established upon the earth as existed formerly, rather than to cover fully a discussion of priesthood, we shall not discuss this matter further at this time other than to point out that all these offices in the priesthood were found in the Church established by Jesus Christ in the Meridian of Time. To quote Paul:

> For every *high priest* taken from among men is ordained for men in things pertaining to God, that he may offer both gifts and sacrifices for sins. (Heb. 5:1.)
>
> So also Christ glorified not himself to be made an *high priest,* but he that said unto him, Thou art my Son, to day have I begotten thee.
>
> As he saith also in another place, Thou art a priest for ever after the order of Melchizedec. (Heb. 5:5-6.)
>
> Wherefore, holy brethren, partakers of the heavenly calling, consider the Apostle and High Priest of our profession, Christ Jesus. (Heb. 3:1.)

From these quotations it is apparent that not only was Jesus an "apostle and high priest" but that his brethren shared this "heavenly calling" with him, and that "every *high priest* taken from among men is ordained for men in things pertaining to God."

Where are the Apostles and high priests in the churches of today? Why have they been done away with?

Patriarch or Evangelist

The calling of a patriarch or an evangelist is to bless the people or members of the Church. We read of evangelists in the New Testament but find nothing there to indicate what the particular duties of this calling in the priesthood are. This information has come to us only through the revelations of the Lord to the Prophet Joseph Smith. The Lord instructed the twelve Apostles of his Church in this dispensation "to ordain evangelical ministers, as they shall be designated unto them by revelation" in all large branches of the Church. (See D. & C. 107:39.) Then he explained how this order of priesthood was confirmed to be handed down from father to son, indicating further that this order was instituted in the days of Adam and came down by lineage through the patriarchs:

It is the duty of the Twelve, in all large branches of the church, to ordain *evangelical ministers,* as they shall be designated unto them by revelation—

The order of this priesthood was confirmed to be handed down from father to son, and rightly belongs to the literal descendants of the chosen seed, to whom the promises were made.

This order was instituted in the days of Adam and came down by lineage in the following manner: . . . (D. & C. 107:39-41; see also verses 41-57 for priesthood lineage from Adam to Noah, and by whom and when each patriarch was ordained.)

The Prophet Joseph Smith made this explanation concerning the calling of an evangelist or patriarch:

An Evangelist is a Patriarch, even the oldest man of the blood of Joseph or of the seed of Abraham. Wherever the Church of Christ is established in the earth, there should be a Patriarch for the benefit of the posterity of the Saints, as it was with Jacob in giving his patriarchal blessing unto his sons, etc. (D. H. C., Vol. 3, p. 381.)

And again, verily I say unto you, let my servant William be appointed, ordained, and anointed, as a counselor unto my servant Joseph, in the room of my servant Hyrum, that my servant Hyrum may take the office of Priesthood and *Patriarch,* which was appointed unto him by his father, by blessing and also by right;

That from henceforth he shall hold the keys of the *patriarchal* blessings upon the heads of all my people,

> That whoever he blesses shall be blessed, and whoever he curses shall be cursed. . . . (D. & C. 124:91-93.)

One of the most striking illustrations of the exercise of this calling as recorded in the Bible is when Jacob blessed his twelve sons:

> And Jacob called unto his sons, and said, Gather yourselves together, that I may tell you that which shall befall you in the last days.
>
> Gather yourselves together, and hear, ye sons of Jacob; and hearken unto Israel your father. (Gen. 49:1-2.)

Then follows the individual blessings pronounced upon the heads of his twelve sons. The great *patriarch* Isaac blessed his sons, Jacob and Esau. (See Gen. Chap. 27.)

Paul referred to Abraham as a patriarch:

> Now consider how great this man was, unto whom even the *patriarch* Abraham gave the tenth of the spoils. (Heb. 7:4.)

Paul spoke of the calling of an evangelist but did not indicate what the work of an evangelist is:

> And he gave some, apostles; and some, prophets; and some, *evangelists;* and some, pastors and teachers. (Eph. 4:11.)

Timothy was called to be an evangelist:

> But watch thou in all things, endure affliction, do the work of an *evangelist,* make full proof of thy ministry. (II Tim. 4:5.)

Notwithstanding these very plain references in both the Old and New Testaments indicating that the Lord has placed patriarchs or evangelists in his Church in times past, we would not know what their particular calling in the priesthood is except through the revelations of the Lord to the Prophet Joseph Smith in re-establishing his Church in this dispensation.

Why has this holy calling of patriarch been done away with by the churches? Tens of thousands of Latter-day Saints have been comforted and inspired by the blessings of the Lord unto them through his patriarchs of this dispensation. And the knowledge of the calling and ministry of a patriarch we did not receive through study of the scriptures, but by the revelations of the Lord to his prophets in this our day.

The Seventy

From the revelations of the Lord to the Prophet Joseph Smith, we learn the duties and calling of the seventy:

The *Seventy* are also called to preach the gospel, and to be especial witnesses unto the Gentiles and in all the world—thus differing from other officers in the church in the duties of their calling.

And they form a quorum, equal in authority to that of the Twelve special witnesses or Apostles just named. (D. & C. 107: 25-26.)

The *Seventy* are to act in the name of the Lord, under the direction of the Twelve or the traveling high council, in building up the church and regulating all the affairs of the same in all nations, first unto the Gentiles and then to the Jews. (D. & C. 107:34.)

And it is according to the vision showing the order of the *Seventy*, that they should have seven presidents to preside over them, chosen out of the number of the *seventy;*

And the seventh president of these presidents is to preside over the six;

And these seven presidents are to choose other *seventy* besides the first *seventy* to whom they belong, and are to preside over them;

And also other *seventy*, until seven times *seventy*, if the labor in the vineyard of necessity requires it.

And these *seventy* are to be traveling ministers, unto the Gentiles first and also unto the Jews.

Whereas other officers of the church, who belong not unto the Twelve, neither to the *Seventy*, are not under the responsibility to travel among all nations, but are to travel as their circumstances shall allow, notwithstanding they may hold as high and responsible offices in the church. (D. & C. 107:93-98.)

When one compares this complete explanation of the calling and duties and organization of the seventy with the meager account contained in the Bible, he is convinced of the need for instruction and revelation from the Lord in these matters, since the Bible fails to give a sufficient account of the duties and calling of the seventy. Again we obtained this information and instruction by revelation from heaven, and we use the Bible to prove its truth.

This is what the Bible has to say about the calling of a seventy:

> After these things the Lord appointed other *seventy* also, and sent them two and two before his face into every city and place, whither he himself would come.
>
> Therefore said he unto them, The harvest truly is great, but the labourers are few: pray ye therefore the Lord of the harvest, that he would send forth labourers into his harvest. . . .
>
> And the *seventy* returned again with joy, saying, Lord, even the devils are subject unto us through thy name. (Luke 10:1-2, 17.)

From the first verse above, it is apparent that the Lord had previously appointed seventy or this account would not say that he "appointed *other seventy.*" Of these "other seventy" we have no account in the Bible. However, the Bible does account for the calling of seventy of the elders of Israel under Moses, but this, no doubt, refers only to the number of elders called, rather than to the office of seventy:

> And the Lord said unto Moses, Gather unto me *seventy* men of the elders of Israel, whom thou knowest to be the elders of the people, and officers over them; and bring them unto the tabernacle of the congregation, that they may stand there with thee.
>
> And I will come down and talk with thee there: and I will take of the spirit which is upon thee, and will put it upon them; and they shall bear the burden of the people with thee, that thou bear it not thyself alone. (Num. 11:16-17.)

It will be noted that the seventy are a traveling quorum even as the Quorum of the Twelve Apostles, and that their special calling is to assist the twelve Apostles in carrying on and directing the missionary work of the Church. Since they are also special witnesses of the Lord Jesus Christ in all the world, "first unto the Gentiles, and then to the Jews," what a loss to the world that they are no more to be found in the churches of the day. This is one more reason why a restoration was necessary.

The Elder

The term, "elder," has a dual usage in the Church of Jesus Christ. It is used as a title referring to any man holding the Melchizedek Priesthood; it also designates one of the offices of the Melchizedek Priesthood:

. . . *An apostle is an elder*, and it is his calling to baptize;

And to ordain other *elders*, priests, teachers, and deacons;

And to administer bread and wine—the emblems of the flesh and blood of Christ—

And to confirm those who are baptized into the church, by the laying on of hands for the baptism of fire and the Holy Ghost, according to the scriptures;

And to teach, expound, exhort, baptize, and watch over the church;

And to confirm the church by the laying on of the hands, and the giving of the Holy Ghost;

And to take the lead of all meetings.

The elders are to conduct the meetings as they are led by the Holy Ghost, according to the commandments and revelations of God. (D. & C. 20:38-45.)

The office of an *elder* comes under the priesthood of Melchizedek.

The Melchizedek Priesthood holds the right of presidency, and has power and authority over all the offices in the church in all ages of the world, to administer in spiritual things. (D. & C. 107:7-8.)

An *elder* has a right to officiate in his stead when the high priest is not present.

The high priest and *elder* are to administer in spiritual things, agreeable to the covenants and commandments of the church; and they have a right to officiate in all these offices of the church when there are no higher authorities present. (D. & C. 107:11-12.)

Verily, I say unto you, saith the Lord of Hosts, there must needs be presiding *elders* to preside over those who are of the office of an *elder*. (D. & C. 107:60.)

Again, the duty of the president over the office of *elders* is to preside over ninety-six *elders*, and to sit in council with them, and to teach them according to the covenants.

This presidency is a distinct one from that of the seventy, and is designed for those who do not travel into all the world. (D. & C. 107:89-90.)

Thus the calling of an elder differs from that of the seventy in that he is called to the ministry at home to officiate in the organizations of the Church, to preside, teach, expound, etc., while the seventy is to be a traveling missionary to all nations and unto all people.

Let us now read what the Bible has to offer concerning the elder:

The *elders* which are among you I exhort, *who am also an elder,* and a witness of the sufferings of Christ, and also a partaker of the glory that shall be revealed:

Feed the flock of God which is among you, taking the oversight thereof, not by constraint, but willingly; not for filthy lucre, but of a ready mind;

Neither as being lords over God's heritage, but being ensamples to the flock. (I Peter 5:1-3.)

Let the *elders* that rule well be counted worthy of double honour, especially they who labour in the word and doctrine. (I Tim. 5:17.)

And when they had ordained them *elders* in every church, and had prayed with fasting, they commended them to the Lord, on whom they believed. (Acts 14:23.)

And the apostles and *elders* came together for to consider of this matter. (Acts 15:6.)

Is any sick among you? let him call for the *elders* of the church; and let them pray over him, anointing him with oil in the name of the Lord:

And the prayer of faith shall save the sick, and the Lord shall raise him up; and if he have committed sins, they shall be forgiven him. (James 5:14-15.)

For this cause left I thee in Crete, that thou shouldest set in order the things that are wanting, and ordain *elders* in every city, as I had appointed thee. (Titus 1:5.)

Because of the numerous references in the New Testament to the calling of an elder, for our present purpose it seems unnecessary to examine those of the Old Testament. These all seem quite in accord with the calling and ministry of an elder as established by the Lord in his Church of this dispensation. However, we find nothing in the Bible to indicate how many elders are necessary to constitute a quorum, nor how it should be organized.

No doubt the more abundant explanation of the duties and calling of an elder in the New Testament accounts, at least in part, for the fact that we find more officers called elders in the churches of today; although who can say that they are more important than seventies and high priests, of whom one hears but little or nothing at all? This, of course, might be expected when one depends entirely on the written word and rejects the principle of continuous revelation.

Bishop

The Lord explained to the Prophet Joseph Smith the calling and responsibilities of a bishop:

The second priesthood is called the Priesthood of Aaron, because it was conferred upon Aaron and his seed, throughout all their generations.

Why it is called the lesser priesthood is because it is an appendage to the greater, or the Melchizedek Priesthood, and has power in administering outward ordinances.

The *bishopric* is the presidency of this priesthood, and holds the keys or authority of the same.

No man has a legal right to this office, to hold the keys of this priesthood, except he be a literal descendant of Aaron.

But as a high priest of the Melchizedek Priesthood has authority to officiate in all the lesser offices, he may officiate in the office of *bishop* when no literal descendant of Aaron can be found, provided he is called and set apart and ordained unto this power by the hands of the Presidency of the Melchizedek Priesthood. (D. & C. 107:13-17.)

Also the duty of the president over the Priesthood of Aaron is to preside over forty-eight priests, and sit in council with them, to teach them the duties of their office, as given in the covenants—

This president is to be a *bishop;* for this is one of the duties of this priesthood. (D. & C. 107:87-88.)

After giving instructions and directions concerning the duties of the Melchizedek Priesthood and the blessings coming to the Church through its administration, the Lord said:

Wherefore, the office of a *bishop* is not equal unto it; for the office of a *bishop* is in administering all temporal things;

Nevertheless a *bishop* must be chosen from the High Priesthood, unless he is a literal descendant of Aaron;

For unless he is a literal descendant of Aaron he cannot hold the keys of that priesthood.

Nevertheless, a high priest, that is, after the order of Melchizedek, may be set apart unto the ministering of temporal things, having a knowledge of them by the Spirit of truth;

And also to be a judge in Israel, to do the business of the church, to sit in judgment upon transgressors upon testimony as it shall be laid before him according to the laws, by the assistance of his counselors, whom he has chosen or will choose among the elders of the church.

This is the duty of a *bishop* who is not a literal descendant of Aaron, but has been ordained to the High Priesthood after the order of Melchizedek.

Thus shall he be a judge, even a common judge among the inhabitants of Zion, or in a stake of Zion, or in any branch of the church where he shall be set apart unto this ministry, until the borders of Zion are enlarged and it becomes necessary to have other *bishops* or judges in Zion or elsewhere.

And inasmuch as there are other *bishops* appointed they shall act in the same office. (D. & C. 107:68-75.)

And inasmuch as ye impart of your substance unto the poor, ye will do it unto me; and they shall be laid before the *bishop* of my church and his counselors, two of the elders, or high priests, such as he shall appoint or has appointed and set apart for that purpose. (D. & C. 42:31.)

In latter-day revelations the Lord has said more pertaining to the calling and duties of a bishop, but this seems sufficient for our present needs.

We shall now consider what the Bible has to offer on this matter:

For a *bishop* must be blameless, as the steward of God; not self-willed, not soon angry, not given to wine, no striker, not given to filthy lucre;

But a lover of hospitality, a lover of good men, sober, just, holy, temperate;

Holding fast the faithful word as he hath been taught, that he may be able by sound doctrine both to exhort and to convince the gainsayers. (Titus 1:7-9.)

This is a true saying, If a man desire the office of a *bishop*, he desireth a good work.

A *bishop* then must be blameless, the husband of one wife, vigilant, sober, of good behaviour, given to hospitality, apt to teach;

Not given to wine, no striker, not greedy of filthy lucre; but patient, not a brawler, not covetous;

One that ruleth well his own house, having his children in subjection with all gravity;

(For if a man know not how to rule his own house, how shall he take care of the church of God?)

Not a novice, lest being lifted up with pride he fall into the condemnation of the devil.

Moreover he must have a good report of them which are without; lest he fall into reproach and the snare of the devil. (I Tim. 3:1-7.)

Paul and Timotheus, the servants of Jesus Christ, to all the saints in Christ Jesus which are at Philippi, with the *bishops* and deacons. (Phil. 1:1.)

From these references, it is apparent that there is much more said of the necessary qualifications of a bishop than is said of the nature of his duties and ministry. About all we can find is that "by sound doctrine" he should be able to both "exhort and to convince the gainsayers." Paul infers to Timothy that it is the calling of a bishop to "take care of the church of God," but no specific instructions are given to indicate what is really meant by this order.

Again, if we had to depend upon the information contained in the Bible we would know but little about this very important calling. We are compelled to look to modern revelation if we would be informed concerning the office of bishop.

The Priest

We have already indicated that the calling of a priest is an office in the Aaronic Priesthood; that the bishop presides over this priesthood; and that the bishop himself is the president of the priest's quorum, consisting of forty-eight members. (See D. & C. 107:15, 87-88.)

> The *priest's* duty is to preach, teach, expound, exhort, and baptize, and administer the sacrament,
>
> And visit the house of each member, and exhort them to pray vocally and in secret and attend to all family duties.
>
> And he may also ordain other *priests*, teachers, and deacons.
>
> And he is to take the lead of meetings when there is no elder present. . . .
>
> In all these duties the *priest* is to assist the elder if occasion requires. (D. & C. 20:46-49, 52.)
>
> Every elder, *priest*, teacher, or deacon is to be ordained according to the gifts and callings of God unto him; and he is to be ordained by the power of the Holy Ghost, which is in the one who ordains him. (D. & C. 20:60.)
>
> And behold, the high priest should travel, and also the elders, and also the lesser *priests*; but the deacons and teachers should be appointed to watch over the church, to be standing ministers unto the church. (D. & C. 84:111.)

The New Testament is almost silent on the calling and duties of a priest.

Zacharias, the father of John the Baptist was a *priest* after the order of Aaron, and served in the temple in the priest's office. (See Luke 1:5-8.)

The Prophet Micah refers to a time to come when the spiritual leaders of the people should make his people to err, and added:

> The heads thereof judge for reward, and the *priests* thereof teach for hire, and the prophets thereof divine for money: yet will they lean upon the Lord, and say, Is not the Lord among us? none evil can come upon us. (Mic. 3:11.)

John the Revelator wrote concerning those whom the Lord had washed of their sins in his blood:

> And hath made us kings and *priests* unto God and his Father; to him be glory and dominion for ever and ever. (Rev. 1:6.)

We will have to turn elsewhere than to the Bible to learn the duties of the priest's office as they were administered under the direction of Christ and his Apostles.

John the Baptist administered under this authority and taught his followers that one mightier than he would come who would baptize them with the Holy Ghost, for the Aaronic Priesthood held not the power to confer the Holy Ghost by laying on of hands, as he explained to Joseph Smith and Oliver Cowdery. (See P. of G. P., Joseph Smith 2:70.)

It would seem that we are justified in assuming that Philip also served under this same authority since he baptized the people of Samaria, but it appears to have been necessary for Peter and John to go there to confer the Holy Ghost by laying on of hands. (See Acts 8:4-20.) The reading of the ancient scriptures does not make this plain. We have to turn to modern revelation for this explanation. If this assumption is not correct, what explanation can be given for the fact that Philip preached Christ unto the people of Samaria and baptized them, and yet could not confer upon them the Holy Ghost, but had to send for Peter and John?

The Teacher

The latter-day revelations of the Lord attach much significance to the office of *teacher* in the Church. Note the detailing of responsibilities, quorum organization, duties of members, and how carefully these are set forth in their relationship to other priesthood offices:

The *teacher's* duty is to watch over the church always, and be with and strengthen them;

And see that there is no iniquity in the church, neither hardness with each other, neither lying, backbiting, nor evil speaking;

And see that the church meet together often, and also see that all members do their duty.

And he is to take the lead of meetings in the absence of the elder or priest—

And is to be assisted always, in all his duties in the church, by the deacons, if occasion requires.

But neither *teachers* nor deacons have authority to baptize, administer the sacrament, or lay on hands;

They are, however, to warn, expound, exhort, and teach, and invite all to come unto Christ.

Every elder, priest, *teacher,* or deacon is to be ordained according to the gifts and callings of God unto him; and he is to be ordained by the power of the Holy Ghost, which is in the one who ordains him. (D. & C. 20:53-60.)

And also the duty of the president over the office of the *teachers* is to preside over twenty-four of the teachers, and to sit in council with them, teaching them the duties of their office, as given in the covenants. (D. & C. 107:86.)

And behold, the high priests should travel, and also the elders, and also the lesser priests; but the deacons and *teachers* should be appointed to watch over the church, to be standing ministers unto the church. (D. & C. 84:111.)

The following reference will indicate how little information the Bible gives us with respect to the calling of a teacher, although there is sufficient to indicate that this was one of the offices in the former Church of Christ:

And he gave some, apostles; and some, prophets; and some, evangelists; and some, pastors and *teachers*. (Eph. 4:11.)

Here again we could not have known the duties and responsibilities of the teacher if we had had to depend upon the Bible.

The Deacon

The nature of the calling and of the responsibilities of the *deacon* have likewise come to light through the revelations of the Lord in this dispensation:

And again, verily I say unto you, the duty of a president over the office of a *deacon* is to preside over twelve *deacons*, to sit in council with them, and to teach them their duty, edifying one another, as it is given according to the covenants. (D. & C. 107:85.)

And [the teacher] is to be assisted always, in all his duties in the church, by the *deacons*, if occasion requires.

But neither teachers nor *deacons*, have authority to baptize, administer the sacrament, or lay on hands;

They are, however, to warn, expound, exhort, and teach, and invite all to come unto Christ.

Every elder, priest, teacher, or *deacon* is to be ordained according to the gifts and callings of God unto him; and he is to be ordained by the power of the Holy Ghost, which is in the one who ordains him. (D. & C. 20:57-60.)

And again, the offices of teacher and *deacon* are necessary appendages belonging to the lesser priesthood, which priesthood was confirmed upon Aaron and his sons. (D. & C. 84:30.)

While reference to the office of deacon is made in the following quotations from the Bible, there is very little specific information on this calling in the Aaronic Priesthood:

Paul and Timotheus, the servants of Jesus Christ, to all the saints in Christ Jesus which are at Philippi, with the bishops and *deacons.* (Phil. 1:1.)

Likewise must the *deacons* be grave, not doubletongued, not given to much wine, not greedy of filthy lucre;

Holding the mystery of the faith in a pure conscience.

And let these also first be proved; then let them use the office of a *deacon,* being found blameless. (I Tim. 3:8-10.)

The Biblical account of the responsibilities and function of the deacon is almost wholly lacking in detail. Except for meager references to the office, we should have known nothing about such a position in the Church if we were compelled to rely upon the Bible alone for guidance. The revelations of the Lord to the Prophet Joseph Smith indicate, unerringly, his will concerning the deacon in the Church.

Additional Officers in the Church

As the Church has grown and developed, and acting under authority of the keys of the priesthood and the inspiration of the Lord, the First Presidency of the Church and the Quorum of the Twelve Apostles have added the following named offices, which we do not find mentioned in the Bible:

(a) *Assistants to the Quorum of Twelve Apostles.*

Because of the multiplicity of the duties of the Quorum of the Twelve Apostles in directing the work of the Church today among the present 592 stakes of Zion and 101 missions (December 31, 1972), the First Presidency has called and appointed some assistants to the Quorum of the Twelve Apostles. At this writing there are eighteen presiding high priests serving in this capacity.

The First Presidency made this explanation at the time these Assistants to the Quorum of the Twelve Apostles were called during the General Conference of the Church, April 6, 1941: "It has been decided to appoint Assistants to the Twelve, who shall be High Priests, who shall be set apart to act under the direction of the Twelve in the performance of such work as the First Presidency and the Twelve may place upon them."

(b) *The First Seven Presidents of the Seventy.*

A careful consideration of the calling and organization of the Seventy as we have herein discussed, and as outlined by the Lord in a revelation to the Prophet Joseph Smith, (See D. & C. 107: 93-97) indicates that there should be seven presidents to preside over all the quorums of Seventy in the Church until these quorums might even number seven times seventy; that these presidents act under the direction of the Twelve Apostles. This council of the First Seven Presidents of Seventy was organized according to a revelation from the Lord to the Prophet Joseph Smith, January 19, 1841. (See D. & C. 124:138-139.)

(c) *The Presiding Bishopric.*

The Presidng Bishopric consists of three high priests, chosen, ordained, and set apart as bishops, to preside over all the Aaronic Priesthood of the Church, and in connection with stake presidents, hold jurisdiction over the duties of other bishops in the Church. They also administer the temporal affairs of the Church under the direction of the First Presidency.

The Rights and the Exercise of Priesthood Authority

With this glorious delegation of priesthood authority to officers functioning within the kingdom of God in these latter-days, there is a tremendous responsibility for one's actions under these divine commissions. Such authority must, of necessity, be exercised in righteousness if the officer would please God and avoid condemnation. The Lord realized this and took into account the human tendency to exercise authority in unrighteousness unless carefully taught how to function under the specifications of divine approval.

Consider well the following revelations from our Heavenly Father through the Prophet Joseph Smith as he set forth the standards for the exercise of priesthood authority. We know of nothing ever written on the subject of government as inspiring and as impressive:

For whoso is faithful unto the obtaining these two priesthoods of which I have spoken, and the magnifying their calling, are sanctified by the Spirit unto the renewing of their bodies.

They become the sons of Moses and of Aaron and the seed of Abraham, and the church and kingdom, and the elect of God.

And also all they who receive this priesthood receive me, saith the Lord;

For he that receiveth my servants receiveth me;

And he that receiveth me receiveth my Father;

And he that receiveth my Father receiveth my Father's kingdom; therefore all that my Father hath shall be given unto him.

And this is according to the oath and covenant which belongeth to the priesthood.

Therefore, all those who receive the priesthood, receive this oath and covenant of my Father, which he cannot break, neither can it be moved.

But whoso breaketh this covenant after he hath received it, and altogether turneth therefrom, shall not have forgiveness of sins in this world nor in the world to come. (D. & C. 84:33-41.)

Wherefore, now let every man learn his duty, and to act in the office in which he is appointed, in all diligence.

He that is slothful shall not be counted worthy to stand, and he that learns not his duty and shows himself not approved shall not be counted worthy to stand. . . . (D. & C. 107:99-100.)

Behold, there are many called, but few are chosen. And why are they not chosen?

Because their hearts are set so much upon the things of this world, and aspire to the honors of men, that they do not learn this one lesson—

That the rights of the priesthood are inseparably connected with the powers of heaven, and that the powers of heaven cannot be controlled nor handled only upon the principles of righteousness.

That they may be conferred upon us, it is true; but when we undertake to cover our sins, or to gratify our pride, our vain ambition, or to exercise control or dominion or compulsion upon the souls of the children of men, in any degree of unrighteousness, behold, the heavens withdraw themselves; the Spirit of the Lord is grieved; and when it is withdrawn, Amen to the priesthood or the authority of that man.

Behold, ere he is aware, he is left unto himself, to kick against the pricks, to persecute the saints, and to fight against God.

We have learned by sad experience that it is the nature and disposition of almost all men, as soon as they get a little authority, as they suppose, they will immediately begin to exercise unrighteous dominion.

Hence many are called, but few are chosen.

No power or influence can or ought to be maintained by virtue of the priesthood, only by persuasion, by longsuffering, by gentleness and meekness, and by love unfeigned;

By kindness, and pure knowledge, which shall greatly enlarge the soul without hypocrisy, and without guile—

Reproving betimes with sharpness, when moved upon by the Holy Ghost; and then showing forth afterwards an increase of love toward him whom thou hast reproved, lest he esteem thee to be his enemy;

That he may know that thy faithfulness is stronger than the cords of death.

Let thy bowels also be full of charity towards all men, and to the household of faith, and let virtue garnish thy thoughts unceasingly; then shall thy confidence wax strong in the presence of God; and the doctrine of the priesthood shall distil upon thy soul as the dews from heaven.

The Holy Ghost shall be thy constant companion, and thy scepter an unchanging scepter of righteousness and truth; and thy dominion shall be an everlasting dominion, and without compulsory means it shall flow unto thee forever and ever. (D. & C. 121:34-46.)

But ye are a chosen generation, *a royal priesthood,* an holy nation, a peculiar people; that ye should shew forth the praises of him who hath called you out of darkness into his marvellous light. (I Pet. 2:9.)

You may search the world over and you will find no people today who answer this description as do the Latter-day Saints, for they truly have a "royal priesthood," where every worthy male member of the Church over twelve years of age may be a bearer thereof, laboring for the upbuilding of the kingdom of God in the earth, showing forth "the praises of him who hath called you out of darkness into his marvelous light."

One cannot consider this matter without being impressed that the churches of the world today are missing much by not having this authority and information, nor can they get it from reading the Bible. One should not be surprised that there was no uniformity of organization in the churches of the day, at the time the Lord restored his priesthood again to the earth, through his prophet, Joseph Smith. While the Bible makes plain most of the officers that should be in the church of Christ, it fails to explain the duties of the various officers. This information had to come through the revelations of the Lord in this dispensation.

Helps and Governments in the Church

It is evident that in the Church which Jesus organized while he was upon the earth, he not only placed the Aaronic and Melchizedek Priesthoods, with their various officers and members, as we have discussed, but he also placed in the Church "helps" and "governments" as the Apostle Paul indicates, although what these "helps" and "governments" are, the scriptures do not indicate:

> And God hath set some in the church, first apostles, secondarily prophets, thirdly teachers, after that miracles, then gifts of healings, *helps, governments, diversities of tongues.* (I Cor. 12:28.)

We will now briefly consider the "helps" and "governments" the Lord has placed in his Church in this dispensation. Books could be written, and have been written, explaining the nature of these "helps" and what they have accomplished, but our purpose will be served by merely calling attention to them.

The membership of The Church of Jesus Christ of Latter-day Saints, numbering over 2,930,810 souls, is organized into wards and branches in the stakes of Zion, and into branches and districts in the missions of the Church. As of December 31, 1970, there are 537 stakes of Zion with an average membership of approximately 5,000 each. In the stakes there are 4,158 wards and 764 branches, with an average membership of approximately 480. There are eighty-eight missions in the Church with branch membership ranging from a few families to several hundred members. New stakes are being organized almost monthly, through the division of present existing stakes, or the creation of new stakes consisting of branches taken from the missions of the Church.

Priesthood Correlation, Regional Representatives, and General Boards

As envisioned in a broad program of Church correlation undertaken in the 1960's, four operating priesthood programs were designated by the First Presidency and the Quorum of the Twelve. These correlated programs placed directly with the priesthood the responsibility of home teaching, missionary work, genealogical and temple work, and the welfare program.

To implement these priesthood programs, along with the work of the auxiliary organizations, all the stakes in the Church have been organized into regions. These regions are the Church units through which training and direction are given to stake and ward officers.

Regional meetings are held twice each year in each region. Designated stake and ward officers are invited to attend and receive training and direction in the operation of the priesthood and auxiliary programs.

To assist the general authorities in the operation of Church programs, regional representatives of the Twelve are appointed to serve in the various regions. These brethren represent the general authorities and serve on much the same basis as do stake presidents, giving their full Church service time to their positions.

Each auxiliary organization in the Church is headed by a general board, working under the direction of the First Presidency and the Quorum of the Twelve Apostles. They have the duty and responsibility to prepare outlines for activities and courses of study, which in turn are submitted to the stakes and wards. These general boards visit the regions of the Church once each year.

The Stake Organization

A stake organization consists of the following: A presidency of three high priests; a high council of twelve high priests; a stake clerk; one or more patriarchs; a high priests' quorum with the stake presidency serving as its presidency, with a secretary; one or more quorums of seventy, each with seven presidents and a secretary; elders' quorums with a presidency and a secretary; home missionaries appointed to fill preaching engagements each month to the wards of the stake; Melchizedek Priesthood committee to correlate the activities of Home Teaching, Missionary Work, Genealogy, Welfare, and the Melchizedek Priesthood Mutual Interest Association through the Melchizedek Priesthood quorums of the stake; committees for correlating the activities of the Aaronic Priesthood including the Aaronic Priesthood Mutual Improvement Association in the wards of the stake; old folks committee; music committee; a women's Relief Society, Sunday School, and the Primary Association, each with a presidency, a secretary, and a board to direct the activities of these auxiliaries in the wards and branches of the stake.

The Ward Organization

A ward organization is the unit that deals directly with the membership of the Church residing within ward boundaries, and is presided over by a bishop and two counselors, with a clerk or clerks to assist them. The bishopric directs the work of the Aaronic Priesthood quorums, keeps all quorums and auxiliaries fully organized, and sees that all the members are given an opportunity to labor in whatever capacity they are best qualified for, according to their special gifts and talents. The bishopric in the ward has the responsibility of the buildings and grounds, all temporal affairs, including the care of the poor and the underprivileged.

The ward organization and auxiliaries follow closely the pattern of the stake, except that in place of boards, each organization has teachers, who conduct the classes of the auxiliaries as the members meet from week to week. An average ward requires approximately eighty-five teachers in the auxiliaries in addition to the presiding officers, home teachers, and the Relief Society visiting teachers, with the latter two teaching groups visiting in the homes of the saints at least each month.

In the wards of the Church at the end of 1972 there were approximately 140,941 Sunday School teachers; 81,141 Primary teachers; 87,668 teachers in the Aaronic Priesthood MIA; and 181,361 Relief Society teachers, including those who visit the homes of the Saints monthly, or a grand total of approximately 489,111 teachers in the organizations of the Church. Astounding as this figure is, it becomes the more a wonder when it is recalled that there are approximately 783,266 male members of the Church who have been ordained to the Aaronic and Melchizedek Priesthoods and who have the authority and privilege to work in the vineyard of the Lord for the salvation and exaltation of his sons and daughters. These combined totals provide approximately 1,470,243 opportunities for service within the Church, which means that nearly forty percent of the total membership of the Church may be given opportunities for individual growth and for the blessing of their fellow men through services to one another. None of these receive monetary compensation for the service they render.

Opportunity and Work for All

Since the Lord set up the organization of his Church, as Paul has said, "For the perfecting of the saints, for the work of the ministry, for the edifying of the body of Christ," (Eph. 4:12) it is difficult to understand how such an objective could be better achieved than through such a perfect organization as he has caused to be placed in his Church in this dispensation. Such an organization also provides an opportunity for every member of the Church to devote his talents for the building up of the kingdom of God in the earth. Why should not every man who loves the Lord enjoy such a privilege? In what other way can one so effectively develop or add to his talents? Remember Jesus' parable of the man traveling into a far country, who called his own servants, and delivered unto them his goods. (See Matt. 25:14-30.) It would seem, therefore, that the organization of The Church of Jesus Christ of Latter-day Saints would be most incomplete did it not provide an opportunity for all its members to develop their talents, through the service they are called upon, and permitted, to render.

Is there any other organization to compare with it in the world? This could not possibly be the work of man—it must be from God!

CHAPTER 13

THE MISSION OF ELIJAH

Elijah's Coming Foretold

The next major event we will consider in the "restitution of all things" (Acts 3:19-21) is the coming of Elijah in fulfilment of the prophecy of Malachi:

> Behold, I will send you Elijah the prophet before the coming of the great and dreadful day of the Lord:

> And he shall turn the heart of the fathers to the children, and the heart of the children to their fathers, lest I come and smite the earth with a curse. (Mal. 4:5-6.)

To which church in all the world today can one go, other than The Church of Jesus Christ of Latter-day Saints, and be told of Elijah's coming in fulfilment of this prophecy? His coming is of the utmost importance in the sight of God in fulfilling his purposes among the children of men in establishing his latter-day kingdom. Unless Elijah were to come and fulfill his mission of turning the heart of the fathers to the children and the heart of the children to their fathers, the Lord would come and "smite the earth with a curse."

The Lord promised that he would send Elijah, the prophet, "before the coming of the great and dreadful day of the Lord," and who is there who can stay his hand and prevent him from fulfilling his promise? If one is privileged to live upon the earth in the day of Elijah's coming, should he not want to know all about it and what message he had to bring to justify his being sent from the courts on high to prevent the earth from being smitten with a curse?

Attempted Explanation of the Fulfilment of Malachi's Prophecy

The following statement regarding the fulfilment of Malachi's prophecy is interesting:

> The book concludes with an appeal to remember the law of Moses (probably Deuteronomy, whose ritual and ethical demands had been violated), and with a promise of the return of Elijah who had left the world about 400 years before; a promise which suggests that the age of the prophets is now felt to be over; and when he comes his business will be to restore harmony in the homes which had been ruined by divorce; otherwise the land would be smitten by destruction. (From *The Abingdon Bible Commentary* by Eiselen, Lewis, and Downey. Used by permission of Abingdon-Cokesbury Press.)

How could Elijah "restore harmony in the homes which had been ruined by divorce"? In too many cases a third party is involved before there is a divorce and usually another marriage follows. The explanation in the commentary is a poor guess, and that is all. We would know no more about Elijah's coming and the nature of his mission, except for the fact that he did come and visit Joseph Smith and Oliver Cowdery in the Kirtland Temple in the state of Ohio, April 3, 1836.

Moroni's Version of Malachi's Prophecy—Its Subsequent Fulfilment

At the time the Angel Moroni visited Joseph Smith September 21, 1823, he quoted many passages of scripture which he said would shortly be fulfilled. Among them was the fourth chapter of Malachi to which we have just referred, though with a little variation from the way it reads in our Bible. He quoted the fifth and sixth verses thus:

> ... Behold, I will reveal unto you the Priesthood, by the hand of Elijah the prophet, before the coming of the great and dreadful day of the Lord.

... And he shall plant in the hearts of the children the promises made to the fathers, and the hearts of the children shall turn to their fathers. If it were not so, the whole earth would be utterly wasted at his coming. (P. of G. P. Joseph Smith 2:38-39.)

Following the dedication of the Kirtland Temple, April 3, 1836, the Savior, Moses, Elias, and Elijah appeared to Joseph Smith and Oliver Cowdery. After recounting the visit of the Savior, and of Moses, and of Elias, Joseph Smith had this to say concerning the visit of Elijah:

... another great and glorious vision burst upon us; for Elijah the prophet, who was taken to heaven without tasting death, stood before us, and said:

Behold, the time has fully come, which was spoken of by the mouth of Malachi—testifying that he (Elijah) should be sent, before the great and dreadful day of the Lord come—

To turn the hearts of the fathers to the children, and the children to the fathers, lest the whole earth be smitten with a curse—

Therefore, the keys of this dispensation are committed into your hands; and by this ye may know that the great and dreadful day of the Lord is near, even at the doors. (D. & C. 110:13-16.)

When the keys of this dispensation for the turning of the heart of the fathers to the children, and the heart of the children to their fathers, had been committed, by Elijah, into the hands of Joseph Smith and Oliver Cowdery, they proceeded to explain the new and strange doctrine of *baptism for the dead* to their associates and the membership of the Church. They made it plain that the children here upon the earth can be baptized for their loved ones who have passed away without enjoying this privilege. The knowledge of this great truth has caused the "heart of the children" to turn "to their fathers," and the children to seek out their genealogy so they can be baptized for their kindred dead. It was for this purpose that the Lord sent Elijah back to this earth as promised by Malachi, and as announced by Moroni to Joseph Smith.

All Things in Heaven and on Earth to be Gathered Together

In a revelation to the Prophet Joseph Smith in September 1830, the Lord had this work of the living for the dead in mind as part of the gospel of the last dispensation. After explaining how he had sent Peter, James, and John to ordain Joseph and Oliver Apostles and special witnesses and to hold the keys of his kingdom in this, the Dispensation of the Fulness of Times, he added:

> ... in the which I will gather together in one all things, both which are in heaven, and which are on earth;
>
> And also with all those whom my Father hath given me out of the world. (D. & C. 27:13-14.)

It is evident that the Dispensation of the Fulness of Times should consist of a work both in heaven and upon earth, since the Lord had decreed that in this dispensation he would "gather together in one all things, both which are in heaven, and which are on earth," and also all whom the Father had given to him "out of the world." This bringing together, in one, naturally calls for one organization, a plan, and indicates how far reaching and complete this gospel dispensation must be; why Elijah was to be sent to commit the keys held by him for this great accomplishment.

What the Lord had in mind to do in this respect in this dispensation, he also made known to Paul:

> Having made known unto us the mystery of his will, according to his good pleasure which he hath purposed in himself:
>
> That in the dispensation of the fulness of times he might gather together in one all things in Christ, both which are in heaven, and which are on earth; even in him. (Eph. 1:9-10.)

This bringing together "all things in Christ, both which are in heaven, and which are on earth," is a very sacred and special ministry, which the Prophet Joseph Smith presented to the Church in some detail:

And now, my dearly beloved brethren and sisters, let me assure you that these are principles in relation to the dead and the living that cannot be lightly passed over, as pertaining to our salvation. For their salvation is necessary and essential to our salvation, as Paul says concerning the fathers—that they without us cannot be made perfect—neither can we without our dead be made perfect.

And now, in relation to the baptism for the dead, I will give you another quotation of Paul, I Corinthians 15:29: *Else what shall they do which are baptized for the dead, if the dead rise not at all? Why are they then baptized for the dead?*

And again, in connection with this quotation I will give you a quotation from one of the prophets, who had his eye fixed on the restoration of the priesthood, the glories to be revealed in the last days, and in an especial manner this most glorious of all subjects belonging to the everlasting gospel, namely, the baptism for the dead; for Malachi says, last chapter, verses 5th and 6th: *Behold, I will send you Elijah the prophet before the coming of the great and dreadful day of the Lord: And he shall turn the heart of the fathers to the children, and the heart of the children to their fathers, lest I come and smite the earth with a curse.*

I might have rendered a plainer translation to this, but it is sufficiently plain to suit my purpose as it stands. It is sufficient to know, in this case, that the earth will be smitten with a curse unless there is a welding link of some kind or other between the fathers and the children, upon some subject or other—and behold what is that subject? It is the baptism for the dead. For we without them cannot be made perfect; neither can they without us be made perfect. Neither can they nor we be made perfect without those who have died in the gospel also; for it is necessary in the ushering in of the dispensation of the fulness of times, which dispensation is now beginning to usher in, that a whole and complete and perfect union, and welding together of dispensations, and keys, and powers, and glories should take place, and be revealed from the days of Adam even to the present time. And not only this, but those things which never have been revealed from the foundation of the world, but have been kept hid from the wise and prudent, shall be revealed unto babes and sucklings in this, the dispensation of the fulness of times. (D. & C. 128:15-18.)

The Gospel Is Preached to the Dead

Now that we have considered what Joseph Smith was able to announce to the world because of the visit of Elijah the Prophet, let us turn to Bible references and observe the close relationship between the two accounts of Elijah's coming and his mission:

Verily, verily, I say unto you, The hour is coming and now is, when the dead shall hear the voice of the Son of God: and they that hear shall live. . . .

Marvel not at this: for the hour is coming, in the which all that are in the grave shall hear his voice. (John 5:25, 28.)

This is a very definite promise, and no one has the right to question its fulfilment. It is clear that Jesus had in mind, when he had completed his mission upon the earth, that the dead should hear his voice:

For Christ also hath once suffered for sins, the just for the unjust, that he might bring us to God, being put to death in the flesh, but quickened by the Spirit:

By which also he went and preached unto the spirits in prison;

Which sometime were disobedient, when once the longsuffering of God waited in the days of Noah, while the ark was a preparing, wherein few, that is, eight souls were saved by water.

The like figure whereunto even baptism doth also now save us (not the putting away of the filth of the flesh, but the answer of a good conscience toward God,) by the resurrection of Jesus Christ. (I Pet. 3:18-21.)

Could a more definite pronouncement be made of the fulfilment of his promise, that the dead and those in their graves shall hear his voice, than was made by Peter indicating that Jesus had preached to the dead who had been disobedient in the days of Noah?

If he preached to those who had been disobedient, the question might logically be asked: "What did he preach?" He had but one message, viz., his gospel of faith, repentance, baptism by immersion for the remission of sins, and the laying on of hands for the gift of the Holy Ghost.

Follow Peter's account of what Christ preached to those spirits who had been disobedient:

> For for this cause was the gospel preached also to them that are dead, that they might be judged according to men in the flesh, but live according to God in the spirit. (I Pet. 4:6.)

Isn't this plain? The gospel was preached to them, and they are to be "judged according to men in the flesh." How can this be? How can a spirit be baptized by immersion for the remission of sins? This can only be done by proxy—the living for the dead. When the gospel is accepted by the departed spirits, their hearts turn to their children upon the earth, who have the privilege of being baptized for their kindred dead so they may go on, and, as Peter states, "live according to God in the spirit." What a beautiful and consistent plan! What a wonderful demonstration of God's justice! The gospel is thus within the reach of all his children, no matter whether they have heard it preached while in mortality or not. The great majority of our father's children have never enjoyed that privilege. It was Paul's understanding of this great principle that caused him to write:

> If in this life only we have hope in Christ, we are of all men most miserable. (I Cor. 15:19.)

The Prophet Isaiah also understood this principle when he declared:

> And it shall come to pass in that day, that the Lord shall punish the host of the high ones that are on high, and the kings of the earth upon the earth.
>
> And they shall be gathered together, as prisoners are gathered in the pit, and shall be shut up in the prison, and after many days shall they be visited. (Isa. 24:21-22.)

In other words, Isaiah saw that they would be visited, as were the disobedient in the days of Noah, and naturally, when visited, it would be to offer them another chance. Jesus also made this clear in speaking of the transgression of his people:

> Agree with thine adversary quickly, whiles thou art in the way with him; lest at any time the adversary deliver thee to the judge, and the judge deliver thee to the officer, and thou be cast into prison.
>
> Verily I say unto thee, Thou shalt by no means come out thence, till thou hast paid the uttermost farthing. (Matt. 5:25-26.)

When they have paid the "uttermost farthing," the implication is that they shall be given another chance, as were those who were disobedient in the days of Noah.

Paul made this declaration concerning the gospel of Christ:

> For I am not ashamed of the gospel of Christ: for it is the power of God unto salvation to every one that believeth; to the Jew first and also to the Greek.
>
> For therein is the righteousness of God revealed from faith to faith: as it is written, The just shall live by faith. (Rom. 1:16-17.)

Paul, or any other man, could well be ashamed of the gospel of Christ if it assigned or condemned to eternal damnation the souls of all our Father's children who have lived upon the earth who have never heard his gospel or even the name of Christ, as many preachers and man-made creeds affirm. Thanks be to God, as Paul indicates, that through his gospel the righteousness or justice of God is revealed. How could this better be done than through the provision he has made that his gospel shall not only be preached to those who live upon the earth, while they so live, but that it shall also be preached to all who are in their graves, and that provision is made, through baptism for the dead, for their complete acceptance of the gospel, that they may be "judged according to men in the flesh, but live according to God in the spirit."

Paul understood how universal would be the preaching of the name of Christ, when he said:

> That at the name of Jesus every knee should bow, of things in heaven, and things in earth, and things under the earth;
>
> And that every tongue should confess that Jesus Christ is Lord, to the glory of God the Father. (Phil. 2:10-11.)

They, of course, cannot do this until his name has been preached to them. Through the restoration of the gospel in this the Dispensation of the Fulness of Times, God has decreed, that he would gather together in one, in Christ, all that is in the heavens above and upon the earth beneath. His worthy servants who have lived upon the earth and received his holy priesthood and have passed away are assigned to preach the gospel in the spirit world as Jesus did to those who were disobedient in the days of Noah. The gospel which is preached to the departed spirits is the same as that which his living servants are commissioned to preach here upon the earth.

Baptism for the Dead

Baptism of the living, for the dead, is performed in the temples of the Lord erected to his name and at his command in this dispensation. Temples will continue to be erected as needed, as the kingdom grows, until baptisms shall have been performed by the living for all the worthy dead who accept the gospel in the spirit world. This work will obviously have to continue throughout the thousand years of the millennium when the Savior will reign upon this earth. At present, we are dependent upon the written records that have been kept. But during the millennium we will have direct communication with the heavens, when all the names and information concerning those who are ready and worthy of baptism will be revealed.

Immediately preceding Paul's statement to the Corinthian saints: "Else what shall they do which are baptized for the dead, if the dead rise not at all? Why are they then baptized for the dead?" (I Cor. 15:29) he described the coming of Christ to reign upon the earth, and the order in which men will be resurrected, with Christ as the "firstfruits":

> Then cometh the end, when he shall have delivered up the kingdom to God, even the Father; when he shall have put down all rule and all authority and power.
>
> For he must reign, till he hath put all enemies under his feet.
>
> The last enemy that shall be destroyed is death. (I Cor. 15:24-26.)

It will be during this time that he will complete his work and put all enemies under his feet and prepare the kingdom to be delivered to his Father and bring together in Christ "all things, both which are in heaven, and which are on earth."

At this time, those who are filthy will remain filthy still. They will all have been given an opportunity to repent, and if they have repented and have "paid the uttermost farthing," they will be given another chance. But there will be some who love darkness more than they love light, and they will remain in darkness.

It was because the Prophets Isaiah and Micah understood that the temples of God in the "last days" would be used for this holy purpose that they declared:

And it shall come to pass in the last days, that the mountain of the Lord's house shall be established in the top of the mountains, and shall be exalted above the hills; and all nations shall flow unto it.

And many people shall go and say, Come ye, and let us go up to the mountain of the Lord, to the house of the God of Jacob; and he will teach us of his ways, and we will walk in his paths: for out of Zion shall go forth the law, and the word of the Lord from Jerusalem. (Isa. 2:2-3; see also Micah 4:1-2.)

This declaration by Isaiah and Micah has been literally fulfilled. Converts to the Church from all nations have gathered with the saints "in the top of the mountains" that they might perform their sacred ordinances in his holy temples.

Latter-day Temples

In a revelation given to the Prophet Joseph Smith, January 19, 1841, in which the saints were commanded to build the Nauvoo Temple in the state of Illinois, the Lord said:

... and build a house to my name, for the Most High to dwell therein.

For there is not a place found on earth that he may come to and restore again that which was lost unto you, or which he hath taken away, even the fulness of the priesthood.

For a *baptismal font* there is not upon the earth, that they, my saints, *many be baptized for those who are dead—*

For this ordinance belongeth to my house, and cannot be acceptable to me, only in the days of your poverty, wherein ye are not able to build a house unto me. (D. & C. 124:27-30.)

Then the Prophet Joseph Smith added:

. . . Let us, therefore, as a church and a people, and as
Latter-day Saints, offer unto the Lord an offering in righteousness; and let us present in his holy temple, when it is finished, a
book containing the records of our dead, which shall be worthy
of all acceptation. (D. & C. 128:24.)

To the present time The Church of Jesus Christ of
Latter-day Saints has erected holy temples in the United
States of America, Canada, Switzerland, New Zealand,
and England as follows:

Kirtland, Ohio*
Nauvoo, Illinois**
St. George, Utah
Logan, Utah
Manti, Utah
Salt Lake City, Utah
Laie, Oahu, Hawaii
Cardston, Alberta, Canada
Mesa, Arizona
Idaho Falls, Idaho
Los Angeles, California
Bern, Switzerland
New Zealand
London, England
Oakland, California

We quote from an address by Brigham Young at the
laying of the cornerstone of the Salt Lake Temple:

This morning we have assembled on one of the most solemn,
interesting, joyful, and glorious occasions that have transpired, or
will transpire among the children of men, while the earth contin-
ues in its present organization, and is occupied for its present
purposes. And I congratulate my brethren and sisters that it is
our unspeakable privilege to stand here this day, and minister

————

*This temple still stands but is no longer a sacred edifice
having been desecrated by the enemies of the Church.
**Destroyed by mobs.

before the Lord on an occasion which has caused the tongues and pens of Prophets to speak and write for many scores of centuries which are past. (*Discourses of Brigham Young,* Edition of 1946, p. 412.)

Interpretation of Jesus' Statement to the Thief on the Cross

The statement of Jesus to one of the malefactors who was hanged with him on the cross has caused many to teach and believe that a deathbed confession of guilt would be acceptable to usher one into the kingdom of God. Let us consider that statement:

And one of the malefactors which were hanged railed on him saying, If thou be Christ, save thyself and us.

But the other answering rebuked him, saying, Dost not thou fear God, seeing thou art in the same condemnation?

And we indeed justly; for we receive the due reward of our deeds: but this man hath done nothing amiss.

And he said unto Jesus, Lord, remember me when thou comest into thy kingdom.

And Jesus said unto him, Verily I say unto thee, To day shalt thou be with me in paradise. (Luke 23:39-43.)

Keep in mind the request of the malefactor: "Remember me when thou comest into thy kingdom." Jesus did not promise him that he would take him with him into his kingdom that day, but he did say, "Today shalt thou be with me in paradise." A more detailed study will indicate that paradise is *not* the kingdom of God.

The Apostle Paul made this very plain:

I knew a man in Christ above fourteen years ago, (whether in the body, I cannot tell; or whether out of the body, I cannot tell: God knoweth;) such an one caught up to the third heaven.

And I knew such a man, (whether in the body, or out of the body, I cannot tell: God knoweth;)

How that he was caught up into paradise, and heard unspeakable words, which it is not lawful for a man to utter. (II Cor. 12:2-4.)

From this scripture, it is very evident that paradise is not the first, second, or third heaven. Therefore the place Jesus promised to take the malefactor was a place separate from any one of these three heavens. If Jesus did not take the malefactor to heaven, where did he take him?

Peter answered the question in the statement that when Jesus was "put to death in the flesh, but quickened by the spirit . . . He went and preached to the spirits in prison; Which sometime were disobedient . . . in the days of Noah." (I Pet. 3:18-20.) This is the logical place where He should have taken the malefactor, for notwithstanding the sinner acknowledged his own guilt, and recognized the righteousness of the Savior, he did not understand the gospel, neither had he been obedient thereto. Therefore he, as well as other men who had not obeyed the gospel while in the flesh, had to have the gospel preached to him. When he understands and accepts the gospel in the spirit world, or paradise, the ordinance of baptism and the laying on of hands for the gift of the Holy Ghost can be performed vicariously for him in a temple by some living person.

To further sustain the fact that Jesus did not take the malefactor with him into his kingdom the day of his crucifixion, we refer to the visit of Mary to the sepulchre:

But Mary stood without at the sepulchre weeping: and as she wept, she stooped down, and looked into the sepulchre,

And seeth two angels in white sitting, the one at the head, and the other at the feet, where the body of Jesus had lain.

And they say unto her, Woman, why weepest thou? She saith unto them, Because they have taken away my Lord, and I know not where they have laid him.

And when she had thus said, she turned herself back, and saw Jesus standing, and knew not that it was Jesus.

Jesus saith unto her, Woman, why weepest thou? whom seekest thou? She, supposing him to be the gardener, saith unto him, Sir, if thou have borne him hence, tell me where thou hast laid him, and I will take him away.

Jesus saith unto her, Mary. She turned herself, and saith unto him, Rabboni; which is to say, Master.

Jesus saith unto her, Touch me not; for I am not yet ascended to my Father: but go to my brethren, and say unto them, I ascend unto my Father, and your Father; and to my God, and your God. (John 20:11-17.)

It is very evident that while Jesus promised the malefactor: "To day shalt thou be with me in paradise," that three days later the Savior had not yet ascended to his Father in heaven.

Alma, the Book of Mormon Prophet, gave additional light on the condition and assignment of the soul of man between death and the resurrection, and described conditions in paradise in these words:

Now, concerning the state of the soul between death and the resurrection—Behold, it has been made known unto me by an angel, that the spirits of all men, as soon as they are departed from this mortal body, yea, the spirits of all men, whether they be good or evil, are taken home to that God who gave them life.

And then shall it come to pass, that the spirits of those who are righteous are received into a state of happiness, which is called paradise, a state of rest, a state of peace, where they shall rest from all their troubles and from all care, and sorrow.

And then shall it come to pass, that the spirits of the wicked, yea, who are evil—for behold, they have no part nor portion of the Spirit of the Lord; for behold, they chose evil works rather than good; therefore the spirit of the devil did enter into them, and take possession of their house—and these shall be cast out into outer darkness; there shall be weeping, and wailing, and gnashing of teeth, and this because of their own iniquity, being led captive by the will of the devil.

Now this is the state of the souls of the wicked, yea, in darkness, and a state of awful, fearful looking for the fiery indignation of the wrath of God upon them; thus they remain in this state, as well as the righteous in paradise, until the time of their resurrection. (Alma 40:11-14.)

The Rich Man and Lazarus

The parable of the rich man and Lazarus, bearing on this subject, is often misunderstood:

> And beside all this, between us and you there is a great gulf fixed: so that they which would pass from hence to you cannot; neither can they pass to us, that would come from thence. (Luke 16:26.)

Elder Joseph Fielding Smith of the Council of the Twelve discussed this passage of scripture as follows:

> . . . Before the crucifixion of the Lord there was a great gulf fixed separating the righteous dead from those who had not received the Gospel, and across this gulf no man could pass. (Luke 16:26.) Christ bridged that gulf and made it possible for the word of salvation to be taken to all corners of the kingdom of darkness. In this way the realms of hell were invaded and the dead prepared for the ordinances of the Gospel which must be performed on earth since they pertain to the mortal probation. (*The Way to Perfection*, p. 165.)

Baptism for the Dead Administered in the Original Church of Jesus Christ

Epiphanius, a writer of the fourth century, in speaking of the Marcionites, a sect of Christians to whom he was opposed, said:

> In this country—I mean Asia—and even Galatea, their school flourished eminently; and a traditional fact concerning them has reached us, that when any of them had died without baptism, they used to baptize others in their name, lest in the resurrection they should suffer punishment as unbaptized. (*Heresies* 28.7.)

The following declaration indicates that vicarious baptism of the living for the dead was practiced by some sects of the early Christians:

But even more emphatic than this is the testimony from the records of the Council of Carthage, held in 397 A.D., clearly declaring that the Christians of that date did practice vicarious baptisms for the dead, for in the sixth canon of that council the prevailing church forbids any further administration of baptism for the dead. Why should this canon be formed against this practice if it had no existence among the Christians of those days? (*Utah Genealogical and Historical Magazine,* April 1933, p. 63.)

While this glorious principle has been again restored to the earth in these latter-days, as was so plainly taught in the Church of former days, it was not to be found in any of the churches which existed upon the earth at the time Elijah visited the Prophet Joseph Smith and Oliver Cowdery and bestowed upon them these keys of the priesthood. The churches were united in condemning to eternal damnation all those who had died without accepting Christ, even though they had never heard his name. The churches also proclaimed damnation as the fate of little children who died without the ceremonies of the church, including baptism, even though the children could not act for themselves. This fate was also to apply to the heathen nations who had never heard the name of Christ.

Mrs. Pearl S. Buck, author of *The Good Earth,* and *Sons,* was tried for her membership in the Presbyterian Church because she disagreed with their doctrine that heathen races were damned unless they accepted the Christian gospel.

Trenton, N. J. April 12, 1934. (United Press) Mrs. Pearl S. Buck, who drew on her experience as a Presbyterian Missionary in China to write two "best seller" novels, faces removal as a result of recent writings differing with fundamentalist doctrines of the church, it was revealed at a meeting of the New Brunswick presbytery. Dr. J. Gresham Mechen of Westminster Theological Seminary, Philadelphia, asked what action the board of foreign missions planned to take. Dr. Robert E. Speer, senior secretary of the board, replied that against Mrs. Buck . . . Mrs. Buck's case was one of two under consideration. "The only question remaining is as to the Christian method by which we should proceed," Speer remarked.

The churches have taught that all must be members of the Christian gospel or they will be damned, and yet no opportunity is provided heathen races to become members. Where is the justice of God made manifest in such doctrine?

Need of Salvation for the Dead Recognized

Some ministers, however, have had a realization of the need of the principle of salvation for the dead to satisfy the justice of God.

John Frederick Denison Maurice, Professor of Theology at King's College, London, was unseated because of his alleged unsound theology in regard to eternal punishment published in 1853 in his *Theological Essays.* (See *Encyclopedia Britannica,* 11th edition, Vol. 17, p. 910.) He taught that the revelations of God's love to us in the gospel is incompatible with his permitting any of the creatures he has loved to be consigned to never ending torment. On his deathbed in 1872, his comrade in the ministry broke the sad news that he would no longer preach the gospel. It is said that he mustered all the energy at his command, and rising in his bed, declared, "If I can no longer preach the gospel here, I will preach it in other worlds."

> . . . Henry Ward Beecher . . . . delivered a lecture in Nashville, Tennessee, his subject being, "What Christianity Has Done to Civilize the World," in which he said: "What has Africa done for the world? She has never produced a sage, a philosopher, a poet nor a prophet, and why not? Because the name of Christ and the influence of Christianity are scarcely known in her dark regions. Millions of her children have lived and passed away without hearing the truth. What will become of them? Will they

be forever damned? No, not if my God reigns, for they will hear the gospel in the spirit world." He then proceeded to show by irrefutable evidence that salvation for the dead is a scriptural doctrine.

The writer was not present at the lecture, but another Latter-day Saint Elder was present, and, at the conclusion of the lecture, stepped up to the platform and said: "Mr. Beecher, I have been much interested in your lecture and would like to ask you a question. Jesus said to Nicodemus, 'Except a man be born of water and of the Spirit he cannot enter into the kingdom of God.' Now, how is it possible for a man to be baptized in water when his body has already crumbled in the earth?" The great preacher looked at the interrogator for a moment and then said: "Young man, where do you hail from?" "From the West." "From what part of the West?" "From Salt Lake City," answered the Elder. "Oh," said Mr. Beecher, "You may answer your own question. Good evening," and walked away. Mr. Beecher probably had read enough on the subject of baptism for the dead to know that such a doctrine must be coupled with preaching to departed spirits, but he did not wish to be accused of teaching "Mormonism," so he stopped short of that. He said enough, however, to verify the words of Joseph Smith and also those of the Savior when He said that if men put new wine into old bottles it would break them to pieces, in other words new doctrine into old systems. (Cowley's *Talks on Doctrine*, 1902 edition, pp. 122, 123.)

Professor A. Hinderkoper, a German writer, says: "In the second and third centuries every branch and division of the Christian church, so far as their record enables us to judge, believed that Christ preached to the departed spirits." (Ben E. Rich, *Scrapbook of Mormon Literature*, pp. 321-322.)

Dr. S. Parkes Cadman, a famous radio preacher and former president of the Federated Council of Churches of America, discussed the following question over the radio for millions of listeners:

Question—What, in your opinion, becomes of those souls who in this life had no opportunity of accepting or rejecting the truth as it is found in the Gospels?

Answer—Those who never heard the name of Jesus since human beings first appeared on the earth constitute the vast majority who have lived and died here. Moreover, hundreds of millions now living are in the same condition. Imagination cannot conceive their endless array.

Even today multitudes exist in Christian lands who because of the circumstances of their birth and upbringing are almost as ignorant of the New Testament faith as were the ancient Greeks who never heard of Christ. Think also of the hosts of innocent children who pass on before arriving at conscious responsibility for their own lives.

Even when dimly understood, your question would be unbearably oppressive if none except those who have intelligently and voluntarily believed in Christ are hereafter admitted to the Divine Presence. If, as we are taught to believe, the incalculable myriads of human beings who have occupied, or, now occupy this life, exist for eternity, and must spend it somewhere, how can we limit the redemptive efficacy of divine love to the brief span of man's mortal existence here?

Consider the issue as it affects the fate of those near and dear to you. Then apply its significance to all mankind. It is our consolation and hope that since God is the Father of us all, not one soul is lost to His sight, and none because of less importance to Him. "His mercy endureth forever." The creeds which confine the operations of that mercy to the life that now is do injustice to its saving virtue, and injure the cause in behalf of which they were set up. (*Millennial Star,* August 13, 1936, p. 514.)

Notwithstanding many of these ministers felt the need of a work being done for the dead, none had a definite program to propose, and neither would The Church of Jesus Christ of Latter-day Saints except for the fact that God revealed such information by sending Elijah to the Prophet Joseph Smith. We therefore received it by revelation and not by reading the Bible. We take the Bible to show that this principle was taught therein.

Why should not members of the present-day Christian denominations, who love their relatives, feel as the heathen king as expressed in this narrative:

A heathen king about to accept Christianity for himself and people, on learning that his ancestors could not be saved, said,

"Then to hell I will go with them." (James E. Talmage, *Vitality of Mormonism*, p. 249.)

Joseph Smith, in speaking of the responsibility the Lord has placed upon us to see that our dead receive the blessings of the gospel, said:

The greatest responsibility in this world that God has laid upon us is to seek after our dead. . . .

Those Saints who neglect it, in behalf of their deceased relatives, do it at the peril of their own salvation. (Joseph Fielding Smith, *The Way to Perfection*, pp. 149, 154.)

Fruits of the Mission and Work of Elijah

What evidence have we that the promise of Malachi has been fulfilled? If Joseph Smith and Oliver Cowdery had spoken a falsehood when they said Elijah came to them, then the hearts of the children would not have turned to their fathers. No one else has claimed that Elijah committed these keys to him. The hearts of the children were not turned to their fathers before the proclamation by Joseph and Oliver.

. . . It is well to know in this connection that in 1836 there were no genealogical societies in this land or in Europe. Save for the keeping of pedigrees of royal and noble families, very little attention was being paid to the records of the dead in any Christian country. The first organized effort to collect and file genealogies of the common people was made shortly after the coming of Elijah. This was the formation of the New England Historic and Genealogical Society. In 1844, this society was incorporated. Its chief purpose is to gather and publish data in relation to American Families. The New York Genealogical and Biographical Society, was incorporated in 1869. The Pennsylvania Genealogical Society, The Maine Genealogical Society, together with other like societies in Maryland, New Hampshire, New Jersey, Rhode Island, Connecticut and most of the other states of the Union, have all been organized since 1836. A great many societies have also been organized in Great Britain and on the continent of Europe, but all of them since the keys of the Priesthood were returned to the earth which planted in the hearts of the children the promises made to their fathers. (Joseph Fielding Smith, *The Way to Perfection*, pp. 168-169.)

Thousands and tens of thousands of genealogical records have been compiled. The spirit of turning the hearts of the children to their fathers has swept the whole earth since Elijah came to accomplish his promised mission. While this spirit cannot be seen, the operation thereof has touched the hearts of men and women the world over. They do not know why they are compiling genealogical records, yet this work has made rapid strides—really it is "a marvellous work and a wonder" in and of itself. The following experiences illustrate the operation of this spirit:

While the author was serving as president of the Southern States Mission, a new convert went into the library at Jacksonville, Florida, looking for the genealogy of his people and found a book prepared by a relative—a judge in Texas. The foreword read something like this:

> This book has been prepared at great cost of time, effort and money on the part of my wife and myself. Why we have done it we do not know, but we trust in the providence of the Almighty it may serve a useful purpose.

While serving as president of the Hollywood Stake in Los Angeles some years ago, the author had the privilege of attending a social gathering of stake genealogical workers at which there was also in attendance the chairman of the Library Board of Los Angeles. In discussing this subject, he said his hobby was gathering genealogy; that he had his vault full of records and manuscripts which had cost him thousands and thousands of dollars. He said he did not know what good the information would be to him when gathered but that he had a mania therefor and could not let it alone.

Some years ago, while the author was serving as president of the Portland, Oregon, branch of the Northwestern States Mission, he met a man who had been traveling for months gathering genealogical data of his people. His home was in the East, but at this time his search and investigation had brought him to Portland. He said he could not understand his interest in the matter, but he could not let it alone.

It would have been as difficult for these men to understand that they were being driven on by the spirit Elijah brought to this earth, as it would have been for Columbus to understand that it was the spirit of the Lord that was to lead him to this land of America, as we have pointed out. (See I Nephi 13:12.)

In the words of William Cowper:

God moves in a mysterious way, his wonders to perform.
He plants his footsteps in the sea, and rides upon the storm.

Marvelous are the manifestations of divine assistance in helping the Latter-day Saints to obtain the genealogical data necessary to enable them to perform baptisms in the temples of the Lord for their kindred dead. We will not, however, attempt to relate these experiences in this discussion.

It is sufficient to know that with respect to record keeping, the establishment of genealogical libraries and family organizations and the preparation of genealogical books and records, there has been a great change in the world since Elijah visited Joseph Smith and Oliver Cowdery, and conferred the keys of turning "the heart of the children to their fathers."

Again, this is not something any man could have achieved of himself, nor could he have done through reading the Bible. This was done by God as a part of the "restitution of all things, which God hath spoken by the

mouth of all the holy prophets since the world began."
(See Acts 3:21.)

Already, The Church of Jesus Christ of Latter-day
Saints has one of the largest and best genealogical libraries in the world. The Church has been microfilming
many of the genealogical records of the nations of the
world with particular emphasis being placed on the
records of Europe.

For the preservation of these records the Church has
carved from granite mountains only 22 miles from Salt
Lake City a giant series of storage vaults. There is nearly
700 feet of solid granite above the six huge vaults which
have been carved almost 500 feet into the heart of the
granite. The natural temperature in the storage area is 57
to 58 degrees Fahrenheit the year around, and the natural humidity is always 40 to 50 percent. These conditions
are perfect for microfilm storage.

It is safe to predict that in the not too far distant
future, the Church Genealogical Library will not only be
the best in the world but will also be a repository of most
all other genealogical libraries.

Surely Elijah must be well pleased with what has
been accomplished in this world because by revelation
the keys of this priesthood were revealed by him to
Joseph Smith and Oliver Cowdery on the third day of
April, 1836, in the temple at Kirtland, Ohio.

Chapter 14

MARRIAGE FOR TIME AND FOR ALL ETERNITY

Marriage for Time Includes Bill of Divorcement at Death

At the time the gospel was restored through the Prophet Joseph Smith, there was not a church in the world, as far as we have been able to learn, which taught that the marriage covenant was intended to extend beyond death; hence the wording of the marriage ceremony as performed by the ministers of that day and until the present time: "Until death do you part." A careful consideration of the wording of this marriage covenant will reveal the fact that it is not only a marriage covenant but also a bill of divorcement because it clearly releases one from the other at the death of either. Thus they have entered into no covenant or agreement with each other beyond the death of one party, neither has the minister attempted to bind them together beyond the death of either. Therefore, all obligations to each other are fulfilled upon the death of either.

The Lord intended that the marriage covenant should be for time and for all eternity and the practice of marrying "until death do you part," did not originate with the Lord, or his servants, but is a man-made doctrine. Therefore, all men and women who have died without having been sealed to each other for time and for all eternity, by the power of the holy priesthood, have no claim upon each other after they are dead, neither have they claim upon their children, for they have not been born under the covenant of eternal marriage. In order that the purposes of the Lord should not be defeated, and that he should not come "and smite the earth with a curse," it became necessary, in restoring the gospel in this dispensation, to restore the keys of the priesthood whereby living children can be vicariously married for their dead parents, and be sealed to them as their children, even as they can be baptized for them, for as the Apostle Paul said: "They without us should not be made perfect." (Heb. 11:40.) This is one of the great truths the Lord has revealed in these latter days, which makes his work in very deed a marvelous work and a wonder.

Eternal Marriage as Revealed Through the Prophet Joseph Smith

In the celestial glory there are three heavens or degrees;

And in order to obtain the highest, a man must enter into this order of the priesthood (meaning the new and everlasting covenant of marriage);

And if he does not, he cannot obtain it.

He may enter into the other, but that is the end of his kingdom; he cannot have an increase. (D. & C. 131:1-4.)

For behold, I reveal unto you a new and an everlasting covenant; and if ye abide not that covenant, then are ye damned; for no one can reject this covenant and be permitted to enter into my glory. (D. & C. 132:4.)

When the Lord indicated that if one does not enter into this everlasting covenant of marriage he will be "damned," he did not mean that he is consigned to eternal burning in a lake of fire and brimstone, as most Christians understand damnation. He simply informed the people that the progress of such an individual is stopped; he cannot have eternal increase and hence he cannot enter into "my glory." The Apostle Paul understood this principle as evidenced by his statement:

Nevertheless neither is the man without the woman, neither the woman without the man, in the Lord. (I Cor. 11:11.)

A man may get along all right without a woman in this world, or a woman without a man, but without each other they cannot enter into his glory in the world to come:

And again, verily I say unto you, if a man marry a wife by my word, which is my law, and by the new and everlasting covenant, and it is sealed unto them by the Holy Spirit of promise, by him who is anointed, unto whom I have appointed this power and the keys of this priesthood; and it shall be said unto them—Ye shall come forth in the first resurrection; and if it be after the first resurrection, in the next resurrection; and shall inherit thrones, kingdoms, principalities, and powers, dominions, all heights and depths—then shall it be written in the Lamb's Book of Life . . . it shall be done unto them in all things whatsoever my servant hath put upon them, in time, and through all eternity; and shall be of full force when they are out of the world. . . . (D. & C. 132:19.)

Therefore, if a man marry him a wife in the world and he marry her not by me nor by my word, and he covenant with her so long as he is in the world and she with him, their covenant and marriage are not of force when they are dead, and when they are out of the world; therefore, they are not bound by any law when they are out of the world.

Therefore, when they are out of the world they neither marry nor are given in marriage; but are appointed angels in heaven; which angels are ministering servants, to minister for those who are worthy of a far more, and an exceeding, and an eternal weight of glory. (D. & C. 132:15-16.)

And again, verily I say unto you, if a man marry a wife, and make a covenant with her for time and for all eternity, if that covenant is not by me or by my word, which is my law, and is not sealed by the Holy Spirit of promise, through him whom I have anointed and appointed unto this power, then it is not valid neither of force when they are out of the world, because they are not joined by me, saith the Lord, neither by my word. . . . (D. & C. 132:18; see also verses 26, 48.)

This glorious principle of eternal marriage did not come to the Prophet Joseph Smith by reading the Bible, but through the revelations of the Lord to him. If members of the Christian churches are "appointed angels in heaven; which angels are ministering servants," as the Lord has indicated, they will receive all they anticipate. But, as we have pointed out, the Lord has prepared a far greater blessing for those who enter "my glory."

Jesus must have had such a principle as this in mind when, after explaining to Nicodemus the need of "being born again" to enter the kingdom of heaven, he said:

... Art thou a master of Israel, and knowest not these things? ...

If I have told you earthly things, and ye believe not, how shall ye believe, if I tell you of heavenly things? (John 3:10, 12.)

Eternal Marriage to be Solemnized in Holy Temples

All the details of "heavenly things" have not been recorded, but many of them have been revealed to his servants, the prophets. In this day, also, the Lord had certain endowments and blessings which he desired to confer upon his servants, which required the building of a house unto him. In a revelation to the Prophet Joseph Smith, the Lord stated:

Yea, verily I say unto you, I gave unto you a commandment that you should build a house, in the which house I design to endow those whom I have chosen with power from on high;

For this is the promise of the Father unto you; therefore I command you to tarry, even as mine apostles at Jerusalem. (D. & C. 95:8-9.)

Before a man can receive the blessings of eternal marriage, he must be ordained an elder in the Melchizedek Priesthood and receive other blessings pertaining to the house of the Lord, to which we have referred, all of which the Lord has indicated shall be administered in his holy temples. As these blessings are made available for the living, they are also made available for the worthy dead.

On the 21st day of January 1836, while the Prophet Joseph Smith and his two counselors in the First Presidency of the Church, together with his father, the Patriarch to the Church, were assembled in the Kirtland Temple, the Prophet had an experience which he related:

> The heavens were opened upon us, and I beheld the celestial kingdom of God, and the glory thereof, whether in the body or out I cannot tell. I saw the transcendent beauty of the gate through which the heirs of that kingdom will enter, which was like unto circling flames of fire; also the blazing throne of God, whereon was seated the Father and the Son. I saw the beautiful streets of that kingdom, which had the appearance of being paved with gold. I saw Fathers Adam and Abraham, and my father and mother, my brother, Alvin, that has long since slept, and marvelled how it was that he had obtained an inheritance in that kingdom, seeing that he had departed this life before the Lord had set His hand to gather Israel the second time, and had not been baptized for the remission of sins.

> Thus came the voice of the Lord unto me, saying—"All who have died without a knowledge of this Gospel, who would have received it if they had been permitted to tarry, shall be heirs of the celestial kingdom of God; also all that shall die henceforth without a knowledge of it, who would have received it with all their hearts, shall be heirs of that kingdom, for I, the Lord, will judge all men according to their works, according to the desire of their hearts." (D.H.C. Vol. 2, p. 380.)

Thus, the blessings of the celestial kingdom are to be made available to all who would have accepted the same had the opportunity been presented to them. Here again is evidence of the justice or righteousness of God. Nevertheless, the ordinances necessary to salvation and exaltation have to be administered unto them vicariously—the living standing as proxies for the dead. These are glorious principles revealed to the earth in these latter days through the Prophet Joseph Smith. Holy ordinances are being performed daily in the temples of the Lord, that the dead "might be judged according to men in the flesh, but live according to God in the spirit." (See I Pet. 4:6.)

This concept makes it easy to understand why the hearts of the fathers would turn to their children and the hearts of the children turn to their fathers, which was a part of the great mission of Elijah. (See Mal. 4:5-6.) How could one be expected to understand this very important matter by reading the Bible only? Elijah had come to make it plain, and to introduce these great truths again to the inhabitants of the earth. This is also one of the great steps in the fulfilment of the promise of Paul:

> That in the dispensation of the fulness of times he might gather together in one all things in Christ, both which are in heaven, and which are on earth; even in him. (Eph. 1:10.)

The Man Is Not Without the Woman, Nor the Woman Without the Man, in the Lord

Our first record of marriage was when the Lord placed Adam in the Garden of Eden:

> And the Lord God said, It is not good that the man should be alone; I will make him an help meet for him. . . .
>
> Therefore shall a man leave his father and his mother, and shall cleave unto his wife: and they shall be one flesh.
>
> And they were both naked, the man and his wife, and were not ashamed. (Gen. 2:18, 24-25.)

Since, therefore, the Lord knew that it was "not good that the man should be alone," before he became subject unto death through transgression, why should men assume that it will be good for man to be alone when he is redeemed from the effects of the fall through the great atonement of the Lord, Jesus Christ—when his body is resurrected from the grave, since, "As in Adam all die, even so in Christ shall all be made alive." (I Cor. 15:22.)

Thus, if man needed "an help meet" before he was subject to death through his transgression, he should need a help meet when his body is restored, through the resurrection, to its former state.

Let us now consider the statement of the Lord: "And they shall be one flesh." (See Gen. 2:24.)

It is evident that the Lord did not have in mind, in this case, that they should be one in purpose and desire, for he makes himself clear as to what this oneness should consist of: viz., "one flesh." This can only be understood when we consider man's mission in the earth. The greatest power God has given unto man is the power of reproducing his kind. This a man cannot do without a woman; hence the statement of the Lord: "And they shall be one flesh."

Jesus understood this principle fully as we learn from his statement:

> For this cause shall a man leave his father and mother, and cleave to his wife;
>
> And they twain shall be one flesh: so then they are no more twain, but one flesh.
>
> What therefore God hath joined together, let not man put asunder. (Mark 10:7-9.)

Thus Jesus gave us to understand that both man and wife should "be one flesh." He adds: "so then they are no more twain, but one flesh." Why then should men attempt to separate them at death when their bodies of flesh and bone are to come forth from the grave?

> Nevertheless neither is the man without the woman, neither the woman without the man, in the Lord. (I Cor. 11:11.)

In other words, so far as the Lord is concerned, man and woman are not "twain, but one flesh."

> Wives, submit yourselves unto your own husbands, as unto the Lord.

> For the husband is the head of the wife, even as Christ is the head of the church: and he is the saviour of the body.

> Therefore as the church is subject unto Christ, so let the wives be to their own husbands in every thing.

> Husbands, love your wives, even as Christ also loved the church, and gave himself for it. (Eph. 5:22-25.)

There will never come a time when Christ will cease to be the head of the Church. Remember, that the husband is the head of the wife, even as Christ is the head of the Church.

> For this cause shall a man leave his father and mother, and shall be joined unto his wife, and they two shall be one flesh. . . .

> Nevertheless let every one of you in particular so love his wife even as himself; and the wife see that she reverence her husband. (Eph. 5:31, 33.)

The Apostle Peter understood that the husband and wife would inherit eternal life together and not separately. After referring to Abraham and Sarah, Peter said:

> Likewise, ye husbands, dwell with them according to knowledge, giving honour unto the wife, as unto the weaker vessel, and as being *heirs together* of the grace of life; that your prayers be not hindered. (I Pet. 3:7.)

The Prophet Isaiah described conditions as they shall exist upon the earth when the earth is renewed and receives its paradisiacal glory:

> For, behold, I create new heavens and a new earth: and the former shall not be remembered, nor come into mind. . . .

And I will rejoice in Jerusalem, and joy in my people: and the voice of weeping shall be no more heard in her, nor the voice of crying.

There shall be no more thence an infant of days, nor an old man that hath not filled his days; for the child shall die an hundred years old; but the sinner being an hundred years old shall be accursed.

And *they shall build houses, and inhabit them;* and they shall plant vineyards, and eat the fruit of them.

They shall not build, and another inhabit; they shall not plant, and another eat: for as the days of a tree are the days of my people, and mine elect shall long enjoy the work of their hands.

They shall not labour in vain, nor bring forth for trouble: for they are the seed of the blessed of the Lord, *and their offspring with them.*

And it shall come to pass, that before they call, I will answer; and while they are yet speaking, I will hear.

The wolf and the lamb shall feed together, and the lion shall eat straw like the bullock: and dust shall be the serpent's meat. They shall not hurt nor destroy in all my holy mountain, saith the Lord. (Isa. 65:17, 19-25.)

We gather from Isaiah's prophecy that, when the Lord creates a new heaven and a new earth, then shall "the seed of the blessed of the Lord, and their offspring with them," build houses and inhabit them and plant vineyards and eat the fruit therefrom. How can anyone figure out anything other than the organization of family groups? What else can one understand from the statement, "the seed of the blessed of the Lord, and their offspring with them"? Who will occupy the houses when built if not families?

How can righteous men and women who have teamed together in the rearing of their children, and sacrificed for them and for each other, believe that "The righteousness [or justice] of God" would put an end to their association and companionship? Not so, if they are married for eternity by the priesthood of God, for they without us cannot be made perfect nor we without them. This is the Lord's plan and he gave it to his children, for his children—it is divine.

The Family Unit in the Millennium

The Lord has also revealed, through the Prophet Joseph Smith, that in the resurrection we will receive our children who have died in infancy and have the privilege of rearing them to manhood and womanhood:

> And the earth shall be given unto them for an inheritance; and they shall multiply and wax strong, and their children shall grow up without sin unto salvation.
>
> For the Lord shall be in their midst, and his glory shall be upon them, and he will be their king and their lawgiver. (D. & C. 45:58-59.)

The above has reference to conditions during the millennial reign of the Lord for a thousand years upon this earth.

> And there shall be no sorrow because there is no death.
>
> In that day an infant shall not die until he is old; and his life shall be as the age of a tree;
>
> And when he dies he shall not sleep, that is to say in the earth, but shall be changed in the twinkling of an eye, and shall be caught up, and his rest shall be glorious. (D. & C. 101:29-31.)

Thus The Church of Jesus Christ of Latter-day Saints stands alone in teaching the doctrine of the eternal duration of the marriage covenant and family unit. How can anyone in whose heart burns a true love for the wife of his bosom, and for his own children, do other than want to believe this doctrine? What could eternity offer to interest one unless he could enjoy it with those whom he has loved in mortality and with whom he has spent his life?

At the close of the Apostle Paul's wonderful sermon on the resurrection he exclaimed:

O death, where is thy sting? O grave, where is thy victory?

The sting of death is sin; and the strength of sin is the law. (I Cor. 15:55-56.)

Had Paul not understood that death was but a brief separation from those whom we love and that there would be a reuniting of loved ones in the resurrection, he might well have said: "The sting of death is eternal separation from those we have loved in life." But Paul understood the truth, for he had been caught up into the third heaven and the paradise of God. (See II Cor. Chapter 12.)

Regardless of the teachings of their churches to the contrary, there are many who believe they will be united again with their loved ones.

Anderson M. Baten dedicated a poem to his beloved wife, Beulah, entitled, *The Philosophy of Life,* which expresses his faith that his marriage tie would extend beyond the grave:

I wed thee forever, not for now;
Nor for the sham of earth's brief years.
I wed thee for the life beyond the tears,
Beyond the heart pain and the clouded brow.
Love knows no grave, and it will guide us, dear,
When life's spent candles flutter and burn low.

In an interview the author had with a prominent minister, the minister admitted that his church held out no hopes of the reuniting of family ties beyond the grave, and then added: "But in my heart I find stubborn objections. Take for instance the kitten. When you take it away from the cat, in a few days the mother cat has forgotten all about it. Take the calf away from the cow and in a few days the cow has forgotten all about the calf. But when you take a child away from his mother, though she lives to be a hundred years old, she never forgets the child of her bosom. I find it difficult to believe that God created such love to perish in the grave."

Scriptures Dealing with Marriage Misunderstood

The misunderstanding with respect to the eternal nature of the marriage covenant and the family unit is largely the result of man's misinterpretation of some of the scriptures. Truth will always be truth, no matter when and by whom it is discussed.

The following statement by Jesus has been very much misunderstood:

> The same day came to him the Sadducees, which say that there is no resurrection, and asked him,
>
> Saying, Master, Moses said, If a man die, having no children, his brother shall marry his wife, and raise up seed unto his brother.
>
> Now there were with us seven brethren: and the first, when he had married a wife, deceased, and, having no issue, left his wife unto his brother:
>
> Likewise the second also, and the third, unto the seventh.
>
> And last of all the woman died also.
>
> Therefore in the resurrection whose wife shall she be of the seven? for they all had her.
>
> Jesus answered and said unto them, Ye do err, not knowing the scriptures, nor the power of God.
>
> For in the resurrection they neither marry, nor are given in marriage, but are as the angels of God in heaven. (Matt. 22:23-30.)

The late Dr. James E. Talmage, of the Quorum of the Twelve Apostles, explained the Saviour's answer to the question of the Sadducees, who deny there is any resurrection:

> The Lord's meaning was clear, that in the resurrected state there can be no question among the seven brothers as to whose wife for eternity the woman shall be, since all except the first had

married her for the duration of mortal life only, and primarily for the purpose of perpetuating in mortality the name and family of the brother who first died. Luke records the Lord's words as follows in part: "But they which shall be accounted worthy to obtain that world, and the resurrection from the dead, neither marry, nor are given in marriage: Neither can they die any more: for they are equal unto the angels; and are the children of God, being the children of the resurrection." In the resurrection there will be no marrying nor giving in marriage; for all questions of marital status must be settled before that time, under the authority of the Holy Priesthood, which holds the power to seal in marriage for both time and eternity. (James E. Talmage, *Jesus The Christ*, p. 548.)

To this explanation add the Lord's own words in a revelation to the Prophet Joseph Smith at Nauvoo, Illinois, recorded July 12, 1843, relating to the new and everlasting covenant of marriage:

Therefore, if a man marry him a wife in the world, and he marry her not by me nor by my word, and he covenant with her so long as he is in the world and she with him, their covenant and marriage are not of force when they are dead, and when they are out of the world; therefore, they are not bound by any law when they are out of the world.

Therefore, when they are out of the world they neither marry nor are given in marriage; but are appointed angels in heaven; which angels are ministering servants, to minister for those who are worthy of a far more, and an exceeding and an eternal weight of glory.

For these angels did not abide my law; therefore, they cannot be enlarged, but remain separately and singly, without exaltation, in their saved condition, to all eternity; and from henceforth are not gods, but are angels of God forever and ever. (D. & C. 132:15-17.)

Jesus must have had this very thought in mind when he answered the Sadducees who did not believe in the resurrection and whose marriage vows were for this world only. By his answer, Jesus "put the Sadducees to silence" for he knew the purpose of their question, for they "tempted him." And when he had answered them, "neither durst any man from that day forth ask him any more questions."

We have already pointed out that marriage is a ceremony belonging to this world, and hence the Lord has made provision for the living to perform this ceremony vicariously for the dead, when their marriage has not been performed by one having priesthood authority to bind both for time and for all eternity.

Compare the limited promise made to those whose marriage vows are for this world only, with the promise, contained in the same revelation, made to those who covenant in marriage for time and for all eternity:

> . . . it shall be done unto them in all things whatsoever my servant hath put upon them, in time, and through all eternity; and shall be of full force when they are out of the world; and they shall pass by the angels, and the gods, which are set there, to their exaltation and glory in all things, as hath been sealed upon their heads, which glory shall be a fulness and a continuation of the seeds forever and ever. (D. & C. 132:19.)

With this glorious truth revealed anew to men upon this earth, they really have something to live for, and something to die for. We doubt if there ever has been a truth revealed to man upon this earth as comforting as the revelation of the Lord to the Prophet Joseph Smith, known as the new and everlasting covenant of marriage. (See D. & C. 132:4.)

It should be noted that this glorious truth is a part of the promised "restitution of all things, which God hath spoken by the mouth of all his holy prophets since the world began." (See Acts 3:21.)

Do not these truths justify the coming of Elijah? How could "the heart of the fathers" be turned "to the children, and the heart of the children to their fathers" more effectively than to seal them together in holy family relationships forevermore?

CHAPTER 15

THE GATHERING OF ISRAEL

Moses Restores the Keys for the Gathering of Israel

When the Angel Moroni visited Joseph Smith during the night of September 21, 1823, he quoted the eleventh chapter of Isaiah and emphasized that it was soon to be fulfilled. Let us now give special consideration to the following as quoted by Moroni:

> And in that day there shall be a root of Jesse, which shall stand for an ensign of the people; to it shall the Gentiles seek: and his rest shall be glorious.
>
> And it shall come to pass in that day, that the Lord shall set his hand again the second time to recover the remnant of his people, which shall be left, from Assyria, and from Egypt, and from Pathros, and from Cush, and from Elam, and from Shinar, and from Hameth, and from the islands of the sea.
>
> And he shall set up an ensign for the nations, and shall assemble the outcasts of Israel, and gather together the dispersed of Judah from the four corners of the earth. (Isa. 11:10-12.)

From this scripture we learn that the events described were to be in the future: "The Lord shall set his hand again the second time to recover the remnant of his people." There could not be a "second time" unless there had been a first. The first time was when the Lord led Israel out of Egyptian bondage and captivity. When did the Lord set his hand the "second time" to recover the remnant of his people? This we will now consider. From the above scripture we learn that three important events were to transpire: (1) He shall set up an ensign for the nations; (2) he shall assemble the outcasts of Israel; (3) he shall gather together the dispersed of Judah from the four corners of the earth.

It is clear there are to be two gathering places—one for Israel and one for Judah.

When the Angel Moroni informed Joseph Smith, not yet eighteen years of age, that these events were about to come to pass, that the Lord would use him as an instrument in their accomplishment, it truly was a great assignment for a youth of his age.

We have referred to the occasion when the Savior and other heavenly messengers appeared to Joseph Smith and Oliver Cowdery in the Kirtland Temple, April 3, 1836, nearly thirteen years after the Angel Moroni had quoted to Joseph Smith the eleventh chapter of Isaiah, indicating that it was about to be fulfilled. We quote from the account of these visitations:

> After this vision closed, the heavens were again opened unto us; and Moses appeared before us, and committed unto us the keys of the gathering of Israel from the four parts of the earth, and the leading of the ten tribes from the land of the north. (D. & C. 110:11.)

Since Moses was the prophet the Lord raised up to lead Israel out of the land of Egypt and gave him power to perform such mighty miracles before Pharaoh, even to the leading of the children of Israel through the Red Sea on dry land, it seems very appropriate that Moses should hold the keys of the gathering of Israel when the Lord would "set his hand again the second time to recover the remnant of his people." These were the keys Moses committed to Joseph Smith and Oliver Cowdery.

The Division and Scattering of Israel

When speaking of Israel, most people have the Jews in mind, and when referring to the gathering of Israel, they have in mind the return of the Jews to the land of Jerusalem. It should be remembered that the Jews, the descendants of Judah, represent but one of the twelve branches, or tribes, of the house of Israel—the family of Jacob.

The twelve tribes of Israel were divided under two great heads, Judah, comprising the smaller group, and Israel, the larger group:

> And Joab gave up the sum of the number of the people unto the king: and *there were in Israel eight hundred thousand* valiant men that drew the sword; and *the men of Judah were five hundred thousand men.* (II Sam. 24:9.)

> And the Lord said, I will remove Judah also out of my sight, as I have removed Israel, and will cast off this city Jerusalem which I have chosen, and the house of which I said, My name shall be there. (II Kings 23:27.)

> . . . I will not utterly destroy the house of Jacob, saith the Lord.

> For, lo, I will command, and I will *sift the house of Israel among all nations,* like as corn is sifted in a sieve, yet shall not the least grain fall upon the earth. (Amos 9:8-9.)

In the seventh and eighth chapters we considered America as the land of Joseph, and the Book of Mormon as a history of the Lord's dealings with that branch of the house of Israel. We will now consider the gathering of the house of Israel in the latter days.

We should keep in mind the words of Amos, just quoted, to the effect that the Lord would "sift the house of Israel *among all nations,*" which means that the gathering of latter-day Israel would have to be from all nations, into which they had been sifted for the Lord has decreed that "not the least grain fall upon the earth."

Israel to be Gathered in This Dispensation

The Tenth Article of Faith of The Church of Jesus Christ of Latter-day Saints reads:

We believe in the literal gathering of Israel and in the restoration of the Ten Tribes; that Zion will be built upon this (the American) continent; that Christ will reign personally upon the earth; and, that the earth will be renewed and receive its paradisiacal glory.

Prior to the organization of The Church of Jesus Christ of Latter-day Saints on April 6, 1830, Joseph Smith and Oliver Cowdery had learned of the gathering of Israel that was to take place upon this land of America in this dispensation. They learned this truth through their work in translating the Book of Mormon from the golden plates.

We quote from the words of the Savior to the Nephites when he visited them in this land of America following his resurrection:

And verily I say unto you, I give unto you a sign, that ye may know the time when these things shall be about to take place— that I shall gather in, from their long dispersion, my people, O house of Israel, *and shall establish again among them my Zion;*

And behold, this is the thing which I will give unto you for a sign—for verily I say unto you that when these things which I declare unto you, and which I shall declare unto you hereafter of myself, and by the power of the Holy Ghost which shall be given unto you of the Father, shall be made known unto the Gentiles that they may know concerning this people who are a remnant of the house of Jacob, and concerning this my people who shall be scattered by them;

Verily, verily, I say unto you, when these things shall be made known unto them of the Father, and shall come forth of the Father, from them unto you;

For it is wisdom in the Father that they should be established in this land, and be set up as a free people by the power of the Father, that these things might come forth from them unto a remnant of your seed, that the covenant of the Father may be fulfilled which he hath covenanted with his people, O house of Israel;

Therefore, when these works and the works which shall be wrought among you hereafter shall come forth from the Gentiles, unto your seed which shall dwindle in unbelief because of iniquity;

For thus it behooveth the Father that it should come forth from the Gentiles, that he may show forth his power unto the Gentiles, for this cause that the Gentiles, if they will not harden their hearts, that they may repent and come unto me and be baptized in my name and know of the true points of my doctrine, that they may be numbered among my people, O house of Israel;

And when these things come to pass that thy seed shall begin to know these things—it shall be a sign unto them, that they may know that the work of the Father hath already commenced unto the fulfilling of the covenant which he hath made unto the people who are of the house of Israel. . . .

For in that day, for my sake shall the Father work a work, which shall be a great and a marvelous work among them; and there shall be among them those who will not believe it, although a man shall declare it unto them. . . .

And my people who are a remnant of Jacob shall be among the Gentiles, yea, in the midst of them as a lion among the beasts of the forest, as a young lion among the flocks of sheep, who, if he go through both treadeth down and teareth in pieces, and none can deliver. . . .

But if they will repent and hearken unto my words, and harden not their hearts, *I will establish my church among them, and they shall come in unto the covenant and be numbered among this the remnant of Jacob, unto whom I have given this land for their inheritance;*

And they shall assist my people, the remnant of Jacob, and also as many of the house of Israel as shall come, that they may build a city, which shall be called the New Jerusalem.

And then shall they assist my people that they may be gathered in, who are scattered upon all the face of the land, in unto the New Jerusalem.

And then shall the power of heaven come down among them; and I also will be in the midst.

And then shall the work of the Father commence at that day, even when this gospel shall be preached among the remnant of this people. Verily I say unto you, *at that day shall the work of the Father commence among all the dispersed of my people, yea, even the tribes which have been lost, which the Father hath led away out of Jerusalem.*

Yea, the work shall commence among all the dispersed of my people, with the Father, to prepare the way *whereby they may come unto me*, that they may call on the Father in my name.

Yea, and then shall the work commence, with the Father, among all nations, in preparing the way whereby his people may be gathered home to the land of their inheritance.

And they shall go out from all nations; and they shall not go out in haste, nor go by flight, for I will go before them, saith the Father, and I will be their rearward. (III Nephi 21: 1-7, 9, 12, 22-29.)

In considering the above declaration, it should be remembered that the Book of Mormon was published and given to the world in 1830, the year the Church was organized, when Joseph Smith was only twenty-four years old. And yet this statement covers all the essential points with respect to the gathering of latter-day Israel, to wit:

1. That the New Jerusalem would be established in the land of America

2. That The Church of Jesus Christ would be established in the land of America

3. That the Church would be established among the gentiles. (We have already pointed out how Israel was to be scattered among the gentile nations.)

4. That at the time that his Church would be established among the gentiles in this land of America, it would be a sign that the time had arrived, "That I shall gather in, from their long dispersion, my people, O house of Israel, and shall establish among them my Zion"

5. That the accomplishment of these things shall precede the second coming of the Christ: "And I also will be in the midst"

6. That at that time, the Lord would set his hand to gather his people from among all nations: "Yea, and then shall the work commence, with the Father, among all nations, in preparing the way whereby His people may be gathered home to the land of their inheritance"

7. These declarations of the Savior confirm the statements of

the prophets already referred to, to the effect that Israel would be sifted among all nations.

The Prophet Ether had a clear understanding of the gathering of Israel in the latter-days and of the establishment of a New Jerusalem in this land of America, and the rebuilding of the Jerusalem of old by the Jews:

And now I, Moroni, proceed to finish my record concerning the destruction of the people of whom I have been writing.

For behold, they rejected all the words of Ether; for he truly told them of all things, from the beginning of man; and that after the waters had receded from off the face of this land it became a choice land above all other lands, a chosen land of the Lord; wherefore the Lord would have that all men should serve him who dwell upon the face thereof;

And that it was the place of the New Jerusalem, which should come down out of heaven, and the holy sanctuary of the Lord.

Behold, Ether saw the days of Christ, and he spake concerning a New Jerusalem upon this land.

And he spake also concerning the house of Israel, and the Jerusalem from whence Lehi should come—after it should be destroyed it should be built up again, a holy city unto the Lord; wherefore, it could not be a new Jerusalem for it had been in a time of old; but it should be built up again, and become a holy city of the Lord; and it should be built unto the house of Israel.

And that a New Jerusalem should be built up upon this land, unto the remnant of the seed of Joseph, for which things there has been a type.

For as Joseph brought his father down into the land of Egypt, even so he died there; wherefore, the Lord brought a remnant of the seed of Joseph out of the land of Jerusalem, that he might be merciful unto the seed of Joseph that they should perish not, even as he was merciful unto the father of Joseph that he should perish not.

Wherefore, the remnant of the house of Joseph shall be built upon this land; and it shall be a land of their inheritance; and they shall build up a holy city unto the Lord, like unto the Jerusalem of old; and they shall no more be confounded, until the end come when the earth shall pass away.

And there shall be a new heaven and a new earth; and they shall be like unto the old save the old have passed away, and all things have become new.

And then cometh the New Jerusalem; and blessed are they who dwell therein, for it is they whose garments are white through the blood of the Lamb; and they are they who are numbered among the remnant of the seed of Joseph, who were of the house of Israel.

And then also cometh the Jerusalem of old; and the inhabitants thereof, blessed are they, for they have been washed in the blood of the Lamb; and they are they who were scattered and gathered in from the four quarters of the earth, and from the north countries, and are partakers of the fulfilling of the covenant which God made with their father, Abraham.

And when these things come, bringeth to pass the scripture which saith, there are they who were first, who shall be last; and there are they who were last, who shall be first.

And I was about to write more, but I am forbidden; but great and marvelous were the prophecies of Ether; but they esteemed him as naught and cast him out; and he hid himself in the cavity of a rock by day, and by night he went forth viewing the things which should come upon the people. (Ether 13:1-13.)

The Prophet Ether who wrote the above was a descendant of Jared, in fact, the twenty-eighth generation:

Which Jared came forth with his brother and their families, with some others and their families, [to the land of America about 2200 B.C.] from the great tower, at the time the Lord confounded the language of the people, and swore in his wrath that they should be scattered upon all the face of the earth; and according to the word of the Lord the people were scattered. (Ether 1:33.)

There are many other valuable references in the Book of Mormon, which space and time make it seem unwise to refer to. However, from these it is evident that through the translation of the Book of Mormon, Joseph Smith and Oliver Cowdery had a clear understanding of the Lord's plan to gather scattered Israel in the latter days from the "four quarters of the earth" whither they had been scattered, and ultimately to establish a New Jerusalem in this land of America.

In September 1830, only five months after the Church was organized, and five and a half years before Moses brought the keys of the gathering of Israel and committed them to Joseph Smith and Oliver Cowdery, the Lord, in a revelation to the Prophet Joseph Smith, made a very definite statement on this subject:

And ye are called to bring to pass the gathering of mine elect; for mine elect hear my voice and harden not their hearts;

Wherefore the decree hath gone forth from the Father that they shall be gathered in unto one place upon the face of this land, to prepare their hearts and be prepared in all things against the day when tribulation and desolation are sent forth upon the wicked. (D. & C. 29:7-8.)

Thus, the first elders of the Church were "called to bring to pass the gathering of mine elect," so that from the very beginning of the Church, the Latter-day Saints have been "gathering." Their first place of gathering was at Kirtland, Ohio.

In a revelation from the Lord to the Prophet Joseph Smith, December 16, 1833, the Lord made plain that his people are to be gathered together:

Behold, it is my will, that all they who call on my name, and worhip me according to mine everlasting gospel, should gather together, and stand in holy places;

And prepare for the revelation which is to come, when the veil of the covering of my temple, in my tabernacle, which hideth the earth, shall be taken off and all flesh shall see me together. . . .

That the work of the gathering together of my saints may continue, that I may build them up unto my name upon holy places; for the time of harvest is come, and my word must needs be fulfilled.

Therefore, I must gather together my people, according to the parable of the wheat and the tares, that the wheat may be secured in the garners to possess eternal life, and be crowned with celestial glory, when I shall come in the kingdom of my Father to reward every man according as his work shall be. (D. & C. 101:22-23, 64-65.)

The following quotations from the revelations of the Lord to the Prophet Joseph Smith are given merely to confirm the statements already made:

That my covenant people may be gathered in one in that day when I shall come to my temple. And this I do for the salvation of my people. (D. & C. 42:36.)

And again, the Lord shall utter his voice out of heaven, saying: Hearken, O ye nations of the earth, and hear the words of that God who made you.

O, ye nations of the earth, how often would I have gathered you together as a hen gathereth her chickens under her wings, but ye would not! (D. & C. 43:23-24.)

And it shall come to pass that the righteous shall be gathered out from among all nations, and shall come to Zion, singing with songs of everlasting joy. (D. & C. 45:71.)

And even so will I gather mine elect from the four quarters of the earth even as many as will believe in me, and hearken unto my voice. (D. & C. 33:6.)

And Israel shall be saved in mine own due time; and by the keys which I have given shall they be led, and no more be confounded at all. (D. & C. 35:25.)

And again, I say unto you, I give unto you a commandment, that every man, both elder, priest, teacher, and also member, go to with his might, with the labor of his hands, to prepare and accomplish the things which I have commanded.

And let your preaching be the warning voice, every man to his neighbor, in mildness and in meekness.

And go ye out from among the wicked. Save yourselves. Be ye clean that bear the vessels of the Lord. . . . (D. & C. 38:40-42.)

Wherefore, prepare ye, prepare ye, O my people; sanctify yourselves; gather ye together, O ye people of my church, upon the land of Zion, all you that have not been commanded to tarry.

Go ye out from Babylon. Be ye clean that bear the vessels of the Lord.

Call your solemn assemblies, and speak often one to another. And let every man call upon the name of the Lord.

Yea, verily I say unto you again, the time has come when the voice of the Lord is unto you: Go ye out of Babylon; gather ye out from among the nations, from the four winds, from one end of heaven to the other.

Send forth the elders of my church unto the nations which are afar off; unto the islands of the sea; send forth unto foreign lands; call upon all nations, first upon the Gentiles, and then upon the Jews.

And behold, and lo, this shall be their cry, and the voice of the Lord unto all people: Go ye forth unto the land of Zion, that the borders of my people may be enlarged, and that her stakes may be strengthened, and that Zion may go forth unto the regions round about. (D. & C. 133:4-9.)

This last revelation was given November 3, 1831, only a year and seven months after the Church was organized. There is no question, in the re-establishment of his Church in the earth in these latter-days, but what the Lord definitely had in mind that his people should be gathered out of the nations and be gathered together in one place, as the above quotations so clearly indicate.

Latter-day Gathering of Scattered Israel

While the Lord has indicated that his Zion of the latter-days, to which Israel would be gathered, would be in the land of America, and that the New Jerusalem would be built upon this land, it is obvious that such a gathering could not be to but one city. In fulfilment of the command of the Lord in this matter, the Latter-day Saints have built over six hundred cities, to which have been gathered converts to the new faith from many countries. This gathering has been continuous from the organization of the Church unto the present time.

At the first gathering place of the Saints in this dispensation which was Kirtland, Ohio, they erected their first temple to the Most High.

The second gathering was in Missouri, where they laid the cornerstones for two temples, one at Independence and the other at Far West. But the Saints were compelled to leave Missouri because of cruel persecutions. However, until this day, the Church anticipates the time when its members will return and build a temple and the city of Zion to the Most High, at Independence, Missouri.

From Missouri, the Saints went to Nauvoo, Illinois, where they built a city of some 20,000 souls, and erected a beautiful temple to their God. It was while they were located here that the Prophet Joseph Smith and his brother, Hyrum, were martyred in cold blood by a wicked mob in Carthage jail, Illinois, on June 27, 1844. Soon after this, the Saints were compelled to leave Nauvoo, and their homes were devastated and their beautiful new temple was burned by their enemies. From there they turned their faces to the valleys of the Rocky Mountains, stopping at Winter Quarters, Iowa, only long enough to make preparations for their journey across the plains. The first main company arrived in what is now Salt Lake City, Utah, July 24, 1847. Since that time the headquarters of the Church have been established in Salt Lake City.

Leading of the Ten Tribes From the Land of the North

When Moses committed the keys of the gathering of Israel to the Prophet Joseph Smith and Oliver Cowdery, he added:

. . . and the leading of the ten tribes from the land of the North. (D. & C. 110:11.)

On this subject, the Lord has added the following in his revelation to the Prophet Joseph Smith:

And the Lord, even the Savior, shall stand in the midst of his people, and shall reign over all flesh.

And they who are in the north countries shall come in remembrance before the Lord; and their prophets shall hear his voice, and shall no longer stay themselves; and they shall smite the rocks, and the ice shall flow down at their presence.

And an highway shall be cast up in the midst of the great deep.

Their enemies shall become a prey unto them,

And in the barren deserts there shall come forth pools of living water; and the parched ground shall no longer be a thirsty land.

And they shall bring forth their rich treasures unto the children of Ephraim, my servants.

And the boundaries of the everlasting hills shall tremble at their presence.

And there shall they fall down and be crowned with glory, even in Zion, by the hands of the servants of the Lord, even the children of Ephraim.

And they shall be filled with songs of everlasting joy.

Behold, this is the blessing of the everlasting God upon the tribes of Israel, and the richer blessing upon the head of Ephraim and his fellows. (D. & C. 133:25-34.)

Where these lost tribes and their prophets are we do not know, except as the Lord has said that they are "in the north countries."

He Shall Gather Together the Dispersed of Judah

We have considered the gathering of Israel to the Zion of the Lord upon this land of America in this dispensation. We should now give some consideration to the matter of gathering together the "dispersed of Judah," to which Isaiah referred, (See Isaiah 11:10-12) and which the Angel Moroni quoted to Joseph Smith when he visited him on the night of September 21, 1823:

Let them, therefore, who are among the Gentiles flee unto Zion.

And let them who be of Judah flee unto Jerusalem, unto the mountains of the Lord's house.

Go ye out from among the nations, even from Babylon, from the midst of wickedness, which is spiritual Babylon. (D. & C. 133:12-14.)

Joseph Smith, the prophet, stated that the prayer he offered at the dedication of the Kirtland Temple on March 27, 1836, was given to him by revelation. We quote from that prayer the following:

But thou knowest that thou hast a great love for the children of Jacob, who have been scattered upon the mountains for a long time, in a cloudy and dark day.

We therefore ask thee to have mercy upon the children of Jacob, that Jerusalem, from this hour, may begin to be redeemed;

And the yoke of bondage may begin to be broken off from the house of David;

And the *children of Judah* may begin to return to the lands which thou didst give to Abraham, their father. (D. & C. 109:61-64.)

In March 1832, the Prophet Joseph Smith received a revelation explaining part of the Revelation of John:

Q. What is to be understood by the two witnesses, in the eleventh chapter of Revelation?

A. They are two prophets that are to be raised up to the Jewish nation in the last days, at the time of the restoration, and to prophesy to the Jews after they are gathered and have built the city of Jerusalem in the land of their fathers. (D. & C. 77:15.)

On March 7, 1831, at Kirtland, Ohio, the Lord gave a revelation to the Prophet Joseph Smith, showing him things covering many generations:

And now ye behold this temple which is in Jerusalem, which ye call the house of God, and your enemies say that this house shall never fall.

But, verily I say unto you, that desolation shall come upon this generation as a thief in the night, and this people shall be destroyed and scattered among all nations.

And this temple which ye now see shall be thrown down that there shall not be left one stone upon another.

And it shall come to pass, that this generation of Jews shall not pass away until every desolation which I have told you concerning them shall come to pass.

Ye say that ye know that the end of the world cometh; ye say also that ye know that the heavens and the earth shall pass away;

And in this ye say truly, for so it is; but these things which I have told you shall not pass away until all shall be fulfilled.

And this I have told you concerning Jerusalem; and when that day shall come, shall a remnant be scattered among all nations;

But they shall be *gathered again;* but they shall remain until the times of the Gentiles be fulfilled. (D. & C. 45:18-25.)

Apostle Orson Hyde Dedicated the Holy Land for the Return of the Jews

With the restoration of the gospel to the gentiles in this dispensation, it was evident that the "times of the Gentiles" would soon be fulfilled. Therefore, the Prophet Joseph Smith and his counselors, as the presidency of the Church, sent Elder Orson Hyde, one of the Twelve Apostles of the Church on a mission to Jerusalem, there to dedicate the Holy Land for the ultimate return thereto of Judah's scattered remnants according to the predictions of ancient prophets, for the rebuilding of Jerusalem, for rearing there a temple to the Lord.

On Sunday morning, October 24, 1841, Apostle Orson Hyde went up on the Mount of Olives and there performed the ceremony of dedication which had been assigned him. We quote from Elder Hyde's dedicatory prayer:

O Thou! who art from everlasting to everlasting, eternally and unchangeably the same, even the God who rules in the heavens above, and controls the destinies of men on the earth, wilt Thou condescend, through Thine infinite goodness and royal favor, to listen to the prayer of Thy servant which he this day offers up unto Thee in the name of Thy holy child Jesus, upon this land where the Sun of Righteousness set in blood, and Thine Anointed One expired. . . .

Now, O Lord! Thy servant has been obedient to the heavenly vision which Thou gavest him in his native land; and under the shadow of Thine outstretched arm, he has safely arrived in this place to dedicate and consecrate this land for the gathering together of Judah's scattered remnants, according to the predictions of the holy prophets—for the building up of Jerusalem again after it has been trodden down by the Gentiles so long, and for rearing a temple in honor of Thy name. . . .

O Thou, who didst covenant with Abraham, Thy friend, and who didst renew that covenant with Isaac, and confirm the same unto Jacob with an oath, that Thou wouldst not only give them this land for an everlasting inheritance, but that Thou wouldst also remember their seed forever. Abraham, Isaac, and Jacob, have long since closed their eyes in death, and made the grave their resting-place. Their children are scattered and dispersed abroad among the nations of the Gentiles like sheep that have no shepherd, and are still looking forward for the fulfillment of those promises which Thou didst make concerning them; and even this land, which once poured forth nature's richest bounty, and flowed, as it were, with milk and honey, has, to a certain extent, been smitten with barrenness and sterility since it drank from murderous hands the blood of Him who never sinned.

Grant, therefore, O Lord, in the name of Thy well-beloved Son, Jesus Christ, to remove the barrenness and sterility of this land, and let springs of living water break forth to water its thirsty soil. Let the vine and the olive produce in their strength, and the fig tree bloom and flourish. Let the land become abundantly fruitful when possessed by its rightful heirs; let it again flow with plenty to feed the returning prodigals who come home with a spirit of grace and supplication; upon it let the clouds distil virtue and richness, and let the fields smile with plenty. Let the flocks and the herds greatly increase and multiply upon the mountains and the hills; and let Thy great kindness conquer and subdue the unbelief of Thy people. Do Thou take from them their stony heart, and give them a heart of flesh; and may the sun of Thy favor dispel the cold mists of darkness which have beclouded their atmosphere. Incline them to gather in upon this land according to Thy Word. Let them come like clouds and like doves to their windows. Let the large ships of the nations bring them from the distant isles; and let kings become their nursing fathers, and queens, with motherly fondness, wipe the tear of sorrow from their eye.

Thou, O Lord, didst once move the heart of Cyrus to show favor unto Jerusalem and her children. Do Thou now also be pleased to inspire the hearts of kings and the powers of the earth to look with friendly eye towards this place, and with a desire to see Thy righteous purposes executed in relation thereto. Let them know that it is Thy good pleasure to restore the kingdom unto Israel—raise up Jerusalem as its capitol, and constitute her people a distinct nation and government, with David Thy servant, even a descendant from the loins of ancient David, to be their king.

Let that nation or that people who shall take an active part in behalf of Abraham's children, and in the raising of Jerusalem, find favor in Thy sight. Let not their enemies prevail against them, neither let pestilence or famine overcome them, but let the glory of Israel overshadow them, and the power of the Highest protect them; while that nation or kingdom that will not serve Thee in this glorious work must perish, according to Thy word—"Yea, those nations shall be utterly wasted." (Joseph S. Hyde, compiler, *Orson Hyde Pamphlet*, pp. 26-28.)

Concerning his visit to Jerusalem, Elder Hyde reported:

I have found many Jews who listened with intense interest. The idea of the Jews being restored to Palestine is gaining ground in Europe almost every day. . . . Many of the Jews who are old go to this place to die, and many are coming from Europe into this Eastern world. The great wheel is unquestionably in motion and the word of the Almighty has declared that it shall roll. (Joseph S. Hyde, compiler, *Orson Hyde Pamphlet*, p. 29.)

Elder Hyde further stated:

In the early part of March last (1841), I retired to my bed one evening as usual, and while contemplating and enquiring out, in my own mind, the field of my ministerial labors for the then coming season, the vision of the Lord, like clouds of light, burst upon my view. The cities of London, Amsterdam, Constantinople, and Jerusalem all appeared in succession before me; and the Spirit said unto me, here are many of the children of Abraham whom I will gather to the land that I gave to their fathers, and here also is the field of your labors. . . . (Joseph S. Hyde, compiler, *Orson Hyde Pamphlet*, p. 5.)

The Spirit of Gathering Spreads Over the Earth

We call attention to the fact that because Moses brought the keys of the gathering of Israel back to earth, The Church of Jesus Christ of Latter-day Saints, as previously indicated, has builded over six hundred cities in the western part of the United States, in the process of gathering the seed of Israel from among the Gentile nations of the earth. These converts to the new faith have not been asked or persuaded to emigrate to America, but this unseen power rests upon them as they receive the gift of the Holy Ghost by the laying on of hands of those who have authority to bestow it. Of their own accord they desire to gather with the saints of the Lord in his latter-day Zion. Shortage of finance and immigration restrictions by the United States government seem to be the only things that hold them back. They are willing to forsake loved ones and friends and their business pursuits. No man could put such desires into their hearts—they must come from God.

Likewise, observe how the hearts of the children of Judah have turned to the land of their fathers. For a remarkable description of how the hearts of the children of Judah have turned to Palestine, their promised land, we refer the reader to the book *Behind the Silken Curtain*, by Bartley C. Crum, published by Simon and Schuster, Inc., 1947. Mr. Crum was appointed in December 1945 by President Harry S. Truman as a member of the Anglo-American Committee on Palestine, and in discharge of his assignment, along with other members of the committee, spent four months touring Europe and the Holy Land. The committee visited the camps of displaced persons, consisting principally of Jews, in the principal cities in Europe. In answer to questionnaires, they found that most of the remaining million Jews (six million having been killed by the Germans) were desirous of returning to Palestine. In one city, for instance, a poll of 18,311 displaced persons in the area was taken. Of the 18,311, thirteen said they wished to remain in Europe, 17,712 said they wished to go to Palestine. Some were asked to indicate their second choice if they could not go to Palestine and hundreds answered: "Crematorium."

They also visited with Dr. Chaim Weizmann, President of both the Jewish Agency for Palestine and the World Zionist Organization, at Jerusalem, and were told by him that it was their belief in a *"mystical force"* that would return the Jews to the land of Israel, that had kept them alive.

And this "mystical force" that has turned the hearts of the Jews of every country to the land of Israel, did not come from man, but after centuries of being "sifted among the nations," the Lord sent Moses back to this earth with the keys for the gathering of Israel, which keys Moses committed to Joseph Smith and Oliver Cowdery. Thus the spirit of gathering has been poured out upon the nations of Israel, making possible the fulfilment of the prediction of Isaiah which Moroni quoted to Joseph Smith:

> And he shall set up an ensign for the nations, and shall assemble the outcasts of Israel, and gather together the dis-

persed of Judah from the four corners of the earth. (Isa. 11:12.)

Does not all this justify the coming of the Prophet Moses as a part of the promised—

> ... restitution of all things, which God hath spoken by the mouth of all his holy prophets since the world began. (Acts 3:21.)

The Prophet Joseph Smith received these truths through the revelations of the Lord in this, the Dispensation of the Fulness of Times, and we take the Bible to show that it is all in accord therewith.

CHAPTER 16

ISRAEL IN THE LATTER DAYS

The Prophecies of Jeremiah Concerning the Gathering of Israel

Let us now consider what the Bible has to offer in confirmation of the truths revealed to and through the Prophet Joseph Smith bearing on the gathering of scattered Israel:

Therefore, behold, the days come, saith the Lord, that it shall no more be said, The Lord liveth, that brought up the children of Israel out of the land of Egypt;

But, The Lord liveth, that brought up the children of Israel from the land of the north, and from all the lands whither he had driven them: and I will bring them again into their land that I gave unto their fathers.

Behold, I will send for many fishers, saith the Lord, and they shall fish them; and after will I send for many hunters, and they shall hunt them from every mountain, and from every hill, and out of the holes of the rocks. (Jer. 16:14-16.)

Thus, we note that Jeremiah was privileged to see how complete the gathering of Israel should be to the lands the Lord had given "unto their fathers." We have already pointed out that America is the land of Joseph, or Ephraim, and that Judah is to be gathered again to the land of Palestine. This latter-day gathering, as seen by Jeremiah, was far to exceed in magnitude the leading of Israel out of the land of Egypt. This is very evident at this writing, and the end is not yet. The Lord was to send fishers and hunters to "hunt them from every mountain, and from every hill, and out of the holes in the rocks," showing how completely he would fulfil his promise, that after Israel should be sifted among the nations, "yet shall not the least grain fall upon the earth." (See Amos 9:8-9.)

Turn, O backsliding children, saith the Lord; for I am married unto you: and I will take you one of a city, and two of a family, and I will bring you to Zion:

And I will give you pastors according to mine heart, which shall feed you with knowledge and understanding. (Jer. 3:14-15.)

Israel to be Gathered in Small Numbers

From these prophecies it will be seen that Jeremiah realized that as Israel had been "sifted among the nations," the Lord would gather them, not in great multitudes, but "one of a city and two of a family," and that when he would bring them to Zion, he would give them "pastors according to mine heart, which shall feed you with knowledge and understanding." In other words, he would lead them to Zion where he had established his Church and kingdom, and restored his priesthood, so that they could be fed "with knowledge and understanding."

And now therefore thus saith the Lord, the God of Israel, concerning this city, whereof ye say, It shall be delivered into the hand of the king of Babylon by the sword, and by the famine, and by the pestilence;

Behold, *I will gather them out of all countries,* whither I have driven them in mine anger, and in my fury, and in great wrath; and I will bring them again unto this place, and I will cause them to dwell safely:

And they shall be my people, and I will be their God: . . .

For thus saith the Lord; Like as I have brought all this great evil upon this people, *so will I bring upon them all the good that I have promised them.*

And fields shall be bought in this land, whereof ye say, It is desolate without man or beast; it is given into the hand of the Chaldeans.

Men shall buy fields for money, and subscribe evidences, and seal them, and take witnesses in the land of Benjamin, and in the places about Jerusalem, and in the cities of Judah, and in the cities of the mountains, and in the cities of the south: *for I will cause their captivity to return, saith the Lord.* (Jer. 32:36-38, 42-44.)

Again, Jeremiah, about 640 B.C. was given to see, and make prophetic announcement of, the very things we are privileged to behold as a part of the great gospel Dispensation of the Fulness of Times, as it was committed to the earth by the God of Israel and his holy prophets.

Judah to be Gathered to Jerusalem

Jerusalem was to be taken from the Jews and they were to be scattered among all nations, and then they were to be regathered: "Behold, I will gather them out of all countries. . . . and I will bring them again unto this place, and I will cause them to dwell safely." The Lord added: "So will I bring upon them all the good that I have promised them."

Note further: "And fields shall be bought in this land, whereof ye say, It is desolate without man or beast." It was a land of desolation when Apostle Orson Hyde went there in 1841 and dedicated the land for the gathering of the Jews. We now know that the Jews are returning with their wealth from all nations to purchase fields and the land as Jeremiah saw so many centuries ago.

Ephraim to be Gathered to the Land of America

We have considered the prophecies of Jeremiah with respect to the gathering of the Jews to the land of their inheritance in Palestine. Let us now consider what he saw and foretold concerning the gathering of the seed of Joseph or Ephraim, who were given the land of America for their inheritance:

> For there shall be a day, that the watchmen upon the mount Ephraim shall cry, Arise ye and let us go up to Zion unto the Lord our God.
>
> For thus saith the Lord; Sing with gladness for Jacob, and shout among the chief of the nations: publish ye, praise ye, and say, O Lord, save thy people, the remnant of Israel.
>
> Behold, I will bring them from the north country, and gather them from the coasts of the earth, and with them the blind and the lame, the woman with child and her that travaileth with child together: a great company shall *return thither*.
>
> They shall come with weeping, and with supplications will I lead them: I will cause them to walk by the rivers of waters in a straight way, wherein they shall not stumble: for I am a father to Israel, and Ephraim is my firstborn.
>
> Hear the word of the Lord, O ye nations, and declare it in the isles afar off, and say, He that scattered Israel will gather him and keep him, as a shepherd doth his flock.
>
> For the Lord hath redeemed Jacob, and ransomed him from the hand of him that was stronger than he.
>
> Therefore they shall come and sing in the height of Zion, and shall flow together to the goodness of the Lord, for wheat, and for wine, and for oil, and for the young of the flock and of the herd: and their soul shall be as a watered garden; and they shall not sorrow any more at all.
>
> Then shall the virgin rejoice in the dance, both young men and old together: for I will turn their mourning into joy, and will comfort them, and make them rejoice from their sorrow.
>
> And I will satiate the soul of the priests with fatness, and my people shall be satisfied with my goodness, saith the Lord. (Jer. 31:6-14.)

Properly understood, the Prophet Jeremiah, here wrote a portion of the history of The Church of Jesus Christ of Latter-day Saints, approximately 2500 years before it occurred, and while but briefly stated, it is very accurate.

This was a cry from "the watchmen upon mount Ephraim. . . . Arise ye and let us go up to Zion unto the Lord our God." This has nothing to do with Judah as the prophet further indicated: "For I am a father to Israel, and Ephraim is my firstborn."

In chapter seven we pointed out that the birthright was taken from Reuben, the firstborn of the twelve sons of Israel, and was given to Joseph and then passed from Joseph to his son Ephraim. (See I Chron. 5:1-2.) Therefore, this was to be a gathering of the descendants of Joseph and Ephraim, "to Zion unto the Lord our God."

"Sing with gladness for Jacob." Why? Because the day of his redemption was nigh.

"Shout among the chief of the nations." The Elders of this Church had been (1846) sent to Great Britain, the Scandinavian countries, Germany, etc., the chief nations, and had gathered in many converts to Nauvoo, Illinois.

"I will bring them . . . a great company shall return *thither*." This was something the Lord was going to do. Note that Jeremiah does not say that they will return *hither* or to the place where this prediction was made, but *thither*, or to a distant place. He understood that Joseph was to be given a new land in the "utmost bounds of the everlasting hills." (See Gen. 49:22-26; Deut. 33:13-17.)

Latter-day Saints Fulfill Jeremiah's Prophecy

A "great company" was to "return thither," and with them "the blind and the lame, the woman with child and her that travaileth with child together," and "they shall come with weeping, and with supplications will I lead them." About twenty thousand Latter-day Saints were driven out of Nauvoo, and with them "the blind and the lame, the woman with child." They did not leave their beautiful homes because they wanted to, hence they came "weeping" and with "supplications" unto the Lord, and healed them as he had promised.

"I will cause them to walk by the rivers of waters in a straight way, wherein they shall not stumble." In their trek from Nauvoo across the great American desert to the great Salt Lake Valley, the saints traveled about six hundred miles along the North Platte River, as Jeremiah had seen.

"Therefore they shall come and sing in the height of Zion." At this writing (1972) the Tabernacle Choir, consisting of approximately 375 unpaid voices broadcasts weekly "from the crossroads of the west," and they are in their 44th year of a weekly nation-wide broadcast. This represents but a small part of the singing that is done "from the height of Zion."

"And shall flow together to the goodness of the Lord, for wheat, and for oil, and for wine, and for the young of the flock and of the herd." Compare this promise with the blessing pronounced upon the head of Joseph by Moses, when he referred to the land of Joseph:

> And of Joseph he said, *Blessed of the Lord be his land,* for the precious things of heaven, for the dew, and for the deep that coucheth beneath.
>
> And for the precious fruits brought forth by the sun, and for the precious things put forth by the moon,
>
> And for the chief things of the ancient mountains, and for the precious things of the lasting hills,
>
> And for the precious things of the earth and fulness thereof . . . (Deut. 33:13-16; See also the blessing of Jacob unto his son Joseph: Gen. 49:22-26.)

It is easy to believe that Joseph's land was to be "choice above all other lands," as the Book of Mormon indicates, when one notes how many times Moses uses the word "precious" in describing the land and its blessings. One will find these predictions in actual fulfilment as he travels among the Saints in the valleys of the Rocky Mountains.

Continuing our analysis of the prophecy of Jeremiah: "And they shall not sorrow any more at all. Then shall the virgin rejoice in the dance, both young men and old together: for I will turn their mourning into joy, and will comfort them, and make them rejoice from their sorrow." To understand how completely this has been fulfilled, one needed but to attend the testimony meetings of the Saints, after their arrival in the valleys of the Rocky Mountains, and there hear them express their gratitude to the Lord for having brought them here. And then attend their dances and see how the young and the old "rejoice in the dance." Practically every ward or branch or congregation of Latter-day Saints have, adjoining their chapel, a recreation hall where the young and the old do rejoice together in the dance, and where other activities are carried on for their enjoyment. Surely the Lord has turned "their mourning into joy," and has comforted them and made "them to rejoice from their sorrow."

"And I will satiate the soul of the priests with fatness, and my people shall be satisfied with my goodness." While the members of the priesthood in The Church of Jesus Christ of Latter-day Saints are not paid for their services, and thousands of them have left their families for years at a time to do missionary work in the nations of the earth, paying their own expenses and without remuneration from the Church, yet, in their hearts, they are the best paid of any priests in the world, because of the joy and satisfaction the Lord plants in their hearts, which could not possibly be purchased with money. Thus he has satiated "the soul of the priests with fatness," and his people are satisfied with his goodness.

Where else in all the world, and in all the annals of

history can you find a fulfilment of this prophecy of Jeremiah? He may have seen more when his prophecy was uttered than has already been fulfilled, but one could scarcely hope to find a more literal fulfilment than in the gathering of the Latter-day Saints to the valleys of the mountains in these latter-days.

The Prophecies of Isaiah Concerning Latter-day Israel

Let us now consider the prophecies of Isaiah with respect to the latter-day gathering of Israel. We have already referred to the visit of the Angel Moroni to Joseph Smith, when he quoted the eleventh chapter of Isaiah, saying that it was about to be fulfilled:

And in that day there shall be a root of Jesse, which shall stand for an ensign of the people; to it shall the Gentiles seek . . .

And it shall come to pass in that day, that the Lord shall set his hand again the second time to recover the remnant of his people . . .

And he shall set up an ensign for the nations, and shall assemble the outcasts of Israel, and gather together the dispersed of Judah from the four corners of the earth. (Isa. 11:10-12.)

From the reading of this scripture, it is plain that Isaiah had in mind the gathering of the seed of Joseph that had been scattered among the Gentile nations, as well as the gathering of the "dispersed of Judah." And what the Lord would do in this respect would "stand for an ensign of the people":

And it shall come to pass in the last days, that the mountain of the Lord's house shall be established in the top of the mountains, and shall be exalted above the hills; and all nations shall flow unto it.

And many people shall go and say, Come ye, and let us go up to the mountain of the Lord, to the house of the God of

Jacob; and he will teach us of his ways and we will walk in his paths for out of Zion shall go forth the law, and the word of the Lord from Jerusalem. (Isa. 2:2-3.)

The Lord's House Established in the Top of the Mountains

Only those who are associated with the Church in this dispensation can understand how literally this prophecy has been fulfilled. That the saints might enjoy the privileges of the sealing ordinances performed in the "house of the God of Jacob," they have gathered from the nations of the earth where the missionaries have carried the message of the revealed gospel of the Lord Jesus Christ. The law of the Lord is going forth out of Zion, as will ultimately the "word of the Lord from Jerusalem."

This establishment of the "Lord's house" in the "top of the mountains," and the gathering of all nations unto it would precede the judgments of the Lord which would be followed by a day when, "nation shall not lift up sword against nation, neither shall they learn war any more." (See Isa. 2:4.) With the close of World War II we are all hopeful that we are approaching the day when the condition Isaiah foretold may be anticipated. At least we know that it has not yet been fulfilled.

Coming of the Railroad and Airplane Speeds the Gathering of Israel

In fixing this time in our day, Isaiah seemed to indicate that the gathering should take place in the day of the railroad, train, and the airplane:

> And he will lift up an ensign to the nations from far, and will hiss unto them from the end of the earth: and, behold, they shall come with speed swiftly:

> None shall be weary nor stumble among them; none shall slumber nor sleep; neither shall the girdle of their loins be loosed, nor the latchet of their shoes be broken:

Whose arrows are sharp, and all their bows bent, their horses' hoofs shall be counted like flint, and their wheels like a whirlwind:

Their roaring shall be like a lion, and they shall roar like young lions: yea, they shall roar, and lay hold of the prey, and shall carry it away safe, and none shall deliver it. (Isa. 5:26-29.)

Since there were no such things as trains and airplanes in that day, Isaiah could hardly have mentioned them by name, but he seems to have described them in unmistakable words. How better could "their horses' hoofs be counted like flint, and their wheel like a whirlwind" than in the modern train? How better could "Their roaring . . . be like a lion" than in the roar of the airplane? Trains and airplanes do not stop for night. Therefore, was not Isaiah justified in saying: "none shall slumber nor sleep; neither shall the girdle of their loins be loosed, nor the latchet of their shoes be broken"? With this manner of transportation the Lord can really "hiss unto them from the end of the earth," that "they shall come with speed swiftly."

Isaiah also understood that this gathering would be to the mountains, and that the Lord would cause the desert to rejoice and blossom as the rose. In this respect, it is remarkable what part "water" was to play in redeeming the desert and the wilderness as the gathering place of latter-day Israel, as the prophets described it:

The wilderness and the solitary place shall be glad for them; and the *desert shall rejoice, and blossom as the rose.*

It shall blossom abundantly, and rejoice even with joy and singing: the glory of Lebanon shall be given unto it, the excellency of Carmel and Sharon, they shall see the glory of the Lord, and the excellency of our God. . . .

Then the eyes of the blind shall be opened, and the ears of the deaf shall be unstopped.

Then shall the lame man leap as an hart, and the tongue of the dumb sing: *for in the wilderness shall waters break out, and streams in the desert.*

And the parched ground shall *become a pool,* and the thirsty land *springs of water:* in the habitation of dragons, where each lay, shall be grass with reeds and rushes. . . .

And the ransomed of the Lord shall return, and *come to Zion* with *songs and everlasting joy upon their heads:* they shall obtain joy and gladness, and sorrow and sighing shall flee away. (Isa. 35:1-2, 5-7, 10.)

This has, in part at least, been fulfilled. The desert has been made to "rejoice and blossom as the rose." Waters have broken out "in the wilderness," (flowing wells) "and streams in the desert," (irrigation canals) "and the ransomed of the Lord" have returned, "and come to Zion with songs and everlasting joy upon their heads."

Following is one of the songs they sing as they leave their native lands, and anyone who has witnessed their departure will realize what Isaiah meant when he said: "they shall obtain joy and gladness, and sorrow and sighing shall flee away":

COME GO WITH ME

Come go with me beyond the sea, where happiness is true,
Where Joseph's land blest, by God's hand, inviting waits for you.
With joyful hearts you'll understand the blessings that await you
  there.
I know it is the promised land, my home, my home is there.
There, on those everlasting hills, and in the valleys fair,
Beside the gurgling fountain rills, we'll bow in humble prayer,
And praise our God in joyful strains, that we are safely gathered
  there.
I know it is the promised land, my home, my home is there.
There Israel's sons, so long oppressed, are pure, free, happy, too;
And daughters, in true virtue dressed, do wait to welcome you,
To greet you with a kindred hand, and with you every good to
  share.
I know it is the promised land, my home, my home is there.

There, too, are Prophets, Priests and Seers who have the Holy
 Priesthood's powers,
To guide our souls through endless years, and light our darkest
 hours;
Yea, truth, which lighted Enoch's band, is freely to them given
 there.
I know it is the promised land, my home, my home is there.
—C. H. Wheelock.

Isaiah continued his description of the gathering of
Israel and reclaiming of the wilderness:

Fear not: for I am with thee: I will bring thy seed from the
east, and gather thee from the west;

I will say to the north, Give up; and to the south, Keep not
back: bring my sons from far, and my daughters from the ends
of the earth;

Even every one that is called by my name: for I have created
him for my glory, I have formed him; yea, I have made
him. . . .

Behold, *I will do a new thing;* now it shall spring forth; shall
ye not know it? I will even *make a way in the wilderness,* and
rivers in the desert.

The beast of the field shall honour me, the dragons and the
owls; because *I give waters in the wilderness, and rivers in the
desert,* to give *drink to my people, my chosen.*

This people have I formed for myself; they shall shew forth
my praise. (Isa. 43:5-7, 19-21.)

Does Introduction of Irrigation Fulfil Prophecy?

"Behold, *I will do a new thing.*" What is this new
thing the Lord speaks of through the mouth of Isaiah?
Could one of the new things not be the great system of
"irrigation," which the Lord inspired his servants to teach
unto his people when they entered the valleys of the
mountains, that made possible the fulfilment of his promises: To cause the desert to "rejoice, and blossom as the
rose," "make a way in the wilderness, and rivers in the
desert?" The great irrigation canals are larger than many
rivers as they flow through the desert, bringing thousands

and tens of thousands of acres of otherwise arid land, under cultivation.

Even the beasts of the field—and the dragons and the owls shall honor him, "because I give waters in the wilderness, and rivers in the desert, to give drink to my people, my chosen." Thus, when the Lord would do this new thing, it would be for his people, his chosen, for said he, "This people have I formed for myself; they shall shew forth my praise." What the Lord has thus done, in this "new thing" has blessed his "people," his "chosen" with such a measure of prosperity, that they have been able to send most of their old and young men on missions to the peoples of all nations, bearing witness of the restoration of the gospel in this dispensation. No doubt this is what the Lord had in mind for them to do, when he said, "This people have I formed for myself; *they shall shew forth my praise."* They become the "fishers" and "hunters" mentioned by Jeremiah, whom the Lord said he would send out to hunt Israel "from every mountain, and from every hill, and out of the holes of the rocks." (See Jer. 16:14-16.)

The Prophet Isaiah continued:

I will open *rivers* in high places, and *fountains* in the midst of the valleys: I will make the *wilderness a pool of water,* and the dry land *springs of water.*

I will plant in the wilderness the cedar, the shittah tree and the myrtle, and the oil tree; I will set in the desert the fir tree, and the pine, and the box tree together:

That they may see, and know, and consider, and understand together, that the hand of the Lord hath done this, and the Holy One of Israel hath created it. (Isa. 41:18-20.)

"I will open rivers in high places." This could have reference to the reservoirs built in the canyons to impound the winter run-off of water, so it can be used for summer irrigation.

"And fountains in the midst of the valleys." If you have seen some of the flowing wells that have been drilled in some of the dry valleys, you can understand this part of the prophecy. All these fulfilments of prophecy have so changed the wilderness, that it has been possible to plant the various types of trees that otherwise would not grow.

"That they may see, and know, and consider, and understand together, that the hand of the Lord hath done this, and the Holy One of Israel hath created it." All this, therefore, may be regarded as the work of the Holy One of Israel, for the benefit of gathered Israel in the latter-days.

The Desert Made to Blossom as the Rose

The Lord must have had a great deal to do with the development of this western empire, for when Brigham Young and the pioneers were enroute to the Salt Lake Valley, they met Jim Bridger, an early western trapper, who said: "Mr. Young, I would give a thousand dollars if I knew an ear of corn could be ripened in the Great Basin." (*See Discourses of Brigham Young,* p. 481.)

As late as 1843, three years before the exodus, the opinion held by the majority in the United States was that the whole territory of the Rocky Mountains was not worth a "pinch of snuff." Such was the expression made by Senator George H. McDuffie, of South Carolina, in the Senate that year. Discussing the settlement of Oregon, he said:

> Who are to go there, along the line of military posts, and take possession of the only part of the territory fit to occupy—that part upon the seacoast, a strip less than one hundred miles in width. Why, sir, of what use will this be for agricultural purposes? I would not for that purpose give a pinch of snuff for the whole territory. I wish to God we did not own it. (*Congressional Globe,* 27th Congress, 3rd Session, pp. 198-201.)

About the time Senator McDuffie made this statement, the Prophet Joseph Smith made the following statement:

> I prophesied that the Saints would continue to suffer much affliction, and would be driven to the Rocky Mountains, many would apostatize, others would be put to death by our persecutors or lose their lives in consequence of exposure or disease, and some of you will live to go and assist in making settlements and build cities, and see the Saints become a mighty people in the midst of the Rocky Mountains. (D.H.C., Vol. 5, p. 85.)

Since the Lord could make such a worthless land as described by Senator McDuffie to "blossom as a rose," and see the saints "become a mighty people in the midst of the Rocky Mountains," surely these are even greater accomplishments than when the Lord parted the Red Sea and led Israel of old through on dry land.

In light of these Biblical prophecies, it seems perfectly logical that in the "restitution of all things," (See Acts 3:21) Moses should be sent by the Father to restore the keys of the gathering of Israel, for surely this, in and of itself, constitutes a marvelous work and a wonder.

We therefore ask: Why did the prophets make such predictions, if we are not to look for their fulfilment? Have they been fulfilled? If so, when, and where, and by what people, if not by The Church of Jesus Christ of Latter-day Saints? We should remember the words of Peter:

> We have also a more sure word of prophecy; whereunto ye do well that ye take heed, as unto a light that shineth in a dark place, until the day dawn, and the day star arise in your hearts:
>
> Knowing this first, that no prophecy of the scripture is of any private interpretation.
>
> For the prophecy came not in old time by the will of man:

but holy men of God spake as they were moved by the Holy Ghost. (II Pet. 1:19-21.)

It thus becomes our privilege and responsibility to announce to the honest seeker after truth that many of these prophecies have been fulfilled and others are in the course of fulfilment, as a part of the great latter-day gospel dispensation.

The Book of Mormon prophets understood the value of the prophecies of Isaiah, and that it would be given to the Lord's people to understand them in the day that they would be fulfilled:

For the eternal purposes of the Lord shall roll on, until all his promises shall be fulfilled.

Search the prophecies of Isaiah. . . . (Mormon 8:22-23.)

But behold, I proceed with mine own prophecy, according to my plainness; in the which I know that no man can err; nevertheless, *in the days that the prophecies of Isaiah shall be fulfilled men shall know of a surety, at the times when they shall come to pass.*

Wherefore, they are of worth unto the children of men, and he that supposeth that they are not, unto them will I speak particularly; and confine the words unto mine own people; *for I know that they shall be of great worth unto them in the last days; for in that day shall they understand them;* wherefore, for their good have I written them. (II Nephi 25:7-8.)

Again, all this the Prophet Joseph Smith received through the revelations of the Lord to him, and from the Prophet Moses who was sent to him with the keys of this great gathering dispensation. We take the Bible to prove that the truths thus revealed are in accord therewith.

According to the statement of the commentator to which we referred in the first chapter, The Church of Jesus Christ of Latter-day Saints, in announcing the return of Moses with a message from God, has the greatest message that could possibly be broadcast to the world.

CHAPTER 17

THE COMING OF ELIAS

We have referred to the occasion when Joseph Smith and Oliver Cowdery were visited by the Prophets Moses and Elijah in the Kirtland Temple, April 3, 1836. Of the events following the visit of Moses, the Prophet Joseph Smith wrote:

> After this, Elias appeared, and committed the dispensation of the gospel of Abraham, saying that in us and our seed all generations after us should be blessed. (D. & C. 110:12.)

Because of Abraham's faithfulness, the Lord bestowed upon him a great blessing and chose him as his representative in the earth. The covenant being that all who received the Gospel from that time henceforth should be named his "seed," whether they were his literal children or accepted the truth and were numbered as his children by adoption. That covenant is given more clearly in the Book of Abraham in The Pearl of Great Price than it is in Genesis:

> My name is Jehovah, and I know the end from the beginning; therefore my hand shall be over thee.
>
> And I will make of thee a great nation, and I will bless thee above measure, and make thy name great among all nations, and thou shalt be a blessing unto thy seed after thee, that in their hands they shall bear this ministry and Priesthood unto all nations;
>
> And I will bless them through thy name, for as many as receive this Gospel shall be called after thy name, and shall be accounted thy seed, and shall rise up and bless thee, as their father;
>
> And I will bless them that bless thee, and curse them that curse thee; and in thee (that is, in thy Priesthood) and in thy seed (that is, thy Priesthood), for I give unto thee a promise that this right shall continue in thee, and in thy seed after thee (that is to

say, the literal seed, or the seed of the body) shall all the families of the earth be blessed, even with the blessings of the Gospel, which are the blessings of salvation, even of eternal life. (Abraham 2:8-11.)

The commitment of "the dispensation of the Gospel of Abraham" by the Prophet Elias was therefore of great significance, that the promises of Jehovah unto the seed of Abraham, and to those who should be numbered as his children by adoption through their having accepted the gospel, might be fully realized.

Elias and the Spirit of Elias

Because of what Jesus said concerning John the Baptist, when he sent two of his disciples to inquire of Christ: "Art thou he that should come, or do we look for another?" (Matt. 11:3) some have taught that John and Elias were one and the same person. Let us consider the statement of Jesus in regard to this matter:

But what went ye out for to see? A prophet? yea, I say unto you, and more than a prophet.

For this is he, of whom it is written, Behold, I send my messenger before thy face, which shall prepare thy way before thee . . .

And if ye will receive it, this is Elias, which was for to come. (Matt. 11:9-10, 14.)

The Lord gave the Prophet Joseph Smith to understand this matter when he explained that one who is sent to prepare the way is "an Elias," not the Prophet Elias, but a preparer of the way. Thus in that sense, John the Baptist was an Elias, or a preparer of the way; the one who was sent to "Prepare ye the way of the Lord." (Isa. 40:3.)

This explanation is in full accord with the statement of the angel to Zacharias when he was promised that his wife, Elisabeth, should bear him a son, whose name should be called John:

And thou shalt have joy and gladness; and many shall rejoice at his birth. . .

And many of the children of Israel shall he turn to the Lord their God.

And he shall go before him *in the spirit and power of Elias*, to turn the hearts of the fathers to the children, and the disobedient to the wisdom of the just; to make ready a people prepared for the Lord. (Luke 1:14, 16-17.)

Thus the angel of the Lord indicated that John would go before the Lord "in the spirit and power of Elias," and this he did, but not as the Prophet Elias who appeared with Moses and Elijah to Joseph Smith and Oliver Cowdery in the Kirtland Temple April 3, 1836. This is further attested in the fact that John had previously visited Joseph Smith and Oliver Cowdery May 15, 1829, and ordained them to the Aaronic Priesthood.

In August 1830, nearly six years before the visit of Elias in the Kirtland Temple, the Lord, in a revelation to the Prophet Joseph Smith, made reference to the importance of the keys held by Elias:

Behold, this is wisdom in me, wherefore, marvel not, for the hour cometh that I will drink of the fruit of the vine with you on the earth, and with Moroni, whom I have sent unto you to reveal the Book of Mormon, containing the fulness of my everlasting gospel, to whom I have committed the keys of the record of the stick of Ephraim;

And also with Elias, to whom I have committed the keys of bringing to pass the restoration of all things spoken by the mouth of all the holy prophets since the world began, concerning the last days;

And also John the son of Zacharias, which Zacharias he (Elias) visited and gave promise that he should have a son, and his name should be John, and he should be filled with the spirit of Elias. (D. & C. 27:5-7.)

Elijah, Elias, and John, Three Persons

To many, Elijah, Elias and John the Baptist are one and the same person. From the revelations of the Lord to the Prophet Joseph Smith, and the personal appearance of these three great prophets to Joseph Smith and Oliver Cowdery, all uncertainty and lack of understanding have been removed, for now we know that each was a separate and distinct personage, a prophet of the Lord.

This information, therefore, was not obtained from the reading of the Bible alone, but through the visits of these three prophets to this earth in this "the Dispensation of the Fulness of Times." This was another step in the fulfillment of the words of the Apostle Peter that heaven must receive the Christ "until the times of restitution of all things, which God hath spoken by the mouth of all his holy prophets since the world began." (Acts 3:19-21.)

Chapter 18

THE TRUE CHURCH, A MISSIONARY CHURCH

The claims of The Church of Jesus Christ of Latter-day Saints are of such a nature that the things the Lord himself has revealed from heaven, and through ancient prophets who have visited this earth and committed the keys of their dispensations to the Prophet Joseph Smith, must be proclaimed to the world. Else how can the world know of these things? How can scattered Israel be gathered to the lands of their inheritance? How can the gospel be preached in all the world for a witness unto all nations before the end shall come?

> How then shall they call on him in whom they have not believed? and how shall they believe in him of whom they have not heard? and how shall they hear without a preacher?
>
> And how shall they preach, except they be sent? as it is written, How beautiful are the feet of them that preach the gospel of peace, and bring glad tidings of good things! (Rom. 10:14-15.)

It is evident that Paul understood the Lord would send "preachers" or missionaries, to teach the people of the world the things He would have them know. Paul also understood that these preachers could not appoint themselves, for he said, "And how shall they preach, except they be sent?"

The magnitude of this responsibility might well be understood by referring again to the vision John the Revelator saw concerning the restoration of the gospel in these latter-days:

> After this I looked, and, behold, a door was opened in heaven: and the first voice which I heard was as it were of a trumpet talking with me; which said, Come up hither, and I will shew thee things which must be *hereafter.* (Rev. 4:1.)

> And I saw another angel fly in the midst of heaven, having the everlasting gospel to preach unto them that dwell on the earth, and to every nation, and kindred, and tongue, and people. (Rev. 14:6.)

When John was shown the "things which must be hereafter," he saw that "the everlasting gospel," (and there can be no other gospel) which should be brought to this earth by an angel flying in the midst of heaven should be preached "unto them that dwell on the earth, and to every nation, and kindred and tongue, and people." Thus, none of the inhabitants of the earth are overlooked or omitted. What a tremendous responsibility and assignment! But, when the Lord has a work to do, he always makes provision for it to be done. He made such provision in the restoration of the gospel in this, the Dispensation of the Fulness of Times, through the Prophet Joseph Smith.

The great missionary work of this Church has gone forward, in many cases by great sacrifice. Men have left their wives and children at home while they have spent an average of more than two years in the mission field, either in the United States or to the nations of the earth and the islands of the sea. Many men have filled three, four or more missions. Some have remained as long as ten years in the mission field at a time— all at their own expense, with such assistance as the people among whom they have labored have been willing to render in the matter of food and lodging but not by the payment of money. Many wives have worked to earn money to be able to support their husbands while in the mission field. Many young men have left their new brides at home to answer the call of the Lord to fill a mission.

Missionaries do not select the mission to which they shall be sent, but go where they are asked to go. Thus approximately 200,000 missionaries have rendered such service to the Lord, his Church, and their fellow men. At the present time (1972) there are over 17,000 missionaries in the mission fields of the Church. Many of these young men have served years in the armed forces of their country. But they have looked forward from their boyhood days to the time when they could fill a mission for their Church. Therefore, when the opportunity has presented itself, even though they have been away from home and loved ones already for years, they are willing and happy to go again in order to answer this call from the Lord. It is the universal testimony of these missionaries, upon their return to their loved ones, that the time they have spent in the mission field, bearing witness of the restoration of the gospel in these latter-days and the truth of the Book of Mormon and the divine calling of the Prophet Joseph Smith, has been the happiest time of their lives.

We learned recently of a young man who made provision, when entering active military service of his country, that should he not be privileged to return to his loved ones and his Church, so that he could fill a mission, that his savings sent home to his parents should be used to send some other young man in his stead, who otherwise might not be financially able. Since he did not return, one has been sent as requested.

When one is converted to the truth through the work of a missionary, he, in turn, wants to fill a mission to repay, in a measure, for the new joy that comes to him through conversion to the truth. Thus, there are but few homes of the members of this Church that have not contributed to the great missionary cause of the Church, and many homes have to their credit the fact that the father and all his sons, and often his daughters, have filled missions for the Church. Only recently the author learned of two families who are maintaining four sons each in the mission field at the same time.

The Voice of Warning Unto All People

On November 1, 1831, the Lord gave a special revelation to the Prophet Joseph Smith which he, himself, called: "My preface unto the book of my commandments,":

Hearken, O ye people of my church, saith the voice of him who dwells on high, and whose eyes are upon all men; yea, verily I say: Hearken ye people from afar; and ye that are upon the islands of the sea, listen together.

For verily the voice of the Lord is unto *all men,* and there is none to escape; and there is no eye that shall not see, neither ear that shall not hear, neither heart that shall not be penetrated. . . .

And the voice of warning shall be unto all people, by the mouths of my disciples, whom I have chosen in these last days.

And they shall go forth and none shall stay them, for I the Lord have commanded them. . . .

And verily I say unto you, that they who go forth, bearing these tidings unto the inhabitants of the earth, to them is power given to seal both on earth and in heaven, the unbelieving and rebellious;

Yea, verily, to seal them up unto the day when the wrath of God shall be poured out upon the wicked without measure—

Unto the day when the Lord shall come to recompense unto every man according to his work, and measure to every man according to the measure which he has measured to his fellow man.

Wherefore the voice of the Lord is unto the ends of the earth, that all that will hear may hear:

Prepare ye, prepare ye for that which is to come, for the Lord is nigh;

And the anger of the Lord is kindled, and his sword is bathed in heaven, and it shall fall upon the inhabitants of the earth.

And the arm of the Lord shall be revealed; and the day cometh that they who will not hear the voice of the Lord, neither the voice of his servants, neither give heed to the words of the prophets and apostles, shall be cut off from among the people; . . .

That the fulness of my gospel might be proclaimed by the weak and the simple unto the ends of the world, and before kings and rulers. (D. & C. 1:1-2, 4-5, 8-14, 23.)

It will thus be seen that, with the restoration of the gospel and the establishment of his Church in this dispensation, the Lord makes it plain that the gospel is to be carried to the entire world, including the islands of the sea, that "the voice of the Lord is unto all men, and there is none to escape"; that his servants, even though they be sent forth in their weakness, should be given power, "to seal both on earth and in heaven"; that they are to be sent to "Prepare ye, prepare ye for that which is to come, for the Lord is nigh." We are privileged therefore, to live in the day of the preparation of the kingdom for the advent of the King.

In February, 1829, before the Church was organized, in a revelation to the Prophet Joseph Smith, the Lord told him of the marvelous work that was about to come forth and the preparation it would be necessary for his servants to make in order to qualify them for the work:

Now behold, a marvelous work is about to come forth among the children of men.

Therefore, O ye that embark in the service of God, see that ye serve him with all your heart, might, mind and strength, that ye may stand blameless before God at the last day.

Therefore, if ye have desires to serve God ye are called to the work;

For behold the field is white already to harvest; and lo, he that thrusteth in his sickle with his might, the same layeth up in store that he perisheth not, but bringeth salvation to his soul;

And faith, hope, charity and love, with an eye single to the glory of God, qualify him for the work.

Remember faith, virtue, knowledge, temperance, patience, brotherly kindness, godliness, charity, humility, diligence.

Ask, and ye shall receive, knock and it shall be opened unto you. Amen. (D. & C. Sec. 4.)

In another revelation in 1829 the Lord said:

Wherefore, you are called to cry repentance unto this people.

And if it so be that you should labor all your days in crying repentance unto this people, and bring, save it be one soul unto me, how great shall be your joy with him in the kingdom of my Father!

And now, if your joy will be great with one soul that you have brought unto me into the kingdom of my Father, how great will be your joy if you should bring many souls unto me! (D. & C. 18:14-16.)

On February 9, 1831, the Lord gave a revelation to some of the elders of the Church, through the Prophet Joseph Smith, dealing with missionary work:

Hearken, O ye elders of my church, who have assembled yourselves together in my name, even Jesus Christ the Son of the living God, the Savior of the world; inasmuch as ye believe on my name and keep my commandments.

Again I say unto you, hearken and hear and obey the law which I shall give unto you.

For verily I say, as ye have assembled yourselves together according to the commandment wherewith I commanded you, and are agreed as touching this one thing, and have asked the Father in my name, even so ye shall receive.

Behold, verily I say unto you, I give unto you this first commandment, that ye shall go forth in my name, every one of you, excepting my servants Joseph Smith, Jun., and Sidney Rigdon. . . .

And ye shall go forth in the power of my Spirit, preaching my gospel, two by two, in my name, lifting up your voices as with the sound of a trump, declaring my word like unto angels of God.

And ye shall go forth baptizing with water, saying: Repent ye, repent ye, for the kingdom of heaven is at hand. (D. & C. 42:1-4, 6-7.)

From that time to the present, the elders of the Church have been going "two by two," as the Lord commanded. He further made it plain in this same revelation, that no one shall go forth to preach his gospel unless he be ordained:

Again, I say unto you, that it shall not be given to any one to go forth to preach my gospel, or to build up my church, except he be ordained by some one who has authority, and it is known to the church that he has authority and has been regularly ordained by the heads of the church. (D. & C. 42:11.)

The Lord instructed every man who is warned to warn his neighbor:

Behold, I sent you out to testify and warn the people, and it becometh every man who hath been warned to warn his neighbor.

Therefore, they are left without excuse, and their sins are upon their own heads. (D. & C. 88:81-82.)

The Lord gave many other instructions and directions to the elders of his Church with respect to the great responsibility resting upon them in carrying the gospel message to all the inhabitants of the earth, most of which are contained in the Doctrine and Covenants. They are too numerous to refer to further in this discussion.

The Prophet Nephi, who lived on the American continent about 600 years B. C., was privileged to see our day and the coming forth of the record of his people (The Book of Mormon) unto the gentiles in the latter-days:

And blessed are they who shall seek to bring forth my Zion at that day, for they shall have the gift and the power of the Holy Ghost; and if they endure unto the end they shall be lifted up at the last day, and shall be saved in the everlasting kingdom of the Lamb; and whoso shall publish peace, yea, tidings of great joy, how beautiful upon the mountains shall they be. (I Nephi 13:37.)

No other Church, except the Church which Jesus established in the Meridian of Time, has ever undertaken such a responsibility of missionary work, carrying the gospel of Jesus Christ to "every nation, kindred, tongue and people" as has The Church of Jesus Christ of Latter-day Saints.

The missionaries of this Church are going from door to door, city to city, state to state, and nation to nation, in carrying out the instructions of the Lord as received from him through the restoration of the gospel. They have been doing this ever since the organization of the Church. They will continue to do so until the head of the Church, Jesus Christ, shall come in the clouds of heaven to claim his Kingdom.

Preaching the Kingdom of God

Jesus gave to his disciples the signs of his second coming and of the end of the world:

And this gospel of the kingdom shall be preached in all the world for a witness unto all nations; and then shall the end come. (Matt. 24:14.)

Jesus fully understood the necessity of the preaching of the Gospel unto all nations, and that this could only be done by great sacrifice, as evidenced by His own statements:

And he said to them all, If any man will come after me, let him deny himself, and take up his cross daily, and follow me.

For whosoever will save his life shall lose it: but whosoever will lose his life for my sake, the same shall save it. (Luke 9:23-24.)

We read further in the same chapter:

And it came to pass, that, as they went in the way, a certain man said unto him, Lord, I will follow thee whithersoever thou goest.

And Jesus said unto him, Foxes have holes, and birds of the air have nests; but the Son of man hath not where to lay his head. (Luke 9:57-58.)

In other words, it would appear that Jesus wanted to make it plain to this "certain man," and all other men who might want to follow him in the ministry in the future, (and we take it that this is the reason the statement became scripture) that he had nothing to offer them in the way of monetary consideration for following him, not even a place to lay their heads.

The Savior continued:

And he said unto another, Follow me. But he said, Lord, suffer me first to go and bury my father.

Jesus said unto him, Let the dead bury their dead: but go thou and preach the kingdom of God. (Luke 9:59-60.)

In other words, Jesus wanted it to be understood that nothing was to stand in the way of preaching the kingdom of God, not even the care of one's dead—or the saying of farewell:

And another also said, Lord, I will follow thee; but let me first go bid them farewell, which are at home at my house.

And Jesus said unto him, No man, having put his hand to the plough, and looking back, is fit for the kingdom of God. (Luke 9:61-62.)

It is thus to be seen that nothing seemed to be as important in the sight of the Lord as to "preach the kingdom of God." Jesus continued to emphasize the importance of this missionary work, or the preaching of the kingdom of God:

After these things, the Lord appointed other seventy also,

and sent them two and two before his face into every city and
place, whither he himself would come.

Therefore said he unto them, The harvest truly is great, but
the labourers are few: pray ye therefore the Lord of the harvest,
that he would send forth labourers into his harvest. (Luke 10:1-2.)

We learn from this how great is the harvest and how
few are the laborers. Nevertheless, men must be "appointed" and "sent"—they do not appoint or send themselves. He sent them "two and two." This is the way the
missionaries of The Church of Jesus Christ of Latter-day
Saints have served ever since the organization of the
Church.

Jesus then instructed the seventy in their missionary
labors, how they should travel, what they should take
with them, and what they should say, indicating what
they should do when they enter a home upon which their
"peace shall rest":

And in the same house remain, eating and drinking such
things as they give: for the labourer is worthy of his hire. Go not
from house to house.

And into whatsoever city ye enter, and they receive you, eat
such things as are set before you:

And heal the sick that are therein, and say unto them, The
kingdom of God is come nigh unto you. (Luke 10:7-9.)

From this statement of the Master, the ministers of
the churches of the day have justified themselves in
preaching for hire, "for the labourer is worthy of his
hire." But it will be noted that Jesus makes it plain that
this hire is to accept food and lodging from those unto
whom they preach the gospel of the kingdom, while going from house to house as missionaries.

Jesus continued:

He that heareth you heareth me; and he that despiseth you
despiseth me; and he that despiseth me despiseth him that sent
me.

> And the seventy returned again with joy, saying, Lord, even the devils are subject unto us through thy name. (Luke 10:16-17.)

It will be noted that the "seventy returned again with joy," and so have the 180,000 missionaries of this dispensation who have been "appointed" and "sent" with the message of the restored gospel to the nations of the earth.

Consider now for a moment the organization of the churches of our day. What provision have they made that the "gospel of the kingdom shall be preached in all the world for a witness unto all nations"? (See Matt. 24:14.) If any one sect has the truth, it is not only necessary that it teach that truth to heathen nations, as some attempt to do in a very weak manner, but that it should teach the truth to the members of other sects, for we must "all come in the unity of the faith":

> That we henceforth be no more children, tossed to and fro, and carried about with every wind of doctrine, by the sleight of men, and cunning craftiness, whereby they lie in wait to deceive. (Eph. 4:14.)

Every truthful man must admit that so-called Christians of today have not "come in the unity of the faith." Has Christ failed? Has he changed his doctrines? No! but men have changed them.

The day will yet come that Jesus taught his disciples to pray for: "Thy kingdom come, thy will be done in earth as it is in heaven." But such a day could never come without the Lord sending his servants into all the world to preach "the everlasting gospel, to them that dwell on the earth, and to every nation, and kindred, and tongue, and people." (Rev. 14:6.)

Consider what a power the professed Christian churches would be in the world if all their ministers were duly called of God and were teaching the same doctrines and working unitedly together for the establishment of his kingdom.

In the Apostle Paul's instruction to the membership of the Church at Corinth, he said:

> Now I beseech you, brethren, by the name of our Lord Jesus Christ, that ye all speak the same thing, and that there be no divisions among you; but that ye be perfectly joined together in the same mind and in the same judgment. (I Cor. 1:10.)

It is apparent that the so-called Christian ministers of today have departed far from Paul's instruction in this matter. No wonder the heathen nations are confused when Christianity is offered to them.

Since the leadership of the priesthood seems to belong to Joseph, the son of Jacob, and his seed, it is proper that the gospel, including the priesthood, should have been restored in these latter-days to a descendant of Joseph. Let us refer to Moses' promise to Joseph:

> His glory is like the firstling of his bullock, and his horns are like the horns of unicorns: with them he shall push the people together to the ends of the earth: and they are the ten thousands of Ephraim, and they are the thousands of Manasseh. (Deut. 33:17.)

Moses' promise has been undergoing its fulfilment for over one hundred years. The seed of Joseph, under a new commitment of the priesthood of God, has been gathering or pushing "the people together to the ends of the earth: and they are the ten thousands of Ephraim and they are the thousands of Manasseh." It will be noted, therefore, that this contemplates a great missionary program. We wonder, if, at the time Moses made this prediction, there could have been a place in all the world that would have seemed to be nearer "the ends of the earth," than in Ephraim's mountains—the valleys of the Rocky Mountains.

In our discussion of the gathering of Israel, reference was made to the prophecy of Jeremiah, wherein he indicated that the latter-day gathering of Israel should far overshadow in magnitude the leading of the children of Israel out of the land of Egypt, which could only be accomplished through a great missionary program:

> Behold, I will send for many fishers, saith the Lord, and they shall fish them; and after will I send for many hunters, and they shall hunt them from every mountain, and from every hill, and out of the holes of the rocks. (Jer. 16:16.)

When the Lord calls his servants and makes them "fishers" and "hunters," he really does something for them that no mortal man can do of his own power. They are called to go forth "in the spirit and power of Elias," as was John the Baptist of old, for they are sent to prepare the way for the coming of the Lord.

Every Nation to Hear the Word of the Lord

Following the crucifixion and resurrection of Jesus, and immediately preceding his ascension, his last commission to his disciples was:

> Go ye therefore, and teach all nations, baptizing them in the name of the Father, and of the Son, and of the Holy Ghost:
>
> Teaching them to observe all things whatsoever I have commanded you: and, lo, I am with you alway, even unto the end of the world. Amen. (Matt. 28:19-20.)

Jesus has never rescinded this instruction nor his promise. Therefore, whenever the Church of Jesus Christ is upon the earth, with authority to officiate in his name, this promise will follow those who are sent to "teach all nations." No one is better able to testify of the truth of this fact than the missionaries of The Church of Jesus Christ of Latter-day Saints. Books could be written of the wonderful manner in which the missionaries have been sustained in their ministry. The way has been opened up whereby the missionaries have been led to the honest seeker after truth in their efforts to gather scattered Israel, for truly they have been sent to "fish" and "hunt" them from every mountain, and from every hill, and out of the holes of the rocks. (Jer. 16:16.)

To illustrate how the Savior has kept his promise: "and lo, I am with you alway, even unto the end of the world," we quote from a vision the Prophet Joseph Smith received in the Kirtland Temple on Thursday, January 21, 1836:

> . . . I saw the Twelve Apostles of the Lamb, who are now upon the earth, who hold the keys of this last ministry, in foreign lands standing together in a circle, much fatigued, with their clothes tattered and feet swollen, with their eyes cast downward, and Jesus standing in their midst, and they did not behold Him. The Savior looked upon them and wept.
>
> I also beheld Elder M'Lellin in the south, standing upon a hill, surrounded by a vast multitude, preaching to them, and a lame man standing before him supported by his crutches; he threw them down at his word and leaped as an hart, by the mighty power of God. Also, I saw Elder Brigham Young standing in a strange land, in the far south and west, in a desert place, upon a rock in the midst of about a dozen men of color, who appeared hostile. He was preaching to them in their own tongue, and the angel of God standing above his head, with a drawn sword in his hand, protecting him, but he did not see it. (D.H.C. Vol. 2, p. 381.)

Under this mighty promise the great missionary work of his Church is going forward in the earth, gaining momentum year after year. The number of missionaries is increasing, and shall continue to increase until the kingdoms of this world shall become the kingdom of our God, and Christ shall come to claim his kingdom as the prophets have declared.

The missionary program of The Church of Jesus Christ of Latter-day Saints is one of the greatest spiritual movements and undertakings this world has ever known.

The Prophet Joseph Smith did not receive this great assignment from reading the scriptures, but by the revelations of the Lord in this, the Dispensation of the Fulness of Times.

To those, therefore, who are sent in his name in this dispensation, the promise is the same as made by Jesus to the seventy of old:

> He that heareth you heareth me; and he that despiseth you despiseth me; and he that despiseth me despiseth him that sent me. (Luke 10:16.)

CHAPTER 19

FUNDAMENTAL DIFFERENCES BETWEEN SALVATION AND EXALTATION

One Heaven and One Hell

One of the greatest errors in the teachings of the Christian religions is the doctrine of one heaven and one hell, so that all who go to heaven share and share alike, and all who fail to go to heaven are sent to hell where they share and share alike.

This thought has led many to feel that while their lives may not be all they should be, they are as good as, or better than, the average. Thus they feel that all will be well with them. If this doctrine be true, it is obvious that a line would have to be drawn somewhere, and the closer one came to the line the less would be the difference or distinction between those who would cross the line and enter heaven and those who would not quite qualify, and therefore would be sent to hell. Such a doctrine does not have the motivating and stimulating power to impel or encourage men to do the best they can, but rather to satisfy themselves by doing as well as the average man. Such a doctrine places no value on anything more than average devotion and obedience to the commandments of the Lord, or the development of one's talents and their useful devotion to his service.

Many Mansions, or Degrees, in Heaven

Jesus taught his disciples:

In my Father's house are many mansions: if it were not so, I would have told you. I go to prepare a place for you. (John 14:2.)

If there were but one heaven, and all who go there share and share alike, how inconsistent for Jesus to even suggest going to prepare a place for his disciples, and then to add: "In my Father's house are *many* mansions."

Since, therefore, there are many mansions in his Father's house, it is well that we give consideration to them.

The Apostle Paul informed us that he knew a man in Christ who was caught up to the *third heaven*. A careful reading of this scripture will reveal the fact that Paul, himself, was that man:

> I knew a man in Christ above fourteen years ago, (whether in the body, I cannot tell; or whether out of the body, I cannot tell: God knoweth;) such an one caught up to the *third heaven*.

> And I knew such a man, (whether in the body, or out of the body, I cannot tell: God knoweth;)

> How that he was caught up into *paradise*, and heard unspeakable words, which it is not lawful for a man to utter. (II Cor. 12:2-4.)

It is obvious that there could not be a third heaven unless there is a first and a second heaven. We, therefore, have three heavens, paradise, and the hell so often spoken of in the scriptures, making at least five places to which we may go after death.

Paul gave a most wonderful description of the resurrection:

> There are also celestial bodies, and bodies terrestrial: but the glory of the celestial is one, and the glory of the terrestrial is another.

> There is one glory of the sun, and another glory of the moon, and another glory of the stars: for one star differeth from another star in glory.

> So also is the resurrection of the dead. . . . (I Cor. 15:40-42.)

What could be more plain? There is a glory of the sun, or celestial glory; another glory like the moon, or the terrestrial glory; and another glory like the stars, or, as we will learn, the telestial glory; and since "one star differeth from another star in glory," so also "is the resurrection of the dead." From this we learn that the great multitude in the resurrection will be likened unto the stars in heaven, and just as their works have differed in importance and faithfulness here upon the earth, so also shall their condition in the resurrection differ, even as the stars in heaven differ in glory.

Celestial Glory

When Paul saw this vision of the third heaven and of paradise, he declared that he "heard unspeakable words, which it is not lawful for man to utter." We have no account that Paul ever described in detail what he saw in this vision, for he was not permitted "to utter" what he saw. We have no record from the vision of Paul of the qualifications necessary to entitle one to obtain the various heavens or paradise. Such qualifications, however, were revealed to Joseph Smith, the Prophet, and Sidney Rigdon, at Hiram, Ohio, February 16, 1832. The prophet was permitted to record *much* of what he saw. We commend the reading of this entire revelation, known as "The Vision," recorded in the seventy-sixth Section of the Doctrine and Covenants, from which we quote:

We, Joseph Smith, Jun., and Sidney Rigdon, being in the Spirit on the sixteenth day of February, in the year of our Lord one thousand eight hundred and thirty-two—

By the power of the Spirit our eyes were opened and our understandings were enlightened, so as to see and understand the things of God—

Even those things which were from the beginning before the world was, which were ordained of the Father, through his

Only Begotten Son, who was in the bosom of the Father, even from the beginning:

Of whom we bear record; and the record which we bear is the fulness of the gospel of Jesus Christ, who is the Son, whom we saw and with whom we conversed in the heavenly vision. . . .

And again we bear record—for we saw and heard, and this is the testimony of the gospel of Christ concerning them who shall come forth in the resurrection of the just—

They are they who received the testimony of Jesus, and believed on his name and were baptized after the manner of his burial, being buried in the water in his name, and thus according to the commandment which he has given—

That by keeping the commandments they might be washed and cleansed from all their sins, and receive the Holy Spirit by the laying on of the hands of him who is ordained and sealed unto this power;

And who overcome by faith, and are sealed by the Holy Spirit of promise, which the Father sheds forth upon all those who are just and true.

They are they who are the church of the Firstborn.

They are they into whose hands the Father has given all things—

They are they who are priests and kings, who have received of his fulness, and of his glory;

And are priests of the Most High, after the order of Melchizedek, which was after the order of Enoch, which was after the order of the Only Begotten Son.

Wherefore, as it is written, they are gods, even the sons of God—

Wherefore, all things are theirs, whether life or death, or things present or things to come, all are theirs and they are Christ's, and Christ is God's.

And they shall overcome all things.

Wherefore, let no man glory in man, but rather let him glory in God, who shall subdue all enemies under his feet.

These shall dwell in the presence of God and his Christ forever and ever.

These are they whom he shall bring with him, when he shall come in the clouds of heaven to reign on the earth over his people.

These are they who shall have part in the first resurrection.

These are they who shall come forth in the resurrection of the just.

These are they who are come unto Mount Zion, and unto the city of the living God, the heavenly place, the holiest of all.

These are they who have come to an innumerable company of angels, to the general assembly and church of Enoch, and of the Firstborn.

These are they whose names are written in heaven, where God and Christ are the judge of all.

These are they who are just men made perfect through Jesus the mediator of the new covenant, who wrought out this perfect atonement through the shedding of his own blood.

These are they whose bodies are celestial, whose glory is that of the sun, even the glory of God, the highest of all, whose glory the sun of the firmament is written of as being typical. (D. & C. 76:11-14, 50-70.)

Terrestrial Glory

And again, we saw the terrestrial world, and behold and lo, these are they who are of the terrestrial, whose glory differs from that of the church of the Firstborn who have received the fulness of the Father, even as that of the moon differs from the sun in the firmament.

Behold, these are they who died without law;

And also they who are the spirits of men kept in prison, whom the Son visited, and preached the gospel unto them, that they might be judged according to men in the flesh;

Who received not the testimony of Jesus in the flesh, but afterwards received it.

These are they who are honorable men of the earth, who were blinded by the craftiness of men.

These are they who receive of his glory, but not of his fulness.

These are they who receive of the presence of the Son, but not of the fulness of the Father.

Wherefore, they are bodies terrestrial, and not bodies celestial, and differ in glory as the moon differs from the sun.

These are they who are not valiant in the testimony of Jesus; wherefore, they obtain not the crown over the kingdom of our God.

And now this is the end of the vision which we saw of the terrestrial, that the Lord commanded us to write while we were yet in the Spirit. (D. & C. 76:71-80.)

Telestial Glory

And again, we saw the glory of the telestial, which is that of the lesser, even as the glory of the stars differ from that of the glory of the moon in the firmament.

These are they who received not the gospel of Christ, neither the testimony of Jesus.

These are they who deny not the Holy Spirit.

These are they who are thrust down to hell.

These are they who shall not be redeemed from the devil until the last resurrection, until the Lord, even Christ the Lamb, shall have finished his work.

These are they who receive not of his fulness in the eternal world, but of the Holy Spirit through the ministration of the terrestrial;

And the terrestrial through the ministration of the celestial.

And also the telestial receive it of the administering of angels who are appointed to minister for them, or who are appointed to be ministering spirits for them; for they shall be heirs of salvation.

And thus we saw, in the heavenly vision, the glory of the telestial, which surpasses all understanding;

And no man knows it except him to whom God has revealed it. (D. & C. 76:81-90.)

Variation in the Degrees of Glory—With Definitions

It will be observed that *all* who inherit *any one of the glories* herein described "shall be heirs of salvation." (See verse 88.) But what a difference in the reward or glory that awaits them—just as much difference as there is between the glory or light of the sun and the moon, or the moon and the stars.

It should be remembered, however, that only "they who are the church of the Firstborn," are heirs of celestial glory (See D. & C. 76:54), and they are the ones "he shall bring with him, when he shall come in the clouds of heaven to reign on the earth over his people." (verse 63) and the ones "who shall have part in the first resurrection." (verse 64. See also D. & C. 45:54.)

Hence the gospel is to be preached to every creature that he might obtain celestial glory if he will.

The prophet continued His description of the difference in these glories:

> And thus we saw the glory of the terrestrial which excels in all things the glory of the telestial, even in glory, and in power, and in might, and in dominion.
>
> And thus we saw the glory of the celestial, which excels in all things—where God, even the Father, reigns upon his throne forever and ever;
>
> Before whose throne all things bow in humble reverence, and give him glory forever and ever.
>
> They who dwell in his presence are the church of the Firstborn; and they see as they are seen, and know as they are known, having received of his fulness and of his grace;
>
> And he makes them equal in power, and in might, and in dominion.
>
> And the glory of the celestial is one, even as the glory of the sun is one.
>
> And the glory of the terrestrial is one, even as the glory of the moon is one.
>
> And the glory of the telestial is one, even as the glory of the stars is one; for as one star differs from another star in glory, even so differs one from another in glory in the telestial world;
>
> For these are they who are of Paul, and of Apollos, and of Cephas.
>
> These are they who say they are some of one and some of another—some of Christ and some of John, and some of Moses, and some of Elias, and some of Esaias, and some of Isaiah, and some of Enoch;
>
> But received not the gospel, neither the testimony of Jesus, neither the prophets, neither the everlasting covenant.
>
> Last of all, these all are they who will not be gathered with the saints, to be caught up unto the church of the Firstborn, and received into the cloud.

These are they who are liars, and sorcerers, and adulterers, and whoremongers, and whosoever loves and makes a lie.

These are they who suffer the wrath of God on earth.

These are they who suffer the vengeance of eternal fire.

These are they who are cast down to hell and suffer the wrath of Almighty God, until the fulness of times, when Christ shall have subdued all enemies under his feet, and shall have perfected His work;

When he shall deliver up the kingdom, and present it unto the Father, spotless, saying: I have overcome and have trodden the wine-press alone, even the wine-press of the fierceness of the wrath of Almighty God.

Then shall he be crowned with the crown of his glory, to sit on the throne of his power to reign forever and ever.

But behold, and lo, we saw the glory and the inhabitants of the telestial world, that they were as innumerable as the stars in the firmament of heaven, or as the sand upon the seashore;

And heard the voice of the Lord, saying: These all shall bow the knee, and every tongue shall confess to him who sits upon the throne forever and ever;

For they shall be judged according to their works, and every man shall receive according to his own works, his own dominion, in the mansions which are prepared;

And they shall be servants of the Most High; but where God and Christ dwell they cannot come, worlds without end.

This is the end of the vision which we saw, which we were commanded to write while we were yet in the Spirit.

But great and marvelous are the works of the Lord, and the mysteries of his kingdom which he showed unto us, which surpass all understanding in glory, and in might, and in dominion;

Which he commanded us we should not write while we were yet in the Spirit, and are not lawful for man to utter;

Neither is man capable to make them known, for they are only to be seen and understood by the power of the Holy Spirit, which God bestows on those who love him, and purify themselves before him;

To whom he grants this privilege of seeing and knowing for themselves;

That through the power and manifestation of the Spirit, while in the flesh, they may be able to bear his presence in the world of glory.

And to God and the Lamb be glory, and honor, and dominion forever and ever. Amen. (D. & C. 76:91-119.)

Sons of Perdition

In this vision the Lord also indicated who the Sons of Perdition are:

And this we saw also, and bear record, that an angel of God who was in authority in the presence of God, who rebelled against the Only Begotten Son whom the Father loved and who was in the bosom of the Father, was thrust down from the presence of God and the Son,

And was called Perdition, for the heavens wept over him—he was Lucifer, a son of the morning.

And we beheld, and lo, he is fallen! is fallen, even a son of the morning!

And while we were yet in the Spirit, the Lord commanded us that we should write the vision; for we beheld Satan, that old serpent, even the devil, who rebelled against God, and sought to take the kingdom of our God and his Christ—

Wherefore, he maketh war with the saints of God, and encompasseth them round about.

And we saw a vision of the sufferings of those with whom he made war and overcame, for thus came the voice of the Lord unto us:

Thus saith the Lord concerning all those who know my power, and have been made partakers thereof, and suffered themselves through the power of the devil to be overcome, and to deny the truth and defy my power—

They are they who are the sons of perdition, of whom I say that it had been better for them never to have been born;

For they are vessels of wrath, doomed to suffer the wrath of God, with the devil and his angels in eternity;

Concerning whom I have said there is no forgiveness in this world nor in the world to come—

Having denied the Holy Spirit after having received it, and having denied the Only Begotten Son of the Father, having crucified him unto themselves and put him to an open shame.

These are they who shall go away into the lake of fire and brimstone, with the devil and his angels—

And the only ones on whom the second death shall have any power;

Yea, verily, the only ones who shall not be redeemed in the due time of the Lord, after the sufferings of his wrath. (D. & C. 76:25-38.)

In commenting on this glorious vision, one of the most inspiring and enlightening the Lord ever revealed unto his prophets with permission to record, the Prophet Joseph Smith wrote:

Nothing could be more pleasing to the Saints upon the order of the Kingdom of the Lord, than the light which burst upon the world through the foregoing vision. Every law, every commandment, every promise, every truth, and every point touching the destiny of man, from Genesis to Revelation, where the purity of the Scriptures remains unsullied by the folly of men, go to show the perfection of the theory (of different degrees of glory in the future life) and witnesses the fact that *that document is a transcript from the records of the eternal world.* The sublimity of the ideas; the purity of the language; the scope for action; the continued duration for completion, in order that the heirs of salvation may confess the Lord and bow the knee; the rewards for faithfulness, and the punishments for sins, are so much beyond the narrow-mindedness of men, that every honest man is constrained to exclaim: *"It came from God."* (D.H.C. Vol. 1, pp. 252-253.)

All Are Heirs of Salvation

When it is understood from this vision, that those who inherit even the telestial glory "shall be heirs of salvation," it is easy to understand an axiom among the Latter-day Saints— "Salvation without exaltation is damnation." Even so, the Prophet Joseph Smith points out the glories of the telestial world—"And thus we saw, in the heavenly vision, the glory of the telestial, which surpasses all understanding; And no man knows it except him to whom God has revealed it." (D. & C. 76:89-90.) What then must be the glory and the exaltation of the celestial kingdom! The gospel of Jesus Christ is given to prepare men for celestial glory.

The information contained in The Vision makes plain these scriptures from the Bible:

> And I saw the dead, small and great, stand before God; and the books were opened: and another book was opened, which is the book of life: and the dead were judged out of those things which were written in the books, according to their works.
>
> And the sea gave up the dead which were in it; and death and hell delivered up the dead which were in them: and they were judged every man according to their works. (Rev. 20:12-13.)

Now, since every man is to be judged according to his works, even those who are in hell, it will make it easy to understand the "justice" of God, for otherwise he could not be just. It will also make it easy to understand how one can receive a glory like the sun, while another receives a glory like the moon, and many others a glory like the stars, and yet know God is just. This statement of Jesus also becomes easy to understand:

> Enter ye in at the strait gate: for wide is the gate, and broad is the way, that leadeth to destruction, and many there be which go in thereat:
>
> Because strait is the gate, and narrow is the way, which leadeth unto life, and few there be that find it. (Matt. 7:13-14.)

The Apostle Paul understood that every man would receive according to his works:

> Be not deceived; God is not mocked: for whatsoever a man soweth, that shall he also reap.
>
> For he that soweth to his flesh shall of the flesh reap corruption; but he that soweth to the Spirit shall of the Spirit reap life everlasting.
>
> And let us not be weary in well doing: for in due season we shall reap, if we faint not. (Gal. 6:7-9.)

Paul further explains what "the righteous judgment of God" is:

> But after thy hardness and impenitent heart treasurest up unto thyself wrath against the day of wrath and revelation of the righteous judgment of God;
>
> Who will render to every man according to his deeds:
>
> To them who by patient continuance in well doing seek for glory and honour and immortality, eternal life:
>
> But unto them that are contentious, and do not obey the truth, but obey unrighteousness, indignation and wrath,
>
> Tribulation and anguish, upon every soul of man that doeth evil, of the Jew first, and also of the Gentile;
>
> But glory, honour, and peace, to every man that worketh good, to the Jew first, and also to the Gentile:
>
> For there is no respect of persons with God. (Rom. 2:5-11.)

No other method of judgment could be righteous. God surely "will render to every man according to his deeds." Even God cannot reward a man for what he does not do.

Saved by Grace

Some of the teachings of Paul are quite difficult for many to understand as Peter explained:

> And account that the long-suffering of our Lord is salvation; even as our beloved brother Paul also according to the wisdom given unto him hath written unto you;
>
> As also in all his epistles, speaking in them of these things; *in which are some things hard to be understood,* which they that are unlearned and unstable wrest, as they do also the other scriptures, unto their own destruction. (II Pet. 3:15-16.)

Remembering, therefore, Peter's warning that some of Paul's writings are "hard to be understood," let us consider the latter's teachings on the subject of "Grace":

> Even when we were dead in sins, hath quickened us together with Christ, (by grace ye are saved;)

And hath raised us up together, and made us sit together in heavenly places in Christ Jesus:

That in the ages to come he might shew the exceeding riches of his grace in his kindness toward us through Christ Jesus.

For *by grace are ye saved* through faith; and that not of yourselves: it is the gift of God:

Not of works, lest any man should boast. (Eph. 2:5-9.)

It is evident that none of our works or anything we can do can affect the Grace of God which is a free gift. But this does not alter the fact, as we have just pointed out from the writings of Paul, that the "righteous judgment of God; . . . will render to every man according to his deeds."

What then is this "grace" Paul speaks of by which we are saved, and that "Not of works, lest any man should boast"?

This represents what Jesus has done for us which we could not possibly have done for ourselves, among which are included:

1. He created this earth upon which we are privileged to live and gain experience. (See John 1:1-14.)

2. He atoned for the transgression of our first parents which brought death into the world, thus bringing to pass the resurrection from the grave, or the reuniting of our bodies and spirits in the resurrection. (See I Cor. 15:22.)

3. By giving us his everlasting gospel, "he became the author of eternal salvation unto all them that *obey* him." (See Heb. 5:9.)

All these glorious gifts, and many more which could be mentioned, come to us through His "grace" as free gifts, and not of works lest any man should boast. (See Eph. 2:8-9.)

Nevertheless, to obtain these "graces," and the gift of "eternal salvation," we must remember that this gift is only to "all them that obey him." (Heb. 5:9.)

Paul's further thinking on this matter is conclusive:

Be not deceived; God is not mocked: for whatsoever a man soweth, that shall he also reap. (Gal. 6:7.)

Take the farmer, as an illustration. No matter how much land he owns, he cannot expect to reap unless he sows. But when the farmer has prepared his land and sowed his seed, and cultivated and irrigated the land, and harvested the crop, is he entitled to all the credit? He did all the work and is entitled to reap as he has sowed, and the result of his effort will be his reward. But no matter how hard the farmer may have worked, he could not have harvested his crop through his own effort since there are other factors to be considered:

1. Who provided him the fertile soil?

2. Who put the germ of life into the seeds he planted?

3. Who caused the sun to warm the soil and cause the seed to germinate and grow?

4. Who caused the rain to fall or the snows to fill the watersheds to give drink to his growing crops?

None of these things could the farmer have done or supplied for himself. They represent the free gift of grace, and yet the farmer will reap as he has sowed.

Paul's statement has been very much misunderstood, both by preachers and laity. Preachers have freely taught that salvation might be obtained as by the snap of the fingers, as one prominent minister expressed himself to the writer; that salvation comes through a lip confession of a belief in Christ, even though not accompanied by obedience to his commandments and works of righteousness. Such doctrine is obviously out of harmony with truth.

It was such interpretations of the scripture that Peter warned against when he said: "which they that are unlearned and unstable wrest, as they do also the other scriptures, unto their own destruction." (See II Pet. 3:16.)

Many have thus been led astray and have contented themselves with a lip confession of faith, "to their own destruction."

The enemy of all righteousness, could not hope to succeed more effectively in thwarting the purposes of the Master and his gospel, than to persuade men that all the blessings the Lord has prepared, through his grace, for his children, can be obtained through their lip acknowledgment that he is the Christ. We have pointed out that those whose glory will be telestial, or like the stars, will be heirs of salvation. However, it should be kept in mind that the gospel of Jesus Christ is not given alone for man's salvation but for his exaltation as well. This is what all lovers of truth should aspire to—the glory which has been spoken of as "the glory of the sun."

Exaltation Dependent Upon Good Works

This explanation of "grace" as a free gift of God, which cannot be obtained through our works, as contrasted with obedience to the gospel, will help to understand properly the following scriptures:

> Not every one that saith unto me, Lord, Lord, shall enter into the kingdom of heaven; but he that doeth the will of my Father which is in heaven. (Matt. 7:21.)

> Therefore whosoever heareth these sayings of mine, and doeth them, I will liken him unto a wise man, which built his house upon a rock:

> And the rain descended, and the floods came, and the winds

blew, and beat upon that house; and it fell not: for it was founded upon a rock.

And every one that heareth these sayings of mine, and doeth them not, shall be likened unto a foolish man, which built his house upon the sand:

And the rain descended, and the floods came, and the winds blew, and beat upon that house; and it fell: and great was the fall of it. (Matt. 7:24-27.)

For the Son of man shall come in the glory of his Father with his angels; and then he shall reward every man according to his works. (Matt. 16:27.)

The Apostle James understood the importance of being "doers of the word, and not hearers only":

But be ye doers of the word, and not hearers only, deceiving your own selves. (James 1:22.)

What doth it profit, my brethren, though a man say he hath faith, and have not works? can faith save him?

If a brother or sister be naked, and destitute of daily food,

And one of you say unto them, Depart in peace, be ye warmed and filled; notwithstanding ye give them not those things which are needful to the body; what doth it profit?

Even so faith, if it hath not works, is dead, being alone.

Yea, a man may say, Thou hast faith, and I have works: shew me thy faith without thy works, and I will shew thee my faith by my works.

Thou believest that there is one God; thou doest well: the devils also believe, and tremble.

But wilt thou know, O vain man, that faith without works is dead? (James 2:14-20.)

James makes it clear that to believe in God is not sufficient, for the devils do as much, and that "faith without works is dead." A farmer might just as well believe that he can harvest a crop without planting. Such faith is dead; it will not produce a harvest without works.

Consider Jesus' parable of the sower:

But other fell into good ground, and brought forth fruit, some an hundredfold, some sixtyfold, some thirtyfold. (Matt. 13:8.)

Also his parable:

> For the kingdom of heaven is as a man travelling into a far country, who called his own servants, and delivered unto them his goods.
>
> And unto one he gave five talents, to another two, and to another one; to every man according to his several ability; and straightway took his journey. (Matt. 25:14-15.)

When the lord returned to conduct an accounting with his servants, the one who had received five talents had won another five; the one who had received two talents had won other two. To each of these their lord said:

> ... Well done, thou good and faithful servant: thou hast been faithful over a few things, I will make thee ruler over many things; enter thou into the joy of thy lord. (Matt. 25:21.)

But to him who had received one talent and hid it, the lord said:

> ... Thou wicked and slothful servant, thou knewest that I reap where I sowed not, and gather where I have not strawed:
>
> Thou oughtest therefore to have put my money to the exchangers, and then at my coming I should have received mine own with usury.
>
> Take therefore the talent from him, and give it unto him which hath ten talents.
>
> For unto every one that hath shall be given, and he shall have abundance: but from him that hath not shall be taken away even that which he hath.
>
> And cast ye the unprofitable servant into outer darkness: there shall be weeping and gnashing of teeth. (Matt. 25:26-30.)

How useless is one's faith without his works. What a glorious award awaits those who deal profitably with the talents they receive!

How inconsistent is the thought that all who do good are rewarded alike, and all who do evil are punished alike. How difficult it would be to draw the line between the two groups. Hence, the need of "many mansions" in our Father's kingdom, where each will be rewarded according to his works.

Salvation Defined

The writer was asked the following question by a minister of the gospel: "Can a man be saved before he dies, or must he die to be saved?"

The answer was, "If you will explain what you mean by being saved, I will try to answer your question."

It has been the writer's experience that few Christians have any definite concept of salvation, other than to escape eternal burning, and this minister seemed totally at a loss to explain salvation.

It was explained that if we had not made ourselves worthy to come upon this earth before we were born, and take upon ourselves bodies, we would have been cast out of heaven with Satan, since he took with him one third of the spirits. (See Jude, verse 6; Rev. 12:7-12; Rev. 12:4.)

It was pointed out that we may be saved every day that we live, for as we learn the laws of God and obey them, we free ourselves from the consequences of a broken law, and entitle ourselves to the blessings predicated upon obedience to divine law. The following latter-day scriptures are quoted to point out this truth:

There is a law, irrevocably decreed in heaven before the foundations of this world, upon which all blessings are predicated—

And when we obtain any blessing from God, it is by obedience to that law upon which it is predicated. (D. & C. 130:20-21.)

And unto every kingdom is given a law; and unto every law there are certain bounds also and conditions.

All beings who abide not in those conditions are not justified. (D. & C. 88:38-39.)

For all who will have a blessing at my hands shall abide the law which was appointed for that blessing, and the conditions thereof, as were instituted from before the foundation of the world. (D. & C. 132:5.)

"It is impossible for a man to be saved in ignorance." (D. & C. 131:6.) Thus it will be seen that, while "Where no law is there is no transgression," (See Rom. 4:15.) it is also "impossible for a man to be saved in ignorance." Therefore, a man must know the law to be able to be rewarded for keeping it, and to be relieved of the consequences of a broken law, even though he may be forgiven for transgressing where no law has been given to him. Hence, as we continue our quest to know and understand the laws of God, and obey them, we increase the measure of our salvation or exaltation.

The writer further explained to the reverend gentleman that since we believe in eternal progression and that "a man is saved no faster than he gets knowledge," (D.H.C., Vol. 4, p. 588) that salvation to a Latter-day Saint is not an end but a process, since we shall never cease to gain knowledge.

The minister replied that he had never heard such a reasonable explanation. All this, we have obtained through the revelations of the Lord to the Prophet Joseph Smith, in this, the Dispensation of the Fulness of Times.

All men are to receive "according to their works," (see Rev. 20:12.) which requires that suitable places shall be prepared for the souls of all men. Hence the statement of Jesus: "In my Father's house are many mansions." (See John 14:2.) The gospel of Jesus Christ provides a plan whereby men can not only be saved, but can also be exalted in the celestial kingdom, "In the day when God shall judge the secrets of men by Jesus Christ according to my gospel." (Rom. 2:16.)

How well do the words of John Oxenham indicate the need of three degrees of glory, or three heavens, which Paul described:

> To every man there openeth
> A way, and ways, and a way,
> And the high soul climb the high way
> And the low soul gropes the low;
> And in between, on the misty flats,
> The rest drift to and fro.
> But to every man there openeth
> A high way and a low,
> And every man decideth
> The way his soul shall go.

CHAPTER 20

WHENCE COMETH MAN?

Man in the Spirit World

One of the most beautiful truths that has been revealed to man through the restoration of the gospel in this dispensation, and one that sheds much light on so many matters, is the knowledge that all men lived with God and his Son, Jesus Christ, in the spirit world before they came here upon the earth.

This new and yet old doctrine is beautifully described in a Latter-day Saint hymn, entitled *O My Father,* with lyrics by Eliza R. Snow:

O my Father, Thou that dwellest in the high and glorious place!
　　When shall I regain Thy presence, and again behold Thy
　　　　face?
In Thy holy habitation, did my spirit once reside;
　　In my first primeval childhood, was I nurtured near Thy
　　　　side?
For a wise and glorious purpose Thou hast placed me here on
　　　　earth,
　　And withheld the recollection of my former friends and
　　　　birth,
Yet oft-times a secret something whispered, "You're a stranger
　　　　here";
　　And I felt that I had wandered from a more exalted sphere.
I had learned to call Thee Father, thro' Thy Spirit from on high;
　　But until the Key of Knowledge was restored, I knew not
　　　　why.
In the heav'ns are parents single? No; the tho't makes reason
　　　　stare!
　　Truth is reason, truth eternal, tells me I've a mother there.

When I leave this frail existence, when I lay this mortal by,
   Father, Mother, may I meet you in your royal courts on
      high?
Then at length, when I've completed all you sent me forth to
   do,
      With your mutual approbation let me come and dwell with
         you.

On May 6, 1833, in a revelation given through the Prophet Joseph Smith, the Lord said:

> Man was also in the beginning with God. Intelligence, or the light of truth, was not created or made, neither indeed can be. (D. & C. 93:29.)

To further illustrate this truth, in teaching the members of the Church, the Prophet Joseph Smith took a ring and explained that if you cut the ring it has a beginning and an end, but if you do not cut it, it has no beginning and hence no end. Since the intelligences of men are, therefore, without beginning, they also can have no end.

The Council in Heaven

The Prophet Joseph Smith gave us a translation of some ancient records, the writings of Abraham while he was in Egypt, that had fallen into his hands and which came from the catacombs of Egypt. To Abraham the Lord revealed the truth that the intelligences or spirits of men existed with God, before the world was created. A council was held in heaven, where a plan was formulated for the creation of the earth, upon which the intelligences or spirits might dwell, and also for their redemption:

> Now the Lord had shown unto me, Abraham, the intelligences that were organized before the world was; and among all these there were many of the noble and great ones;
>
> And God saw these souls that they were good, and he stood in the midst of them, and he said: These I will make my rulers;

for he stood among those that were spirits, and he saw that they were good; and he said unto me: Abraham, thou art one of them; thou wast chosen before thou wast born.

And there stood one among them that was like unto God, and he said unto those who were with him: We will go down, for there is space there, and we will take of these materials, and we will make an earth whereon these may dwell;

And we will prove them herewith, to see if they will do all things whatsoever the Lord their God shall command them;

And they who keep their first estate shall be added upon; and they who keep not their first estate shall not have glory in the same kingdom with those who keep their first estate; and they who keep their second estate shall have glory added upon their heads for ever and ever.

And the Lord said: Whom shall I send? And one answered like unto the Son of Man: Here am I, send me. And another answered and said: Here am I, send me. And the Lord said: I will send the first.

And the second was angry, and kept not his first estate; and, at that day, many followed after him. (P. of G. P., Abraham 3:22-28.)

It will be seen that the spirits of all men were in the beginning with God; that already they had distinguished themselves, so that the Lord, as he stood among "many of the noble and great ones," said: "These I will make my rulers . . . and he said unto me: Abraham, thou art one of them, thou wast chosen before thou was born."

Note the Lord's promise that "they who keep their first estate shall be added upon." This first estate is the life we lived in the spirit world before we were born. Abraham was chosen before he was born, and we will learn that others were also.

Consider again the Lord's words: "and they who keep not their first estate shall not have glory in the same kingdom with those who keep their first estate." When the Lord chose the offer of his Son, Jesus, "the second was angry, and kept not his first estate; and, at that day, many followed after him."

Thus, it was Satan, and a third of the hosts of heaven who kept not their first estate. They were, therefore, cast down to the earth and deprived of the privilege of taking upon themselves bodies, remaining bodies of spirit only, so they "shall not have glory in the same kingdom with those who keep their first estate." The Lord made this plain in a revelation to the Prophet Joseph Smith in September 1830:

> And it came to pass that Adam, being tempted of the devil— for, behold, the devil was before Adam, for he rebelled against me, saying, Give me thine honor, which is my power; and also a *third part* of the hosts of heaven turned he away from me because of their agency;
>
> And they were thrust down, and thus came the devil and his angels. (D. & C. 29:36-37.)

It is evident, therefore, that the spirits of all men existed in the presence of God before this world was created, and that they counseled together regarding the creation of the earth upon which they may dwell. Because the plan of Jesus Christ was accepted, giving man his free agency, and because Satan's plan was rejected, Lucifer rebelled and was cast out of heaven. A third of the spirits followed him and were cast out with him as the scriptures attest.

It is reasonable to assume that, of those who remained, there was as much difference in their faithfulness and intelligence as we find among those same spirits after they came upon this earth. Hence, Abraham's statement that God stood in the midst of them and said, "These I will make my rulers; for he stood among those that were spirits, and he saw that they were good; and he said unto me: Abraham, thou art one of them; thou wast chosen before thou was born." (See P. of G. P., Abraham 3:23.)

Satan and His Angels

Let us now consider what the Bible has to offer concerning Satan and his angels or the third of the spirits who were cast out of heaven with him:

And there was war in heaven: Michael and his angels fought against the dragon; and the dragon fought and his angels,

And prevailed not; neither was their place *found any more in heaven.*

And the great dragon was cast out, that old serpent, called the Devil, and Satan, which deceiveth the whole world: he was cast out into the earth, and his angels were cast out with him. (Rev. 12:7-9.)

And his tail drew the third part of the stars of heaven, and did cast them to the earth: and the dragon stood before the woman which was ready to be delivered, for to devour her child as soon as it was born. (Rev. 12:4.)

And the angels which kept not their first estate, but left their own habitation, he hath reserved in everlasting chains under darkness unto the judgment of the great day. (Jude, verse 6.)

How art thou fallen from heaven, O Lucifer, son of the morning! how art thou cut down to the ground, which didst weaken the nations! . . .

They that see thee shall narrowly look upon thee, and consider thee, saying, Is this *the man* that made the earth to tremble, that did shake kingdoms? (Isa. 14:12, 16.)

Thus we see that Satan and his followers were cast down to the earth; that they were formerly angels but failed to keep "their first estate," so they became devils; that Satan was just as much *a man* in the spirit world, as were those spirits who have been given bodies through birth into this world.

The Apostle Peter also understood this great truth:

For if God spared not the angels that sinned, but cast them down to hell, and delivered them into chains of darkness, to be reserved unto judgment. (II Pet. 2:4.)

The Sons of God Shouted for Joy

The Lord gave Job to understand that "all the sons of God shouted for joy," (Job 38:7) when the foundations of the earth were laid. Therefore, they must have had the ability to understand and to shout, and to experience joy, while yet experiencing only a spiritual existence:

> Then the Lord answered Job out of the whirlwind, and said,
> Who is this that darkeneth counsel by words without knowledge?
> Gird up now thy loins like a man; for I will demand of thee, and answer thou me.
> Where wast thou when I laid the foundations of the earth? declare, if thou hast understanding.
> Who hath laid the measures thereof, if thou knowest? or who hath stretched the line upon it?
> Whereupon are the foundations thereof fastened? or who laid the corner stone thereof;
> When the morning stars sang together, and all the sons of God shouted for joy? (Job 38:1-7.)

The Apostle Paul understood this principle, and the fact that the Lord was acquainted with all the spirits of men before they dwelt upon the earth. Therefore, he could wisely and justly appoint "the bounds of their habitation" upon the earth:

> And hath made of one blood all nations of men for to dwell on all the face of the earth, and hath determined the times before appointed, and the bounds of their habitation. (Acts 17:26.)

Prophets Chosen Before Birth

This thought gives purpose to life and indicates at least the "noble and great" spirits among whom the Lord stood, including Abraham's spirit, whom also he chose to be his leaders. It indicates that prophets may have an appointed time to come upon the earth to perform the work or mission to which they have been called or assigned in the spirit world, as for example, the Prophet Jeremiah, who was chosen before he was born:

Then the word of the Lord came unto me, saying,

Before I formed thee in the belly I knew thee; and before thou camest forth out of the womb I sanctified thee, and I ordained thee a prophet unto the nations. (Jer. 1:4-5.)

The spirit of Joseph Smith, like Jeremiah, was also one of the "noble and great" ones. The Lord appointed unto him his work, and reserved him to come forth in this dispensation to be a prophet and seer unto the nations. That is why the Lord called Joseph Smith while yet a boy, because he knew Joseph and knew of his integrity and greatness.

The Prophet Lehi, who came to America from Jerusalem about 600 B.C., explained this to his son, Joseph:

And now I speak unto you, Joseph, my last-born. Thou wast born in the wilderness of mine afflictions; yea, in the days of my greatest sorrow did thy mother bear thee.

And may the Lord consecrate also unto thee this land, which is a most precious land, for thine inheritance and the inheritance of thy seed with thy brethren, for thy security forever, if it so be that ye shall keep the commandments of the Holy One of Israel.

And now, Joseph, my last-born, whom I have brought out of the wilderness of mine afflictions, may the Lord bless thee forever, for thy seed shall not utterly be destroyed.

For behold, thou art the fruit of my loins; and I am a descendant of Joseph who was carried captive into Egypt. And great were the covenants of the Lord which he made unto Joseph.

Wherefore, Joseph truly saw our day. And he obtained a promise of the Lord, that out of the fruit of his loins the Lord God would raise up a righteous branch unto the house of Israel; not the Messiah, but a branch which was to be broken off, nevertheless, to be remembered in the covenants of the Lord that the Messiah should be made manifest unto them in the latter days, in the spirit of power, unto the bringing of them out of darkness unto light—yea, out of hidden darkness and out of captivity unto freedom.

For Joseph truly testified, saying: A seer shall the Lord my God raise up, who shall be a choice seer unto the fruit of my loins.

Yea, Joseph truly said: Thus saith the Lord unto me: A choice seer will I raise up out of the fruit of thy loins; and he shall be esteemed highly among the fruit of thy loins. And unto him will I give commandment that he shall do a work for the fruit of thy loins, his brethren, which shall be of great worth unto them, even to the bringing of them to the knowledge of the covenants which I have made with thy fathers.

And I will give unto him a commandment that he shall do none other work, save the work which I shall command him. And I will make him great in mine eyes; for he shall do my work.

And he shall be great like unto Moses, whom I have said I would raise up unto you, to deliver my people, O house of Israel.

And Moses will I raise up, to deliver thy people out of the land of Egypt.

But a seer will I raise up out of the fruit of thy loins; and unto him will I give power to bring forth my word unto the seed of thy loins—and not to the bringing forth of my word only, saith the Lord, but to the convincing them of my word, which shall have already gone forth among them.

Wherefore, the fruit of thy loins shall write; and the fruit of the loins of Judah shall write; and that which shall be written by the fruit of thy loins, and also that which shall be written by the fruit of the loins of Judah, shall grow together, unto the confounding of false doctrines and laying down of contentions, and establishing peace among the fruit of thy loins, and bringing them to the knowledge of their fathers in the latter days, and also to the knowledge of my covenants, saith the Lord.

And out of weakness he shall be made strong, in that day when my work shall commence among all my people, unto the restoring thee, O house of Israel, saith the Lord.

And thus prophesied Joseph, saying: Behold, that seer will the Lord bless; and they that seek to destroy him shall be confounded; for this promise, which I have obtained of the Lord, of the fruit of my loins, shall be fulfilled. Behold, I am sure of the fulfilling of this promise;

And his name shall be called after me; and it shall be after the name of his father. And he shall be like unto me; for the thing, which the Lord shall bring forth by his hand, by the power of the Lord shall bring my people unto salvation. (II Nephi 3:1-15.)

The Antemortal Calling and Ordination of Jesus

In the calling and appointment of Abraham, Jeremiah, Joseph Smith, and, no doubt, many others, the Lord was only following the pattern he had adopted with respect to his Only Begotten Son, Jesus Christ. Read Peter's explanation:

But with the precious blood of Christ, as of a lamb without blemish and without spot:

Who verily was foreordained before the foundation of the world, but was manifest in these last times for you. (I Pet. 1:19-20.)

Thus Jesus was called and ordained before the foundation of the world. It was then that the gospel was prepared and accepted, even before man was placed upon the earth:

In hope of eternal life, which God, that cannot lie, promised before the world began. (Titus 1:2.)

Here we have the reason why the gospel is called "the everlasting gospel," (See Rev. 14:6) because it was prepared "before the world began."

This is also the reason we read of "the Lamb slain from the foundation of the world." (See Rev. 13:8.) Not that Jesus was actually "slain from the foundation of the world," but in the gospel plan then prepared, this was a part of the plan and when his plan was accepted and Lucifer's plan was rejected he freely offered himself to be slain.

Jesus the Creator Before He Was Born

Let us now consider Christ as the creator of this world before he was born in the flesh:

In the beginning was the Word, and the Word was with God, and the Word was God.

The same was in the beginning with God.

All things were made by him; and without him was not any thing made that was made.

In him was life; and the life was the light of men.

And the light shineth in darkness; and the darkness comprehended it not. . . .

That was the true Light, which lighteth every man that cometh into the world.

He was in the world, and the world was made by him, and the world knew him not. . . .

And the Word was made flesh, and dwelt among us, (and we beheld his glory, the glory as of the only begotten of the Father,) full of grace and truth. (John 1:1-5, 9-10, 14.)

It is difficult for us to realize that when the only begotten of the Father took upon himself a body of flesh and bones, notwithstanding the fact that he was the creator of this world, he had to learn to walk and talk as all other children who are born into this world. This is no doubt what Paul had in mind when he said:

For we know in part, and we prophesy in part.

But when that which is perfect is come, then that which is in part shall be done away.

When I was a child, I spake as a child, I understood as a child, I thought as a child: but when I became a man, I put away childish things.

For now we see through a glass, darkly; but then face to face: now I know in part; but then shall I know even as I am known. (I Cor. 13:9-12.)

When we are born into this world, we only have a vague recollection of our pre-existent life. By the inspiration of the Spirit "we see through a glass darkly" and we "know in part" but ultimately our previous knowledge will be restored to us, when that which is perfect comes and then we shall know even as also we are known. Here we have the reason why the world did not recognize Jesus when he came in the flesh:

He was in the world, and the world was made by him, and the world knew him not. (John 1:10.)

But ultimately the veil of darkness, or forgetfulness, that deprives us of the recollection of our existence in the spirit world before this earth was made and of the acquaintances we had there, will be lifted. Then we will see as we are seen and know as we are known and as we were known before earth life. This experience came to Jesus while yet in the flesh. At the age of twelve he was reasoning with the doctors in the temple when Joseph and Mary found him:

And he went down with them, and came to Nazareth, and was subject unto them: but his mother kept all these sayings in her heart.

And Jesus increased in wisdom and stature, and in favour with God and man. (Luke 2:51-52.)

We should remember that before Jesus was born he created this world. Had he brought with him the knowledge and wisdom he then had, it would have been impossible for him to increase "in wisdom." Yet God added unto him as he increased in years, and removed the veil of darkness that hid from him a recollection of His experiences in the spirit world:

I have glorified thee on the earth: I have finished the work which thou gavest me to do.

And now, O Father, glorify thou me with thine own self with the glory which I had with thee before the world was. (John 17:4-5.)

He sought no reward for his work in this world except the place of glory he had with the Father "before the world was":

I came forth from the Father, and am come into the world: again, I leave the world, and go to the Father. (John 16:28.)

Could anything be written with greater plainness?

What and if ye shall see the Son of man ascend up where he was before? (John 6:62.)

With this knowledge restored, Jesus recalled seeing "Satan as lightning fall from heaven." (See Luke 10:18.)

Satan and His Angels Retain Their Knowledge of the Spirit World

It should be remembered that the devil and his angels, when cast down to this earth, (see Rev. 12:9) were not deprived of the knowledge they had while in the spirit world because they did not take upon themselves bodies of flesh and blood and therefore they seek to possess the bodies of those who "kept their first estate" and who are privileged to come upon the earth and take upon themselves bodies.

Consider the experience Jesus had with the man possessed by unclean spirits, whom no man could bind with chains:

But when he saw Jesus afar off, he ran and worshipped him,

And cried with a loud voice, and said, What have I to do with thee, Jesus, thou Son of the most high God? I adjure thee by God, that thou torment me not.

For he said unto him, Come out of the man, thou unclean spirit.

And he asked him, What is thy name? And he answered, saying, My name is Legion: for we are many. (Mark 5:6-9.)

We learn from this that the unclean spirits needed no introduction to Jesus. They knew him. They called him by name: "Jesus, thou Son of the most high God."

It is because the spirits cast out of heaven with Satan

have retained their knowledge and recollection of what happened there before they were cast out, that they knew Jesus and the power given to him. Therefore, they not only obey his commands, but the commands of those sent by him, who bear his priesthood; for instance, the seventy whom Jesus sent into every land whither he himself should come:

> And the seventy returned again with joy, saying, Lord, even the devils are subject unto us through thy name. (Luke 10:17.)

It is because of this knowledge and acquaintance these spirits brought with them that they moved upon Herod to issue an order that all children "from two years old and under," should be slain. (See Matt. 2:16.) Jesus had done nothing to justify such an order being issued, since he was yet only an infant in the flesh, but Satan knew what his mission was to be and from the day of his birth he sought in every possible manner to prevent him from its accomplishment.

The same was true with respect to the mission of Joseph Smith. We have already quoted from his own story, showing how Satan sought to destroy him when but a boy of fourteen years, when he went into the woods to pray. Many other boys of that age had prayed without Satan molesting them. Joseph had not yet had any manifestation from the Lord. Therefore, except for Satan's knowledge and acquaintance which he brought with him from the spirit world, he would not have known that Joseph Smith was different from any other young boy, but he knew who "the noble and great" spirits were. Remember, "there was war in heaven," and Satan led one host, and he knew who the leading spirits of the opposition were.

Because the Lord knew Satan would seek to destroy Joseph Smith and cut short his mission, he moved upon

Moroni to instruct Joseph Smith who recounted the instructions as follows:

> He called me by name, and said unto me that he was a messenger sent from the presence of God to me, and that his name was Moroni; that God had a work for me to do; and that my name should be had for good and evil among all nations, kindreds, and tongues, or that it should be both good and evil spoken of among all people. (P. of G. P., Joseph Smith 2:33.)

To those who know of the great work Joseph Smith did and the wonderful truths he taught, and the nobility of his character, it is easy to understand that the only reason he should be "evil spoken of among all people," is because of Satan's decree to destroy the work of the Lord. In this respect Joseph Smith shared a similar fate with his great Master, and with several of the Apostles of old, to the ultimate giving of his life for his testimony to the world.

The Brother of Jared Looked Upon Jesus While Yet in the Spirit

There is much speculation in the minds of men as to what a spirit really is and its form. We have already pointed out in this chapter that "Man was also in the beginning with God. Intelligence, or the light of truth, was not created or made, neither indeed can be." (D. & C. 93:29.)

We are also taught that these intelligences, of which God is the greatest, (See P. of G. P., Abraham 3:18-19) have been given spiritual bodies and, subsequently, have been given mortal bodies after the same pattern and form as their spirit bodies.

Jesus explained this great truth to the brother of Jared when he appeared before him while yet in the spirit:

And it came to pass that when the brother of Jared had said these words, behold, the Lord stretched forth his hand and touched the stones one by one with his finger. And the veil was taken from off the eyes of the brother of Jared, and he saw the finger of the Lord; and it was as the finger of a man, like unto flesh and blood; and the brother of Jared fell down before the Lord, for he was struck with fear.

And the Lord saw that the brother of Jared had fallen to the earth; and the Lord said unto him: Arise, why hast thou fallen?

And he saith unto the Lord: I saw the finger of the Lord, and I feared lest he should smite me; for I knew not that the Lord had flesh and blood.

And the Lord said unto him: because of thy faith thou hast seen that I shall take upon me flesh and blood; and never has man come before me with such exceeding faith as thou hast; for were it not so ye could not have seen my finger. Sawest thou more than this?

And he answered: Nay; Lord show thyself unto me.

And the Lord said unto him: Believest thou the words which I shall speak?

And he answered: Yea, Lord I know that thou speakest the truth, for thou art a God of truth, and canst not lie.

And when he had said these words, behold, the Lord showed himself unto him, and said: Because thou knowest these things ye are redeemed from the fall; therefore ye are brought back into my presence; therefore I show myself unto you.

Behold, I am he who was prepared from the foundation of the world to redeem my people. Behold, I am Jesus Christ.*

––––

*This statement by the Savior was explained by the late President Franklin D. Richards of the Council of the Twelve Apostles, and is printed here for the information of those who may desire more light on the subject:

Jesus Christ has not only this name, but He has many titles. By searching the scriptures we find twenty or thirty of them. Some of them are "Almighty God, Jehovah, the Son of God, the Christ." Isaiah said concerning Him: "His name shall be called Wonderful, Counselor, the Mighty God, the Everlasting Father, the Prince of Peace." John refers to Him as the "Word of God, King of Kings and Lord of Lords."

Now this name Father is a wonderful name. We understand, generally, that it means one who becomes a father of children. There is a beginning to fatherhood. There was a beginning to the creation of the earth, and there is a beginning to the creation of a man's family; but that is not the only sense in which the word father is used. In the scriptures it is often used in a more general sense, e.g., Joseph said to his brethren, "He (God) has

I am the Father and the Son. In me shall all mankind have light, and that eternally, even they who shall believe on my name; and they shall become my sons and my daughters.

And never have I showed myself unto man who I have created, for never has man believed in me as thou hast. Seest thou that ye are created after mine own image? Yea, even all men were created in the beginning after mine own image.

Behold, this body, which ye now behold, is the body of my spirit; and man have I created after the body of my spirit; and even as I appear unto thee to be in the spirit will I appear unto my people in the flesh. (Ether 3:6-16.)

After giving this account, Moroni added:

And now, as I, Moroni, said I could not make a full account of these things which are written, therefore it sufficeth me to say that Jesus showed himself unto this man in the spirit, even after the manner and in the likeness of the same body even as he showed himself unto the Nephites. (Ether 3:17.)

All Mankind are Begotten Sons and Daughters Unto God

Thus, if our eyes were touched as were the eyes of the brother of Jared, so that we could see the spirits of

----

made me a father to Pharaoh." Why? Because He had given him the power, the wisdom and the understanding to lay up food during the seven years of plenty, sufficient to save not only Egypt, but the neighboring nations in the time of their terrible necessity. In the scriptures Satan is called the father of lies, the father of deceit, of misrepresentation, of contention and strife. George Washington is called the father of this nation. His skill, his warlike prowess, and his readiness to stand at the head of his people, "first in war, first in peace, and first in the hearts of his countrymen," made him the father of his country. Thus Professor Morse is the father of telegraphy, and Mr. Watt the father of steam power development. We see by the foregoing that the meaning of father in this general and broad sense is a creator, a controller, a manager.

The Prophet Mosiah has told us that because of the Spirit, Christ is the Father, and because of His having been born in the flesh, He is the Son, and therefore is called "the very Eternal Father of heaven and earth," which really means that He is the very Eternal Creator of heaven and earth. In the beginning He created the heavens and the earth.

If we turn to the first chapter of John's Revelation, we find that great glory and dominion will be given unto Him "who hath made us kings and priests unto God and his Father." So we see that He does not assume to be the Father of All, but He is the Father of heaven and earth, and is to make men kings and priests unto himself and his Father; knowing that He and his Father are two persons, as is distinctly maintained in all the scriptures. (Franklin L. West, *Life of Franklin D. Richards*, pp. 185-187.)

those with whom we associated in the pre-existent world
before they enter the mortal body, we would see that
they are in the same form and likeness of the mortal
body, and that the spirit possesses all the attributes of
man—the power to speak; the power to think; the power
to choose; the power to rejoice, etc.; that the mortal body
is only the house in which the spirit lives; and that the
spiritual bodies "are begotten sons and daughters unto
God":

> And now, after the many testimonies which have been given
> of him, this is the testimony, last of all, which we give of him:
> That he lives!
>
> For we saw him, even on the right hand of God; and we
> heard the voice bearing record that he is the Only Begotten of
> the Father—
>
> That by him, and through him, and of him, the worlds are
> and were created, and the inhabitants thereof are *begotten sons
> and daughters unto God.* (D. & C. 76:22-24.)

In this remarkable revelation from the Lord to the
Prophet Joseph Smith and Sidney Rigdon, February 16,
1832, we are taught that we are all "begotten sons and
daughters unto God." What a glorious thought, for then
we are justified in assuming that, being literally his sons
and daughters, we are endowed with the possibilities of
becoming like him.

All Mankind Are Brothers and Sisters in the Spirit

The Apostle Paul understood and taught that God is
the father of our spirits, even as we are children of our
earthly fathers in the flesh:

> Furthermore we have had fathers of our flesh which cor-
> rected us, and we gave them reverence: shall we not much
> rather be in subjection unto the *Father of Spirits*, and live? (Heb.
> 12:9.)
>
> For in him we live, and move, and have our being; as certain
> also of your own poets have said, For we are also his *offspring.*

Forasmuch then as we are the *offspring of God,* we ought not to think that the Godhead is like unto gold, or silver, or stone, graven by art and man's device. (Acts 17:28-29.)

Paul also understood that Christ was not only the Only Begotten Son of God in the flesh, but that he was also the firstborn in the spirit:

In whom we have redemption through his blood, even the forgiveness of sins:

Who is the image of the invisible God, the firstborn of every creature. (Col. 1:14-15.)

This gives us to understand the wonderful relationship of our being literally spirit brothers and sisters of our elder brother, Jesus Christ. Jesus understood this relationship when he said to Mary Magdalene, following her visit to the sepulchre when she found the stone taken away:

. . . Touch me not; for I am not yet ascended to my Father: but go to my brethren, and say unto them, I ascend unto *my Father, and your Father;* and to my God, and your God. (John 20:17.)

Such a concept gives real meaning to the salutation Jesus gave to his disciples when he taught them to pray: "Our Father which art in heaven . . ." (Matt. 6:9.)

Jesus did not want to claim God as his father only, but he wanted all men to realize their relationship to him—"Our Father."

Jesus further emphasized this truth:

Be ye therefore perfect, even as your Father which is in heaven is perfect. (Matt. 5:48.)

In the eighth chapter of Proverbs, Wisdom seemed to be speaking, and she indicated that before the earth was, she rejoiced in the habitable parts of the Lord's earth, or the abode of spirits, and that her delights were with the sons of men. Therefore, the sons of men must have been there before this earth was:

The Lord possessed me in the beginning of his way, before his works of old.

I was set up from everlasting, from the beginning, or ever the earth was.

When there were no depths, I was brought forth; when there were no fountains abounding with water.

Before the mountains were settled, before the hills was I brought forth:

While as yet he had not made the earth, nor the fields, nor the highest part of the dust of the world.

When he prepared the heavens, I was there: when he set a compass upon the face of the depth:

When he established the clouds above: when he strengthened the fountains of the deep:

When he gave to the sea his decree, that the waters should not pass his commandment: when he appointed the foundations of the earth:

Then I was by him, as one brought up with him: and I was daily his delight, rejoicing always before him;

Rejoicing in the habitable part of his earth; and my delights were *with the sons of men*. (Prov. 8:22-31.)

Death Marks Man's Return to the World of Spirits

When we realize the truth of this scripture, that before the earth was, we were "brought up with him" and were "daily his delight, rejoicing always before him . . . in the habitable part of his earth," or the world of spirits, it really gives comfort and meaning to the thought of returning home when our spirits leave our bodies in death:

Then shall the dust return to the earth as it was: and the spirit shall return unto God who gave it. (Eccl. 12:7.)

they who keep their second estate shall have glory added upon their heads for ever and ever. (P. of G. P., Abraham 3:24-26.)

Thus the reason for the creation of the earth was to prepare a place whereon the spirits God had begotten may dwell, that he may "prove them herewith, to see if they will do all things whatsoever the Lord their God shall command them."

Condition of Those Who Kept Not Their First Estate

We have already considered the condition of those spirits who "keep not their first estate," and who were cast out of heaven with Satan and who constitute the third of the hosts of heaven cast out as spirits with him and are thus deprived of the privilege of taking upon themselves bodies of flesh and blood. They, therefore, have not "glory in the same kingdom with those who keep their first estate." We probably will never be able to understand in this life, what it means to be deprived of the right and privilege of receiving a body.

When Jesus had cast out the evil spirits from the man whom no man could bind with chains, he asked his name, and the man replied: "Legion: for we are many." (See Mark 5:2-9.) Upon being commanded to leave the body of the man who was possessed, they asked the privilege of entering the bodies of the swine feeding in the field, and when their request was granted, "the herd ran violently down a steep place into the sea." (See Mark 5:13.) It will therefore be seen that because these evil spirits had forfeited the right to bodies of their own, it is so desirable to have a body that they were even willing to enter bodies of swine.

If we can understand the significance of this experience and the lesson it teaches, how can we be sufficiently grateful to our Father in heaven for permitting us to receive our bodies, and for the assurance that after we lay them down in the grave, through the atonement of our Lord, Jesus Christ, we will take them up again in the resurrection.

In a revelation to the Prophet Joseph Smith, the Lord taught:

> For man is spirit. The elements are eternal, and spirit and element, inseparably connected, receive a fulness of joy;
>
> And when separated, man cannot receive a fulness of joy. (D. & C. 93:33-34.)

Thus, the first purpose of earth life is to obtain a body, without which, "man cannot receive a fulness of joy."

The Prophet Lehi also understood the purpose of man's existence:

> Adam fell that men might be; and men are, that they might have joy. (II Nephi 2:25.)

Significance of Our Second Estate

We will now consider the importance of keeping our second estate, which is earth life. May what we have learned concerning the fate of those spirits which kept not their first estate, inspire us with a desire and a will to keep our second estate, that we may have glory added upon our heads for ever and ever.

We should bear in mind that we are here upon this earth with free agency, to be proved to see if we will do all things whatsoever the Lord our God shall command us; for it was to afford us this opportunity that the Lord created the earth. He declared to Moses:

> For behold, this is my work and my glory—to bring to pass the immortality and eternal life of man. (P. of G. P., Moses 1:39.)

To the Prophet Joseph Smith the Lord said:

> And, if you keep my commandments and endure to the end you shall have eternal life, which gift is the greatest of all the gifts of God. (D. & C. 14:7.)

... he that receiveth light, and continueth in God, receiveth more light; and that light groweth brighter and brighter until the perfect day. (D. & C. 50:24.)

In order, therefore, for man to prove himself, he must acquire a knowledge and understanding of the commandments of God which are contained in his gospel. Since it is the Lord's work and glory "to bring to pass the immortality and eternal life of man," we must be engaged in the work of the Lord, for the Lord must have instruments for the accomplishment of his purposes:

Remember the worth of souls is great in the sight of God. . . .

And how great is his joy in the soul that repenteth!

Wherefore, you are called to cry repentance unto this people.

And if it so be that you should labor all your days in crying repentance unto this people, and bring, save it be one soul unto me, how great shall be your joy with him in the kingdom of my Father!

And now, if your joy will be great with one soul that you have brought unto me into the kingdom of my Father, how great will be your joy if you should bring many souls unto me! (D. & C. 18:10, 13-16.)

In February 1829, over a year before the Church was organized, the Lord gave a revelation to the Prophet Joseph Smith from which we quote:

Now behold, a marvelous work is about to come forth among the children of men.

Therefore, O ye that embark in the service of God, see that ye serve him with all your heart, might, mind and strength, *that ye may stand blameless before God at the last day.*

Therefore, if ye have desires to serve God ye are called to the work;

For behold the field is white already to harvest; and lo, he that thrusteth in his sickle with his might, the same layeth up in store that he perisheth not, but bringeth salvation to his soul. (D. & C. 4:1-4.)

The Body of Christ

The Apostle Paul explained that we are all members of the body of Christ, through our acceptance of his gospel, and that each receives a gift, though different, yet by the same spirit, and each is responsible for the proper working of the body:

Now there are diversities of gifts, but the same Spirit.

And there are differences of administrations, but the same Lord.

And there are diversities of operations, but it is the same God which worketh all in all.

But the manifestation of the Spirit is given to every man to profit withal.

For to one is given by the Spirit the word of wisdom; to another the word of knowledge by the same Spirit;

To another faith by the same Spirit; to another the gifts of healing by the same Spirit;

To another the working of miracles; to another prophecy; to another discerning of spirits; to another divers kinds of tongues; to another the interpretation of tongues:

But all these worketh that one and the selfsame Spirit, dividing to every man severally as he will.

For as the body is one, and hath many members, and all the members of that one body, being many, are one body: so also is Christ.

For by one Spirit are we all baptized into one body, whether we be Jews or Gentiles, whether we be bond or free; and have been all made to drink into one Spirit.

For the body is not one member, but many.

If the foot shall say, Because I am not the hand, I am not of the body; is it therefore not of the body?

And if the ear shall say, Because I am not the eye, I am not of the body; is it therefore not of the body?

If the whole body were an eye, where were the hearing? If the whole were hearing, where were the smelling?

But now hath God set the members every one of them in the body, as it hath pleased him.

And if they were all one member, where were the body?

But now are they many members, yet but one body.

And the eye cannot say unto the hand, I have no need of thee: nor again the head to the feet, I have no need of you.

Nay, much more those members of the body, which seem to be more feeble, are necessary . . .

Now ye are the body of Christ, and members in particular.

And God hath set some in the Church, first apostles, secondly prophets, thirdly teachers, after that miracles, then gifts of healings, helps, governments, diversities of tongues.

Are all apostles? are all prophets? are all teachers? are all workers of miracles?

Have all the gifts of healing? do all speak with tongues? do all interpret?

But covet earnestly the best gifts: and yet shew I unto you a more excellent way. (I Cor. 12:4-22, 27-31.)

From this epistle of Paul's, we learn that all who are baptized are baptized into one body, whether Jew or Gentile, whether bond or free; and have all been made to drink into one Spirit. Paul explained at length how each member of the body receives a special spiritual gift, and that all members are necessary for the perfect working of the body—that one member cannot say to the other, "I have no need of thee." We learn that there is work for all the members of the Church of Jesus Christ. Each must develop the gift or talent with which the Lord has endowed him. Paul also pointed out that even the most feeble members are necessary.

Man's Obligations to Improve His Talents

The words of Paul may be compared with the parable Jesus taught of the man traveling into a far country, who delivered his goods unto his servants:

For the kingdom of heaven is as a man travelling into a far country, who called his own servants, and delivered unto them his goods.

And unto one he gave five talents, to another two, and to another one; to every man according to his several ability; and straightway took his journey.

Then he that had received the five talents went and traded with the same, and made them other five talents.

And likewise he that had received two, he also gained other two.

But he that had received one went and digged in the earth, and hid his lord's money.

After a long time the Lord of those servants cometh, and reckoneth with them.

And so he that had received five talents came and brought other five talents, saying, Lord, thou deliveredst unto me five talents: behold, I have gained beside them five talents more.

His lord said unto him, Well done, thou good and faithful servant: thou hast been faithful over a few things, I will make thee ruler over many things: enter thou into the joy of thy lord.

He also that had received two talents came and said, Lord, thou deliveredst unto me two talents: behold I have gained two other talents beside them.

His lord said unto him, Well done, good and faithful servant; thou hast been faithful over a few things, I will make thee ruler over many things: enter thou into the joy of thy lord.

Then he which had received the one talent came and said, Lord, I knew thee that thou art an hard man, reaping where thou hast not sown, and gathering where thou hast not strawed:

And I was afraid, and went and hid thy talent in the earth: lo, there thou hast that is thine.

His lord answered and said unto him, Thou wicked and slothful servant, thou knewest that I reap where I sowed not, and gather where I have not strawed:

Thou oughtest therefore to have put my money to the exchangers, and then at my coming I should have received mine own with usury.

Take therefore the talent from him, and give it unto him which hath ten talents.

For unto every one that hath shall be given, and he shall have abundance: but from him that hath not shall be taken away even that which he hath.

And cast ye the unprofitable servant into outer darkness: there shall be weeping and gnashing of teeth. (Matt. 25:14-30.)

Jesus made it plain that each will be required to give an accounting only for the talents or gifts he has received: "for unto whomsoever much is given, of him shall be much required." (See Luke 12:48.) No man can say that he has received nothing. Even though it be but one talent, he will be expected to develop that talent so that when his Lord comes, he will be able to return it with profit. It will also be noted, that unto him "that hath shall be given, and he shall have abundance: but from him that hath not shall be taken away even that which he hath. And cast ye the unprofitable servant into outer darkness: there shall be weeping and gnashing of teeth."

Can you imagine any greater justification for "weeping and gnashing of teeth," than to learn from your Lord, when called to give an accounting for your life here upon the earth, that while you had been faithful in your spirit existence, and had kept your first estate, that you had failed in your second estate, and when you were put to the test to see if you would do all things whatsoever the Lord your God had commanded you, that you had failed? Remember, the Lord said of such: "Cast ye the unprofitable servant into outer darkness."

We have already considered the fate of the spirits who kept not their first estate, but we have not yet seen the end of those who keep not their second estate. The realization of our failure will be multiplied when "that which is perfect is come," and we regain our recollection of our former existence, at which time, we will "see as we are seen and know as we are known."

Jesus taught his followers that the road to greatness was through service to others:

... but whosoever will be great among you, let him be your minister;

And whosoever will be chief among you, let him be your servant. (Matt. 20:26-27.)

Speaking of the Church of Christ in his day, Peter said:

> But ye are a chosen generation, a royal priesthood, an holy nation, a peculiar people; that ye should shew forth the praises of him who hath called you out of darkness into his marvellous light. (I Pet. 2:9.)

It is evident, therefore, that Peter realized the great responsibility that would rest upon the members of the Church, that "royal priesthood" which we have previously discussed, to "shew forth the praises of him who hath called you out of darkness into his marvellous light," unto all men everywhere.

Heirs of Celestial Glory

In the revelation or vision on the three degrees of glory which the Lord gave to Joseph Smith and Sidney Rigdon at Hiram, Ohio, February 16, 1832, the Lord indicated who will be heirs of celestial glory:

> They are they who are the church of the Firstborn.
>
> They are they into whose hands the Father has given all things—
>
> They are they who are priests and kings, who have received of his fulness, and of his glory;
>
> And are priests of the Most High, after the order of Melchizedek, which was after the order of Enoch, which was after the order of the Only Begotten Son.
>
> Wherefore, as it is written, they are gods, even the sons of God—
>
> Wherefore, all things are theirs, whether life or death, or things present, or things to come, all are theirs and they are Christ's, and Christ is God's. (D. & C. 76:54-59.)

It is evident, therefore, that a man must receive the priesthood after the order of Melchizedek to qualify for exaltation in the celestial kingdom.

Again, in a revelation to the Prophet Joseph Smith in September 1832, on the subject of priesthood, the Lord said:

For whoso is faithful unto the obtaining these two priesthoods of which I have spoken, and the magnifying their calling, are sanctified by the Spirit unto the renewing of their bodies.

They become the sons of Moses and of Aaron and the seed of Abraham, and the church and kingdom, and the elect of God.

And also all they who receive this priesthood receive me, saith the Lord. (D. & C. 84:33-35.)

Marriage and Family Relationships in the Eternal Plan

In our study of the subject of marriage, we called attention to the fact that man without woman cannot accomplish the full measure of his creation:

And the Lord God said, It is not good that the man should be alone; I will make him an help meet for him. . . .

And Adam said, This is now bone of my bones, and flesh of my flesh: she shall be called Woman, because she was taken out of Man.

Therefore shall a man leave his father and his mother, and shall cleave unto his wife: and they shall be one flesh. (Gen. 2:18, 23-24.)

It should be remembered that it was before the fall of Adam and Eve that "God said, It is not good that the man should be alone," and that the two should "be one flesh." Since this was true before the fall, and since God considered man and woman "one flesh," how much more important is it that this relationship should exist following the redemption of man from the effects of the fall, when he shall live forever.

The Apostle Paul understood the importance of this matter:

Nevertheless neither is the man without the woman, neither the woman without the man, in the Lord. (I Cor. 11:11.)

This principle was revealed in great plainness to the Prophet Joseph Smith:

In the celestial glory there are three heavens or degrees;

And in order to obtain the highest, a man must enter into this order of the priesthood (meaning the new and everlasting covenant of marriage);

And if he does not, he cannot obtain it.

He may enter into the other, but that is the end of his kingdom, *he cannot have an increase.* (D. & C. 131:4.)

For behold, I reveal unto you a new and an everlasting covenant; and if ye abide not that covenant, then are ye damned; for no one can reject this covenant and be permitted to enter into my glory.

For all who will have a blessing at my hands shall abide the law which was appointed for that blessing, and the conditions thereof, as were instituted from before the foundation of the world.

And as pertaining to the new and everlasting covenant, it was instituted for the fulness of my glory; and he that receiveth a fulness thereof must and shall abide the law, or he shall be damned, saith the Lord God. . . .

Therefore, if a man marry him a wife in the world, and he marry her not by me nor by my word, and he covenant with her so long as he is in the world and she with him, their covenant and marriage are not of force when they are dead, and when they are out of the world; therefore, they are not bound by any law when they are out of the world.

Therefore, when they are out of the world they neither marry nor are given in marriage; but are appointed angels in heaven; which angels are ministering servants, to minister for those who are worthy of a far more, and an exceeding and an eternal weight of glory.

For these angels did not abide my law; therefore, they cannot be enlarged, but remain separately and singly, without exaltation, in their saved condition, to all eternity; and from henceforth are not gods, but are angels of God forever and ever. . . .

And again, verily I say unto you, if a man marry a wife by my word, which is my law, and by the new and everlasting covenant, and it is sealed unto them by the Holy Spirit of promise, by him who is anointed, unto whom I have appointed this power and the keys of this priesthood; and it shall be said unto them—Ye shall come forth in the first resurrection; and if it be after the first resurrection, in the next resurrection; and shall inherit thrones, kingdoms, principalities, and powers, dominions, all heights and depths . . . it shall be done unto them in all things whatsoever my servant hath put upon them, in time, and through all eternity; and shall be of full force when they are out of the world; and they shall pass by the angels, and the gods, which are set there, to their exaltation and glory in all things, as hath been sealed upon their heads, *which glory shall be a fulness and a continuation of the seeds forever and ever.*

Then shall they be gods, because they have no end; therefore shall they be from everlasting to everlasting, because they continue; then shall they be above all, because they have all power, and the angels are subject unto them.

Verily, verily, I say unto you, except ye abide my law ye cannot attain to this glory. (D. & C. 132:4-6, 15-17, 19-21.)

From this revelation, it will be seen that men can become Gods and enjoy a "fulness and a continuation of the seeds forever and ever," only by observing the new and everlasting covenant of marriage, and that without marriage they can only become "ministering servants, to minister for those who are worthy of a far more, and an exceeding, and an eternal weight of glory."

When the Lord said, referring to the new and everlasting covenant of marriage, "and if ye abide not that covenant, then are ye damned," he does not use the term "damned" in the sense that it is usually understood by the modern Christian world, for it will be noted he indicated they "shall be appointed angels in heaven; which angels are ministering servants; to minister for those who are worthy of a far more and an exceeding, and an eternal weight of glory." In verse seventeen of the above quotation, the Lord stated that they shall "remain separately and singly, without exaltation, in their *saved condition.*" Thus even they will be *saved,* but not exalted. The use of the word "damned," therefore, means that one's progress is stopped; (See D. & C. 131:4.) "they cannot be enlarged." (See D. & C. 132:17.)

In our consideration of the mission of Elijah as pertaining to the subject of marriage, we explained how the

Lord has made provision so that "the new and everlasting covenant of marriage," can be vicariously performed in the temples of the Lord for those who have been deprived that privilege in mortality.

Children Are a Heritage of the Lord

In this study of the importance of marriage as a step in our eternal progression, we have noted that this glory "shall be a fulness and a continuation of the seeds forever and ever." (See D. & C. 132:19.)

The Psalmist understood the place of children in the Lord's scheme of things:

Lo, children are an heritage of the Lord: and the fruit of the womb is his reward.

As arrows are in the hand of a mighty man; so are children of the youth.

Happy is the man that hath his quiver full of them. . . . (Ps. 127:3-5.)

In ancient Israel it was considered a reproach for a woman to be barren. Observe Rachel's statement to Jacob:

And when Rachel saw that she bare Jacob no children, Rachel envied her sister; and said unto Jacob, Give me children, or else I die. . . .

And God remembered Rachel, and God hearkened to her, and opened her womb.

And she conceived, and bare a son; and said, God hath taken away my reproach. (Gen. 30:1, 22-23.)

Consider the promise made to Abraham and Sarah, when Abraham was a hundred years old and Sarah was ninety, that she should bear a son and that his name should be Isaac:

And I will bless her, and give thee a son also of her: yea, I will bless her, and she shall be a mother of nations; kings of people shall be of her. (Gen. 17:16.)

It will be noted that this particular blessing the Lord gave to Abraham and to Sarah, his wife, made possible the fulfilment of this further promise:

And the Lord said, Shall I hide from Abraham that thing which I do;

Seeing that Abraham shall surely become a great and mighty nation, and all the nations of the earth shall be blessed in him? (Gen. 18:17-18.)

Without a posterity, therefore, the blessings the Lord had in store for Abraham could not have been fully realized: "And all the nations of the earth shall be blessed in him." And Sarah was to "be a mother of nations; kings of people shall be of her."

As all nations of the earth were to be blessed in Abraham and his seed, and as Sarah was to become a mother of nations, and kings of people were to be of her, so is the new and everlasting covenant of marriage necessary that every faithful man may lay the foundation of his kingdom through his wife and his posterity.

There are many faithful people who have done all they consistently could to prove themselves worthy of the choicest blessings of the Lord who have been deprived the privilege of having children in this life, through no fault of their own. On the other hand, there are many who have borne children whose lives have been such that they will be entirely unworthy of them in the eternal worlds. The Lord has provided a millennium, during which time, no doubt, necessary adjustments will be made.

Purpose of Man's Existence upon the Earth

The purpose of man's existence here upon the earth may therefore be summed up as follows:

1. To be proved by God "to see if they will do all

things whatsoever the Lord their God shall command them." (See P. of G. P., Abraham 3:25.)

2. To receive a body of flesh and bones, for the body and spirit when separated "cannot receive a fulness of joy." (See D. & C. 93:33-34.)

3. To prove that they can keep their second estate, even as they have kept their first estate, that they may have "glory added upon their heads for ever and ever." (See P. of G. P., Abraham 3:26.)

4. To develop the gifts and talents to which they are born heirs, that they may be able to give proper accounting of their stewardship; that the Lord may be able to say: "Well done, thou good and faithful servant: thou hast been faithful over a few things, I will make thee ruler over many things: enter thou into the joy of thy lord." (See Matt. 25:21.)

5. To meet the requirements to become heirs of celestial glory, by becoming "priests of the Most High, after the order of Melchizedek." (See D. & C. 76:57.)

6. To be sealed to a companion for time and all eternity by one having authority of the Lord, through the Holy Priesthood, for "neither is the man without the woman, neither the woman without the man, in the Lord." (See I Cor. 11:11.) For without such sealing ordinance of marriage one cannot obtain the highest degree of celestial glory, (See D. & C. 131:1-4.) "which glory shall be a fulness and a continuation of the seeds for ever and ever." (See D. & C. 132:19.)

7. To have children, for "Lo, children are an heritage of the Lord: and the fruit of the womb is his reward. . . . Happy is the man that hath his quiver full of them." (Ps. 127:3,5.)

Again, we are indebted to the revelations of the Lord to the Prophet Joseph Smith in the restoration of the gospel, in this, the Dispensation of the Fulness of Times, to make plain the purpose of man's existence here upon this earth.

CHAPTER 22

WHERE IS MAN GOING?

Man Stands Bewildered

Nothing is more conducive to arriving nowhere than to be going nowhere. That's the spot where, with no guide posts, and little urge, one arrives with utmost certainty.

(Author unknown.)

What is the end of the journey? Many and conflicting are the philosophies and explanations given in answer to this question. The Church should explain, since the Church is to bring to us the word of the Lord and reveal the purpose of life. The Church should be able to speak in definite terms. Why should not a son of God know the purposes and plans of his Heavenly Father? Without this knowledge, religion would be very incomplete. To the lack of this information must be attributed much of the unbelief in the world today, and much of the inactivity in religious matters.

So far as we know there has never been found a tribe so ignorant, so low, so uncultured, that it did not hold in some form the belief that there was that in man which death could not destroy. Is this delusion, or is it a whisper of the eternal Spirit telling of the deathlessness of man?

(Author unknown.)

The great controversy, however, arises over what it is in man that death cannot destroy, and the condition of that life after death.

We have referred to a questionnaire prepared by the School of Education for the Northwestern University in February, 1934, which was answered by five hundred ministers of whom 460, or ninety-two percent were in favor of teaching that those who die go right on living, without making any explanation as to how, or in what form; the thought being that whatever leaves the body at the time of death will continue to live, no reference being made, however, to the possibility of a resurrection. (See *The Deseret News,* February 8, 1934.)

It is this inability of the churches to speak in positive terms that accounts for such articles as the one written by Channing Pollock, entitled, "Heaven Doesn't Matter." After philosophizing on the different kinds of heavens people expect to obtain and referring to Aunt Jane, he wrote: "Shall we like her, or ourselves, as disembodied spirits? I've never thought of myself as a materialist, but the things I've enjoyed all seem to have required body and mind."

Then he added:

> In the resurrection, there is to be no marriage or giving in marriage—and that's a big drawback, too. Personally, I can't conceive a heaven without it. My own ego is so inextricably blended with that of my wife, and my own happiness has been so long a part of hers. Nor would it help much to be vaguely associated with her in spirit. Married life is made up of so many physical and mental contacts, of so many shared fears and hopes, sorrows and joys, pains and comfortings that both of us, and millions of other wives and husbands could not help missing terribly in any conceivable resort of souls. (*North American Review,* reprinted in *The Reader's Digest,* January 1937.)

If there is a Church other than The Church of Jesus Christ of Latter-day Saints which believes and teaches that the family unit of husband, wife, and children will endure in organized form, beyond the grave, the author does not know of it. During a conversation with a prominent minister in the mission field, he admitted that his church did not hold out a promise or assurance of the continuation of the marriage tie or family unit, but he stated, "In my own mind, I find stubborn objections to the stand taken by my church in this matter."

In Senator Albert J. Beveridge's book, *The Young Man and the World,* the Senator pointed out how completely men want to believe in the fundamentals of the Christian religion. As an example, he referred to the following statement made to him by "a man whose name is known to the railroad world as one of the ablest transportation men in the United States":

> I would rather be sure that when a man dies he will live again with his conscious identity, than to have all the wealth of the United States, or to occupy any position of honor or power the world could possibly give.

Through the restoration of the gospel and the new revelations of the Lord to the Prophet Joseph Smith all doubts have been removed on these important questions:

> As in Adam all die, even so in Christ shall all be made alive. (I Cor. 15:22.)

We will lose our bodies in death for a brief span, but they will be returned to us more beautiful than we have ever known them before, and they will be as real and tangible as they are now:

> When the Savior shall appear we shall see him as he is. We shall see that he is a man like ourselves.
>
> And that same sociality which exists among us here will exist among us there, only it will be coupled with eternal glory, which glory we do not now enjoy. (D. & C. 130:1-2.)
>
> The soul shall be restored to the body, and the body to the soul; yea, and every limb and joint shall be restored to its body; yea, even a hair of the head shall not be lost; but all things shall be restored to their proper and perfect frame. (Alma 40:23.)

Joseph Smith's Description of the Angel Moroni

We have never seen a person who has been clothed with "eternal glory," but the Prophet Joseph Smith described such a man, Moroni, when he appeared to him:

... immediately a personage appeared at my bedside, standing in the air, for his feet did not touch the floor.

He had on a loose robe of most exquisite whiteness. It was a whiteness beyond anything earthly I had ever seen; nor do I believe that any earthly thing could be made to appear so exceedingly white and brilliant. His hands were naked, and his arms also, a little above the wrist; so, also, were his feet naked, as were his legs, a little above the ankles. His head and neck were also bare. I could discover that he had no other clothing on but this robe, as it was open, so that I could see into his bosom.

Not only was his robe exceedingly white, but his whole person was glorious beyond description, and his countenance truly like lightning. . . . (P. of G. P., Joseph Smith 2:30-32.)

This is the description of a prophet who lived in the land of America about four hundred years after the resurrection of the Christ, and who had been resurrected for the work the Lord had planned for him to do. There was nothing mystical about him. He was a resurrected man, endowed with "eternal glory," which we do not yet enjoy but which is promised to all faithful followers of the Christ, and which made his very personage and countenance defy description. It is easy to understand, therefore, how the "same sociality" which we now enjoy, can be enjoyed by those who have been endowed with "eternal glory."

John Beholds the Angel of the Lord

When the angel of the Lord was sent to John the Revelator upon the Isle of Patmos, John was so impressed with his personage that he fell down to worship before the feet of the angel which showed him these things:

Then saith he unto me, See thou do it not: for *I am thy fellowservant, and of thy brethren the prophets,* and of them which keep the sayings of this book: worship God. (Rev. 22:9.)

Thus, the angel was but one of the brethren, a real man, but so wonderful that John would gladly have knelt and worshiped him, had the angel not forbidden him.

The "same sociality" we possess here, we will possess there, and we will know each other as we have known each other here.

The Body of Jesus Is Resurrected

Jesus' resurrection was real, the body and spirit having actually been reunited, as the women fully realized when they came to the sepulchre upon the first day of the week:

Now upon the first day of the week, very early in the morning, they came unto the sepulchre, bringing the spices which they had prepared, and certain others with them.

And they found the stone rolled away from the sepulchre.

And they entered in, and found not the body of the Lord Jesus.

And it came to pass, as they were much perplexed thereabout, behold, two men stood by them in shining garments:

And as they were afraid, and bowed down their faces to the earth, they said unto them, Why seek ye the living among the dead?

He is not here, but is risen: remember how he spake unto you when he was yet in Galilee,

Saying, The Son of man must be delivered into the hands of sinful men, and be crucified, and the third day rise again.

And they remembered his words,

And returned from the sepulchre, and told all these things unto the eleven, and to all the rest.

It was Mary Magdalene, and Joanna, and Mary the mother of James, and other women that were with them, which told these things unto the apostles.

And their words seemed to them as idle tales, and they believed them not.

Then arose Peter, and ran unto the sepulchre; and stooping down, he beheld the linen clothes laid by themselves, and departed, wondering in himself at that which was come to pass. . .

And as they thus spake, Jesus himself stood in the midst of them, and saith unto them, Peace be unto you.

But they were terrified and affrighted, and supposed that they had *seen a spirit.*

And he said unto them, Why are ye troubled? and why do thoughts arise in your hearts?

Behold my hands and my feet, that it is I myself: handle me, and see; *for a spirit hath not flesh and bones,* as ye see me have.

And when he had thus spoken, he shewed them his hands and his feet.

And while they yet believed not for joy, and wondered, he said unto them, *Have ye here any meat?*

And they gave him a piece of a broiled fish, and of an honeycomb.

And he took it, and did eat before them. (Luke 24:1-12, 36-43.)

This is undoubtedly the greatest event ever recorded in history. No wonder the words of the women seemed to the Apostles "as idle tales, and they believed them not." Had Jesus not permitted them to behold his body and feel the wounds there, they might still have assumed that they had seen a spirit. But Jesus had to assure them that a "spirit hath not flesh and bones, as ye see me have." To further attest the fact that he had the same body that had been laid in the sepulchre, Jesus said: "Have ye here any meat? And they gave him a piece of a broiled fish, and of an honeycomb. And he took it, and did eat before them."

It was in this same body that Jesus ministered among his disciples, following his resurrection; and in which he appeared to the Nephites (See III Nephi, chapter 11); and in which he appeared to Joseph Smith, while he was but a boy, in the woods on his father's farm at Palmyra, New York; and in which he will again appear with all his holy angels when he comes to claim his kingdom as he has promised.

Jesus himself was to be but the "firstfruits" of the resurrection:

> But every man in his own order: Christ the firstfruits; afterward they that are Christ's at his coming. (I Cor. 15:23.)

Following His resurrection the graves of others were opened, and they came forth:

> And the graves were opened; and many bodies of the saints which slept arose,
>
> And came out of the graves after his resurrection, and went into the holy city, and appeared unto many. (Matt. 27:52-53.)

What a testimony this must have been to the then living saints to see the graves opened and the sleeping saints in resurrected form come forth and appear to many in the holy city! Who could further doubt the reality of the resurrection and the fact that it did consist of reuniting the spirit and the body?

Bodies of the Saints Resurrected

According to the Book of Mormon, the Nephites received a similar witness:

> Verily I say unto you, I commanded my servant Samuel, the Lamanite, that he should testify unto this people, that at the day that the Father should glorify his name in me that there were many saints who should arise from the dead, and should appear unto many, and should minister unto them. And he said unto them: Was it not so?
>
> And his disciples answered him and said: Yea, Lord, Samuel did prophesy according to thy words, and they were all fulfilled.
>
> And Jesus said unto them: How be it that ye have not written this thing, *that many saints did arise and appear unto many and did minister unto them?*
>
> And it came to pass that Nephi remembered that this thing had not been written.

And it came to pass that Jesus commanded that it should be written; therefore it was written according as he commanded. (III Nephi 23:9-13.)

Thus, through the atonement of Christ, the resurrection of the body will come to all who have lived upon the earth in the flesh:

For as in Adam all die, even so in Christ shall all be made alive.

But every man in his own order: Christ the firstfruits; afterward they that are Christ's at his coming.

Then cometh the end, when he shall have delivered up the kingdom to God, even the Father; when he shall have put down all rule and all authority and power.

For he must reign, till he hath put all enemies under his feet.

The last enemy that shall be destroyed is death.

For he hath put all things under his feet. But when he saith all things are put under him, it is manifest that he is excepted, which did put all things under him.

And when all things shall be subdued unto him, then shall the Son also himself be subject unto him that put all things under him, that God may be all in all. (I Cor. 15:22-28.)

The First and Second Resurrections

When Christ shall come again, he will bring with him those who are his, and they will reign with him a thousand years until he shall have subdued all his enemies and put them under his feet, the last enemy being death. Then there shall be no more death; but the dead who have not died in Christ shall not have part in this first resurrection, but shall come forth from their graves at the end of the thousand years, or Christ's millennial reign, to be judged according to the deeds done in the body:

And I saw an angel come down from heaven, having the key of the bottomless pit and a great chain in his hand.

And he laid hold on the dragon, that old serpent, which is the Devil, and Satan, and bound him a thousand years,

And cast him into the bottomless pit, and shut him up, and set a seal upon him, that he should deceive the nations no more, till the thousand years should be fulfilled: and after that he must be loosed a little season.

And I saw thrones, and they sat upon them, and judgment was given unto them: and I saw the souls of them that were beheaded for the witness of Jesus, and for the word of God, and which had not worshipped the beast, neither his image, neither had received his mark upon their foreheads, or in their hands; *and they lived and reigned with Christ a thousand years.*

But the rest of the dead lived not again until the thousand years were finished. This is the first resurrection.

Blessed and holy is he that hath part in the first resurrection: on such the second death hath no power, but they shall be priests of God and of Christ, and shall reign with him a thousand years.

And I saw the dead, small and great, stand before God; and the books were opened: and another book was opened, which is the book of life: and the dead were judged out of those things which were written in the books, according to their works.

And the sea gave up the dead which were in it; and death and hell delivered up the dead which were in them: and they were judged every man according to their works. (Rev. 20: 1-6, 12-13.)

Many believe that the judgment day of the Lord comes at death. While there is a partial judgment and assignment at the time of death, it must not be confused with the final judgment:

Now, concerning the state of the soul between death and the resurrection—Behold, it has been made known unto me by an angel, that the spirits of all men, as soon as they are departed from this mortal body, yea, the spirits of all men, whether they be good or evil, are taken home to that God who gave them life.

And then shall it come to pass, that the spirits of those who are righteous are received into a state of happiness, which is called paradise, a state of rest, a state of peace, where they shall rest from all their troubles and from all care, and sorrow.

And then shall it come to pass, that the spirits of the wicked, yea, who are evil—for behold, they have no part nor portion of the Spirit of the Lord; for behold, they chose evil works rather than good; therefore the spirit of the devil did enter into them, and take possession of their house—and these shall be cast out into outer darkness; there shall be weeping, and wailing, and gnashing of teeth, and this because of their own iniquity, being led captive by the will of the devil.

Now this is the state of the souls of the wicked, yea, in darkness, and a state of awful, fearful looking for the fiery indignation of the wrath of God upon them; thus they remain in this state, as well as the righteous in paradise, until the time of their resurrection. (Alma 40:11-14.)

The final day of judgment, when men shall be assigned to the kingdom or glory to which they will belong, will not come until the end of the thousand years, after Satan shall have been loosed for a brief season, to try the inhabitants of the earth for the last time:

And when the thousand years are expired, Satan shall be loosed out of his prison.

And shall go out to deceive the nations which are in the four quarters of the earth, Gog and Magog, to gather them together to battle: the number of whom is as the sand of the sea.

And they went up on the breadth of the earth, and compassed the camp of the saints about, and the beloved city; and fire came down from God out of heaven, and devoured them.

And the devil that deceived them was cast into the lake of fire and brimstone, where the beast and the false prophet are, and shall be tormented day and night for ever and ever.

And I saw a great white throne, and him that sat on it, from whose face the earth and the heaven fled away; and there was found no place for them. (Rev. 20:7-11.)

To the Prophet Joseph Smith the Lord revealed the following:

And again, verily, verily, I say unto you that when the thousand years are ended, and men again begin to deny their God, then will I spare the earth but for a little season;

And the end shall come, and the heaven and the earth shall be consumed and pass away, and there shall be a new heaven and a new earth.

For all old things shall pass away, and all things shall become new, even the heaven and the earth, and all the fulness thereof, both men and beasts, the fowls of the air, and the fishes of the sea;

And not one hair, neither mote, shall be lost, for it is the workmanship of mine hand. (D. & C. 29:22-25.)

Building the Kingdom of God upon the Earth Following the First Resurrection

Has anyone the capacity or ability to understand what it will mean to be called forth in the morning of the first resurrection to reign with Christ a thousand years and assist him in establishing his kingdom in the earth, and in conquering or subduing all his enemies, until the last enemy, death, has been conquered? Surely he will only call those who are worthy and have the necessary experience and training, for he will need only the "lifters" and not the "leaners." Hence, Paul's statement that he will bring those that are his, at his coming. (See I Cor. 15:23.)

To the Prophet Joseph Smith the Lord revealed who these are to be:

And again we bear record—for we saw and heard, and this is the testimony of the gospel of Christ concerning them who shall come forth in the resurrection of the just—

They are they who received the testimony of Jesus, and believed on his name and were baptized after the manner of his burial, being buried in the water in his name, and thus according to the commandment which he has given—

That by keeping the commandments they might be washed and cleansed from all their sins, and receive the Holy Spirit by the laying on of the hands of him who is ordained and sealed unto this power;

And who overcome by faith, and are sealed by the Holy Spirit of promise, which the Father sheds forth upon all those who are just and true.

They are they who are the church of the Firstborn.

They are they into whose hands the Father has given all things—

They are they who are priests and kings, who have received of his fulness, and of his glory;

And are priests of the Most High, after the order of Melchizedek, which was after the order of Enoch, which was after the order of the Only Begotten Son.

Wherefore, as it is written, they are gods, even the sons of God—

Wherefore, all things are theirs, whether life or death, or things present, or things to come, all are theirs and they are Christ's, and Christ is God's.

And they shall overcome all things.

Wherefore, let no man glory in man, but rather let him glory in God, who shall subdue all enemies under his feet.

These shall dwell in the presence of God and his Christ forever and ever.

These are they whom he shall bring with him, when he shall come in the clouds of heaven to reign on the earth over his people.

They are they who shall have part in the first resurrection. (D. & C. 76:50-64.)

We see, therefore, that they "are priests of the Most High after the order of Melchizedek," and we have pointed out how this priesthood may be obtained by every faithful male member of the Church over twelve years of age. Since only the men can hold the priesthood, this revelation will help us to understand why husbands and wives are to become "one flesh," (See Gen. 2:24) so that they can enjoy the benefits of the priesthood together. This is what Paul had in mind:

Nevertheless neither is the man without the woman, neither the woman without the man in the Lord. (I Cor. 11:11.)

Peter must have had the same thought:

Likewise, ye husbands, dwell with them according to knowledge, giving honour unto the wife, as unto the weaker vessel, and as being *heirs together* of the grace of life; that your prayers be not hindered. (I Pet. 3:7.)

Thus it is clear that husbands and wives are to be "heirs together" of the blessings the Lord has provided for man.

Another comforting fact is the knowledge that we are to dwell on this earth. When Jesus taught his disciples to pray, after paying due deference to their Heavenly Father, the first thing he taught them to ask for was: "Thy kingdom come. Thy will be done in earth, as it is in heaven." (Matt. 6:10.) While this prayer has been uttered by most Christians through the ages, we question if there have been many who have really believed that it would ever be fully answered. Yet we have just referred to the words of the Apostle Paul describing the work and mission of the Savior during the millennium, during which time he shall "put all enemies under his feet," preparatory to delivering the kingdom up to the Father. The prayer will be answered:

Then cometh the end, when he shall have delivered up the kingdom to God, even the Father; when he shall have put down all rule and all authority and power.

For he must reign, till he hath put all enemies under his feet.

The last enemy that shall be destroyed is death. (I Cor. 15:24-26.)

The Prophet Isaiah also saw the earth and the inhabitants thereof during this period of time, and described them in these words:

For, behold, I create new heavens and a new earth; and the former shall not be remembered, nor come into mind.

But be ye glad and rejoice for ever in that which I create: for, behold, I create Jerusalem a rejoicing, and her people a joy.

And I will rejoice in Jerusalem, and joy in my people: and the voice of weeping shall be no more heard in her, not the voice of crying.

There shall be no more thence an infant of days, nor an old man that hath not filled his days: for the child shall die an hundred years old; but the sinner being an hundred years old shall be accursed.

And they shall build houses, and inhabit them; and they shall plant vineyards, and eat the fruit of them.

They shall not build, and another inhabit; they shall not plant, and another eat: for as the days of a tree are the days of my people, and mine elect shall long enjoy the work of their hands.

They shall not labour in vain, nor bring forth for trouble; *for they are the seed of the blessed of the Lord, and their offspring with them.*

And it shall come to pass, that before they call, I will answer; and while they are yet speaking, I will hear.

The wolf and the lamb shall feed together, and the lion shall eat straw like the bullock: and dust shall be the serpent's meat. They shall not hurt nor destroy in all my holy mountain, saith the Lord. (Isa. 65:17-25, see also Isa. 11:6-9.)

Would it be possible to write with greater plainness of the conditions when the earth is to be renewed, and the wolf and the lamb shall feed together? Note how Isaiah makes plain the fact that "they shall build houses, and inhabit them; and they shall plant vineyards, and eat the fruit of them." Who shall do all this? Families, of course, just as they do now. Isaiah added: "for they are the seed of the blessed of the Lord, and their offspring with them." (Isa. 65:23.)

In a revelation to the Prophet Joseph Smith, the Lord further described this condition:

And in that day the enmity of man, and the enmity of beasts, yea, the enmity of all flesh, shall cease from before my face.

And in that day whatsoever any man shall ask, it shall be given unto him.

And in that day Satan shall not have power to tempt any man.

And there shall be no sorrow because there is no death.

> *In that day an infant shall not die until he is old; and his life shall be as the age of a tree;*
>
> *And when he dies he shall not sleep, that is to say in the earth,* but shall be changed in the twinkling of an eye, and shall be caught up, and his rest shall be glorious. (D. & C. 101:26-31.)

It will, therefore, be noted that there is to be no more death; that "an infant shall not die until he is old," at which time he shall not sleep in the earth but shall be "changed in the twinkling of an eye."

Again the Lord revealed to the Prophet Joseph Smith:

> And at that day, when I shall come in my glory, shall the parable be fulfilled which I spake concerning the ten virgins.
>
> For they that are wise and have received the truth, and have taken the Holy Spirit for their guide, and have not been deceived —verily I say unto you, they shall not be hewn down and cast into the fire, but shall abide the day.
>
> *And the earth shall be given unto them for an inheritance;* and they shall multiply and wax strong, and *their children shall grow up without sin unto salvation.*
>
> For the Lord shall be in their midst, and his glory shall be upon them, and he will be their king and their lawgiver. (D. & C. 45:56-59.)

There is nothing difficult to understand, or mythical, about this promise; since we are to live upon this earth, and are to multiply, and our children "shall grow up without sin unto salvation."

Daniel saw the coming of this kingdom of God in the latter days:

> I saw in the night visions, and, behold, one like the Son of man came with the clouds of heaven, and came to the Ancient of days, and they brought him near before him.
>
> And there was given him dominion, and glory, and a kingdom, that all people, nations, and languages, should serve him: his dominion is an everlasting dominion, which shall not pass away, and his kingdom that which shall not be destroyed. (Dan. 7:13-14.)

But the saints of the most High shall take the kingdom, and possess the kingdom for ever, even for ever and ever. . . .

Until the Ancient of days came, and judgment was given to the saints of the most High; and the time came that the saints possessed the kingdom. . . .

And the kingdom and dominion, and the greatness of the kingdom under the whole heaven, shall be given to the people of the saints of the most High, whose kingdom is an everlasting kingdom, and all dominions shall serve and obey him. (Dan. 7:18, 22, 27.)

When these promises find their fulfilment, it will be a great day in the history of this world—the prayer Jesus taught his disciples, will have found its fulfilment:

Thy kingdom come. Thy will be done in earth, as it is in heaven. (Matt. 6:10.)

Work to be Done During the Millennium

Mention has been made of the nature of the work that will be carried on between the membership of the Church living upon the earth, and the resurrected saints, as there will then be freedom of communion between them, during the thousand years of the personal reign of the Savior of the world among his people. Brief reference has been made thereto in considering the keys brought by Elijah, in carrying on the vicarious work of the living for the dead in the temples of the Lord, as pertaining to baptism, laying on of hands for the gift of the Holy Ghost, ordination to the priesthood, endowments, and the sealing of parents to each other for time and all eternity, and the sealing of their children to them.

President Brigham Young described the work to be done during the millennium:

In the Millennium, when the Kingdom of God is established on the earth in power, glory and perfection, and the reign of wickedness that has so long prevailed is subdued, and the Saints of God will have the privilege of building their temples, and of entering into them, becoming, as it were, pillars in the temples of God, and they will officiate for their dead. Then we will see our friends come up, and perhaps some that we have been acquainted with here. If we ask who will stand at the head of the resurrection in this last dispensation, the answer is—Joseph Smith, Junior, the Prophet of God. He is the man who will be resurrected and receive the keys of the resurrection, and he will seal this authority upon others, and they will hunt up their friends and resurrect them when they shall have been officiated for, and bring them up. And we will have revelations to know our forefathers clear back to Father Adam and Mother Eve, and we will enter into the temples of God and officiate for them. Then man will be sealed to man until the chain is made perfect back to Adam, so that there will be a perfect chain of Priesthood from Adam to the winding-up scene.

This will be the work of the Latter-day Saints in the Millennium. (*Discourses of Brigham Young*, p. 116.)

Gospel to be Preached During the Millennium

The millennium will also be the greatest day for preaching the gospel this world has ever known. Follow the words of Jesus Christ to his servant, Joseph Smith, in February, 1831.

Again I say, hearken ye elders of my church, whom I have appointed: Ye are not sent forth to be taught, but to teach the children of men the things which I have put into your hands by the power of my Spirit;

And ye are to be taught from on high. Sanctify yourselves and ye shall be endowed with power, that ye may give even as I have spoken.

Hearken ye, for, behold, that great day of the Lord is nigh at hand.

For the day cometh that the Lord shall utter his voice out of heaven; the heavens shall shake and the earth shall tremble, and the trump of God shall sound both long and loud, and shall say to the sleeping nations: Ye saints arise and live; *ye sinner stay and sleep until I shall call again.*

Wherefore gird up your loins lest ye be found among the wicked.

Lift up your voices and spare not. Call upon the nations to repent, both old and young, both bond and free, saying: *Prepare yourselves for the great day of the Lord;*

For if I, who am a man, do lift up my voice and call upon you to repent, and ye hate me, what will ye say when the day cometh when the thunders shall utter their voices from the ends of the earth, speaking to the ears of all that live, saying—Repent, and prepare for the great day of the Lord?

Yea, and again, when the lightnings shall streak forth from the east unto the west, and shall utter forth their voices until all that live, and make the ears of all tingle that hear, saying these words—Repent ye, for the great day of the Lord is come?

And again, the Lord shall utter his voice out of heaven, saying: Hearken, O ye nations of the earth, and hear the words of that God who made you.

O, ye nations of the earth, how often would I have gathered you together as a hen gathereth her chickens under her wings, but ye would not!

How often have I called upon you by the mouth of my servants, and by the ministering of angels, and by mine own voice, and by the voice of thunderings, and by the voice of lightnings, and by the voice of tempests, and by the voice of famines and pestilences of every kind, and by the great sound of a trump, and by the voice of judgment, and by the voice of mercy all the day long, and by the voice of glory and honor and the riches of eternal life, and would have saved you with an everlasting salvation, but ye would not!

Behold the day has come, when the cup of the wrath of mine indignation is full.

Behold, verily I say unto you, that these are the words of the Lord your God.

Wherefore, labor ye, labor ye in my vineyard for the last time—for the last time call upon the inhabitants of the earth.

For in mine own due time will I come upon the earth in judgment, and my people shall be redeemed and shall reign with me on earth.

For the great Millennium, of which I have spoken by the mouth of my servants, shall come.

For Satan shall be bound, and when he is loosed again he shall only reign for a little season, and then cometh the end of the earth.

And he that liveth in righteousness shall be changed in the twinkling of an eye, and the earth shall pass away so as by fire.

And the wicked shall go away into unquenchable fire, and their end no man knoweth on earth, nor even shall know, until they come before me in judgment.

Hearken ye to these words. Behold, I am Jesus Christ, the Savior of the world. Treasure these things up in your hearts, and let the solemnities of eternity rest upon your minds.

Be sober. Keep all my commandments. Even so. Amen. (D. & C. 43:15-35.)

When one gives consideration to the promised establishment of the kingdom of God upon this earth, to which we have referred, it gives significance to the promise of our Lord in his sermon on the mount: "Blessed are the meek: for they shall inherit the earth." (Matt. 5:5.) It must not be supposed that death can rob the meek of this promise, for it will be theirs for ever and ever.

Man and the Earth Following the Millennium

Let us now consider briefly the condition of the earth after the thousand year millennial reign of Christ. To the Prophet Joseph Smith the Lord revealed:

The place where God resides is a great Urim and Thummim.

This earth, in its sanctified and immortal state, will be made like unto crystal and will be a Urim and Thummim to the inhabitants who dwell thereon whereby all things pertaining to an inferior kingdom, or all kingdoms of a lower order, will be manifest to those who dwell on it; and this earth will be Christ's. (D. & C. 130:8-9.)

John the Revelator spoke also of this time:

And I saw a new heaven and a new earth: for the first heaven and the first earth were passed away; and there was no more sea.

And I John saw the holy city, *new Jerusalem*, coming down from God out of heaven, prepared as a bride adorned for her husband.

And I heard a great voice out of heaven saying, Behold, the tabernacle of God is with men, and he will dwell with them, and they shall be his people, and God himself shall be with them, and be their God.

And God shall wipe away all tears from their eyes; and there shall be no more death, neither sorrow, nor crying, neither shall there be any more pain: for the former things are passed away.

And he that sat upon the throne said, Behold, I make all things new. And he said unto me, Write: for these words are true and faithful.

And he said unto me, It is done. I am Alpha and Omega, the beginning and the end. I will give unto him that is athirst of the fountain of the water of life freely.

He that overcometh shall inherit all things; and I will be his God, and he shall be my son. . . .

And he carried me away in the spirit to a great and high mountain, and shewed me that great city, the *holy Jerusalem*, descending out of heaven from God.

Having the glory of God: and her light was like unto a stone most precious, even like a jasper stone, clear as crystal. (Rev. 21:1-7, 10-11.)

Please note in verse two that John saw "the holy city, new Jerusalem, coming down from God out of heaven." In verse ten, he saw "that great city, the holy Jerusalem, descending out of heaven from God." The first, "new Jerusalem," is the Jerusalem which is to be built here in America as part of the gathering of latter-day Israel, and "that great city, the holy Jerusalem," is the one that Jesus loved.

The Prophet Ether among the Nephites here in America, as recorded in the Book of Mormon, was given to understand the difference between the two Jerusalems:

And now I, Moroni, proceed to finish my record concerning the destruction of the people of whom I have been writing.

For behold, they rejected all the words of Ether; for he truly told them of all things, from the beginning of man; and that after the waters had receded from off the face of this land it became a choice land above all other lands, a chosen land of the Lord; wherefore the Lord would have that all men should serve him who dwell upon the face thereof;

And that it was the place of the New Jerusalem, which should come down out of heaven, and the holy sanctuary of the Lord.

Behold, Ether saw the days of Christ, and he spake concerning a *New Jerusalem upon this land.*

And he spake also concerning the house of Israel, and the Jerusalem from whence Lehi should come—after it should be destroyed it should be built up again, a holy city unto the Lord; wherefore, it could not be a new Jerusalem for it had been in a time of old; but it should be built up again, and become a holy city of the Lord; and it should be built unto the house of Israel.

And that a New Jerusalem should be built up upon this land, unto the remnant of the seed of Joseph, for which things there has been a type.

For as Joseph brought his father down into the land of Egypt, even so he died there; wherefore, the Lord brought a remnant of the seed of Joseph out of the land of Jerusalem, that he might be merciful unto the seed of Joseph that they should perish not, even as he was merciful unto the father of Joseph that he should perish not.

Wherefore, the remnant of the house of Joseph shall be built upon this land; and it shall be a land of their inheritance; and they shall build up a holy city unto the Lord, like unto the Jerusalem of old; and they shall no more be condemned, until the end come when the earth shall pass away.

And there shall be a new heaven and a new earth; and they shall be like unto the old save the old have passed away, and all things have become new.

And then cometh the New Jerusalem; and blessed are they who dwell therein, for it is they whose garments are white through the blood of the Lamb; and they are they who are numbered among the remnant of the seed of Joseph, who were of the house of Israel.

And then also cometh the Jerusalem of old; and the inhabitants thereof, blessed are they, for they have been washed in the blood of the Lamb; and they are they who were scattered and gathered in from the four quarters of the earth, and from the north countries, and are partakers of the fulfilling of the covenant which God made with their father, Abraham.

And when these things come, bringeth to pass the scripture which saith, there are they who were first, who shall be last; and there are they who were last, who shall be first. (Ether 13:1-12.)

Reference should be made to the following:

And I saw no temple therein: for the Lord God Almighty and the Lamb are the temple of it.

And the city had no need of the sun, neither of the moon, to shine in it: for the glory of God did lighten it, and the Lamb is the light thereof. (Rev. 21:22-23.)

There are those who do not understand why there should be no temple in this "holy Jerusalem." The fact is that when the thousand years are ended, the temple work will all have been done, and therefore we will have no more use for a temple, just as we learn from verse twenty-three that we will have no further need of the moon by night or the sun by day, "for the glory of God did lighten it, and the Lamb is the light thereof." (See Rev. 22:23.)

Man's Celestial and Eternal Home

Thus shall the earth in its celestialized form become the abode of those who are worthy of celestial glory, whose names are written in the Lamb's book of life:

And there shall in no wise enter into it any thing that defileth, neither whatsoever worketh abomination, or maketh a lie: but they which are written in the Lamb's book of life. (Rev. 21:27.)

To the Prophet Joseph Smith, by revelation, the Lord gave this further light:

Nevertheless, he that endureth in faith and doeth my will, the same shall overcome, and shall receive an inheritance upon the earth when the day of transfiguration shall come;

When the earth shall be transfigured, even according to the pattern which was shown unto mine apostles upon the mount; of which account the fulness ye have not yet received. (D. & C. 63:20-21.)

> And again, verily I say unto you, the earth abideth the law of a celestial kingdom, for it filleth the measure of its creation, and transgresseth not the law—
>
> Wherefore, it shall be sanctified; yea, notwithstanding it shall die, it shall be quickened again, and shall abide the power by which it is quickened, and *the righteous shall inherit it.* (D. & C. 88:25-26.)
>
> But blessed are the poor who are pure in heart, whose hearts are broken, and whose spirits are contrite, for they shall see the kingdom of God coming in power and great glory unto their deliverance; for the fatness of the earth shall be theirs.
>
> For behold, the Lord shall come, and his recompense shall be with him, and he shall reward every man, and the poor shall rejoice;
>
> And their generations shall inherit the earth from generation to generation, forever and ever. . . . (D. & C. 56:18-20.)

Therefore, with our friends and our families in our resurrected bodies, through our faithfulness, we may inherit this earth "from generation to generation, forever and ever."

John, the Revelator, also beheld this glorious event in vision:

> And I heard a great voice out of heaven saying, Behold, the tabernacle of God is with men, and he will dwell with them, and they shall be his people, and God himself shall be with them, and be their God.
>
> And God shall wipe away all tears from their eyes; and there shall be no more death, neither sorrow, nor crying, neither shall there be any more pain: for the former things are passed away. . . .
>
> He that overcometh shall inherit all things; and I will be his God, and he shall be my son. (Rev. 21:3-4, 7.)

It will be noted that this discussion attempts only to indicate what shall become of those who overcome all things, and thus make themselves worthy of celestial glory, or that glory spoken of as being like unto the sun, the Lord having made plain that they shall inherit this earth "from generation to generation, forever and ever."

Of those not worthy to inherit celestial glory, the Lord said, in a revelation to the Prophet Joseph Smith:

> And they who are not sanctified through the law which I have given unto you, even the law of Christ, must inherit another kingdom, even that of a terrestrial kingdom, or that of a telestial kingdom.
>
> For he who is not able to abide the law of a celestial kingdom cannot abide a celestial glory.
>
> And he who cannot abide the law of a terrestrial kingdom cannot abide a terrestrial glory.
>
> And he who cannot abide the law of a telestial kingdom cannot abide a telestial glory; therefore he is not meet for a kingdom of glory. Therefore he must abide a kingdom which is not a kingdom of glory. (D. & C. 88:21-24.)

Of the sons of perdition, the Lord said:

> . . . they shall go away into everlasting punishment which is endless punishment, which is eternal punishment, to reign with the devil and his angels in eternity, where their worm dieth not, and the fire is not quenched, which is their torment—
>
> And the end thereof, neither the place thereof, nor their torment, no man knows;
>
> Neither was it revealed, neither is, neither will be revealed unto man, except to them who are made partakers thereof. (D. & C. 76:44-46.)

The gospel of the Lord, Jesus Christ, is given unto man to prepare him for celestial glory. The Lord has said concerning those who are not willing to receive the gospel when offered unto them:

> And they who remain shall also be quickened; nevertheless, they shall return again to their own place, to enjoy that which they are willing to receive, because they were not willing to enjoy that which they might have received.
>
> For what doth it profit a man if a gift is bestowed upon him, and he receive not the gift? Behold, he rejoices not in that which is given unto him, neither rejoices in him who is the giver of the gift. (D. & C. 88:32-33.)

Chapter 23

THE SABBATH DAY

Since there has been considerable difference of opinion among Christians as to whether they should worship on the seventh day of the week (Saturday), the sabbath of the Jews, or the first day of the week (Sunday), the day upon which Christ arose from the tomb, called in Holy Writ, the Lord's day, it seems proper that in the restoration of his Church in this dispensation, the Lord should express himself on this subject. He did so in a revelation to the Prophet Joseph Smith given in Zion, Jackson County, Missouri, August 7, 1831, from which we quote:

> And that thou mayest more fully keep thyself unspotted from the world, thou shalt go to the house of prayer and offer up thy sacraments upon my holy day;
>
> For verily this is a day appointed unto you to rest from your labors, and to pay thy devotions unto the Most High;
>
> Nevertheless thy vows shall be offered up in righteousness on all days and at all times;
>
> But remember that on this, the Lord's day, thou shalt offer thine oblations and thy sacraments unto the Most High, confessing thy sins unto thy brethren, and before the Lord. (D. & C. 59:9-12.)

From this revelation, we learn that the Lord designates "the Lord's day" as "my holy day." Again, it is through the revelation of the Lord to his prophet of this dispensation that this truth is made plain, rather than through a study of ancient scriptures or of history. However, let us turn to the scriptures of old to learn that this revelation of the Lord in the reestablishment of his Church upon the earth in this dispensation, in no way conflicts with instructions and revelations given by the Lord through his prophets of former days.

History of the Sabbath Day

Let us pursue a brief study of the history of the sabbath day:

> And on the seventh day God ended his work which he had made; and he rested on the seventh day from all his work which he had made.
>
> And God blessed the seventh day, and sanctified it: because that in it he had rested from all his work which God created and made. (Gen. 2:2-3.)

From this account it is clear that "God blessed the seventh day, and sanctified it: because that in it he had rested from all his work." But from a study of the scriptures it would appear that the first commandment given through any of the prophets, that the people should observe this as a day of worship, was given through Moses about 2500 years after the creation. In Deuteronomy we learn why God gave the commandment to the children of Israel at that time:

> The Lord our God made a covenant with us in Horeb.
>
> The Lord made not this covenant with our fathers, but with us, even us, who are all of us here alive this day. . . .
>
> Keep the sabbath day to sanctify it, as the Lord thy God hath commanded thee. . . .
>
> And remember that thou wast a servant in the land of Egypt, and that the Lord thy God brought thee out thence through a mighty hand and by a stretched out arm: therefore the Lord thy God commanded thee to keep the sabbath day. (Deut. 5:2-3, 12, 15.)

From this scripture it is apparent that this was a new covenant the Lord made with Israel in Horeb; that he made not this covenant with their fathers; that he made this covenant that they might remember that they were servants in the land of Egypt, and that the Lord their God brought them out through a mighty hand and by a stretched-out arm, therefore the Lord their God commanded them to keep the sabbath day.

This commandment to observe the sabbath day was incorporated in the law of Moses, as were also the sabbatic year and the forty-ninth and the fiftieth-year sabbath.

Speaking of the law of Moses, the Apostle Paul stated:

> Wherefore the law was our schoolmaster to bring us unto Christ, that we might be justified by faith. (Gal. 3:24.)

If the law of Moses, therefore, were the schoolmaster to bring us unto Christ, it would seem perfectly reasonable to assume that when Christ had come, there would be no further need of the schoolmaster.

Israel's Sabbath to Cease

When we understand that the law of Moses, including its sabbaths, was a schoolmaster to bring us unto Christ, we are better able to understand why the Lord permitted his prophet, Hosea, to declare that he would cause Israel's sabbaths to cease:

> I will also cause all her mirth to cease, her feast days, her new moons, and her sabbaths, and all her solemn feasts. (Hos. 2:11.)

Can we accept the scriptures as the word of God and question that this prophecy of Hosea should be fulfilled and that the Lord would truly cause Israel's sabbaths to cease? When Hosea's prophecy was fulfilled, the way was obviously opened for the introduction of a new sabbath.

A New Sabbath, the Lord's Day

The Savior understood that a change was to be made in the sabbath:

> And he said unto them, The sabbath was made for man, and not man for the sabbath:

> Therefore the Son of man is Lord also of the sabbath. (Mark 2:27-28.)

Jesus did not come to break the law but to fulfil it. Thus in him, the Jewish sabbath was fulfilled, as was the remainder of the law of Moses, which was the "schoolmaster to bring us unto Christ." Hence, when Christ came, he became also Lord of the Sabbath. He, himself, declared that he came to fulfil the law:

> Think not that I am come to destroy the law, or the prophets: I am not come to destroy, but to fulfil. (Matt. 5:17.)

Since Jesus came to fulfil the law, why then should some still want to retain it? Why should they not prefer to accept that which Jesus brought to take the place of the law, which includes the new sabbath, the first day of the week, or the Lord's day, (Sunday) the day upon which Jesus arose from the tomb? "The Lord's day," is the day he directed his saints in this dispensation to worship him. (See D. & C. 59:12.)

John, the beloved disciple of the Lord, while banished upon the Isle of Patmos, "for the word of God, and for the testimony of Jesus Christ," wrote:

> I was in the Spirit on *the Lord's day*, and heard behind me a great voice, as of a trumpet. (Rev. 1:10.)

Why should this day be called, "The Lord's day," if it were not a sacred day? Remember, "The Son of man is Lord also of the sabbath." (Mark 2:28.)

Because the sabbath day was changed, the Apostle Paul realized that the saints would be criticized, as they were for other practices to which the Jews objected:

> Let no man therefore judge you in meat, or in drink, or in respect of an holyday, or of the new moon, or of the sabbath days. (Col. 2:16.)

This warning from the Apostle Paul would have been entirely uncalled for were the saints worshiping on the Jewish sabbath, for the Jews then would have had no occasion to judge them on this matter.

The Saints Worshiped on the First Day of the Week

There is no record that the saints observed the Jewish sabbath as a day of worship following the resurrection of the Savior. The Apostles did, however, meet with the Jews in their synagogues on their sabbath to teach them the gospel. (See Acts 13:13-44; 17:1-2.)

The records are quite complete, however, indicating that the saints often met to worship on the first day of the week (Sunday), the Lord's day, or the day that Jesus arose from the tomb:

> Then the same day at evening, being the first day of the week, when the doors were shut where the disciples were assembled for fear of the Jews, came Jesus and stood in the midst, and saith unto them, Peace be unto you. (John 20:19.)

> And after eight days again his disciples were within, and Thomas with them: then came Jesus, the doors being shut, and stood in the midst, and said, Peace be unto you. (John 20:26.)

> And upon the first day of the week, when the disciples came together to break bread, Paul preached unto them, ready to depart on the morrow; and continued his speech until midnight. (Acts 20:7.)

> Now concerning the collection for the saints, as I have given order to the churches of Galatia, even so do ye.

> Upon the first day of the week let every one of you lay by him in store, as God hath prospered him, that there be no gatherings when I come. (I Cor. 16:1-2.)

The following scripture is particularly significant since the "day of Pentecost" was the day following the Jewish sabbath:

> And when the day of Pentecost was fully come, they were all with one accord in one place.

And suddenly there came a sound from heaven as of a rushing mighty wind, and it filled all the house where they were sitting.

And there appeared unto them cloven tongues like as of fire, and it sat upon each of them.

And they were all filled with the Holy Ghost, and began to speak with other tongues, as the Spirit gave them utterance. (Acts 2:1-4; see also Lev. 23:15-16.)

What consistent explanation can be given for the fact that the saints met to worship on the first day of the week (Sunday), the Lord's day, the day upon which the Savior rose from the tomb, instead of Saturday, the Jewish sabbath, except that the Lord did cause the Jewish sabbaths to cease as the Prophet Hosea declared he would? Jesus instituted a new sabbath, "the Lord's day," thus becoming "Lord also of the sabbath."

The Greek Bible Designates the First Day of the Week as a Sabbath

This conclusion is further sustained by the fact that the first day of the week (Sunday) is called a sabbath eight times in the original Greek Bible. Had the Bible, therefore, been correctly translated, much of the present confusion in this matter would have been eliminated. Why would the first day of the week (Sunday) be called a sabbath in the Bible if it were not a sabbath? And how did it become a sabbath other than as we have explained?

In the end of the sabbath, as it began to dawn toward the first day of the week ... (Matt. 28:1: In Greek, "Sabbath" instead of "first day of the week.")

This text may be confusing because of its reference to two sabbaths, unless one keeps in mind the fact that the Christian sabbath (first day of the week) follows immediately the Jewish sabbath (seventh day of the week.) Hence the reference to two sabbaths.

> And very early in the morning the first day of the week . . . (Mark 16:2: In Greek, "Sabbath" instead of "first day of the week.")
>
> Now when Jesus was risen early the first day of the week . . . (Mark 16:9: In Greek, "Sabbath" instead of "first day of the week.")
>
> Now upon the first day of the week . . . (Luke 24:1: In Greek, "Sabbath" instead of "first day of the week.")
>
> The first day of the week . . . (John 20:1: In Greek, "Sabbath" instead of "first day of the week.")
>
> Then the same day at evening, being the first day of the week . . . (John 20:19: In Greek, "Sabbath" instead of "first day of the week.")
>
> And upon the first day of the week . . . (Acts 20:7: In Greek "Sabbath" instead of "first day of the week.")
>
> Upon the first day of the week . . . (I Cor. 16:2: In Greek "Sabbath" instead of "first day of the week.")

From the foregoing, it should be clear that the writers of the New Testament fully understood that the first day of the week (Sunday) was a sabbath day, and that it was the day upon which the saints met to worship.

Early Christians Worshiped on the First Day of the Week

The early Church historians stated that the first day of the week, the day on which the Lord arose from the tomb, was held sacred by the Christians as a day of worship. This, together with the evidence we have already submitted, refutes the claims of some that the change from Saturday to Sunday was instituted by Constantine, Emperor of Rome:

> . . . It is indeed true, that Constantine's life was not such as the precepts of Christianity required; and it is also true that he remained a catechumen (unbaptized Christian) all his life, and was received to full membership in the church, by baptism at Nicomedia only a few days before his death.

Footnote 25: . . . That Constantine, long before this time, A. D. 324, declared himself a Christian, and was acknowledged as such by the churches, is certain. It is also true, he had for a long time performed the religious acts of an unbaptized Christian, that is, of a catechumen; for he attended public worship, fasted, prayed, observed the Christian Sabbath and the anniversaries of the martyrs, and watched on the vigils of Easter, etc. (*Mosheim's Church History,* Book 2, Century 4, Part 1, Chap. 1:8.)

. . . The Christians of this century, in piety, assembled for the worship of God and for their advancement on the first day of the week, the day on which Christ reassumed his life; for that this day was set apart for religious worship by the apostles them- selves, and that, after the example of the church at Jerusalem, it was generally observed, we have unexceptionable testimony. (*Mosheim's Church History,* Book 1, Century 1, Part 2, Chap. 4:4.)

Those who were brought up in the ancient order of things, have come to the possession of a new hope, no longer observing the Sabbath (Jewish or seventh day), but living in the observance of the Lord's day (first day) on which also our life was sprung by him and his death. (Epistle to the Magnesians, 101 A. D., Chap. 9, *Ignatius.*)

On one day, the first day of the week, we assembled our- selves together. (*Barderaven,* A.D. 130.)

. . . And on the day which is called Sunday, there is an assembly in the same place of all who live in cities, or in country districts; and the records of the Apostles, or the writings of the Prophets, are read as long as we have time. . . Sunday is the day on which we all hold our common assembly, because it is the first day on which God, when He changed the darkness and matter, made the world; and Jesus Christ our Savior, on the same day, rose from the dead . . . (Justin Martyr, *Apologies,* 1:67, A.D. 140.)

He, in fulfilment of the precept according to the gospel, keeps the Lord's day. (*Clement of Alexandria,* Book 7, Chap. 12, A.D. 193.)

We neither accord with the Jews in their peculiarities in regard to food nor in their sacred days. (*Apologies,* Sec. 21, A.D. 200.)

We ourselves are accustomed to observe certain days, as for example, the Lord's day. (*Origen,* Book 3, Chap. 23, A.D. 201.)

But why is it, you ask, that we gather on the Lord's day to celebrate our solemnities? Because that was the way the Apostles also did. (*De Fuga* XIV:11, 141, 200 A. D.)

It will thus be seen that through the revelations of the Lord to the Prophet Joseph Smith in directing his saints of this dispensation to observe the Lord's day (Sunday), the first day of the week, as a day of worship, he only confirmed his approval of the practice of the saints of former days, as fully sustained by Holy Writ and the early church historians. If they had been in error in abandoning the seventh day (Saturday), the Jewish sabbath, in favor of the Lord's day (Sunday), the first day of the week, the Lord would surely have so indicated, for in restoring the gospel he did not hesitate to correct mistakes that had been made by alleged church leaders through the ages.

CHAPTER 24

PREDESTINATION AND FOREORDINATION

All Lived in the Spirit World

One of the much misunderstood teachings of the holy scriptures is the principle of predestination, as taught by Calvin, one of the early reformers. Had he understood the principle of pre-existence, that we all lived in the spirit world before we were born here upon the earth, it would have enabled him to understand how men could be *foreordained,* called, and chosen before they were born to do certain work here upon the earth without being predestined. He would also have understood how, because of the Lord's acquaintance with the spirits of all his children, he could know in advance what they would do under given circumstances and conditions, even as earthly parents may know largely how their own children will react to given experiences.

But the holy scripture does not sustain the extreme stand taken by many of that thought, that some are predestined to eternal life, and that regardless of what they do, they will achieve it, while others are predestined to eternal damnation, and if so predestined, there is nothing they can do about it; that every act of our lives is predetermined before we are born, and that we cannot deviate therefrom; that whatever happens to us in life is the will of the Lord.

Such a belief would hold the Lord responsible for all the wickedness, disobedience, and unrighteousness in the world. If man is without free agency and choice, then God who created man, must have done the choosing, and hence he and not man is responsible for the life of man.

The explanation usually given is that all men are born fit subjects of eternal damnation, but that by the principle of grace, those whom the Lord elects to predestine or foreordain, may obtain salvation—none others. These we usually call fatalists.

Scriptures Difficult to Understand

The following explanation should be helpful in understanding some of the scriptures pertaining to the doctrine of predestination.

Peter warned that Paul had made some statements on this subject which are very difficult to understand for those who do not have the spirit of prophecy and those who have not studied deeply:

> And account that the longsuffering of our Lord is salvation; even as our beloved brother Paul also according to the wisdom given unto him hath written unto you;
>
> As also in all his epistles, speaking in them of these things; in which are some things hard to be understood, which they that are unlearned and unstable wrest, as they do also the other scriptures, unto their own destruction. (II Pet. 3:15-16.)

Let us now consider some of Paul's statements:

> For this is the word of promise, At this time will I come, and Sarah shall have a son.
>
> And not only this; but when Rebecca also had conceived by one, even by our father Isaac;
>
> (For the children being not yet born, neither having done any good or evil, that the purpose of God according to election might stand, not of works, but of him that calleth;)
>
> It was said unto her, The elder shall serve the younger.
>
> As it is written, Jacob have I loved, but Esau have I hated.
>
> What shall we say then? Is there unrighteousness with God? God forbid. (Rom. 9:9-14.)

From a casual reading of this scripture, one would be inclined to assume that it was before Jacob and Esau were born that the Lord said: "Jacob have I loved, but Esau have I hated." Let us see what the Lord did say before they were born:

> And the Lord said unto her, [Rebekah] Two nations are in thy womb, and two manner of people shall be separated from thy bowels; and the one people shall be stronger than the other people; and the elder shall serve the younger. (Gen. 25:23.)

Thus, before these twin boys were born, the Lord knew what spirits he was sending to become Rebekah's sons and the manner of spirits he would send through them as their posterity, and he knew which one would be born first:

> And hath made of one blood all nations of men for to dwell on all the face of the earth, and hath determined the times before appointed, and the bounds of their habitation. (Acts 17:26.)

Even so the Lord had determined this to be the time and place for Esau and Jacob to be born, and he knew them and the nature of their lives and what they would do under the circumstances and conditions surrounding them. Therefore, the Lord was able to say, even before they were born: "And the elder shall serve the younger."

Now when did the Lord say: "Jacob have I loved, but Esau have I hated"?

Following are the words of the Lord to his Prophet Malachi spoken approximately thirteen hundred years after Jacob and Esau were born:

> The burden of the word of the Lord to Israel by Malachi.
>
> I have loved you, saith the Lord. Yet ye say, Wherein hast thou loved us? Was not Esau Jacob's brother? saith the Lord; yet I loved Jacob,

> And I hated Esau, and laid his mountains and his heritage
> waste for the dragons of the wilderness. (Mal. 1:1-3.)

Thus, thirteen hundred years after their birth, the Lord could well make such a statement. We will not take time to review the life of Jacob, other than to remind the reader that the Lord changed his name to Israel because of his faithfulness, and he now stands at the head of the house of Israel, while Paul gives us this account of Esau's unfaithfulness:

> Lest there be any fornicator, or profane person, as Esau, who
> for one morsel of meat sold his birthright. (Heb. 12:16.)

Now let us consider another of Paul's statements which is often misunderstood. Contenders for the principle of predestination often refer to Romans, chapter nine, as "A *Bible* within a *Bible*":

> Nay but, O man, who art thou that repliest against God?
> Shall the thing formed say to him that formed it, Why hast thou
> made me thus?
>
> Hath not the potter power over the clay, of the same lump
> to make one vessel unto honour, and another unto dishonour?
>
> What if God, willing to shew his wrath, and to make his
> power known, endured with much longsuffering the vessels of
> wrath fitted to destruction;
>
> And that he might make known the riches of his glory on
> the vessels of mercy, which he had afore prepared unto glory.
> (Rom. 9:20-23.)

From this scripture, it is reasoned that the Lord (the potter) has the power from the same lump of clay to make one a vessel unto honor, and another unto dishonor, and that the thing formed cannot say to him that formed it: "Why hast thou made me thus?" Let us, in connection with this statement, consider another of Paul's statements bearing on this same subject:

But in a great house there are not only vessels of gold and of silver, but also of wood and of earth; and some to honour, and some to dishonour.

If a man therefore purge himself from these, he shall be a vessel unto honour, sanctified, and meet for the master's use, and prepared unto every good work. (II Tim. 2:20-21.)

From this statement of Paul's to Timothy, it is very clear that no matter what may be one's handicaps or limitations in life, that by purging himself, he may become "a vessel unto honour, sanctified, and meet for the master's use, and prepared unto every good work."

The Parable of the Talents

This is only a different way of teaching what Jesus taught in the parable of the man traveling into a far country, who called his own servants and delivered unto them his goods:

And unto one he gave five talents, to another two, and to another one; to every man according to his several ability; and straightway took his journey. (Matt. 25:15.)

Then he returned and held an accounting with them. The one who received five talents, returned ten; the one who received two, returned four, and both were rewarded as faithful servants, but the one who received but one buried it in the earth, and of him the Master said:

Take therefore the talent from him, and give it unto him which hath ten talents. (Matt. 25:28.)

Therefore, as Paul said, the thing formed cannot say to him that formed it, "Why hast thou made me thus?"

One may have received five talents, another two and another one, but in the sight of the Lord, it does not matter so much what one has received, as what he does with that which he has been given.

Clay in the Potter's Hand

Jeremiah discussed the work of the potter:

The word which came to Jeremiah from the Lord, saying,

Arise, and go down to the potter's house, and there I will cause thee to hear my words.

Then I went down to the potter's house, and, behold, he wrought a work on the wheels.

And the vessel that he made of clay was marred in the hand of the potter: so he made it again another vessel, as seemed good to the potter to make it.

Then the word of the Lord came to me, saying,

O house of Israel, cannot I do with you as this potter? saith the Lord. Behold, as the clay is in the potter's hand, so are ye in mine hand, O house of Israel.

At what instant I shall speak concerning a nation, and concerning a kingdom, to pluck up, and to pull down, and to destroy it;

If that nation, against whom I have pronounced, turn from their evil, I will repent of the evil that I thought to do unto them.

And at what instant I shall speak concerning a nation, and concerning a kingdom, to build and to plant it;

If it do evil in my sight, that it obey not my voice, then I will repent of the good, wherewith I said I would benefit them. (Jer. 18:1-10.)

It is apparent, therefore, that no matter what may be the characteristics of a nation, if it will turn from its evil, the Lord will repent of the evil that he thought to do unto it, and vice versa, showing that all nations and people have free agency and according to their choice, the Lord will do unto them.

Paul's Discussion of Pharaoh

In Paul's discussion of Pharaoh, it may appear that the ruler had no free will but was raised up for a certain purpose, and that he was without choice:

For the scripture saith unto Pharaoh, Even for this same purpose have I raised thee up, that I might shew my power in thee, and that my name might be declared throughout all the earth.

Therefore hath he mercy on whom he will have mercy, and whom he will he hardeneth. (Roman. 9:17-18; see also Exod. 9:16.)

To understand this statement of Paul's one must keep in mind the principle of pre-existence of spirits— that the spirits of all men lived with God in the spirit world before they were born in the flesh; that the Lord sent certain of the noble and great spirits at a particular time to do a certain work. To illustrate, let us consider the call of the Prophet Jeremiah:

Then the word of the Lord came unto me, saying,

Before I formed thee in the belly I knew thee; and before thou camest forth out of the womb I sanctified thee, and ordained thee a prophet unto the nations. (Jer. 1:4-5.)

In like manner, the Lord knew Pharaoh before he was born, and understood his character and how he would respond to certain circumstances and situations, so as indicated, for a special purpose the Lord raised him up that he might show his power in him. But this did not force Pharaoh in any way to do the things he did, any more than a nation is forced to do what it does. Pharaoh took his time in making up his mind to free the children of Israel:

And Moses and Aaron came in unto Pharaoh, and said unto him, Thus saith the Lord God of the Hebrews, How long wilt thou refuse to humble thyself before me? let my people go, that they may serve me. (Exod. 10:3.)

So Pharaoh was chosen by the Lord and sent into this world at his particular time because the Lord knew him and how he would meet the situation into which he was placed, but he still had the right to exercise his free will.

Salvation Available to All

Another of Paul's statements that is sometimes misunderstood was made to the Ephesians:

> For by grace are ye saved through faith; and that not of yourselves: it is the gift of God:
>
> Not of works, lest any man should boast. (Eph. 2:8-9.)

It is clear that we are saved by grace, for Jesus did for us what we could not have done for ourselves, hence it is not by our works, but through his grace which is made effective to those who accept his gospel and live its teachings. However, Paul understood the difference between universal and individual salvation, which is confusing to many, and therefore makes it difficult for some to understand certain scriptures. Said he:

> For as in Adam all die, even so in Christ shall all be made alive. (I Cor. 15:22.)

Thus, regardless of any act of ours, we shall all be made alive in the resurrection because of the atonement of Christ; but we may be resurrected and yet not be saved in the sense in which that word is so often used in the scriptures. Paul fully understood this as evidenced also in his statement to Titus:

> For the grace of God that bringeth salvation hath appeared to all men. (Titus 2:11.)

Therefore, if all men are not saved, it will be because they, in the exercise of their free will, do not accept of his gift of grace.

From Paul's statement to Timothy it is evident he understood that salvation was available to all men:

> For this is good and acceptable in the sight of God our Saviour;
>
> Who will have all men to be saved, and to come unto the knowledge of the truth. (I Tim. 2:3-4.)

Since, therefore, "God our Savior . . . will have all men to be saved, and to come unto the knowledge of the truth," there is only one reason why all men will not be saved and that is because they have the right to choose for themselves and may choose evil instead of good. Hence there is no group predestined to be saved, for God "will have all men to be saved." How then could he have a predestined group?

That salvation is available to all who will obey the Christ, Paul further made plain in his epistle to the Hebrews:

> Though he were a Son, yet learned he obedience by the things which he suffered;
>
> And being made perfect, *he became the author of eternal salvation unto all them that obey him.* (Heb. 5:8-9.)

Since, therefore, Christ learned obedience by the things which he suffered, so must all men obey him if they would have eternal salvation.

It is plain that Paul understood that the "free gift" was made available to "all men." Hence, no predestined few, but all are to receive according to their works:

> Therefore as by the offence of one judgment came upon all men to condemnation; even so by the righteousness of one the *free gift* came upon *all men* unto justification of life. (Rom. 5:18.)
>
> For we must all appear before the judgment seat of Christ; that every one may receive the things done in his body, according to that he hath done, whether it be good or bad. (II Cor. 5:10.)

Paul further informs us what the "righteous judgment of God" is, and that "there is no respect of persons with God":

> But after thy hardness and impenitent heart treasurest up unto thyself wrath against the day of wrath and revelation of the righteous judgment of God;
>
> Who will render to every man according to his deeds:
>
> To them who by patient continuance in well doing seek for glory and honour and immortality, eternal life:

But unto them that are contentious, and do not obey the truth, but obey unrighteousness, indignation and wrath,

Tribulation and anguish, upon every soul of man that doeth evil, of the Jew first, and also of the Gentile;

But glory, honour, and peace, to every man that worketh good, to the Jew first, and also to the Gentile:

For there is no respect of person with God. (Rom. 2:5-11.)

In his ministry, Jesus made it clear that his gospel of salvation was for all:

And he spake this parable unto them, saying,

What man of you, having an hundred sheep, if he lose one of them, doth not leave the ninety and nine in the wilderness, and go after that which is lost, until he find it?

And when he hath found it, he layeth it on his shoulders, rejoicing.

And when he cometh home, he calleth together his friends and neighbours, saying unto them, Rejoice with me; for I have found my sheep which was lost.

I say unto you, that likewise joy shall be in heaven over one sinner that repenteth, more than over ninety and nine just persons, which need no repentance.

Either what woman having ten pieces of silver, if she lose one piece, doth not light a candle, and sweep the house, and seek diligently till she find it?

And when she hath found it, she calleth her friends and her neighbours together, saying, Rejoice with me; for I have found the piece which I had lost.

Likewise, I say unto you, there is joy in the presence of the angels of God over one sinner that repenteth. (Luke 15:3-10.)

After Jesus had prayed unto his Father for his Apostles, he added:

Neither pray I for these alone, but for them also which shall believe on me through their word;

That they all may be one; as thou, Father, art in me, and I in thee, that they also may be one in us: that the world may believe that thou hast sent me. (John 17:20-21.)

Apostles Invited All unto Salvation

Jesus sent his Apostles into all the world, inviting all nations to accept his gospel:

> And he said unto them, Go ye into all the world, and preach the gospel *to every creature.*
>
> He that believeth and is baptized shall be saved; but he that believeth not shall be damned. (Mark 16:15-16.)

If a certain number were predestined to be saved and only they could be saved, how unreasonable for Jesus to instruct his Apostles to "preach the gospel to every creature."

John the Revelator saw the power that would be given to the Lamb of God to make war with the kings of this world, and with the Lamb were the *called,* the *chosen,* and the *faithful:*

> These shall make war with the Lamb, and the Lamb shall overcome them: for he is Lord of lords, and King of kings: and they that are with him are *called,* and *chosen,* and *faithful.* (Rev. 17:14.)

The gospel of salvation has thus been placed within reach of all our Father's children, and each is given the right to choose for himself as expressed in the poet's words:

> Know this, that every soul is free
> To choose his life and what he'll be;
> For this eternal truth is given,
> That God will force no man to heaven.
> He'll call, persuade, direct aright,
> And bless with wisdom, love and light;
> In nameless ways be good and kind,
> But never force the human mind.
> Freedom and reason make us men,
> Take these away, what are we then?
> Mere animals, and just as well
> The beasts may think of heaven or hell.
> —Wm C. Gregg.

Chapter 25

THE WORD OF WISDOM
The Lord's Law of Health

It is impossible to estimate the good that would result from the world accepting the revelation given by the Lord to his Church in this dispensation, through his prophet, Joseph Smith, at Kirtland, Ohio, February 27, 1833, known as the Word of Wisdom:

A Word of Wisdom, for the benefit of the council of high priests, assembled in Kirtland, and the church, and also the saints in Zion—

To be sent greeting; not by commandment or constraint, but by revelation and the word of wisdom, showing forth the order and will of God in the temporal salvation of all saints in the last days—

Given for a principle with promise, adapted to the capacity of the weak and the weakest of all saints, who are or can be called saints.

Behold, verily, thus saith the Lord unto you: In consequence of evils and designs which do and will exist in the hearts of conspiring men in the last days, I have warned you, and forewarn you, by giving unto you this word of wisdom by revelation—

That inasmuch as any man drinketh wine or strong drink among you, behold it is not good, neither meet in the sight of your Father, only in assembling yourselves together to offer up your sacraments before him.

And, behold, this should be wine, yea, pure wine of the grape of the vine, of your own make.

And, again, strong drinks are not for the belly, but for the washing of your bodies.

And again, tobacco is not for the body, neither for the belly, and is not good for man, but is an herb for bruises and all sick cattle, to be used with judgment and skill.

And again, hot drinks are not for the body or belly.

And again, verily I say unto you, all wholesome herbs God hath ordained for the constitution, nature, and use of man—

Every herb in the season thereof, and every fruit in the season thereof; all these to be used with prudence and thanksgiving.

Yea, flesh also of beasts and of the fowls of the air, I, the Lord have ordained for the use of man with thanksgiving; nevertheless they are to be used sparingly;

And it is pleasing unto me that they should not be used, only in time of winter, or of cold, or famine.

All grain is ordained for the use of man and of beasts, to be the staff of life, not only for man but for the beasts of the field, and the fowls of heaven, and all wild animals that run or creep on the earth;

And these hath God made for the use of man only in times of famine and excess of hunger.

All grain is good for the food of man; as also the fruit of the vine; that which yieldeth fruit, whether in the ground or above the ground—

Nevertheless, wheat for man, and corn for the ox, and oats for the horse, and rye for the fowls and for swine, and for all beasts of the field, and barley for all useful animals, and for mild drinks, as also other grain.

And all saints who remember to keep and do these sayings, walking in obedience to the commandments, shall receive health in their navel and marrow to their bones;

And shall find wisdom and great treasures of knowledge, even hidden treasures;

And shall run and not be weary, and shall walk and not faint.

And I, the Lord, give unto them a promise, that the destroying angel shall pass by them, as the children of Israel, and not slay them. Amen. (D. & C. Section 89.)

The Cost of Forbidden Indulgences

It will be noted that the first purpose of this revelation was the "showing forth the order and will of God in the temporal salvation of all saints in the last days."

As near as we have been able to obtain the figures, the things which God indicated in this revelation are not good for man, i.e., wine or strong drinks, tobacco, hot drinks (coffee and tea), cost the citizens of the United States during the year 1963, approximately the following:

Wine and strong drinks	$11,100,000,000
Tobacco	8,100,000,000
Coffee and Tea	2,650,000,000

$21,850,000,000*

It should be remembered that the Lord, who knows all things, has indicated that "strong drinks are not for the belly, but for the washing of your bodies"; and that "tobacco is not for the body, neither for the belly, and is not good for man, but is an herb for bruises and all sick cattle, to be used with judgment and skill"; and that "hot drinks [coffee and tea] are not for the body or belly." All these things which the Lord has indicated are not good for the body are but narcotics, which weaken rather than strengthen the body—they are but stimulants. Hence the people of the United States are spending nearly twenty-two billion dollars annually for that which weakens rather than strengthens their bodies.

This amount is tremendous. Think what could be done with it! Surely the wisdom of God in giving this revelation to his Church cannot be questioned. Obedience to the Word of Wisdom becomes a temporal salvation to all who observe the Lord's law.

The American Liquor Bill

To better understand the figures we have given, and to show what the Lord had in mind when he gave this revelation for "the temporal salvation of all saints in the last days," consider the following, which does not account for expenditures for tobacco, coffee and tea, but only for alcoholic beverages:

With licensed liquor places so numerous and so conveniently located, the American people spent more than seven billion dollars for alchoholic drinks in 1944. Notice, it is seven

————

*Figures taken from "The U. S. Book of Facts, Statistics and Information," published by Pocket Books, Inc., New York, N. Y.

billion, not seven million! In 1944 the American people spent for liquors approximately as much as they paid for all cultural, religious, and charitable work combined in a similar period of time! And that, too, in the face of the fact that Americans are not tight-fisted in their gifts for education, religion, and charity.

Add up all the money spent for all educational purposes in the United States, 1941-42, including that spent on all public and private schools, teachers' schools and normal colleges, schools for deaf, blind, mentally deficient, and delinquents, and the federal schools for Indians; add to that all the expenditures for the year for all of our six thousand public libraries, our sixteen hundred college and university libraries, and our twenty-eight hundred public school libraries.

Then add to that all the expenditures, gifts, and bequests to organized religion for the year 1942, as reported in June 1944; add next all expenditures from the American Red Cross funds by the national organization and the 3,757 chapters from January 1, 1942, to February 28, 1945; add the total income of the National Foundation for Infantile Paralysis for the eight-month period ending May 31, 1944; add the expenditures for the United States Health Service; add the expenditure by the forty-eight state governments for certain benefits in 1941, such as public safety, health, hospitals, and institutions for the handicapped, public welfare, corrections, and recreation.

Add also all the expenditure of the federal government during the fiscal year of 1944 under the Social Security Act, including old-age assistance, aid to dependent children, aid to blind, unemployment compensation administration; add the Department of Labor expenditure for maternal and child health service, for crippled children; add, finally, the United States Veterans' Administration expenditures during the fiscal year 1944.

When all these vast expenditures are added together you have the sum of $7,039,914,950. This amount is approximately the same as that spent by the American people for alcoholic beverages during 1944!

Another fact related to this seven-billion-dollar expenditure for liquor will arouse businessmen as to its fearful economic drain. Seven billion dollars spent annually for liquors means seven billion dollars syphoned each year out of the cash registers of legitimate business to fill the pockets of the brewers and the distillers. And, yet, as staggering as is the financial cost of alcoholic beverages, the nefarious traffic is guilty of worse crimes than just striking an economic blow.

Right now one of the unpardonable sins of the liquor traffic is that while millions, literally millions, of people in Europe and Asia are starving to death, America used 4,147,555,000 pounds of grain and 238,655,000 pounds of sugar, syrup, and molasses in the manufacture of distilled and fermented liquors in 1944. According to the American Business Men's Research Foundation, 5,341,701 acres of land were required to grow the grain and sugar products used in producing the more than 10,000,000,000 quarts of alcoholic liquors consumed in 1944.

The grain destroyed in the making of distilled liquors and beer in 1943 would have fed 4,223,054 civilians for a whole year at the rate of three pounds a day each. Allowing five and one-half pounds a day (Major-General E. B. Gregory's estimate before the United States Senate hearing, April 14, 1943) for soldiers, this grain would have fed an army of 2,303,000 for an entire year. (Rev. M. E. Lazenby, "Facing Liquor Facts," printed in *The Christian Advocate*.)

Evils and Designs of Conspiring Men

The next reason the Lord gives for giving this revelation to his Church is "In consequence of evils and designs which do and will exist in the hearts of conspiring men in the last days, I have warned you, and forewarn you, by giving unto you this word of wisdom by revelation." Now what are these evils and designs which do and will exist in the hearts of conspiring men? It must be the tremendous amount of money the Lord saw they would spend in the last days in advertising to induce his children to use these things which are not good for man. It is estimated that over one hundred million dollars are spent in advertising strong drink alone, and there must have been more than this amount spent in advertising coffee and tea. As a result of this advertising of liquor alone, Mr. Lazenby continued:

Thinking people easily see the results of such a stupendous advertising campaign. It will mean, first of all, more drinkers.

That is the purpose of the campaign—to get more men and women and young people to drink. It will mean more and more money taken from the channels of legitimate business. It will mean more hunger, more suffering, more poverty, more broken homes, more abandoned and orphaned children, more accidents, more deaths, more insanity, more disease, more suicides, more immorality, more sin. Does America want this? We would better face the facts as they are, and put a stop to the most nefarious traffic known to this nation.

From this, and considering the amounts spent for the advertising of tobacco, coffee, and tea, it is apparent that the Lord acted very wisely in February 1833, when he gave this revelation to his Church of this dispensation, warning them of the "evils and designs which do and will exist in the hearts of conspiring men in the last days."

Wine or Strong Drink

Observe how the following statements of eminent persons confirm the Lord's statement that "wine or strong drink . . . is not good":

Some Little Known Scientific Facts About Liquor

1. Alcohol is not a stimulant. It is a depressant of the central nervous system, the brain and spinal cord.

2. Alcohol is a subtle and deadly habit-forming drug. Beverage alcohol, whether disguised as beer, wine, or whiskey is a "narcotic," as are ether and chloroform. Alcohol has toxic or poisonous effects whenever used, these effects being chiefly if not exclusively due to action on the brain and other parts of the central nervous system . . . mild or severe, acute or chronic according to the amount of alcohol consumed.

3. As a food, alcohol has no value. It provides some heat and energy, no vitamins, and is an expensive source of energy.

4. As a medicine, alcohol may be used as a sedative or a depressant, but not as a reliable stimulant for circulation, respiration, or digestion. Safer medicines are replacing alcohol as depressants.

5. Habitual users of alcohol are numerous, many becoming alcoholics who require medical and psychiatric treatment. It is estimated that there are 750,000 alcoholics in the United States and 2,250,000 on the way. Women alcoholics are steadily increasing in number in this country. (An alcoholic is one who has become physically ill from habitual drinking of alcohol and whose system demands more and more of the drug. He becomes a different personality from his former self and disintegrates into a slave to the thirst.)

6. The bodily functions are not improved by alcohol. Mental acuteness and accuracy of judgment are impaired, and in chronic alcoholics the brain cells may actually degenerate. No student is helped to proficiency of physical or intellectual performance by drinking the poison, whether in mild or large amounts.

7. Alcohol is the cause of various diseases, and is a contributing factor in others. From 10,000 to 12,000 alcoholic patients are given psychiatric treatment in Bellevue Hospital (New York City) annually. (Haven Emerson, M.D., "Summary of Scientific Findings Regarding Beverage Alcohol," published in *The International Student,* 1945.)

To put alcohol in the human brain is like putting sand in the bearings of an engine. (Thomas A. Edison.)

The ravages of drink are greater than those of war, pestilence and famine combined. (Gladstone.)

Drink has drained more blood, hung more crepe, sold more homes, plunged more people into bankruptcy, armed more villains, slain more children, snapped more wedding rings, defiled more innocent, blinded more eyes, twisted more limbs, dethroned more reason, wrecked more manhood, dishonored more womanhood, broken more hearts, blasted more lives, driven more to suicide, and dug more graves than any other poison scourge that ever swept its death-dealing wave across the world. (Evangeline Boothe.)

Tobacco Is Not for the Body

The following statements confirm the announcement made by the Lord in this revelation that "tobacco is not for the body . . . and is not good for man":

The boy who begins cigarette smoking never enters the life of the world. When other boys are taking hold of the world's work he is concerned with the sexton and undertaker.

Cigarette smoking boys are like wormy apples—They drop before the harvest time. The cigarette becomes the master; the smoker its slave. (David Starr Jordan.)

No man or boy who smokes cigarettes can work in my laboratory. There are enough degenerates in the world without manufacturing more by means of cigarettes. (Thomas A. Edison.)

Our hearts are saddened and our eyes filled with tears at the sight of the mangled and crippled human wrecks left as an aftermath of war; but these do not compare in horror with the innumerable multitudes of hereditary defectives left in the wake of the vast army of cigarettes. Is it fair to make the man or woman of tomorrow—our posterity—pay the fiddler for our pleasures today? (Dr. George Thomason, M.D.)

You have seen pictures of military cemeteries near great battlefields.

Upon every headstone is chiseled the inscription: "Killed in action."

If one knew nothing about war, these headstones would be sufficient to impress upon him that war is deadly—that it kills.

How much would you know about tobacco if, upon the tombstone of everyone killed by it were inscribed, "Killed by tobacco"?

You would know a lot more about it than you do now, but you would not know all, because tobacco does more than *kill*. It *halfkills*. It has its victims in the cemeteries and in the streets. It is bad enough to be dead, but it is a question if it is sometimes worse to be half-dead—to be nervous, irritable, unable to sleep well, with efficiency cut in two and vitality ready to snap at the first great strain. . . .

Let me tell you how tobacco kills. Smokers do not all drop dead around the cigar lighters in tobacco stores. They go away and, years later, die of something else. From the tobacco trust's point of view, that is one of the finest things about tobacco. Its victims do not die on the premises, even when sold the worst cigars. They go away, and when they die, the doctors certify that they died of something else—pneumonia, heart disease, typhoid fever, or what not.

In other words, tobacco kills indirectly and escapes the blame.

What killed General Grant? Why, of course you know—cancer. But what caused the cancer in his throat? Do you know? Smoking caused it. General Lee could not get Grant, but tobacco got him.

What killed President McKinley? An assassin's bullet, you say. Partly right and partly wrong. McKinley was shot, but his wound need not have proved fatal. Thousands of men, hurt worse, have survived. But they had good hearts. When a great strain comes, strong hearts are necessary to bring the sufferers through alive. McKinley, when he was born, had a strong heart, but the tobacco habit got him and left his heart muscles soft and flabby. When McKinley had need of a strong heart he went down because he had nothing to keep him up. He had smoked up his most vital strength.

Woodrow Wilson when old was seized by an ailment that brought him almost to the point of death. For hours he was unconscious and for weeks his physicians could not say whether he would live or die. He had need of a good heart. In his hour of need he had a good heart. If Mr. Wilson had been a smoker, Mr. Marshall might have been President.

In the African jungle, Theodore Roosevelt was stricken with such a fever that he begged his son and other companions to save themselves by leaving him to die. He, too, had need of a strong heart—and he had one. Mr. Roosevelt never used tobacco. His African illness was so serious that he returned to America emaciated and shaken, but he at least had the heart-power to enable him to get back.

But the case for or against tobacco cannot be conclusively proved by what happened to this or that man. The point I am trying to make is that when the pinch comes everyone has need of all the heart-power he can muster—and tobacco weakens heart-power. There is no doubt about that. When one's heart is faltering, no doctor ever prescribes nicotine. Nicotine is a slow poison that strikes at the heart first.

Nicotine, after you have used it awhile, puts you in a condition to be "bumped off" by the first thing that hits you. If you saw some men undermine a building until it was ready to topple into the street, and then saw a woman hit the building with a baby carriage and make it topple, you would not say the woman wrecked the building, would you? Yet when a smoker dies of pneumonia the doctor's death certificate gives pneumonia and not tobacco as the cause of death. And the tombstone man with his chisel says nothing at all. (Luther Burbank, *Tobacco, Tombstones and Profits*.)

Hot Drinks (Tea and Coffee) Are Not for the Body

Note this brief but pointed summary of the harmful effects of tea and coffee:

Coffee and tea, very much alike in their immediate physiological action, both contain dangerous drugs. Like all other such poisons, their effects differ with the quantity given and condition of the user. A person with a sensitive nervous system or one not in full strength is affected most quickly. A small amount of a drug may give a feeling of exhilaration while a large dose may produce death. Nevertheless, the constant taking of small doses of a poisonous drug has a cumulative effect and leads eventually to disease.

The physiological effects of caffeine have been studied experimentally by many investigators, especially in Europe. All have come to practically the same conclusion. All agree that the use of caffeine-containing beverages is harmful to the body and reduces normal health. No principle laid down in the Word of Wisdom has received more complete vindication by progressing science.

Coffee and tea act directly upon the brain. A small dose of caffeine, as found in a cup of coffee, stimulates the mental powers and banishes drowsiness. Connected thought becomes more difficult, for impressions come more rapidly. However, the period of reaction and depression more than offsets the artificially induced brilliance. Throughout a period of a week, month or year, the person who depends upon normal foods, rest and play for the regeneration of the power spent in daily activity will produce more and better work than the person can possibly do who resorts to artificial unnatural stimulation to accomplish the tasks before him.

The wider effect of caffeine upon the brain was put to experimental test by Professor Storm van Leuwen, of the University of Leyden, Holland. A dog was confined in a cage which registered every movement of the animal. After a small dose of caffeine, the movements of the dog increased more than three times; and a very small dose resulted in extreme restlessness during sleep. Caffeine has **the same** effect upon human beings.

All coffee and tea drinkers may suffer, sooner or later, and usually do so, from insomnia, irritability, loss of memory, high blood pressure, headaches and other nervous disorders.

Dr. Hawk administered coffee "over a prolonged period," one to three times daily to 100 normal young men. The nervous system was "very definitely" and unfavorably affected and as a result the mechanical and mental efficiency of the coffee drinker was materially lowered and they became less efficient human machines.

The heart and circulatory system are likewise affected by caffeine. Several investigators have demonstrated that not only are the heartbeats somewhat increased after coffee or tea drinking, but there follows also an irregularity of the heart, and an increase in the blood pressure. This means that more work is placed upon the heart. The increased rate of breathing after a cup of coffee is well known to every coffee user. There is direct action also upon the muscles, which has given rise to the statement that more muscular work may be done by men under the influence of caffeine. This is true, for a brief period, but as with the apparent mental brilliance after coffee drinking, the work done over a longer period of time is greater by the non-user of caffeine. (Dr. John A. Widtsoe, *The Word of Wisdom*, pp. 92-94.)

Herbs and Fruits in the Season Thereof

In the revelation known as the Word of Wisdom, the Lord further stated:

And again, verily I say unto you, all wholesome herbs God hath ordained for the constitution, nature, and use of man—

Every herb in the season thereof, and every fruit in the season thereof; all these to be used with prudence and thanksgiving. (D. & C. 89:10-11.)

Elder Joseph F. Merrill of the Council of the Twelve spoke on this phase of the Word of Wisdom in a radio address delivered December 30, 1945, over Station KSL, Salt Lake City, Utah, from which we quote:

In any modern reliable book on foods and health, such as *How To Live,* by Fisher and Fisk, (the recent edition by Fisher and Haven Emerson), or *Food, Nutrition and Health,* by McCollum and Simmonds, many details may be found, not given in the

Word of Wisdom. Personally, I like to regard these details as fillers to the *Word of Wisdom,* since so far as I have read, all these details are complementary to, and in agreement with, this remarkable document. None of them contradict its statements. For instance, in the document we find the following: "And again, verily I say unto you, all wholesome herbs God hath ordained for the constitution, nature, and use of man. Every herb *in the season thereof* and every fruit *in the season thereof;* all these to be used with prudence and thanksgiving." Modern dietetics, as you undoubtedly know, fully confirm these statements. In fact, in recent years since the discovery of vitamins renewed emphasis has been placed by the newer books upon the value for human food of fruits and vegetables, particularly *fresh fruits and vegetables.* No diet is satisfactory that does not contain a liberal amount of these things.

May I call to your attention the significance of the words *"in the season thereof"* as applied to the use of fruits and vegetables? The full meaning of this expression was doubtless not understood by anyone until after the discovery of vitamins some years ago and of the extremely important role they play in the maintenance of health. But, as is now well known, fresh foods only— *"in the season thereof"*—have their full amount of vitamins. In dried, withered, and processed foods there are, in general, important losses of vitamins, resulting in loss of nutritional value in the foods eaten. A continued insufficient supply of vitamins in the food is followed by poor health and often disease. All of this is new knowledge, acquired, as I understand, during the last forty years. Joseph Smith certainly knew nothing about these things.

The Use of Grains

Elder Merrill also mentioned in his radio talk, and the one preceding it, the experiments of Dr. H. V. McCollum of the University of Wisconsin Experiment Station, as contained in the book, *The Newer Knowledge of Nutrition* by Drs. McCollum and Simmonds, feeding grains to animals, confirming the truth and wisdom of the statements contained in the revelation known as the Word of Wisdom, indicating that the statements by the

Lord in this revelation were far in advance of the knowledge of the time.

The Use of Meat

Concerning the use of meats, the Lord revealed the following:

> Yea, flesh also of beasts and of the fowls of the air, I, the Lord, have ordained for the use of man with thanksgiving; nevertheless they are to be used sparingly;
>
> And it is pleasing unto me that they should not be used, only in times of winter, or of cold, or famine. (D. & C. 89:12-13.)

More could be said on this subject, since it has been widely discussed. However, for our purpose, we quote the following:

> A comparison of the findings of modern science regarding the eating of meat, with the injunction of the Word of Wisdom given over one hundred years ago, is most interesting. Two modern scientists have used almost the exact words employed by the Prophet Joseph Smith. Dr. Mottram, Professor of Physiology in the University of London says:
>
> "Meat is chiefly of value as a source of protein. . . . It is, however, wise to *use it in moderation* (italics ours) and to substitute milk and cheese for it whenever possible. This is true from the points of view of individual and national economy as explained above. The idea that meat promotes energy above all foods is a myth that lingers on. Possibly the myth has its roots in some old folk lore, for the scientific ground, if there ever was any for it, disappeared years ago. . . . To sum up: Meats are dear foods; they could be partly or wholly replaced by cheese and milk."
>
> Another distinguished scientist, Dr. Henry C. Sherman, Professor of Chemistry in Columbia University says:
>
> "The undesirable putrefactive bacteria find a favorable medium in meat. It is partly for this reason that meat should be *eaten sparingly* (italics ours) and when eaten should always be well chewed so as to reduce it to the smallest possible particles in the hope that its putrefactive bacteria will be largely killed by the gastric juice."
>
> Moderation in meat eating is taught by nearly all students of

nutrition. The Word of Wisdom declares that meats are to be used sparingly.

"In Times of Famine and Cold." Meats have the power to sustain life for a time if nothing else is eaten, provided that the blood and internal organs—heart, kidneys, liver and brains— are eaten. Under such conditions, the proteins which normally are body builders are burned and used as energy producers. It is clear therefore that in times of famine there could be no objection to using meat as the only article of diet.

In hot weather the meat intake should be reduced, and vegetable proteins substituted.

Professor Mottram, speaking of climate and meat eating says:

"Proteins are rather wastefully utilized by the body and a point for the vegetarian is that there is less wastefulness with cereal proteins than with meat proteins. A practical outcome is that *in hot weather, or in the tropics*, the proteins should be *cut to the minimum* and vegetable protein practically substituted for animal protein." (italics ours) (Dr. John A. Widtsoe, *The Word of Wisdom*, pp. 216-217.)

The Lord's Promise for Keeping the Word of Wisdom

And all saints who remember to keep and do these sayings, walking in obedience to the commandments, shall receive health in their navel and marrow to their bones . . .

And shall run and not be weary, and shall walk and not faint. (D. & C. 89:18, 20.)

The Latter-day Saints everywhere can bear testimony of the fulfilment of this promise, and what a promise it is! Is there a real parent in all the world who would not want to claim this promise for himself and his children? Those of us who know of its value are humbly grateful to the Lord for having revealed such glorious truths for the guidance and blessing of his people.

Since the evidence of the fulfilment of this promise must come from those who have put it to the test, we will refer to Paul C. Kimball, a young Latter-day Saint student, who had been a Rhodes Scholar at Oxford University, England. He entered Oxford in the fall of 1927. He reported his impressions of the conditions he found as compared with the American schools. He found that the boys at Oxford were left free to do and live about as they pleased, which was so different from the strict discipline they were subjected to in the public schools. Many of them went in for smoking and drinking on a large scale.

Paul found that everyone played some kind of game. After a very unpleasant experience in playing English rugby, he decided to practice rowing. In the spring of 1928 he rowed number five in one of the fastest college boats that had raced at Oxford—a boat that entered in six races and won them all. When he returned to the Varsity the following autumn, a number of groups wanted him to coach for them. At Oxford there were no professional coaches, and a man who had rowed with a successful crew was usually asked to take on a coaching job the following year.

Here we quote from an address by Paul C. Kimball as he related his experience in the Salt Lake Tabernacle May 24, 1931:

> One group of young men came to me and said, "We would like you to coach our crew for rowing. None of us has ever rowed before, but we think you can teach us the rudiments." Truthfully, I felt rather weak at that sort of an offer. I had never done any coaching. However, I accepted their invitation, but said to them, "Now, if I am going to coach you, I am going to make you train according to my rules. I will not have a thing to do with you unless you promise to obey them implicitly." The group said, "Well, that is all right with us. What are your rules?" I said, "First of all, you must stop smoking." They murmured at that and pointed out that they had just left school and apparently thought it would be "big" if they could smoke. I then said, "Secondly, you must refrain from the use of alcoholics of all kinds." Having left their prep school and entered the Varsity, they believed it was their right to have their pint of beer for lunch. I said, "You must cut it out. You must also stop using tea."

Finally I said, "You must also stop using coffee." That did not hurt them so much because they said that English coffee was more like mud than anything else.

After the boys had agreed to my training rules (and it took them a week to make the decision), I took them in hand about the middle of October. I worked with them every afternoon for three hours till February, when they competed against crews from all the other colleges of Oxford. There were approximately fifty crews in the races. My boys were competing against crews composed of men who had been rowing since they were tiny tots. This group that I had was made up of inexperienced boys. From October to February those boys trained. *Not one of them, so far as I know, used a cigaret during this period; not one of them had a cup of tea or coffee, or drank any alcoholic drink.* Then came the day of the first race. No one thought that they had the remotest chance of a victory.

The race was on the Thames at Oxford, over a mile and a quarter course. Two cannons were fired, starting the race. Every crew went as hard as it could. As coach, I had to run along the bank and shout words of encouragement to my crew through a megaphone. By the time I had gone about half the distance I was so tired I could not run much farther. My particular crew had not gained anything, nor had they lost anything thus far during the race; they were just even with their competitors.

I thought, "Well, that's a good thing; I will give them my last word of counsel and advice, and sit down and rest." So I shouted through my megaphone, 'Sprint!' They sprinted beautifully and within a minute had stretched out a hundred feet between them and their nearest competitor. They won their race by three hundred feet, and with ease. Everybody said that the next day they would be beaten.

The next day we tried the same tricks and won the race handily. On all six days, a race being slated for each day, they won by large margins, but not because they were experts. They were not as finished a crew as most of the others, nor were they polished in their technique, but the best thing about them was they had stamina. They had some reserve, even after a hard race.

These boys won their races hands down. People came up to me after and said, "Mr. Kimball, how did you manage to get such success with that crew? They were just novices, and yet they made better crews look weak." I answered, *"I made those boys live right. I made them cut out tobacco, alcohol, tea and coffee. When the sprint came, their lungs were clean; their systems were clean; their blood was clean, and their nerves were strong."*

Paul took another group the next year with the same results. Then he had an opportunity to help coach the Oxford swimming team for two years and saw men victorious both years, and then he added: "I saw success come so many times from living the Word of Wisdom that nothing can change my belief in its value."

Truly did the Lord say: "And shall run and not be weary, and shall walk and not faint." (D. & C. 89:20.)

My experience has shown that tobacco slows up the reflexes of athletes, lowers their morale, and does nothing constructive. Athletes who smoke are the careless type, and do not have the best interests of their team at heart. (The late Knute Rockne, former great coach of Notre Dame University.)

During my twenty years in the big leagues I have seen the careers of several promising young ball players ruined by the use of tobacco. Cigarettes are very bad, and my advice is to let them alone. (Walter Johnson, famous big league pitcher.)

No boy can become a star athlete and use tobacco in any form, because it cuts his wind and affects his heart. (Charles Paddock, noted sprinter.)

Testimonies of a similar character can be found in every Latter-day Saint community, and in the homes of all members who observe this law of health.

Wisdom and Great Treasures of Knowledge

The Word of Wisdom contains two more promises:

And shall find wisdom and great treasures of knowledge, even hidden treasures. (D. & C. 89:19.)

Enter the communities of the Latter-day Saints, or their universities and colleges, and see how many of their young men and women have a personal testimony that

God lives; that Jesus is the Christ, the Redeemer of the world; that God hears and answers prayers; and that Joseph Smith was the Lord's prophet of this dispensation, and you will realize that the Lord has given unto them "wisdom and great treasures of knowledge, even hidden treasures." These hidden treasures of knowledge account for the tens of thousands of Latter-day Saints who fill missions for the Church, for an average period of two years, paying their own expenses and receiving no remuneration therefor. At the close of World War II, it was an inspiration to see the thousands of young Latter-day Saint men who had been in the armed forces of their country from one to four years, who were eager to leave their homes again that the cherished desires of their youth to fill a mission for their Church might be realized. Man cannot put such love for the Lord and his work into the human heart—it must come from God.

The health statistics of the Latter-day Saints, which are discussed in chapter 27 are evidences that the Lord is fulfilling this promise unto his people:

> And I, the Lord, give unto them a promise, that the destroying angel shall pass by them, as the children of Israel and not slay them. (D. & C. 89:21.)

The Human Body, A Temple of God

The Apostle Paul understood the importance of our keeping our bodies clean, since they are temples of the Holy Ghost:

> What? know ye not that your body is the temple of the Holy Ghost which is in you, which ye have of God, and ye are not your own?
>
> For ye are bought with a price; therefore glorify God in your body, and in your spirit, which are God's. (I Cor. 6:19-20.)
>
> Know ye not that ye are the temple of God, and that the Spirit of God dwelleth in you?

If any man defile the temple of God, him shall God destroy; for the temple of God is holy, which temple ye are. (I Cor. 3:16-17.)

There are many who think their bodies are their own and that they can do with them what they will, but Paul makes it plain that they are not their own, for they are bought with a price, and that "If any man defile the temple of God, him shall God destroy; for the temple of God is holy, which temple ye are." This makes it easy to understand why the Lord should give to his prophet of this dispensation, the necessary information for the members of his Church so that they might know how they can live that they may not defile their bodies.

In the light of the terrible waste of money for the use of these narcotics, the injury to the human body through their use, and the spiritual uplift that comes to those who keep their bodies clean through abstaining from their use, how can one question the source from whence this revelation (D. & C. Section 89) came? It was far ahead of the scientific thought of its day. It must have, and did, come from God.

"The Truth Shall Make You Free"

The things which the Lord revealed to the Prophet Joseph Smith in the Word of Wisdom, as not being good for man, i.e., wine and strong drinks, tobacco, and hot drinks (tea and coffee), are all habit forming, and many men and women are greater slaves thereto than were the Israelites to the Egyptians. Nothing that the Lord has given that nourishes our bodies is habit forming. In giving us this Word of Wisdom, therefore, emphasis is given to the words of Jesus:

And ye shall know the truth, and the truth shall make you free. (John 8:32.)

CHAPTER 26

THE LAW OF TITHING

The Lord's Law of Finance

It seems that the Lord had two major objectives in mind in giving to his Church the law of tithing in these latter days:

First: The most equitable manner of financing his Church, for the burden is distributed according to one's ability to pay, the penny of the widow being equal to the gold piece of the rich man.

Second: To test the faith of his people, obedience to the law of tithing being accompanied by a promised blessing. Hence, it is the Lord's law of blessing his people.

The Lord gave to the Prophet Joseph Smith this revelation at Far West, Missouri, July 8, 1838, in answer to his supplication: "O Lord, show unto thy servants how much thou requirest of the properties of thy people for a tithing":

Verily, thus saith the Lord, I require all their surplus property to be put into the hands of the bishop of my church in Zion,

For the building of mine house, and for the laying of the foundation of Zion and for the priesthood, and for the debts of the Presidency of my Church.

And this shall be the beginning of the tithing of my people.

And after that, those who have thus been tithed shall pay one-tenth of all their interest annually; and this shall be a standing law unto them forever, for my holy priesthood, saith the Lord.

Verily I say unto you, it shall come to pass that all those who gather unto the land of Zion shall be tithed of their surplus properties, and shall observe this law, or they shall not be found worthy to abide among you.

And I say unto you, if my people observe not this law, to keep it holy, and by this law sanctify the land of Zion unto me, that my statutes and my judgments may be kept thereon, that it may be most holy, behold, verily I say unto you, it shall not be a land of Zion unto you.

And this shall be an ensample unto all the stakes of Zion. Even so. Amen. (D. & C. Section 119.)

The Purpose and Use of Tithing

While the Saints were attempting to establish Zion in the land of Missouri, they followed this requirement as given by the Lord and placed all their surplus property in the hands of the bishop of his Church in Zion. Since that time they have endeavored to comply with the "standing law" given "unto them forever."

And after that, those who have thus been tithed shall pay one-tenth of all their interest annually; and this shall be a standing law unto them forever, for my holy priesthood, saith the Lord. (D. & C. 119:4.)

In this revelation, the Lord indicated the purpose for which the tithing shall be used:

For the building of mine house, and for the laying of the foundation of Zion and for the priesthood, and for the debts of the Presidency of my Church. (D. & C. 119:2.)

If one is interested to know more in detail what the tithing of the Church is used for, we suggest he note that at each annual April general conference of the Church a complete statement of all the expenditures of the Church for the preceding year is made, which statement is published in full in the Church Section of *The Deseret News* and in *The Improvement Era*.

The Lord further directed who shall be responsible to dispose of the tithing:

. . . it [tithing] shall be disposed of by a council, composed of the First Presidency of my Church, and of the bishop and his council, and by my high council; and by mine own voice unto them, saith the lord. . . . (D. & C. Section 120.)

In a revelation given to the Prophet Joseph Smith at Kirtland, Ohio, September 11, 1831, the Lord made very plain the importance of observing the law of tithing:

> Behold, now it is called today until the coming of the Son of Man, and verily it is a day of sacrifice, and a day for the tithing of my people; for he that is tithed shall not be burned at his coming. (D. & C. 64:23.)

How could one's conscience help but burn within him upon the "coming of the Son of Man," if he realized that he had made no contribution to the expense of establishing God's kingdom in the earth, especially when he came to a realization that all he has he obtained from the Lord, for he created the earth and the fulness thereof, and gave us our lives and our being upon this earth, with a promise that we might "inherit the earth" eternally, if we are faithful. Should we, then, not be willing to pay something for such an inheritance? It is not uncommon for a man in this life to pay money for ten to twenty-five years to purchase a small plot of ground for his use while he lives upon the earth. Should he be less interested in acquiring an eternal inheritance?

Payment of Tithing Develops Faith

The Lord has always understood that to ask one to surrender, as evidence of religious faith, part of what he has acquired of this world's goods, requires a great measure of faith in obedience. Therefore, in order to develop and test the faith of his children, the law of sacrifice has been given unto them even when the Lord did not require their gift for the financing of his Church.

Take, for example, Cain and Abel—to them was given the law of sacrifice:

> . . . Cain brought of the fruit of the ground an offering unto the Lord.
>
> And Abel, he also brought of the firstlings of his flock and of the fat thereof. And the Lord had respect unto Abel and to his offering:
>
> But unto Cain and to his offering he had not respect. And Cain was very wroth, and his countenance fell.
>
> And the Lord said unto Cain, Why art thou wroth? and why is thy countenance fallen?
>
> If thou doest well, shalt thou not be accepted? and if thou doest not well, sin lieth at the door. . . . (Gen. 4:3-7.)

The Lord did not need the fruit of Cain's land or the firstlings of Abel's flock, for they were burned as an offering unto the Lord, but Cain and Abel needed to make this sacrifice to prove their love of God and their faith in him.

A careful reading of this text will indicate that Abel's heart was right so he brought "the firstlings of his flock, and the fat thereof," while Cain's offering was made as Satan commanded. (See P. of G. P., Moses 5:18.) Hence, "the Lord had respect unto Abel and to his offering: But unto Cain and to his offering he had not respect. And Cain was very wroth, and his countenance fell," and darkness entered his heart, and he slew his brother, Abel.

Let us now consider Jesus' experience with the rich young man:

> And, behold, one came and said unto him, Good Master, what good thing shall I do, that I may have *eternal life.*
>
> And he said unto him, Why callest thou me good? there is none good but one, that is, God: but if thou wilt enter into life, keep the commandments.
>
> He saith unto him, Which? . . . (Matt. 19:16-18.)

Then Jesus enumerated most of the Ten Commandments, to which the young man replied:

> . . . All these things have I kept from my youth up: what lack I yet?

Jesus said unto him, *If thou wilt be perfect,* go and sell that thou hast, and give to the poor, and thou shalt have treasure in heaven: and come and follow me.

But when the young man heard that saying, he went away sorrowful: for he had great possessions. (Matt. 19:20-22.)

It should be noted that the rich young man asked: "What good thing shall I do, that I may have eternal life?" Then it was that Jesus told him to keep the commandments. When the young man informed him that he had done this from his youth, Mark tells us that "Jesus beholding him loved him." (Mark 10:21.) How wonderful! Jesus loves every man who keeps the commandments, but Jesus tried to teach him the law of perfection, so in answer to the young man's further question: "What lack I yet?" Jesus said unto him, "If thou wilt be *perfect,* go and sell that thou hast, and give to the poor, and thou shalt have treasure in heaven: and come and follow me."

But when the young man heard that saying, he went away sorrowful: for he had great possessions. (Matt. 19:22.)

In this experience, the Savior taught the rich young man that he should be ready to sacrifice all he had, including his time, and follow Jesus in order to obtain perfection. The gospel of Jesus Christ, as restored to the earth in these latter-days, would not be perfect did it not provide all the requirements for our Father's children to reach perfection, for this is what Jesus taught:

Be ye therefore perfect, even as your Father which is in heaven is perfect. (Matt. 5:48.)

Our consideration of the experience of the rich young man will better enable us to understand this teaching of the Master:

No man can serve two masters: for either he will hate the one, and love the other; or else he will hold to the one, and despise the other. Ye cannot serve God and mammon. (Matt. 6:24.)

Abel chose to serve the Lord, "and the Lord had respect unto Abel and to his offering." Cain apparently, in his heart, had greater feeling for Mammon, and his offering was not accepted. The rich young man could not part with his earthly possessions, thus exercising his right of choice, and "he went away sorrowful: for he had great possessions," thus evidencing the fact that he chose to serve Mammon rather than God, thereby proving that he could not live the law of perfection which Jesus attempted to teach him.

The Church of Jesus Christ provides an opportunity for all men to express their choice. Jesus made this plain:

Therefore take no thought, saying, What shall we eat? or, What shall we drink? or, Wherewith shall we be clothed?

(For after all these things do the Gentiles seek:) for your heavenly Father knoweth that ye have need of all these things.

But seek ye first the kingdom of God, and his righteousness; and all these things shall be added unto you. (Matt. 6:31-33.)

The Law of Tithing in Ancient Israel

The law of tithing was observed by the prophets of Israel. Abraham paid tithing to Melchizedek:

For this Melchisedec, king of Salem, priest of the most high God, who met Abraham returning from the slaughter of the kings, and blessed him;

To whom also Abraham gave a tenth part of all; first being by interpretation King of righteousness, and after that also King of Salem, which is, King of peace; . . .

Now consider how great this man was, unto whom even the patriarch Abraham gave *the tenth* of the spoils. (Heb. 7:1-2, 4.)

The Lord gave this commandment to the children of Israel on Mount Sinai:

And all the *tithe* of the land, whether of the seed of the land, or of the fruit of the tree, is the Lord's: it is holy unto the Lord. (Lev. 27:30.)

Thou shalt truly *tithe* all the increase of thy seed, that the field bringeth forth year by year.

And thou shalt eat before the Lord thy God, in the place which he shall choose to place his name there, the *tithe* of thy corn, of thy wine, and of thine oil, and the firstlings of thy herds and of thy flocks; that thou mayest learn to fear the Lord thy God always. (Deut. 14:22-23.)

Thus the purpose was then as it is now: "that thou mayest learn to fear the Lord thy God always."

And as soon as the commandment came abroad, the children of Israel brought in abundance the firstfruits of corn, wine, and oil, and honey, and of all the increase of the field; and *the tithe* of all things brought they in abundantly. (II Chron. 31:5.)

Honour the Lord with thy substance, and with the firstfruits of all thine increase. (Prov. 3:9.)

Jacob promised a tenth of all the Lord gave him:

And this stone, which I have set for a pillar, shall be God's house: and of all that thou shalt give me I will surely *give the tenth* unto thee. (Gen. 28:22.)

The sons of Levi were appointed to receive the tithes:

And verily they that are of the sons of Levi, who receive the office of the priesthood, have a commandment to take *tithes* of the people according to the law, that is, of their brethren, though they come out of the loins of Abraham. (Heb. 7:5.)

Opposition to the Law of Tithing in Modern Times

When the Latter-day Saints first taught the law of tithing as a part of the gospel of Jesus Christ, they were opposed by clergy and laity alike, on the grounds that tithing belonged to the law of Moses, which was fulfilled in Christ, but that it was not a part of the teachings of the New Testament. It is clear, however, that Jesus taught that they should not neglect the payment of their tithes:

> Woe unto you, scribes and Pharisees, hypocrites! for ye *pay tithe* of mint and anise and cummin, and have omitted the weightier matters of the law, judgment, mercy, and faith: these ought ye to have done, *and not to leave the other undone.* (Matt. 23:23; see also Luke 11:42.)

Opposition, however, has now ceased and many of the churches have attempted to adopt the law of tithing with questionable results.

We know that tithing belongs to the gospel of Jesus Christ, for, as we have already indicated, the Lord gave this principle unto his Church by revelation to his prophet of this dispensation, to "be a standing law unto them forever."

Israel to Return to the Law of Tithing

Furthermore, we have been given to understand the third chapter of Malachi, (which was also given unto the Nephites, III Nephi, chapter 24) which we now consider:

> Behold, I will send my messenger, and he shall prepare the way before me: and the Lord, whom ye seek, shall suddenly come to his temple, even the messenger of the covenant, whom ye delight in: behold, he shall come, saith the Lord of hosts.
>
> But who may abide the day of his coming? and who shall stand when he appeareth? for he is like a refiner's fire, and like fullers' soap:
>
> And he shall sit as a refiner and purifier of silver: and he shall purify the sons of Levi, and purge them as gold and silver, that they may offer unto the Lord an offering in righteousness.
>
> Then shall the offering of Judah and Jerusalem be pleasant unto the Lord, as in the days of old, and as in former years.
>
> And I will come near to you to judgment; and I will be a swift witness against the sorcerers, and against the adulterers, and against false swearers, and against those that oppress the hireling in his wages, the widow, and the fatherless, and that turn aside the stranger from his right, and fear not me, saith the Lord of hosts.

For I am the Lord, I change not; therefore ye sons of Jacob are not consumed. (Mal. 3:1-6.)

This constitutes a very definite promise that the Lord will send his messenger to prepare the way before him, and that he shall suddenly come to his temple. This could have had no relationship to his first coming, for he did not come suddenly to his temple.

But the Lord has sent his messenger in these last days, as we have herein set forth. When Jesus comes the second time to reign upon the earth a thousand years, as he has promised, he will "suddenly come to his temple."

All were able to abide the day of his first coming, but when he shall reappear his judgment will be in his hands, and the wicked will fear his coming, and call upon the rocks to hide them as John the Revelator declared:

And said to the mountain and rocks, Fall on us, and hide us from the face of him that sitteth on the throne, and from the wrath of the Lamb:

For the great day of his wrath is come; and who shall be able to stand? (Rev. 6:16-17.)

Then Malachi tells us that the Lord should come near to judgment (verse 5) all of which pertains not to his first but to his second coming.

The Lord, through his Prophet Malachi, indicated that he, the Lord, does not change and implies that it is for this reason that the sons of Jacob are not consumed (verse 6). (We should not forget the promises of the Lord unto Jacob and his seed, as we have previously discussed.)

Therefore, are we better able to understand why the Lord calls men back to repentance:

Even from the days of your fathers ye are gone away from mine ordinances, and have not kept them. Return unto me, and I will return unto you, saith the Lord of hosts. But ye said, Wherein shall we return?

> Will a man rob God? Yet ye have robbed me. But ye say,
> Wherein have we robbed thee? *In tithes and offerings.*
>
> Ye are cursed with a curse: for ye have robbed me, even this
> whole nation. (Mal. 3:7-9.)

Thus the Lord, speaking to Israel, or the descendants of Jacob, accused them of having gone away from his ordinances, and not having kept them. Then he invited them to return unto him, and in turn, he promised to return unto them. This is no idle promise. How could Israel resist? Then the Lord accused them of having robbed him, even the whole nation of Israel. He then pointed out how they have robbed him: *"In tithes and offerings."*

The whole nation of Jacob, or Israel, as far as we know, had gone astray in the observance of this principle when the Lord sent his messenger to restore the gospel in the latter-days. One of the steps, however, in this restoration was the invitation the Lord would extend unto Israel to return to him in the payment of their tithes and offerings. Read his further promise:

> Bring ye all the *tithes* into the storehouse, that there may
> be meat in mine house, and prove me now herewith, saith the
> Lord of hosts, if I will not open you the windows of heaven, and
> pour you out a blessing, that there shall not be room enough to
> receive it.
>
> And I will rebuke the devourer for your sakes, and he shall
> not destroy the fruits of your ground; neither shall your vine cast
> her fruit before the time in the field, saith the Lord of hosts.
> (Mal. 3:10-11.)

What a promise! How could any person or people with faith in God refuse or neglect to respond to such an invitation!

The Latter-day Saints, among the descendants of Jacob, have responded to this invitation. The Lord has kept his promise and has caused the wilderness and the dry places to become fruitful and to blossom as a rose.

And because of the blessings of the Lord thus received, they have been able to contribute liberally of their means and talents in carrying on the great work of the Church, and in sending missionaries to the nations of the earth to proclaim the glad tidings of the restoration of the gospel to those of our Father's children who have not been privileged to hear it.

When Malachi made this promise of the Lord to those to whom he would send his messenger to prepare the way of his coming, he seemed to see that they would accept the Lord's invitation to return unto him, and described the fulfilment of the Lord's promise unto them:

And all nations shall call you blessed: for ye shall be a delightsome land, saith the Lord of hosts. (Mal. 3:12.)

Sidelights on Tithing

A few years ago while laboring in the mission field, the writer attended a meeting in one of the large cities of the United States, at which an itinerant minister, who was traveling from city to city for this purpose, presented the law of tithing to this particular congregation as a means of getting their church out of debt, using this third chapter of Malachi as his text and explaining to the people that tithing was the Lord's law of blessing his people, and assuring them that if they would but pay their tithing for ten months, they could get their Church out of debt, and the Lord would bless them as he had promised. At the close of the meeting the writer had the privilege of being introduced to this minister, at which time he commented on the fact that he was getting near the truth; that the Latter-day Saints had been practicing the principle of tithing for over a hundred years with much success, but that there was one thing about his address that he could not understand—that if tithing were the Lord's plan for blessing his people, why he didn't ask them to pay their tithing for their entire lives; that if it is good to enjoy the blessings of the Lord for ten months, it would be much better to enjoy them for an entire life-time; to which the minister replied: "We cannot go that far yet; we will do well if we can get them to pay for ten months."

In *Our Sunday Visitor,* January 1, 1939, page 14, there appeared, under the sub-heading, *The Mormons,* the following:

> Almighty God's way—the tithe way—automatically places on people the obligation to give proportionately. This tithe system is still in use in some non-Catholic religious bodies, and most notably among the Mormons. The members of the Mormon Church cannot participate in the services in the Temple unless they are "tithers." They must give not only ten percent of their salaries, but of all their income from investments, and should a rich member of the Mormon Church dispose of property valued at $100,000, he would be compelled to give $10,000 of it to his Church.
>
> The Mormon Church has no financial difficulties. In fact, in Utah, the Mormons refused to accept anything from the United States Government in the form of relief. Their Church took care of all their own while unemployed, simply because the revenue from those who were employed and from an accumulated endowment, was able to take care of those out of work.

While the above statement is somewhat erroneous since no member of the Church is "compelled" to give anything to his Church—tithing being a free-will offering —and when a member sells property, he is only expected to pay tithing on his profit and not on the total amount of the sale, nevertheless it indicates that the Catholic Church recognizes that the Mormon Church is following "Almighty God's way—the tithe way," and the question might be logically asked: Why have the other churches not followed "Almighty God's Way?"

Again, the Lord's way is better than man's way, and we did not obtain the details and the application of this truth through the reading of the scriptures, but by the revelations of the Lord through his prophet of this dispensation.

Blessings Through the Payment of Tithing

Let us refer once more to the third chapter of Malachi. While the Lord invites the descendants of Jacob to return unto him in the payment of their tithes and offerings with the assurance that if they will prove him in so doing, he will open the windows of heaven and pour them out blessings, that there shall not be room enough to receive them, it is reasonable to assume that if the Lord rewarded each one immediately upon his obedience, and punished immediately for disobedience, all would keep his commandments, if only for the hope of gain and in fear of punishment. The Lord knew such a condition might arise, and therefore permitted Malachi to warn against it in these words:

Your words have been stout against me, saith the Lord. Yet ye say, What have we spoken so much against thee?

Ye have said, It is vain to serve God: and what profit is it that we have kept his ordinances, and that we have walked mournfully before the Lord of hosts?

And now we call the proud happy; yea, they that work wickedness are set up; yea, they that tempt God are even delivered.

Then they that feared the Lord spake often one to another: and the Lord hearkened, and heard it, and a book of remembrance was written before him for them that feared the Lord, and that thought upon his name.

And they shall be mine, saith the Lord of hosts, in that day when I make up my jewels; and I will spare them, as a man spareth his own son that serveth him.

Then shall ye return, and discern between the righteous and the wicked, between him that serveth God and him that serveth him not. (Mal. 3:13-18.)

Thus in their reasoning about this matter, they pointed out that the wicked, or proud, were happy, and possibly enjoyed more than those who served the Lord (and we take it that Malachi is still referring to the payment of tithes, since this whole chapter seems to deal with this subject and its importance.)

It seems, therefore, to be the ultimate desire of the Lord that none should be disturbed by present disputations, but that through their faithfulness, their names might be recorded in his book of remembrance, that they might be his when he comes to claim his jewels; with the assurance that they will then return and discern the difference "between him that serveth God and him that serveth him not."

It is our conviction that one who accepts the Lord's invitation to return unto him, makes no greater sacrifice when he pays his tithing than the farmer does when he sows his seed in the ground. Both require faith, and both bring their reward.

TITHING

Not mine to keep—not mine to spend,
   Not mine to give, not mine to lend,
'Tis the Lord's part—'tis the Lord's part,
   A tenth of all I gain.
'Tis His to have, 'tis His to use,
   As He, not I, may please to choose,
'Tis the Lord's part—'tis the Lord's part,
   A tenth of all I gain.
He gives me all and asks this part,
   To test the bigness of my heart,
'Tis the Lord's part—'tis the Lord's part,
   A tenth of all I gain.
His part shall be the first and best,
   Of all the ten with which I am blessed.
'Tis the Lord's part—'tis the Lord's part,
   A tenth of all I gain.
            —George H. Brimhall

Chapter 27

BY THEIR FRUITS YE SHALL KNOW THEM

Our claims to the visitation of the Father and the Son and the visits of other heavenly messengers to restore all things, including the restoration of the holy priesthood, giving us a better philosophy of life and a better understanding of the scriptures, would be of little weight and consequence if the fruits of the Church did not bear witness of the truth of these claims. Jesus said:

Beware of false prophets, which come to you in sheep's clothing, but inwardly they are ravening wolves.

Ye shall know them by their fruits. Do men gather grapes of thorns, or figs of thistles?

Even so every good tree bringeth forth good fruit; but a corrupt tree bring forth evil fruit.

A good tree cannot bring forth evil fruit, neither can a corrupt tree bring forth good fruit.

Every tree that bringeth not forth good fruit is hewn down, and cast into the fire.

Wherefore by their fruits ye shall know them. (Matt. 7:15-20.)

Every Church and people must be willing to stand upon this test.

Ideals and Objectives of the Church

Some of the lofty ideals and objectives of the Church are stated in these quotations:

. . . men are that they might have joy. (II Nephi 2:25.)

The glory of God is intelligence. (D. & C. 93:36.)

As God is, man may become. (Eliza R. Snow, *Biography and Family Record of Lorenzo Snow,* p. 46.)

Whatever principle of intelligence we attain unto in this life, it will rise with us in the resurrection.

And if a person gain more knowledge and intelligence in this life through his diligence and obedience than another, he will have so much the advantage in the world to come. (D. & C. 130:18-19.)

It is impossible for a man to be saved in ignorance. (D. & C. 131:6.)

. . . seek ye diligently and teach one another words of wisdom; yea, seek ye out of the best books words of wisdom; seek learning, even by study and also by faith. (D. & C. 88:118.)

Guided and inspired by such divine injunctions, the Church could be expected to achieve much in the establishment of schools, and in the pursuit of education.

The Place of Education in the Church

Dr. John A. Widtsoe and Elder Richard L. Evans wrote concerning some of the teachings and accomplishments of The Church of Jesus Christ of Latter-day Saints:

Within a year of the organization of the Church, in 1831, provision was made for schools, teachers, and schoolbooks. A little later, in 1833, a school for mature men, known as the School of the Prophets, was conducted. This anticipated the present worldwide movement for adult education. In 1842, when the Missouri refugees were building the city of Nauvoo, a university was founded.

On the trek westward, following the expulsion from Nauvoo, school sessions were held in the moving camps. A few weeks after reaching Salt Lake Valley, school instruction was begun in the sage-encircled, pioneer log cabins. One of the first legislative acts, after provision had been made for roads in the wilderness, was the chartering in 1850 of a university, the first west of the Missouri River.

Since then the people, despite the toil of compelling a stubborn desert to serve civilized man, have fostered the training of the mind, with all the attendant arts and cultures.

The need and value of education have never been forgotten by the Latter-day Saints, despite the material costs.

What are the results of this century-long support of education?

The Latter-day Saints have always been a literate people. The seventh census of the United States was in 1850. In that year the average percentage of illiteracy in the United States was

4.92. The Utah percentage was only 0.25, the lowest of the states and territories cited.

In 1923 a careful educational survey of the stakes of Zion showed that the literacy of the Church was about ninety-seven percent. It was found that about sixty Latter-day Saints in every thousand attended high school—*more than three times the average of the United States at that time;* and that about nine in a thousand were in attendance at colleges and universities—*nearly twice the average for the United States.* The survey also indicated a large preponderance of college graduates, the holders of masters' and doctors' degrees *above any other group of like numbers in America or the world. . . .*

More students graduate from college in Utah, in proportion to the state population, than in any other state. (Dr. John A. Widtsoe and Richard L. Evans, *The Educational Level of the Latter-day Saints, The Improvement Era,* July 1947, pp. 444-445.)

Dr. Widtsoe and Elder Evans then referred to a book, *Education—America's Magic,* by Dr. Raymond M. Hughes, president emeritus of Iowa State College, and William H. Lancelot, professor of education of Iowa State College, in which they made reference to the "approximate position of each state in the educational procession in America."

Measured by the criteria used by them in a survey to determine the position of the states, "Utah has first place among the states by a wide margin."

In the article above referred to, reference was made to Dr. Edward L. Thorndike's study of men and science, as follows:

Dr. Thorndike, professor emeritus of Columbia University, undertook to determine the origin of America's men of achievement and men of science. This was done at the request of the Carnegie Foundation for Educational Advancement. He turned to the three standard compilations: *Who's Who in America, Leaders in Education,* and *American Men of Science.* All who had been found worthy of inclusion in these books were classified according to the place of their birth. The number of distinguished men in achievement or in science or in both in proportion to the population was determined for each state in the Union.

In the number of men of achievement, *Utah was the highest and led the nearest state, Massachusetts, by about twenty percent.* In the number of men of science, *Utah was the highest and led the nearest state, Colorado, by about thirty percent.* In science, certainly, and in achievement, probably, success implies previous education. (*The Improvement Era*, July 1947, p. 446.)

The article by Dr. Widtsoe and Elder Evans then continued:

. . . The Latter-day Saint student conceives his school work to be part of his purposeful preparation for eternal life and joy.

With this doctrine in his mind the Church has always made religion accompany secular education. The training of the whole man has been the objective of Latter-day Saints. In schools maintained by Church funds, religion has always been a part of the curriculum. When the schools become state supported, a system of supplementary seminaries and institutions was organized, supported by Church funds, in which religious training is offered, at convenient, free hours to high school and college students. Moreover, the Church maintains Brigham Young University and the Ricks Junior College, in both of which religion is freely taught.

At the close of the first century since the pioneers undertook to make the great deserts of the West their home, the Latter-day Saints present a picture of educational achievement second to none in America or in the world. (*The Improvement Era*, July 1947, p. 447.)

Health and Other Vital Statistics

Reliable statistics recently gathered indicate a remarkable difference in death from the major causes among the Latter-day Saints, the United States, and the average of six nations— Germany, France, the Netherlands, Sweden, Great Britain, and the United States. . . .

Death per 100,000 of white population from the following diseases:

Cause	(1936) Six Nations	(1944) United States	(1946) Latter-day Saints
Tuberculosis	79.5	33.7	5.5
Cancer	137.5	138.9	60.0
Diseases of the nervous system	117.6	103.7	58.5
Diseases of the circulatory system	224.0	348.7	171.6
Diseases of the respiratory system	118.8	56.3	48.5
Diseases of the digestive system	63.7	51.3	26.5
Kidney diseases	56.9	76.3	24.9
Infant mortality (first year of life, per thousand live births)	51.6	39.8	11.7
Maternity (per thousand live births)	4.5	2.0	

A further indication of a healthy people is their birth rate. The Latter-day Saints have consistently maintained a birth rate of better than thirty a thousand of population.

"In twenty-five of the leading nations on earth, the birth rate, in 1927-28, was twenty-two per thousand population, or about two-thirds of the birth rate among Latter-day Saints."

Statistics for 1946 show that the birth rate for the Latter-day Saints was 33.8 a thousand of population as compared with 20.0 for the United States for 1945 (latest figures available), or better than half again as high.

The excess of births over deaths among the Latter-day Saints for 1946 was almost twenty-eight a thousand as compared with ten for the United States and seven for the six nations previously mentioned, or about three and four times as great respectively.

A high standard of morality also serves as an indicator of a healthy people. The marriage rate for the Church is high, and the divorce rate correspondingly low as compared with the United States and other civilized countries of the world. Latest compilations number marriages at 21.9 a thousand population and divorces at 2.02 a thousand for the Church, as compared with 12.26 for marriages and 3.59 for divorces in the United States as a whole.

Illegitimate birth rates in Utah and Idaho, states of large Latter-day Saint population, are the lowest in the United States, being 10.4 and 10.8 a thousand births respectively. The rate of illegitimacy for the United States is 40.4 a thousand. The latest rate available for the average of twenty-two civilized nations of the world is seventy-four a thousand births. These figures give additional proof of the high degree of morality among our people.

"Insanity is low among the Latter-day Saints—about one-half of the average of the people among whom they live." (Verl F. Scott, Secretary of General Church Information and Statistics Committee, *The Improvement Era*, July 1947, pp. 426-427.)

Latter-day Saints As Colonizers and Nation-Builders

Dr. Thomas Nixon Carver, Professor of Political Economy, Harvard University, in an article, *A Positive Religion,* published in *The Westerner,* April 1930, wrote of the Mormons as colonizers and nation-builders:

Economics has been called the science of statesmanship. Statesmanship is the art of nation-building. One good way to study the art of nation-building is to study it in miniature in the early colonies of the Atlantic coast, *and in the Mormon colonies of Utah.*

I have long been interested in the Mormon polity. It is one of the most interesting and instructive experiments in the world. It throws a great deal of light on the art of nation-building. It, therefore, furnishes a laboratory for the study of the science of statesmanship.

Plutarch tells us that Themistocles was once twitted in a polite gathering because he could not play any musical instrument. He replied that, although he could not fiddle, he could make a small city into a great and glorious one. The Mormon leaders did even better than that. They did not have even a small city to start with. *They started with nothing and built a great and glorious commonwealth. They found a desert and made it bloom and blossom as the rose.*

Such things can be accomplished in only one way. That way is the economizing of man-power. The economy of man-power is, therefore, the key to the whole art of nation-building. It is only by economizing man-power that great masses of material can be moved, that rivers can be dammed, ditches dug, and land irrigated. It is only by economizing man-power that cities can be built, populations fed, and energy be spared for the arts and graces of life.

The Mormons did not even start with a mass of highly educated or skilled man-power. They started, as a general rule, with very commonplace people. These people came from the backwoods, the prairies, and the mountains of this country. From overseas they came, from peasant farms, from coal mines, and from workshops. While they were sturdy, hard-working people, they were not conspicuously gifted or learned.

It was necessary for the Mormon Church to train its own people. They not only began with desert land and had to put everything on it, even water; they also had to start with relatively uneducated people. This double task of developing both land and people could never have been performed except by economizing such man-power as there was, and utilizing it to the nth degree. *The results were a marvel of statesmanship.*

Man-power may be economized, first by cultivating sound, personal habits among the people. "Wherefore will ye spend your money for that which is not bread," asked the scriptures. They who waste their substance in riotous living are wasting more than wealth. They are wasting their own vital energy, their own man-power.

I have never found more sound and wholesome personal habits than among the Mormons. I have never mingled with people who showed fewer signs of dissipation. I have never studied groups of people who seemed better nourished and more healthful. I have never known people who took more pains to educate their children. This gives a clue to the success of the Mormons as colonizers and nation-builders.

Man-power is also economized by discovering hidden talent and giving it a chance to function. Every village Hampden or mute, inglorious Milton is a waste of man-power, the more destructive because the world is always in need of such talent. *Any system of supervision or of teaching which can discover latent genius and make it active is a factor in nation-building. To discover hidden genius is better than to discover a hidden gold mine.*

I have heard and read a number of stories which show that the leaders of Mormonism had an almost uncanny power of discovering hidden talent. Unsuspected skill exists in every large group of people. If it remains unsuspected or inactive, it is a waste of a most valuable kind of man-power. The power to save skill, talent and genius from going to waste, is as near to divine wisdom as anything we are likely to know in this world. Whether this power comes from superior organization, or from superior personal insight, it is equally valuable. *The Mormon Church seems to have possessed it in high degree.*

Man-power is also economized by cooperation, or by working together harmoniously. Every time two or more persons work at cross purposes, each one trying to interfere with the others, there is a waste of man-power. To eliminate that form of waste is one of the major purposes of statesmanship. It may have been sheer necessity of the situation which forced the early Mormons to cooperate or starve. It may have been the bond of a common religion, it may have been superior intelligence and insight. Whatever the source, the result was good.

The Church Welfare Plan

Mr. J. Beharrell of London, England, head of the Wolsey Works on Carpenter's Road, in Stratford, visited Utah and upon his return to England, wrote *The Deseret News* editorial staff at Salt Lake City, Utah, giving unstinted praise to the enterprise and foresight of the Church leaders in outlining and placing into operation, the Church welfare plan:

> The program of the Church in assuming this responsibility will always remain in the memory of the greatest lesson of my visit, a lesson that might be copied with advantage by every country in the world. It sets an example in social, economic and religious life—it proves that where there's a will there's a way— a program that sets as its standard the production of wealth from the soil rather than from the mass production by machine, cannot fail to succeed. (*The Deseret News*, Aug. 22, 1936.)

Demonstrating his own acceptance of the lesson taught him while in Utah, Mr. Beharrell continued:

> In a modest way the example has now been followed in my factory, where every man has been given a plot sufficiently large to cultivate flowers, fruit and vegetables to satisfy the requirements of his family; and this experiment in social welfare, the first of its kind in this country (England), is being followed closely by national organizations who will, I hope, continue and extend its usefulness in other ways. To me, Utah is America, and Salt Lake City is Utah.

During his two-week's visit to Utah, Mr. Beharrell attended a session of the June conference of the Young Men's and Young Women's Mutual Improvement and Primary Associations of the Church, made a study of the Church Welfare plan, and toured the national parks of Southern Utah. All of these experiences he related in a talk to members of the West Ham Rotary Club, upon his return. His concluding words:

> Time does not permit me to tell you all I should like of the Church of the Latter-day Saints, but I must assure you that the popular belief is altogether wrong, for never have I met such a happy band of people, with ideals that were lived every minute of their lives. If ever there was a perfect community it was here. (*Millennial Star*, October 15, 1936.)

We quote from an address by Congressman Pierce of the state of Oregon on the floor of the House.

> I have a thought which I want to present to the Committee, and it has reference to something which is being done in the West to help solve this relief problem. . . .

> The experience from the West upon which I wish to comment is the unique and admirable record of a church.

> The Mormon Church, or Latter-day Saints, with headquarters at Salt Lake City, Utah, has a membership of about 1,000,-000. They are setting an example for the care of their unemployed membership that should be highly praised and given wide publicity.

> The plan of this Church is to find jobs for their own members and keep them off the relief rolls and the W.P.A. The plan should be emulated everywhere. The president of the church, Heber J. Grant, has several times stated that no good member of the Mormon Church should stay on the W.P.A. rolls, apparently thinking it breaks their morale, their ambition and their desire to do anything for themselves. This organization, through its local bodies, or stakes, has held many meetings seeking jobs for those on relief or those likely to apply for relief. I have personally attended some of these meetings and have aided the organization, as I could, to secure jobs for members. So far as I know this

is the only religious organization that is making a really determined effort to meet the problem. The Church is succeeding in
a marvelous way in fitting its membership into the active affairs
of life so that they are not depending upon relief or charity. It
has great warehouses, organized industries and projects, and
co-operative plans which are effective and stimulating to partici-
pants and to observers.

May other organizations imitate the example of the Mormon
Church and make a determined effort that those that come under the influence of their organization will be given jobs, so, in
a satisfactory way, they may earn money to care for themselves.
(*Congressional Record,* January 13, 1939, p. 291.)

We quote from *The Catholic Worker,* which was re-
produced in *The Improvement Era:*

Mormons are personalists! Mormons have taken the lead
from Catholics in caring for their needy. The Church of the
Latter-day Saints has met the crisis in a manner which ought to
shame our so-called Catholic charitable organizations. . . .

In every stake unemployed men and women were set to
work sewing, farming, canning, repairing shoes and clothing,
collecting furniture and gifts from Church members and non-
members.

All work was voluntary. No money was paid. To each man
and woman a work certificate was given. When a worker needs
anything he presents his certificate to the Bishop of his ward
and he is given what he and his family need.

The certificates are not valuated in dollars or cents. Their
value depends upon the size of the family. Single men doing the
same amount of work receive only what they require as
bachelors. . . .

The Church of the Latter-day Saints has set an example
worthy of imitation by their Catholic fellow countrymen. It has
set up . . . "a system under which the curse of idleness would be
done away with, the evils of a dole abolished, and independence, industry, thrift, and self-respect once more established
among our people."

It has accomplished this great task by calling upon every
man, woman, and child in their communities to consider the

welfare of others about them as their own, and to be willing to
work for others not related by ties other than Christian fellowship. It has called upon every man, woman, and child to be
personally responsible for the amelioration of the present crisis.
We repeat, all work was voluntary and personal. No money
was paid in wages. And it was accomplished without calling in
state aid.

We suggest that our Catholic laymen cull a few pages from
the record of the Church of Latter-day Saints. It is a bitter tea
that we must swallow, and brewed by Mormon hands. It may be
hard to take a lesson in Catholic charity and sociology from
non-Catholics, but we trust that in the future we can afford to
play "hookey." (November, 1936)

As it has grown through the years the welfare plan
has been a source of inspiration to many non-Church
members. Comments made by visitors touring Welfare
Square in Salt Lake City have included the following:

NATO Delegate from England: "This has been an extraordinary experience, and it seems to me to be one of the best examples of practical Christianity in the modern world." A Baptist:
"It is a pattern for our Federal Government to attempt to
follow." Non-Church Member: "This is the most wonderful thing
I have ever seen, and hope to come back again." A Hebrew:
"This to my way of thinking is a real religion." Non-Church
Member: "We believe your Church and its members are doing
the great deeds that may some day achieve a true brotherhood
of man." A Baptist: "I find you people truly a work of God." A
Catholic: "A wonderful project and something other faiths might
well copy." A Methodist: "I'm flabbergasted!" An Episcopalian:
"Beyond Belief."

The Church Welfare Plan Abroad

Through its welfare plan the Church has not only
cared for the needs of its members in the United States
and Canada, but has also shipped by trucks, trains, ships
and planes thousands of tons of food and clothing to
members in distress in various parts of the world. The
Church has assisted thousands who were victims of wars,
floods and quakes at home and abroad.

Millions of dollars have been collected by the Church from its members which have been used to assist the needy and distressed throughout the world. This has been accomplished by direct welfare contributions and through the fast days that are observed one day each month. Church members abstain from two meals on those days and give the value of two meals or a more liberal contribution to the Church as fast offerings to assist those in need. In this way all Church families are invited and given an opportunity to participate in assisting others in need or distress.

Comments on the Church and Its Achievements By Those Who Have Visited Among Us

Utah excels in the number of Boy Scouts reached in proportion to the population. There are more boys of advanced rank and a greater percentage of Eagle Scouts than in any other section of America. Utah is setting standards for the whole country. The Mormon Church is the largest factor in this achievement. (George J. Fisher, M.D., New York City, Chief Scout Executive.)

I wish to call your attention to a piece of literature I am just now going through. Two of the choicest pieces of literature in all my collection of pamphlets on church work with young people, I have found here in Utah—they are the Handbooks of the Young Men's and Young Women's Mutual Improvement Association. (Dr. E. C. Branson, University of North Carolina.)

I want to give you some of my impressions of Utah as a sociologist. I am first of all, very favorably impressed with the Mormon Church. I don't know any other place where the young people are so well provided for as here in the State of Utah. I don't understand how the "Mormon" people got the idea of providing for the recreational and social needs of people so much earlier than we sociologists got the idea. The Church was away ahead of us in making this discovery.

I have never met so many fine young people as I have met here in Utah. The "Mormon" people have been decidedly misunderstood in the East. (Dr. E. A. Ross, Sociologist of the University of Wisconsin.)

Rev. Charles Francis Potter, in his book, *The Story of Religion,* p. 527, gave great credit to the accomplishments of those who accepted Joseph Smith as a prophet of the Lord:

> Mormonism is barely a century old and yet is one of the most successful religions on the American continent. . . . All too little is known by non-Mormons, or "Gentiles," of the admirable civilization built up in Utah.
>
> By the use of a system of irrigation, the first in America, the Mormons made the desert an agricultural paradise.
>
> The town planning was intelligently done in a period when in the rest of the country communities merely straggled into existence. The fruits of the early system are now evident in the beauty and prosperity of the cities of Utah.
>
> The first newspaper and the first university west of the Missouri were established by the Mormons.
>
> Their educational system, started early, embraces schools of a high order, literary societies, theaters and libraries.
>
> The culture—and prosperity—levels of Utah are far above those of some other American states. Nor can the culture of Utah be separated from the religion of Mormonism, for that religion is interwoven with the fabric of the life of the state.
>
> *If we are to accept the dictum of Jesus, "By their fruits ye shall know them," we must rate Mormons high.*

Dr. Charles E. Barker, well-known lecturer, and Rotary's ambassador to youth, made the following statement in the Salt Lake Tabernacle on April 21, 1935:

> Two years ago in the east, I was asked by an audience to tell them which group of citizens were making the greatest contributions to civilization as I had witnessed them in my travels about the country. I told them it was a difficult question to answer.
>
> I said that if they had asked me, twenty-one years ago, when I had not traveled about at all and my mind was very provincial and biased, who are the most undesirable class, I would have unhesitatingly said, "The Mormons."
>
> But having traveled about almost every year for sixteen years and having learned to know these people, I have come to feel that the most desirable people, having the highest standards of morality and virtue are the "Mormon" people. (*The Deseret News,* April 27, 1935.)

Dr. and Mrs. Garry Cleveland Myers, famous child psychologists, lectured in Salt Lake City in 1945, and praised the Church program in these words:

> The recreational program of the L.D.S. Church is the best plan of any large organization we know. (*The Deseret News,* February 26, 1945.)

Dr. Myers made a similar statement when visiting Salt Lake City in 1939:

> The youth program of the L.D.S. Church is best in the world. (*The Deseret News,* February 13, 1939.)

Dr. T. T. Brumbaugh, head of Wesley Foundation (student) work for the Methodist Episcopal Church in Japan, after making a tour of colleges and universities in twenty-two states, wrote an article, "Religion Returns to the Campus," which was published in the *Christian Century,* April 20, 1938, with a sub-heading, "Mormons Show the Way," concerning the institutes and seminaries conducted by the Latter-day Saints adjacent to colleges and high schools.

Chaplain Gilmore, Lieutenant Colonel of the 143rd Field Artillery, in speaking to a group of "Mormon" boys at Camp San Luis Obispo, said:

> There is not another regiment, except those coming from Utah, in the entire San Luis Obispo Camp, where four or five young Christians can be called upon to conduct church services. You should thank God that your church trains you for this calling. I have always appreciated attending church services in Utah because of this fact. (*The Deseret News,* March 26, 1941.)

Another outstanding tribute to "The Mormon boys" in uniform during World War II, by Lt. Col. Ira Freeman, post chaplain at Fort Ord, California:

> During several years of service in the United States Army, especially since Pearl Harbor, I have had the privilege of ministering to the needs of many members of the Church of Jesus Christ of Latter-day Saints.

The Mormon boys whom I knew intimately overseas were such outstandingly good soldiers in every sense of the word that I found myself wondering from time to time if they were a specially-selected group, the salt of Utah. But when I came to Fort Ord I had to dismiss that idea.

The Mormon boys on duty at this post have what it takes! There's something about a Mormon soldier! He loves the United States. He is loyal to Almighty God. Apparently, no Mormon lad leaves his religion at home when he accompanies the colors to the battlefield. Undoubtedly, that is the chief reason why it is comparatively easy for them to carry on without shamming, without shirking, without snivelling. Anyway, neither worldliness on the one hand nor the roaring of guns on the other affect their faith in or loyalty to God or country. Naturally, therefore, as an American, I am proud of them.

To further illustrate what I have in mind, I shall refer the reader to something that happened during one of the hottest battles of the Civil War. A Confederate general, while watching his hardhitting North Carolinians storm a strong Union position, exclaimed: "God bless North Carolina troops."

In that sense, the nation's eyes are upon its defenders today. Therefore, in my humble opinion, when the history of this global war has been written and read, and when Uncle Sam is ready to reward "every man according to his works," Americans of all faiths will say: "God bless our Mormon soldiers!"

No matter where you go from here, American soldiers of the Mormon faith, I want you to remember my faith in you is unbounded, that I shall follow you in spirit, that I shall remember you in my prayers. (*The Deseret News,* July 22, 1944.)

The Tabernacle Choir and Organ

The fame of the Tabernacle Choir and organ is spreading further afield every day.

Nowadays, not only are the tourists who pass through Salt Lake City and hear the organ recitals and choir broadcasts impressed with the outstanding quality of music—nor is the list of admirers limited to these and to the hundreds of thousands who hear the weekly radio broadcasts themselves—but nationally known writers on music are telling newspaper readers in distant parts of the country about the choir and organ.

George Mackey, noted choral leader of South Carolina, after visiting Salt Lake City, wrote:

> The Salt Lake City Tabernacle Choir is a voluntary choir of 350 voices, with 180 people on the waiting list. They are all residents of the city or nearby towns, and their work is the best in sacred music. From hymnology through all variations to great oratorios the tremendous chorus, as directed by J. Spencer Cornwall, gives the country's most perfect rendition of sacred compositions. (*Greenville South Carolina News*, August 31, 1941.)

What Others Think of the Mormons

J. Orval Ellsworth, Ph.D., in an article entitled "What Others Think of the Mormons" has provided us with an interesting account of his findings on this subject:

> A personal letter was written to nationally known scientists, educators, and lecturers who were known to have taken part as faculty members of the various summer schools held in Utah. Replies were received from twenty-five such inquiries.
>
> To avoid any possible influence of bias, a colleague of the writer of this article signed the inquiries. In the letter, the writer said: "I have no affiliation with the Mormon Church." The following questions were asked:
>
> What do you consider the two most outstanding characteristics of the Mormon Church:
>
> First, the trait which you regard as an asset, or which reacts to their advantage.
>
> Second, the trait which you regard as a liability, or which reacts to their disadvantage, and which reflects their weakness.
>
> The foregoing may be considered from a moral, intellectual, spiritual, or physical standpoint.
>
> The replies have been compiled and exact quotations used. Some of the writers asked not to be quoted; hence, no names are used.

*   *   *   *   *

The most outstanding characteristic of the Mormon people which would be considered as an asset is their high development of the economic virtues of industry, sobriety, thrift, and mutual helpfulness. I think I have never been among people who possessed these virtues in a higher degree.

I am greatly impressed with the high state of morality among the people, especially those phases of morality which an economist is likely to evaluate highly. The habits of the people seemed unusually simple and wholesome. Their ability to work together on large projects was greater than I have seen elsewhere. There was less profanity and vulgarity than one commonly hears, and I never was in a community in which outsiders were treated with quite so much courtesy and consideration.

* * * * *

I have come to feel, from my several summers in Utah, and my students share this feeling with me, that the Mormons are usually a high grade of people, higher, I think on the average than the general run of people in this country. I think their most outstanding characteristics are their devotion to the truth and their emphasis on a sound mind and a sound body. . . .

As a group they are remarkably abstemious in their habits. Practically none of them use intoxicating liquors, tobacco, tea, or coffee. . . .

You will perhaps think, from the foregoing, that I am a Mormon, or have a tendency to become one. This is very far from being the case. I am a member of the Congregational Church, as all my ancestors have been for many years. Like so many in the East, I was brought up to have a feeling of abhorrence toward the Mormons, but I have long since lived down that feeling and believe that any who had the experience that I have had in Utah would share my feelings as expressed above.

* * * * *

So far as I have observed the Mormon people, they surpass the people in any other part of the country in their high standards of personal conduct. . . . I can only speak in terms of the highest admiration of the efforts which they are making to bring up their boys and girls to be honorable and industrious men and women.

* * * * *

I know of nothing other than an inborn prejudice that was borrowed from a previous generation that might act as a liability or react against them from a moral, intellectual, spiritual, and physical standpoint. I would list the Mormons as an A No. 1 risk.

* * * * *

I have known the Mormon people somewhat for fifty-two years and rather intimately for forty-eight years. They are always thrifty. The Church gives personal attention to all of their people, financially and otherwise. They promote all talent that is discovered.

* * * * *

I was impressed particularly by two things; (1) The seriousness with which they take their religion and apply it to everyday conduct; (2) their universal courtesy to strangers. I was furthermore impressed by their apparent success in keeping the large majority of the children orthodox and free from delinquent tendencies.

. . . They seem to be leading a clean, useful life, with the majority of them apparently more nearly living up to the ideals which they hold than is the case with people with whom I have lived elsewhere.

* * * * *

I was particularly impressed by the cleanness and decency of the young Mormons who have been members of my field parties. Not one of them had any bad habits at all. Very few of them even used tobacco. I found them good workers, cheerful, steady, and reasonable. I do not recall that I ever had a personal altercation or any other kind of difficulty with one of them. I have noticed in the small Mormon villages that there was a general air of contentment and absence of friction. . . . I found the Mormons very kind and hospitable. In very few parts of the country do I recall being treated with such friendliness as in Utah.

* * * * *

Students who have come from Mormon homes to eastern universities have made enviable records. This is true in scholastic work and in music and art.

I would like to mention another thing in connection with their interest in education and that is their high moral standard. As far as I have been able to observe in many classes of society, one will not find, in my opinion, a higher grade of morals than exists among the Mormon people and the children who have been taught in Mormon homes and institutions.

* * * * *

In their towns you'll find less wickedness than in most places; I think much less than in a gentile town that prides itself on its superiority. You know Mormons object to smoking. Well, the six weeks or so I spent in a town of about ten thousand I saw three persons smoking. One was myself, another was an eastern professor, and the third was a man five miles up the canyon fishing. There probably is some smoking among gentiles and backsliders or poor Mormons, for one can buy tobacco. They do not drink tea or coffee. . . . The young people in the college are a wholesome, rather fine-looking, well-mannered, and well-behaved lot.

I believe the Church is building up a sound civilization in that mountain region. (*The Improvement Era.* Oct. 1942, pp. 624, 666, 668-669.)

What more could be said? Recall what Jesus said:

Ye shall know them by their fruits. . . . (Matt. 7:16.)

In the words of Jesus, we say to the world today, as he said when he undertook to establish his Church in the Meridian of Time:

If I do not the works of my Father, believe me not.

But if I do, though ye believe not me, believe the works. . . . (John 10:37-38.)

CHAPTER 28

BY THEIR FRUITS YE SHALL KNOW THEM (Cont'd)

The Followers of Christ to be Persecuted

In light of the superior lives and accomplishments of the faithful members of The Church of Jesus Christ of Latter-day Saints, as discussed only briefly in the preceding chapter, one who does not understand that it is the heritage of the followers of Christ to be persecuted and evil spoken of, would not be able to account for the almost unparalleled persecution to which the members of The Church of Jesus Christ of Latter-day Saints have been subjected. From the very moment that Joseph Smith, at the age of fourteen announced he had seen God the Father and his Son Jesus Christ in holy vision, the forces of evil combined against him and against those whose faith led them to embrace the restored truth. Why he should be so persecuted and evil spoken of was a matter the boy Joseph Smith could not understand. We quote his own statement regarding this matter:

I soon found, however, that my telling the story had excited a great deal of prejudice against me among professors of religion, and was the cause of great persecution, which continued to increase; and though I was an obscure boy, only between fourteen and fifteen years of age, and my circumstances in life such as to make a boy of no consequence in the world, yet men of high standing would take notice sufficient to excite the public mind against me, and create a bitter persecution; and this was common among all the sects—all united to persecute me.

It caused me serious reflection then, and often has since, how very strange it was that an obscure boy, of a little over fourteen years of age, and one, too, who was doomed to the necessity of obtaining a scanty maintenance by his daily labor, should be thought a character of sufficient importance to attract the attention of the great ones of the most popular sects of the day, and in a manner to create in them a spirit of the most bitter persecution and reviling. But strange or not, so it was, and it was often the cause of great sorrow to myself. (P. of G. P., Joseph Smith 2:22-23.)

This persecution and reviling has been the heritage of all those who have believed and accepted the testimony of Joseph Smith.

We have referred to the unseen spirit operating upon the hearts of the children of men through the coming of Elijah, Moses, and Elias, making possible the great redemption work performed by the living for the dead; the gathering of latter-day Israel; and the preaching of the gospel in all the world as a witness unto all nations preparatory to the coming of the Christ in glory with all the holy angels as promised.

We should not overlook the fact that there is also an evil power operating in the world. When Satan was cast down to the earth, he brought with him a third of the spirits of heaven, whose special mission it is to destroy the work of the Lord, and prevent those who come upon the earth from proving themselves worthy to return unto the presence of the Lord. Note the following scriptural declarations:

... Woe to the inhabiters of the earth and of the sea! for the devil is come down unto you, having great wrath, because he knoweth that he hath but a short time. (Rev. 12:12.)

And his tail drew the *third part of the stars of heaven,* and did cast them to the earth: and the dragon stood before the woman which was ready to be delivered, for to devour her child as soon as it was born. (Rev. 12:4.)

And there was war in heaven; Michael and his angels fought against the *dragon;* and the dragon fought *and his angels,*

And prevailed not; neither was their place found any more in heaven.

And the great dragon was cast out, that old serpent, called the Devil, and Satan *which deceiveth the whole world:* he was cast out into the earth, *and his angels were cast out with him.* (Rev. 12:7-9.)

It is therefore apparent that Satan's influence in the world of spirits was so great that he "drew the third part" of the spirits who followed him, "and Satan, which deceiveth the whole world: he was cast out into the earth, and his angels were cast out with him." The Apostle John who wrote this scripture fully understood that Satan would have power to deceive the whole world.

The Prophet Isaiah also testified of Satan's ambition to deceive all mankind:

> How art thou fallen from heaven, O Lucifer, son of the morning! how art thou cut down to the ground, *which didst weaken the nations!*
>
> For thou hast said in thine heart, I will ascend into heaven, *I will exalt my throne above the stars of God:* I will sit also upon the mount of the congregation, in the sides of the north:
>
> I will ascend above the heights of the clouds; *I will be like the most High.*
>
> Yet thou shalt be brought down to hell, to the sides of the pit.
>
> They that see thee shall narrowly look upon thee, and consider thee, saying, Is this the man that made the earth to tremble, that did shake kingdoms;
>
> That *made the world as a wilderness,* and *destroyed the cities thereof;* that opened not the house of his prisoners? (Isa. 14:12-17.)

What a record could be written of Satan's activities to accomplish the very things Isaiah foretold! Lucifer is fallen from heaven; he has weakened the nations; he has decreed to exalt his throne above the stars of God, and to be like the Most High; he has made the world as a wilderness, and destroyed the cities thereof.

John the Revelator declared that Satan's reign upon this earth should be practically universal:

And it was given unto him to make war with the saints, and to overcome them: and power was given him over all kindreds, and tongues, and nations. (Rev. 13:7.)

To be able to hold dominion over the kingdoms of the world, Satan's plan has been to destroy all who in any way can detract from his power. Hence, he has put it into the hearts of men to destroy the prophets and servants of the Lord whose commands he must obey. He put it into the heart of Herod to have all the children under two years of age put to death, in his effort to destroy Jesus, and prevent the establishment of his kingdom in the earth. Failing in this attempt, he continued to influence men to persecute Jesus until he was finally put to death—not because of any evil he had done, but because he stood in the way of Satan's continued supremacy over the kingdoms of this world. A similar fate befell his Apostles except John the Beloved who received the promise from his Master that he might tarry until he should come in his glory. And such, also, was the fate of the saints who were burned as torches and fed to the wild animals by the Romans. None of these had done any harm—they had nothing but blessings in their hearts for all men, but they were dangerous enemies to Satan and the continuation of his power in the earth. Jesus understood that this would be the lot of those who were willing to take upon them his name and follow him:

Think not that I am come to send peace on earth: I came not to send peace, but a sword.

For I am come to set a man at variance against his father, and the daughter against her mother, and the daughter in law against her mother in law.

And a man's foes shall be they of his own household. (Matt. 10:34-36.)

In the restoration of his gospel in these latter-days, the above statement of the Savior is equally true, as many Latter-day Saints can attest. Many have been turned out of their own homes by their own parents for no other reason than the fact that they have joined The Church of Jesus Christ of Latter-day Saints. Without understanding how Satan works upon the minds of men to achieve his purposes and destroy the work of the Lord, such actions cannot be understood. Parents will follow their children even to the gallows, and yet turn their backs upon them when they accept the truth. One mother was so terribly perturbed because her daughter wanted to join the Church that she remarked to the writer:

"I cannot understand it—she has always been the best child we have."

The Faithful to be Afflicted, Killed, Hated for His Name's Sake

When Jesus departed from the temple, he explained to his disciples that there should not be left one stone upon another that should not be thrown down:

> And as he sat upon the mount of Olives, the disciples came unto him privately, saying, Tell us, when shall these things be? and what shall be the sign of thy coming, and of the end of the world? (Matt. 24:3.)

It will be noted that there are three questions asked in the above scripture: (1) when shall the temple be destroyed; (2) what shall be the sign of thy coming; (3) what shall be the sign indicating the end of the world? Then Jesus proceeded to answer these questions. In giving the signs of his second coming, he told them that there shall be wars and rumors of wars; that "nation shall rise against nation, and kingdom against kingdom: and there shall be famines, and pestilences, and earthquakes in divers places." (See Matt. 24:6-7.) Then Jesus added:

All these are the beginning of sorrows.

Then shall they deliver you up to be afflicted, and shall kill you: and ye shall be hated of all nations for my name's sake. (Matt. 24:8-9.)

If, therefore, one believes the words of Jesus, he must believe that his followers who shall be sent to prepare the way for his second coming, shall be delivered up to be afflicted; that they shall be killed, and that they shall be hated of all nations for his name's sake. In this respect The Church of Jesus Christ of Latter-day Saints shares the same fate as The Church of Jesus Christ of former-day saints according to the testimony of Paul, for when he was taken as a prisoner to Rome, he called the chiefs of the Jews together, and they said:

But we desire to hear of thee what thou thinkest: for as concerning this sect, we know that *every where it is spoken against.* (Act 28:22.)

Jesus fully understood that the war which was commenced in heaven, where Satan headed the opposition to truth, would be continued here upon this earth. He said to his disciples:

If the world hate you, ye know that it hated me before it hated you.

If ye were of the world, the world would love his own: but because ye are not of the world, but I have chosen you out of the world, therefore the world hateth you.

Remember the word that I said unto you, The servant is not greater than his lord. If they have persecuted me, they will also persecute you; if they have kept my saying, they will keep yours also.

But all these things will they do unto you for my name's sake. because they know not him that sent me. (John 15:18-21.)

As we are now able to view things, without personalities entering into our consideration, it seems incredible that Jesus, going about "doing good" and blessing the people, should have been subjected to such persecution and finally crucifixion at the hands of those who should have been his friends. Satan saw in the coming of Jesus, the establishment of a movement that would ultimately mean destruction of his power in the earth. Therefore, he put it into the hearts of the selfish spiritual leaders of the people, whom the people were quick to follow, the desire to oppose Jesus and his followers that many may be led away to their destruction. Thus the opposition to Jesus and his followers was motivated by Satan who worked through the spiritual leaders of the people of that day. So has it been in the opposition to the Prophet Joseph Smith, and the work established by the Lord in the earth in this last dispensation, and unto those who have accepted his message—such persecutions, drivings, and ultimate killings, have seldom been recorded in the history of the world. Jesus must have had all this in mind when he said:

> Wherefore, behold, I send unto you prophets, and wise men, and scribes: and some of them ye shall kill and crucify; and some of them shall ye scourge in your synagogues, and persecute them from city to city. (Matt. 23:34.)

Then Jesus pleaded with his people in these words:

> O Jerusalem, Jerusalem, thou that killest the prophets, and stonest them which are sent unto thee, how often would I have gathered thy children together, even as a hen gathereth her chickens under her wings, and ye would not!
>
> Behold, your house is left unto you desolate.
>
> For I say unto you, Ye shall not see me henceforth, till ye shall say, Blessed is he that cometh in the name of the Lord. (Matt. 23:37-39.)

It will be seen that in the persecutions that have been heaped upon the members of The Church of Jesus Christ of Latter-day Saints, that history is but repeating itself. The words of Jesus are being fulfilled; his warning should be heeded by all seekers after truth: "For I say unto you, Ye shall not see me henceforth, till ye shall say,

Blessed is he that cometh in the name of the Lord." Our testimony is that he has again sent his servants in his name in this dispensation; that they have the same message of eternal truth to offer unto all men everywhere.

Our understanding, therefore, of Satan's decree to become "like the Most High" and exalt his throne "above the stars of God" by deceiving "the whole world" and killing the prophets and wise men who are sent unto them, enables us to understand the persecutions to which the prophets and saints of God of this dispensation, as also they of the meridian of time, have been subjected, notwithstanding the sacrifices they have made to prove themselves worthy of the great trust given unto them in the commitment of the gospel in this dispensation, and in carrying the message thereof to all the nations of the earth. Their hearts have been full of love and blessings for all men—they have harmed no one. Judging from human reasoning alone, there has been no justification for the persecutions they have been forced to endure, nor the unfriendly attitude of the world toward them. There can be but one answer and Jesus provided that answer:

> If ye were of the world, the world would love his own: but because ye are not of the world, but I have chosen you out of the world, therefore the world hateth you. (John 15:19.)

Thus one of the signs by which the true followers of the Christ may be known, is, as he said: "And ye shall be hated of all nations for my name's sake." (See Matt. 24:9.)

Persecution Because of Plural Marriage

There may be some who feel that the reason for the unfavorable attitude of the world toward The Church of Jesus Christ of Latter-day Saints is due to its belief in and practice of plural marriage in the early days of the Church. This, however, cannot be true, since Joseph Smith was subjected to persecutions from the time he was a boy of fourteen when he had related to some of the ministers, whom he regarded as his dearest friends, the vision he had received when the Father and the Son appeared to him. From that time on he was ridiculed and reviled; he was imprisoned time and time again, without cause; he was tarred and feathered. He, and those who believed his story, were driven from Ohio, then from Missouri, and finally from Nauvoo, Illinois. All of these trials and persecutions took place before the revelation from the Lord on the subject of plural marriage was made known, even to the members of the Church. The Church was organized April 6, 1830, and the Prophet Joseph Smith recorded the revelation received by him from the Lord on the subject of the eternity of the marriage covenant and the plurality of wives, at Nauvoo, Illinois, July 12, 1843, (D. & C. Section 132) less than a year before his martyrdom, June 27, 1844. The attitude of the Church, therefore, toward this principle was scarcely known publicly until after the Saints were driven from Nauvoo, Illinois, and settled in the Rocky Mountains.

What will the people of the world say when all things are known in their true light and relationship to the Lord and his great work, and when they learn it was the Lord who taught the Prophet Joseph Smith this principle, and that it had a sacred and religious aspect and purpose, rather than having been adopted for the gratification of the lusts of men? Only a few of the members of the Church ever lived the principle of plural marriage— never over three per cent. There must have been something of outstanding worth and conviction to hold 97 per cent of the Church membership true to their testimonies of the divinity of the teachings of the Prophet Joseph Smith, even when they saw some of the members living this principle. It was apparent to them that those who practiced it were among the finest people in the community, and their children were in every way equal to the children of monogamous marriages. Members of the Church most familiar with the fruits of this principle were the least offended by its practice.

Under the inspired leadership of Wilford Woodruff, then president of The Church of Jesus Christ of Latter-day Saints, "The Manifesto," dated September 24, 1890, was issued, advising Latter-day Saints "to refrain from contracting any marriage forbidden by the law of the land." Before a General Conference of the Church, October 6, 1890, President Lorenzo Snow offered the following motion:

> I move that, recognizing Wilford Woodruff as the President of the Church of Jesus Christ of Latter-day Saints, and the only man on the earth at the present time who holds the keys of the sealing ordinances, we consider him fully authorized by virtue of his position to issue the Manifesto which has been read in our hearing, and which is dated September 24th, 1890, and that as a Church in General Conference assembled, we accept his declaration concerning plural marriages as authoritative and binding.

The vote to sustain the foregoing motion was unanimous.

The following year, President Wilford Woodruff, while addressing the saints in Logan, Utah, November 1, 1891, gave a striking account of the "vision and revelation" which led him to issue the Official Declaration known as "The Manifesto":

> The Lord showed me by vision and revelation exactly what would take place if we did not stop this practice. . . .
>
> I know there are a good many men, and probably some leading men, in this Church who have been tried and felt as though President Woodruff had lost the Spirit of God and was

about to apostatize. Now, I want you to understand that he has not lost the Spirit, nor is he about to apostatize. The Lord is with him, and with his people. *He has told me exactly what to do, and what the result would be if we did not do it. . . .* I want to say this: I should have let all the temples go out of our hands; I should have gone to prison myself, and let every other man go there, *had not the God of heaven commanded me to do what I did do;* and when the hour came that I was commanded to do that, it was all clear to me. (*Deseret News,* November 7, 1891.)

Since the date of The Manifesto and its acceptance by the vote of the saints, the Church has taken a definite stand against the practice of plural marriage, even excommunicating from membership in the Church those who have been found guilty of violating instructions on this matter.

CHAPTER 29

SUMMARY

Joseph Smith's Contributions to the Holy Scriptures

After considering carefully the preceding chapters, one might ask what more could have been expected of a true prophet of God than was accomplished by the Prophet Joseph Smith. He made plain precious truths referred to in the Bible, but lost to the world because, no doubt in many cases, of brevity of explanation, inability of laity and clergy to understand, or because they were hidden by the Lord as Jesus said:

> . . . I thank thee, O Father, Lord of heaven and earth, because thou hast hid these things from the wise and prudent, and hast revealed them unto babes.
>
> Even so, Father: for so it seemed good in thy sight. (Matt. 11:25-26.)

Joseph Smith contributed three volumes of scripture to go hand in hand with the Bible: (1) The Book of Mormon, which we have discussed, being a translation of part of the golden plates delivered to him by the Angel Moroni, containing a record of the former inhabitants of the American continents; (2) The Doctrine and Covenants, containing the revelations of the Lord to his Prophets in connection with the restoration of the gospel, and the organization of his Church in its fulness in this the Dispensation of the Fulness of Times; (3) The Pearl of Great Price.*

--- --- ---

*Following is a brief history of the book, the *Pearl of Great Price,* presented here for the reader's information.

. . . "It appears that in the year 1828, a French explorer named Antonio Sebolo, secured permission from Mehemit Ali, the viceroy of Egypt, to explore for antiquities. Three years later, in 1831, Sebolo entered some catacombs near the place where stood formerly the ancient city of Thebes. Eleven of the mummies, found in perfect state of preservation, he carried away with

426 A Marvelous Work and a Wonder

Priesthood Keys Restored

Joseph Smith received the Aaronic Priesthood under the hands of John the Baptist.

He received the Melchizedek Priesthood under the hands of Peter, James and John.

He received the keys of turning "the heart of the fathers to the children, and the heart of the children to their fathers," under the hands of Elijah.

Under the hands of Moses, he received the keys for the gathering of Israel.

Under the hands of Elias, he received the keys of the gospel of the Dispensation of Abraham.

He established The Church of Jesus Christ again upon the earth, by virtue of the keys and ordinations he received, with the same organization that existed in

---

him to Paris. On the way to the French capital, however, M. Sebolo put in at Trieste, where he died after an illness of several days. The mummies were then directed to a nephew named Chandler. Mr. Chandler lived in Philadelphia, Pennsylvania, though it was supposed that his home was in Ireland. After a devious course, the mummies finally came to New York, addressed to Michael H. Chandler. There the caskets were first opened, and the contents examined. 'On opening the coffins,' the Prophet tells us, 'he (Mr. Chandler) discovered that in connection with two of the bodies, was something rolled up with the same kind of linen, saturated with the same bitumen, which when examined, proved to be two rolls of papyrus.' These rolls of papyrus were beautifully written 'with black, and a small part red, ink or paint, in perfect preservation.'

"A stranger standing near at the time of the discovery recommended to Mr. Chandler that he seek out the Mormon Prophet, Joseph Smith, as probably the only man who could render a correct translation of the ancient manuscripts. Mr. Chandler, however, began to exhibit the mummies in the larger cities of the United States. They very soon became objects of peculiar interest. Mr. Chandler was assured by the learned men of the land that both mummies and papyrus were genuine. Indeed, from some he received certificates testifying to the genuineness of his display and to the characters on the papyrus. It was not until July 3, 1835, that Mr. Chandler reached Kirtland with the Egyptian mummies. Immediately, it appears, he sought out the Prophet Joseph Smith. 'There were four human figures,' the latter writes in his history, 'together with . . . hieroglyphic figures and devices.' As Mr. Chandler had been told I could translate them, he brought me some characters, and I gave him the interpretation, and like a gentleman, he gave me the following certificate:

Kirtland, July 6, 1835

'This is to make known to all who may be desirous, concerning the knowledge of Mr. Joseph Smith, Jun., in deciphering the ancient Egyptian

the primitive Church, viz: Apostles, prophets, pastors, teachers, evangelists, etc.

He taught the principles of eternal truth as he received them from the Lord, correcting false doctrines and practices then in existence in the churches.

The Need for a Prophet

The need for a prophet to accomplish these very things has long been felt. A writer for the *New York Herald*, who had visited with the Prophet Joseph Smith in 1842, wrote the following account of his experience which was originally published in his paper:

Joseph Smith is undoubtedly one of the greatest characters of the age. He indicates as much talent, originality and moral courage as Mahomet, Odin, or any of the great spirits that have

—————

hieroglyphic characters in my possession, which I have, in many eminent cities, showed to the most learned. And, from the information that I could ever learn or meet with, I find that of Mr. Joseph Smith, Jun., to correspond in the most minute matters.'

'Michael H. Chandler, Traveling with,
and proprietor of Egyptian mummies.'

"Soon after receiving this certificate from Mr. Chandler some of the Saints in Kirtland purchased from him the mummies and the papyrus. Thereupon, the Prophet, with William W. Phelps and Oliver Cowdery as scribes, began to translate the strange hieroglyphics. To their infinite joy, they found that one of the rolls contained writings of Abraham, whereas the other contained writings of Joseph, who was sold into Egypt. The first of these the Prophet translated, in part. It recounts of the trials of Abraham in the idolatrous home of his fathers, and his miraculous deliverance. It tells also of the creation of the world, and of the spirits before, and reveals the system of astronomy understood by the ancient patriarch. The Book of Abraham, an invaluable and truly authentic record translated by divine inspiration, forms now an important part of the *Pearl of Great Price.*

"It appears that the papyrus-roll containing the writings of Joseph was never translated. The Saints retained possession of the mummies, and carried them along in their wanderings, until they became settled in their new home— Nauvoo, the Beautiful. There, the mummies were displayed in the Nauvoo Mansion, built by the Prophet. After the death of the Prophet, however, the mummies and the papyrus-rolls fell into the hands of the Prophet's family, and were sold. For some time they were exhibited by a syndicate in St. Louis. Thence they were sold to a museum in Chicago. When the great fire swept Chicago in 1870, the museum was destroyed; and with it, presumably, the historic mummies and the sacred records of old. All that we have preserved to us, then, of these interesting papyrus records is contained in the *Pearl of Great Price.* (Osborne J. P. Widtsoe, *The Restoration of the Gospel.* pp. 114-117.)

hitherto produced the revolutions of past ages. In the present infidel, irreligious, ideal, geological, animal-magnetic age of the world, some such singular prophet as Joseph Smith is required to preserve the principle of faith, and to plant some new germs of civilization that may come to maturity in a thousand years. While modern philosophy, which believes in nothing but what you can touch, is overspreading the Atlantic States, Joseph Smith is creating a spiritual system, combined also with morals and industry, that may change the destiny of the race. . . . We certainly want some such prophet to start up, take a big hold of the public mind—and stop the torrent of materialism that is hurrying the world into infidelity, immorality, licentiousness and crime.—George Q. Cannon, *Life of Joseph Smith*, p. 324.

Josiah Quincy, former mayor of Boston, had met the Prophet Joseph Smith, and was impressed with the fact that the world would yet have to account for his claims that he was a prophet sent of God:

It is by no means improbable that some future text-book, for the use of generations yet unborn, will contain a question something like this: What historical American of the nineteenth century has exerted the most powerful influence upon the destinies of his countrymen? And it is by no means impossible that the answer to that interrogatory may be thus written: *Joseph Smith, the Mormon prophet.* And the reply, absurd as it doubtless seems to most men now living, may be an obvious commonplace to their descendants. History deals in surprises and paradoxes quite as startling as this. The man who established a religion in this age of free debate, who was and is to-day accepted by hundreds of thousands as a direct emissary from the Most High,—such a rare human being is not to be disposed of by pelting his memory with unsavory epithets. (Josiah Quincy, *Figures of the Past*, p. 376.)

Let the reader determine whence came such accomplishments, if the Prophet Joseph Smith were not called of God.

Remember, there were those who stood with him in heavenly vision; who received, with him, ordination to the Priesthood and special callings; who beheld the gold plates from which the Book of Mormon was translated; and who heard the voice of the angel declare that they were translated by the gift and power of God. All these special witnesses remained true to their testimonies as long as they lived.

Truths Revealed and Prophecies Fulfilled in This Dispensation

To provide a brief summation, we will mention some of the great truths upon which the Lord has shed his divine light through the instrumentality of the Prophet Joseph Smith:

1. The true personality of God
2. Man's true relationship to God
3. The proper foundation of the Gospel
   a. Faith in the Lord Jesus Christ
   b. Repentance
   c. Baptism by immersion for the remission of sins
   d. Laying on of hands for the gift of the Holy Ghost
4. An understanding of the difference between the Aaronic and Melchizedek Priesthoods (Heb. 7:11-12.)
5. An understanding of the different offices in these two Priesthoods; the duties of each, the number required to form a quorum, etc.
6. The proper organization of the Church and its purpose
7. The correct name which the Church of Jesus Christ should bear
8. That the followers of Christ's Church were and should be called "Saints"
9. Where we came from; that we lived before we were born
10. Why we are here upon the earth
11. The three degrees of glory and what one must do to prepare for celestial glory
12. Who are to come forth in the First Resurrection, and that

the rest of the dead are not to come forth until the end of
the thousand years, which will be the great judgment day

13. That obedience to the ordinances of the gospel is so necessary that the perfect plan of God provides for a vicarious
work of the living for the dead, for the benefit of those to
whom the gospel has not been preached, or who have not
accepted it in this life

14. That the gospel is being preached to the dead and for what
purpose

15. That the millennium of one thousand years has been provided to complete this work, without which, the final judgment day should come at the beginning and not the end
thereof

16. That the condition and time of one's life here upon the
earth is as much the result of a life previously lived as the
life to come will be the result of how we live and what we
do in this life

17. That the Church established by Christ in the meridian of
time should fall into an apostate condition, of which fact
both the ancient prophets and the Apostles of the Master
freely bore witness

18. That the prophets of the Old Testament and the Apostles
of the New Testament, predicted a complete restoration of
"all things which God hath spoken by the mouth of all his
holy prophets, since the world began," (Acts 3:21) rather
than a reformation to correct the false teachings of the
churches

19. The meaning and fulfilment of the following prophecies:
a. "And I saw another angel fly in the midst of heaven,
having the everlasting gospel to preach unto them that
dwell on the earth, and to every nation, and kindred, and
tongue, and people,

"Saying with a loud voice, Fear God, and give glory
to him; for the hour of his judgment is come: and worship
him that made heaven, and earth, and the sea, and the
fountains of waters." (Rev. 14:6-7.)

b. "And he shall send Jesus Christ . . .

"Whom the heaven must receive until the times of
restitution of all things, which God hath spoken by the
mouth of all his holy prophets since the world began."
(Acts 3:20-21.)

c. "Behold, I will send my messenger, and he shall prepare the way before me: and the Lord, whom ye seek shall suddenly come to his temple, even the messenger of the covenant, whom ye delight in: behold, he shall come, saith the Lord of hosts." (Mal. 3:1.)

d. "Wherefore the Lord said, Forasmuch as this people draw near me with their mouth, and with their lips do honour me, but have removed their heart far from me, and their fear toward me is taught by the precept of men:

"Therefore, behold, I will proceed to do a marvellous work among this people, even a marvellous work and a wonder: for the wisdom of their wise men shall perish, and the understanding of their prudent men shall be hid." (Isa. 29:13-14.)

e. "And in the days of these kings shall the God of heaven set up a kingdom, which shall never be destroyed: and the kingdom shall not be left to other people, but it shall break in pieces and consume all these kingdoms, and it shall stand for ever." (Dan. 2:44.)

20. That Elijah has been sent back to this earth, and for what purpose (Mal. 4:5-6.)

21. Why there has been such a marvelous change in the world with respect to genealogical record keeping, genealogical organizations, societies, libraries, and research work

22. That marriage, according to the scriptures, was intended to be eternal

23. That the family unit is to endure beyond the grave

24. Why temples are erected unto the Most High, and what they are used for

25. Where the temple is which Isaiah saw that should be built in the tops of the mountains in the last days (Isa. 2:2-3.)

26. That in case of sickness we should call the elders of the Church to anoint the sick with oil (James 5:14-16.)

27. The command of God to Ezekiel that two sticks (or records) should be kept, one of Judah and his companions and one of Joseph and his companions, and what these two records are (Ezek. 37:15-19.)

28. What people should speak out of the ground with a voice that hath a familiar spirit (Isa. 29:1-4; II Nephi 25:7-8; II Nephi 26:15-17.)

29. What the "sealed book" is to which Isaiah refers (Isa. 29:11-12; II Nephi 27:5-26.)

30. To what people Jesus referred when he said: "Other sheep I have which are not of this fold" (John 10:16; III Nephi 15:11-21.)

31. The promises made to Joseph by his father Jacob, and by Moses, when he was promised a *new land* in "the *utmost* bounds of the everlasting hills," (Gen. 49:22-26; Deut. 33:-13-18.) and where that *new land and the everlasting hills* are to which they referred

32. When and how the cities that are being excavated in Central and South America, came to be buried in the depths of the earth (III Nephi, chapter 8.)

33. Where the civilized people who once inhabited this land of America came from and who they were as evidenced by their great cities and buildings being excavated

34. That there were to be two gathering places, not one, in the last days; one for Judah at Jerusalem and one for Israel or the seed of Joseph, in America (Ether, chapter 13.)

35. The difference between Judah's blessing and Joseph's blessing as pertaining to priesthood. (Heb. 7:4; I Chron. 5:1-2.)

36. That Israel, or the seed of Joseph should be gathered in the last days to that portion of America designated as a wilderness or desert in the mountains and requiring irrigation (Jer. 31:6-13; Isa. 2:2-3; Isa., chapter 35; Isa. 41:18-23; Isa. 43:18-21.)

37. The calling of a patriarch, or evangelist, as he is often called (Gen., chapter 49; Deut., chapter 33; Acts 2:29; Acts 7:8-9; Heb. 7:4; D. & C. 124:91-93.)

38. That Jesus did not baptize little children, nor did any of his Apostles, but "He took them up in his arms, put his hands upon them, and blessed them" (Mark 10:16.)

39. What the Urim and Thummim are, and what they were used for by the prophets of old, and what became of them (I Sam. 28:6; Ezra 2:62-63; Lev. 8:8; Deut. 33:8; Exod. 28:30; Num. 27:21.)

40. That the Lord's plan of financing his kingdom on the earth is by the law of tithing

41. That the Word of Wisdom was given as a revelation by the Lord for the temporal salvation of his people in the latter days, and that it was ahead of science in declaring things which are not good for the body

42. That The Church of Jesus Christ of Latter-day Saints maintains a missionary system as instituted by the Savior, where the missionaries labor without compensation for their services.

Surely all this represents more than the wisdom of man.

A Marvelous Work and a Wonder

Joseph Smith, or any other man, could not have obtained all this information by reading the Bible or studying all the books that have ever been written. It came from God. It is just exactly what Isaiah promised the Lord would do when conditions upon the earth should become as Joseph Smith found them when he went into the woods to pray for light as to which of all the churches he should join.

Consider again the promise of the Lord through Isaiah:

Wherefore the Lord said, Forasmuch as this people draw near me with their mouth, and with their lips do honour me, but have removed their heart far from me, and their fear toward me is taught by the precept of men:

Therefore, behold, I will proceed to do a *marvellous work* among this people, even *a marvellous work and a wonder:* for the wisdom of their wise men shall perish, and the understanding of their prudent men shall be hid. (Isa. 29:13-14.)

It truly is a marvelous work and a wonder. Can you conceive of anything that could be more marvelous or more wonderful?

In the face of it all, the wisdom of their wise men does perish. The world has no satisfactory explanation. In the Church Historian's Office in Salt Lake City, there are more than twenty thousand volumes, large and small, each of which says something about the Prophet Joseph Smith. There are also some two thousand pamphlets on the subject. Many of these represent attempts on the part of non-Mormon writers to explain the conundrum of Joseph Smith and the work he established, but all without avail. All these writings have been accumulated since the birth of Joseph Smith in 1805. In contrast, in the two centuries that have elapsed since the birth of George Washington, it is reported, there are only two thousand six hundred fifty-six volumes written about him in the Library of Congress.

Well did Isaiah predict:

> . . . For the wisdom of their wise men shall perish, and the understanding of their prudent men shall be hid. (Isa. 29:14.)

How could this prediction possibly be more literally fulfilled than in the case of Joseph Smith and the work the Lord established through him?

We emphasized a statement published in the *New York Herald*, which we quoted in this chapter: "Joseph Smith is creating a spiritual system, combined with morals and industry that may change the destiny of the race." This statement was made in 1842, and at this writing, 108 years later (1950), from the present accomplishments of the Church founded under his leadership, it is evident that this prognostication is sure to achieve a complete fulfilment.

It is equally sure that the prediction of Josiah Quincy in 1844, will find its fulfilment i.e., "It is by no means improbable that some future textbook for the use of generations yet unborn, will contain a question something

like this: 'What historical American of the nineteenth century has exerted the most powerful influence upon the
lives of his countrymen?' And it is by no means impossible
that the answer to that interrogatory may be thus written:
'Joseph Smith, the Mormon prophet.' "

The American Religion, A World Religion

Count Leo Tolstoi, the great Russian author, states-
man, and philosopher, held a similar opinion as to the
possible future destiny of the "American religion" founded under the instrumentality of the Prophet Joseph
Smith.

Thomas J. Yates related an experience he had while
a student at Cornell University in 1900. He had the privilege of meeting Dr. Andrew D. White, former president
of Cornell, and at the time, U. S. Ambassador to Germany. Upon learning that Mr. Yates was a Mormon, Dr.
White made an appointment for Mr. Yates to spend an
evening with him, at which time he related to him an
experience he had with Count Tolstoi while serving as U.
S. Foreign Minister to Russia in 1892. Dr. White visited
often with Count Tolstoi, and upon one occasion they
discussed religion. We quote from Elder Yates' account
of this discussion as related to him by Dr. White:

"Dr. White," said Count Tolstoi, "I wish you would tell me
about your American religion."

"We have no state church in America," replied Dr. White.

"I know that, but what about your American religion?"

Patiently then Dr. White explained to the Count that in
America there are many religions, and that each person is free
to belong to the particular church in which he is interested.

To this Tolstoi impatiently replied: "I know all of this, but I
want to know about the *American* religion. Catholicism originated in Rome; the Episcopal Church originated in England; the
Lutheran Church in Germany, but the Church to which I refer

originated in America, and is commonly known as the Mormon
Church. What can you tell me of the teachings of the
Mormons?"

"Well," said Dr. White, "I know very little concerning them.
They have an unsavory reputation, they practice polygamy, and
are very superstitious."

Then Count Leo Tolstoi, in his honest and stern, but lovable
manner, rebuked the ambassador. "Dr. White, I am greatly surprised and disappointed that a man of your great learning and
position should be so ignorant on this important subject. The
Mormon people teach the American religion; their principles
teach the people not only of Heaven and its attendant glories,
but how to live so that their social and economic relations with
each other are placed on a sound basis. If the people follow the
teachings of this Church, nothing can stop their progress—it will
be limitless. There have been great movements started in the
past but they have died or been modified before they reached
maturity. If Mormonism is able to endure, unmodified, until it
reaches the third and fourth generations, it is destined to become
the greatest power the world has ever known." (*The
Improvement Era,* Vol. 42, p. 94.)

Because of his discussion with Count Tolstoi, upon
his return to the United States, Dr. White secured a set of
the Church works and placed them in the Cornell University Library.

Count Tolstoi indicated that "if Mormonism is able
to endure, unmodified, until it reaches the third and
fourth generations, it is destined to become the greatest
power the world has ever known."

There can be no question about its enduring to the
third and fourth generations, as those acquainted with
the present membership of the Church will attest. Therefore, in the words of the count: "It is destined to become
the greatest power the world has ever known."

This is just another way of describing what Daniel
saw in his interpretation of King Nebuchadnezzar's
dream:

But there is a God in heaven that revealeth secrets, and

maketh known to the king Nebuchadnezzar what shall be in the latter days. . . .

And in the days of these kings shall the God of heaven set up a kingdom, which shall never be destroyed: and the kingdom shall not be left to other people, but it shall break in pieces and consume all these kingdoms, and it shall stand for ever. (Dan. 2:28, 44.)

Why should anyone doubt that the Lord will fulfil this promise? Where then is the kingdom to which Daniel refers? It will not come all at once, but, founded by God and not by man, though it had a small beginning, it is destined to fill the whole earth.

Thou sawest till that a stone was cut out without hands, which smote the image upon his feet that were of iron and clay, and brake them to pieces.

. . . and the wind carried them away, that no place was found for them: and the stone that smote the image became a great mountain, and filled the whole earth. (Dan. 2:34-35.)

Why should the world doubt? What greater evidences could God place in the kingdom he was to establish in the latter days, to prove that it is of him and not of man? Why should it take truth so long to travel? It runs true to form. When Jesus came among men and announced himself as the Son of God, the people of the world turned their backs on him. Jesus said, "If the world hate you, ye know that it hated me before it hated you." (John 15:18.)

Assuming that the Prophet Amos spoke the truth when he said: "Surely the Lord God will do nothing, but he revealeth his secret unto his servants the prophets," (Amos 3:7) he surely would not establish the kingdom Daniel saw, without a prophet, neither would he do the marvelous work and a wonder which Isaiah saw, without a prophet. What prophet could have done more to prove his faithfulness to his trust and to his calling than to seal his testimony with his blood, as did the Prophet Joseph Smith?

William George Jordan wrote:

> The man who has a certain religious belief and fears to discuss it, lest it may be proved wrong, is not loyal to his belief, he has but a coward's faithfulness to his prejudices. If he were a lover of truth, he would be willing at any moment to surrender his belief for a higher, better, and truer faith. (*The Power of Truth*, pp. 16-17.)

Jesus expressed this same thought when he said:

> Blessed are they which do hunger and thirst after righteousness: for they shall be filled. (Matt. 5:6.)

God's Promises to the Seeker of Truth

In closing, we suggest to the reader that if he is a lover of truth, that he consider without bias the evidences we have submitted as to the divine calling of the Prophet Joseph Smith and the truth of the Church established under his instrumentality and that he follow the admonition of James, as did the boy Joseph Smith:

> If any of you lack wisdom, let him ask of God, that giveth to all men liberally, and upbraideth not and it shall be given him. (James 1:5.)

We suggest further that the promise contained in the Book of Mormon be put to the test:

> And when ye shall receive these things, I would exhort you that ye would ask God, the Eternal Father, in the name of Christ, if these things are not true; and if ye shall ask with a sincere heart, with real intent, having faith in Christ, he will manifest the truth of it unto you, by the power of the Holy Ghost. (Moroni 10:4.)

The strength of The Church of Jesus Christ of Latter-day Saints, and the power by which it is making such rapid growth, is the individual testimony of its members. They have put this promise to the test, and the Lord has done his part. Why should one be satisfied with anything less than an individual testimony in light of the promises made by James and Moroni in addition to the promise of the Savior of the world:

> Jesus answered them, and said, My doctrine is not mine, but his that sent me.
>
> If any man will do his will, he shall know of the doctrine, whether it be of God, or whether I speak of myself. (John 7: 16-17.)

May each reader of this book share, with the writer, an individual testimony of the truth of these things, which will constitute the Pearl of Great Price, to which Jesus referred, when he said:

> Again, the kingdom of heaven is like unto a merchant man, seeking goodly pearls:
>
> Who, when he had found one pearl of great price, went and sold all that he had, and bought it. (Matt. 13:45-46.)

THE MORNING BREAKS

The morning breaks, the shadows flee;
  Lo! Zion's standard is unfurled.
The dawning of a brighter day,
  Majestic rises on the world.
The clouds of error disappear
  Before the rays of truth divine;
The glory bursting from afar,
  Wide o'er the nations soon will shine.
The Gentiles fulness now comes in,
  And Israel's blessings are at hand;
Lo! Judah's remnant, cleansed from sin,
  Shall in their promised Canaan stand.
Jehovah speaks! let earth give ear,
  And Gentile nations turn and live;
His mighty arm is making bare,
  His covenant people to receive.
Angels from heaven and truth from earth
  Have met, and both have record borne;
Thus Zion's light is bursting forth,
  To bring her ransomed children home.

Written by Parley P. Pratt in 1840

The promised "marvellous work and a wonder" is here among men. The message and the work may be accepted or rejected. The choice is yours. You may never again, in this life, judge such an important matter. Your decision will follow you with its consequences through time and throughout the eternities to come.

INDEX